W9-BKI-308

Contents

for Tuesday

iii

PART IV: HOW IT HAPPENED: THE LEGAL STATUS OF WOMEN AND PEOPLE OF COLOR IN THE UNITED STATES   177

Preface

Racism and Sexism undertakes an integrated study of racism and sexism within the context of class. Such a project poses many difficulties. First and foremost is the complexity of the material being studied and the need to explore the various ways in which race, class, and gender intersect to define, modify, or qualify our realities. In constructing this book, an ongoing concern was how to find a structure that did justice to all these complexities at the same time that it presented each topic with sufficient clarity. My experience teaching about race, class, and gender over a period of years had convinced me that introducing all these topics simultaneously creates serious difficulties. For this reason, I chose to focus on racism and sexism in the first section of this book, and I have examined each phenomenon in itself and in relation to one another but without regard to the way in which issues of class affect them. Section II introduces the concept of class and presents data that reflect some of the ways that class differences, along with differences in race and gender, intersect and mutually determine the economic reality of people's lives. Section III offers three-dimensional accounts of experiences in which a myriad of other factors further modify the impact of race, class, and gender on individuals. The sections that follow include discussions of all these issues in various combinations.

Another concern has been how to portray adequately the unique situation of women of color. Even the very topic we propose, a study of racism and sexism within the context of class, seems both too narrow and too broad to do justice to what many have called the double or triple oppression of women of color—women who simultaneously experience both racism and sexism and who must often contend with the impact of class subordination as well. The readings in this book have been chosen with an awareness of this problem and with the hope that they contribute to the understanding of it.

Furthermore, talking about racism and sexism within the context of class requires that we generalize about the experience of different groups of people, even while we realize that each group and indeed each individual is unique. In order to highlight the similarities in the experiences of some individuals, I often talk about "people of color" and "women of color" even though these terms are not without attendant difficulties. When I refer to "women" in this book instead of to "white women" or "women of color," it is usually because I wish to focus on the particular experiences or the legal status of women as women irrespective of race. In doing so, I use language in much the same way that one might author a guide to "*the* anatomy of *the* cat." There is no such thing as "*the* cat" any more than there is "a woman" or there are "people of color." And yet for purposes of discussion and analysis, it is often necessary to make artificial distinctions that allow us to focus on particular aspects of experience that may not be separable in reality. One assumption that is reflected in the structure and contents of this book is that language both mirrors reality and helps to structure it. It is no wonder then that it is often so difficult to use our language in ways that are adequate to our topics without falling victim to the implicit racism and sexism that has rendered various individuals and groups invisible in the past.

Finally, this book is in many respects incomplete. There will be those who will be disappointed because some particular topic is not included or does not receive the coverage they might wish. Because I believed this was inevitable from the start, I decided to present a core of material that would help people understand the nature of racism and sexism as they interact within our class society. If I have succeeded, it should be possible to build upon this core, moving toward an ever more complex, inclusive, and adequate account of the forces that shape our reality and the steps we must take to transform them in the interests of justice. I will be grateful to readers who call my attention to any shortcomings of this book and who offer concrete suggestions for strengthening future editions.

Many people contributed to this book. First, I owe a profound debt to the old 12th Street Study Group, with whom I first studied Black history and first came to understand the centrality of the issue of race. I am also indebted to the group's members, who provided me with a lasting example of what it means to commit one's life to the struggle for justice for all people.

Next, I owe an equally profound debt to friends and colleagues and students at William Paterson College involved in the various race and gender projects we have carried out for some years now. I have learned a great deal from all of them. I am especially grateful to J. Samuel Jordan and Leslie Agard-Jones of the African Afro-American Studies Department, with whom I have taught and learned and laughed and cried. Les was available throughout every phase of the preparation of this book, and my debt to him is incalculable. I also wish to thank Della Capers of the African Afro-American Studies Department for her constant and professional attention to all the details that make a book like this possible and for her friendship and encouragement.

I am also indebted to Norma Stoltz Chinchilla of California State University, Long Beach, Alma M. Garcia of Santa Clara University, Patricia Samuel of St. Cloud State University, Margaret Stroebel of the University of Illinois at Chicago Circle, Margaret Anderson of the University of Delaware, and Pamela Hawkins of the California State University, Fresno, each of whom commented in great detail on the manuscript and whose thoughtful comments and suggestions have greatly strengthened the book's final form.

Many other people contributed to the book in a variety of ways. Some helped me track down articles or information, others discussed issues, and others were simply part of a broad learning experience that provided the context for the book. My thanks to: Laura Aitken, Janet Falk, Ann Ferguson, Charley Flint, Carol Gruber, Linda Hamalian, Diane Harriford, Lee Hummel, Jean Levitan, Clara Lomas, Gregory Mantsios, Vernon McClean, Mihri Reyes-Napoliello, Gladys Nussenbaum, Phyllis Palmer, Donna Perry, Susan Radner, Bob Rosen, Steve Shalom, Carole Sheffield, Vicki Spellman, Peter Stein, Isabel Tirado, Phyllis Vine, Bill Willis, Arlene Hirschfelder and Dennis White of the Association of American Indian Affairs, and Susan Smith of the National Committee on Pay Equity.

The book has benefited greatly from the professional contributions of many people at St. Martin's Press. In particular, I would like to thank Andrea R. Guidoboni, Patricia Mansfield, Beverly Hinton, and Michael Weber for their work on this book. I would also like to thank the people at Editing, Design & Production, Inc., especially Lilliane Chouinard, for their careful attention to the manuscript.

Finally, I want to thank my family for always being there for me. Alexi and Andrea fill me with hope and make it possible for me to continue even after reading the daily newspaper, and Greg keeps me sane. I would also like to thank Phyllis Simitopoulos for finding all the typos in this edition as she did in my other books.

Paula S. Rothenberg

Introduction

A book that integrates rather than alternates the study of racism and sexism is long overdue. Whereas the sixties and seventies were characterized by a desire for separation and autonomy, the eighties reflect a spirit of cooperation and a sense of shared interests. In part, this attitude is a response to the shrinking resources being made available to bring us closer to race and gender equity. Many of us involved in teaching about race and gender have come to recognize that our survival may well depend upon a combined struggle to oppose cuts and cutbacks. Equally important, and not unrelated, many of us have come to understand that talking about gender without talking about race and class—or talking about race without considering class and gender—is simply another way of obscuring reality instead of coming to terms with it. This book grew out of the belief that an integrated study of racism and sexism, within the context of class, can provide us with a more comprehensive, more accurate, and more useful analysis of the world in which we live out our lives.

Our enterprise is not entirely without potential hazards. Racism and sexism are both comprehensive systems of oppression that deny individuals their personhood. As such, they have much in common that recommends their combined study. They are not, however, identical. This book presents an integrated approach to racism and sexism within the context of class while recognizing that neither phenomenon is reducible to the other. There are important historical and contemporary differences in these forms of oppression, and we seek to recognize these differences and learn from them as well as from their similarities. The same may be said of class. Although introducing the notion of class can often help us understand puzzling differences in the experiences of individuals of the same race or gender, overemphasizing it can obscure the full impact of racism and sexism on people's lives at this moment in history. This book proceeds by integrating race, class, and gender in order to enhance our total understanding, but we must be ever mindful of the need to recognize and learn from difference.

Beginning

Beginning our study together presents some immediate differences from other academic enterprises. Whereas most students in an introductory literature or sociology class do not begin the semester with deeply felt and firmly entrenched attitudes toward the subject they are about to study, almost every student in a course on racism and sexism enters the room with strong feelings. These feelings can either provide the basis for a profoundly passionate and personal study of race and gender that transforms its participants, or they can function as enormous obstacles that prevent our study from ever beginning in earnest. How we begin has critical implications for the success or failure of our enterprise.

It is important that we start by acknowledging the existence of these strong feelings and trying to come to terms with them. Why do we feel so strongly about issues of race and gender? Why is it often difficult to examine critically our thoughts on the nature of women and men, sexuality, the family, racial difference, and equality of opportunity? Can we find a way to share these strong feelings and participate in an honest and open exploration of our attitudes while remaining respectful of and sensitive to the feelings of others? Are we willing to examine our beliefs and evaluate their accuracy? A good way to begin might be for each of us to try to remember when and how we first became aware of gender and race differences in the world and to share our memories with each other. When undertaken seriously and thoughtfully, this process reveals that much of what we believe was learned early in a thoroughly pre-critical context. Once we acknowledge the shaky basis for our attitudes toward race and gender, it may be easier for us to bracket those attitudes temporarily and begin our study of racism and sexism in a changing society.

Structure of the Book

This book begins with definitions. What is "racism?" What is "sexism?" How shall we define these concepts? How shall we recognize instances of each? We are immediately confronted with another difference between this course and traditional courses. In the latter, teachers write definitions on the board, and students copy them down. The definitions are memorized, the problems or issues that define the subject matter are agreed upon, and the remainder of the course is spent examining different ways of solving the problems. In courses about race and gender, definitions provoke all kinds of intense responses and inspire little agreement. Instead of copying them down and memorizing them, students argue, protest, and challenge. Instead of spending the semester solving mutually recognized problems, we spend it trying to agree on what the problems are.

Part I of this book is designed to initiate this process. It allows us to examine fairly formal definitions of racism and sexism in relation to concrete manifestations of them in daily life. This part is not intended to end our discussion of the nature of racism and sexism but to begin it in a concrete and focused way, moving back and forth between theory and practice, using each to test the adequacy of the other.

After this preliminary attempt at definition, we are introduced to the notion of class and begin to examine the concrete impact of race, class, and gender on people's lives in two different ways. Part II provides statistics to paint a picture of differences in opportunity, expectations, and treatment, while Part III presents real-life experiences, which allow us to examine the impact of racism and sexism on people's daily lives. Many of these essays are highly personal, but each points beyond the individual's experience to social policy or practice or culturally conditioned attitudes. These articles should be used to further our discussion of the nature of racism and sexism and of the adequacy of the definitions examined in Part I.

When people first begin to recognize the enormous toll that racism and sexism take on human lives, they are often overwhelmed. How can they reconcile their belief that the United States provides liberty and justice and equal opportunity for all, with the reality presented in these pages? How did it happen? It is at this point that we turn to history.

Part IV highlights important aspects of the history of women and people of color in the United States by focusing on historical documents that reflect the legal status of these groups since the beginning of the Republic. Read in the context of the earlier material describing race, gender, and class differences in contemporary society, history becomes a way of using the past to make sense of the present. Focusing on the *legal* status of women and people of color allows us to telescope hundreds of years of history into manageable size, while still providing us with the historical information we need to make sense of contemporary society.

Our survey of racism and sexism in North America, past and present, has shown us that these phenomena function in a variety of ways. For some, the experiences that Richard Wright describes in "The Ethics of Living Jim Crow" are still all too real, but for most of us they describe a crude, blatant racism that seems incompatible with contemporary practice. How then are racism and sexism perpetuated in contemporary society? Why do these divisions and the accompanying differences in opportunity and achievement continue? How are they reproduced? Why do we have so much difficulty recognizing the reality that lies behind a rhetoric of equality of opportunity and justice for all? Part V offers some suggestions.

An early essay on sex-role conditioning draws an important distinction between discrimination, which frustrates choices already made, and the force of a largely unconscious gender-role ideology, which frustrates the ability to choose.* Our discussion of stereotypes, language, and social control is concerned with analyzing how the way we conceive of others and, equally important, the way we have come to conceive of ourselves help perpetuate racism and sexism. Our discussion then moves beyond the specificity of racist and sexist stereotypes to analyze how our modes of conceptualizing reality itself are conditioned by forces that are not always obvious. Racism and sexism are not merely narrow but identifiable attitudes, policies, and practices that affect individuals' lives. Rather, they operate on a basic level to structure what we come to think of as "reality." In this way, they cause us to limit our possibilities and personhood by internalizing beliefs that distort our perspective and make it more difficult to blame the socioeconomic system that benefits.

Finally, Part VI offers suggestions for moving beyond racism and sexism. These suggestions are not definitive answers. They are offered to stimulate discussion about the kinds of changes we might wish to explore in order to transform society. They offer the reader a variety of ideas about the causes and cures for the pervasive social and economic inequality and injustice this volume documents. They are meant to initiate a process of reflection and debate about these social ills and about the kinds of changes that can help address them. These solutions are neither comprehensive nor definitive simply because we are light-years away from *global* change. Meaningful social change will occur first at the local level as individuals, working together, begin to identify ways in which the institutions of which they are part perpetuate racism and sexism so that they can then seek to alter those institutions. Part VI is meant to provide a framework in which this process of identification and alteration can occur.

*Sandra L. Bem and Daryl Bem: "Homogenizing the American Woman," from *Beliefs, Attitudes, and Human Affairs* by D. J. Bem, Brooks/Cole Publishing Company, Monterey, California, 1970, pp. 89–99.

PART I

Defining "Racism" and "Sexism"

Refusing to hire a qualified person for a job because of race or gender or refusing to rent someone an apartment or sell him or her a house because of race or gender are fairly straightforward examples of discrimination. Most people would agree that such behavior is unfair and unjust. But once we move beyond these clear-cut cases of discrimination, it becomes more difficult to reach a consensus. Is the male supermarket manager or gas-station attendant just being friendly or is he acting in a sexist manner when he calls female customers "Sweetheart?" Is the underrepresentation of people of color in medical schools in the United States de facto proof of racism in the society, or does it result from a lack of qualified applicants? Is it possible that the very criteria for "qualified applicants" for jobs and academic opportunities may themselves reflect a subtle and pervasive racism and sexism? Can individuals and institutions be racist and sexist in the way they function normally, quite apart from their explicit intentions? These are the kinds of questions that will be raised in Part I as we attempt to arrive at some agreement about what constitutes racism and sexism.

Many people find the very words *racism* and *sexism* inflammatory and for this reason prefer to talk about *discrimination*. The members of the United States Commission on Civil Rights, authors of the first selection in this part, do just that. They define the problem in terms of discrimination and present us with a survey of race and gender discrimination, past and present. They begin by citing examples of discrimination by individuals, move on to examine organizational and structural discrimination, and conclude with a discussion of the way in which such treatment forms an interlocking and self-perpetuating *process of discrimination.*

Those who wish to emphasize the interlocking and self-perpetuating nature of discrimination as a process often claim that the term *discrimination* is itself too narrow and limited to do so effectively. They argue that words like *racism, sexism,* and *oppression* are more appropriate because they capture the comprehensive, systemic nature of the phenomena we are studying. They use these terms to point to a complex and pervasive system of beliefs, policies, practices, and attitudes that interrelate with incredible intricacy and subtlety.

The definitions provided in Part I are offered to give the reader an idea of the different ways thinkers have described the complexity of racism and sexism. None of these definitions is offered as *the* definition. In fact, defining racism and sexism is the project of this entire book, not merely the project of this single part. Nevertheless, this larger project requires some preliminary attempt to arrive at a set of working definitions. The examples provided in Selection 2 are a good place to begin. They ask us to move beyond a narrow understanding of discrimination and to think in more complex terms. They offer very different ways of expanding our thinking about the society we live in and how we have come to think about ourselves and others. Because they ask us to assume a critical perspective toward our experience, they are likely to strike some readers as provocative. Quite apart from the differences among them, each of these definitions agree that racism and sexism share the following common elements:

1. *Racism involves the subordination of people of color by white people.* While an individual person of color may discriminate against white people or even hate them, his or her behavior or attitude cannot be called "racist." He or she may be considered *prejudiced* against whites and we may all agree that the person acts unfairly and unjustly, but *racism* requires something more than anger, hatred, or prejudice; at the very least, it requires *prejudice plus power.* The history of the world provides us with a long record of white people holding power and using it to maintain that power and privilege over people of color, not the reverse.

2. *Sexism involves the subordination of women by men.* The reasoning here is fairly similar. While some women may dislike men intensely and treat them unfairly and while some women may be equally guilty of prejudice toward other women, the balance of power throughout most, if not all, of recorded history has allowed men to subordinate women in order to maintain their own privilege. Thus, an individual woman who treats men or women unfairly simply because of their gender may be called *prejudiced* and may be criticized as unjust, but she cannot be guilty of sexism. Of course, it is possible to imagine what it would mean for women to be guilty of sexism (or for people of color to be guilty of racism). If a reversal of power should come

about so that women and people of color somehow gain fairly comprehensive control of the institutions and ideas of society *and* use them to subordinate men and whites, respectively, we will alter our usage accordingly.

3. *Racism and sexism can be either conscious or unconscious, intentional or unintentional.* In Selection 3, Richard Wright describes growing up in the South during the early part of this century and provides us with excellent examples of the kind of blatant, conscious, intentional racism that most of us take as stereotypical. However, once we proceed to the fourth selection, the job of definition becomes more difficult. "'Bias Incident' at Staten Island's Miller Field" presents a disturbing example of racism carried out by a group of people who staunchly affirm, "We're not racists." Why do these people maintain this innocence in light of the incident described? What does their insistence tell us about racism? One lesson to be learned is that it is possible for a person to believe passionately that he or she is not racist or sexist but to be mistaken. Along these same lines, "Hidden Lessons" takes our inquiry further into the unconscious nature of racism and sexism by showing us how even teachers firmly committed to treating boy and girl students "equally" may themselves, unconsciously and unintentionally, be guilty of sexism.

The frequently unconscious and unintentional nature of both racism and sexism should not surprise us. One assumption this book makes is that both racism and sexism pervade American culture, that they are learned at an early age and re-inforced throughout life by a variety of institutions and experiences that are part of growing up and living in the United States. No wonder then that, like those teachers in "Hidden Lessons," even those of us consciously committed to race and gender justice are often guilty of the very behavior or attitudes we reject. No wonder too that there is such a strong desire to deny responsibility for them. Nonetheless, if the articles in Part I are correct, good people with good intentions can do racist and sexist things. The difference between nice people who inadvertently perpetuate racism and sexism and out-and-out racists is that the former generally apologize for their behavior and try to change it, and the latter do not.

Selection 6 introduces the concept of *oppression* to describe the pervasive nature of sexism and racism and helps to further explain why it is possible to be unaware of the forces that subordinate women and people of color and to participate in them unintentionally. Marilyn Frye, the author of the selection, uses the concept to focus on the profoundly comprehensive and personally crippling impact these two phenomena have on people's lives. Frye uses the metaphor of a bird cage to illustrate how sexism imprisons its victims through the interlocking operation of a series of impediments to motion. Taken alone, none of the barriers seems very powerful or threatening; taken together, they construct a cage that appears light and airy, masking the fact that its occupants are trapped as if in a sealed vault. Although Frye focuses exclusively on sexism, it is relatively easy to apply the same metaphor and analysis to explicate racism as well.

Frye follows her discussion of the bird cage metaphor with some examples of seemingly innocent but oppressive practices that will undoubtedly anger some readers. She takes as her paradigm, or model, the "male door-opening ritual" and argues that its meaning and implications go far beyond the conscious intentions of the man who opens the door. Before rejecting her argument out of hand, you might recall the reaction of the individuals in "Bias Incident" who disclaimed all responsibility for racism. Remember, Frye is analyzing the implications of a social ritual, not looking at any individual's motives for following that ritual. The point is that sexism and racism can be perpetuated by people who are just trying to be nice.

The final article in Part I, "Theories of Discrimination," surveys recent attempts to offer a theoretical analysis of the nature of discrimination. It begins with the important point that racism and sexism cannot be equated with pure and simple prejudice. Then, it examines three versions of the most widely held theoretical accounts of how and why racism and sexism function. These theories emphasize the institutional, systemic nature of both racism and sexism and help us understand further how both forms of oppression can be perpetuated by well-intentioned individuals who believe they are treating people fairly and who intend to treat people equally. This selection reiterates many of the points made by the United States Commission on Civil Rights and illustrated by the other readings in Part I. However, instead of merely describing or illustrating these theories, they are used here to try to offer coherent explanations for some of the policies and practices we have examined.

The Problem:
Discrimination

United States Commission on Civil Rights

Making choices is an essential part of everyday life for individuals and organizations. These choices are shaped in part by social structures that set standards and influence conduct in such areas as education, employment, housing, and government. When these choices limit the opportunities available to people because of their race, sex, or national origin, the problem of discrimination arises.

Historically, discrimination against minorities and women was not only accepted but it was also governmentally required. The doctrine of white supremacy used to support the institution of slavery was so much a part of American custom and policy that the Supreme Court in 1857 approvingly concluded that both the North and the South regarded slaves "as beings of an inferior order, and altogether unfit to associate with the white race, either in social or political relations; and so far inferior, that they had no rights which the white man was bound to respect."[1] White supremacy survived the passage of the Civil War amendments to the Constitution and continued to dominate legal and social institutions in the North as well as the South to disadvantage not only blacks,[2] but other racial and ethnic groups as well—American Indians, Alaskan Natives, Asian and Pacific Islanders, and Hispanics.[3]

While minorities were suffering from white supremacy, women were suffering from male supremacy. Mr. Justice Brennan has summed up the legal disabilities imposed on women this way:

> [T]hroughout much of the 19th century the position of women in our society was, in many respects, comparable to that of blacks under the pre-Civil War slave codes. Neither slaves nor women could hold office, serve on juries, or bring suit in their own names, and married women traditionally were denied the legal capacity to hold or convey property or to serve as legal guardians of their own children.[4]

In 1873 a member of the Supreme Court proclaimed, "Man is, or should be, woman's protector and defender. The natural and proper timidity and delicacy

9

which belongs to the female sex evidently unfits it for many of the occupations of civil life."[5] Such romantic paternalism has alternated with fixed notions of male superiority to deny women in law and in practice the most fundamental of rights, including the right to vote, which was not granted until 1920;[6] the Equal Rights Amendment has yet to be ratified.[7]

White and male supremacy are no longer popularly accepted American values.[8] The blatant racial and sexual discrimination that originated in our conveniently forgotten past, however, continues to manifest itself today in a complex interaction of attitudes and actions of individuals, organizations, and the network of social structures that make up our society.

Individual Discrimination

The most common understanding of discrimination rests at the level of prejudiced individual attitudes and behavior. Although open and intentional prejudice persists, individual discriminatory conduct is often hidden and sometimes unintentional.[9] Some of the following are examples of deliberately discriminatory actions by consciously prejudiced individuals. Some are examples of unintentionally discriminatory actions taken by persons who may not believe themselves to be prejudiced but whose decisions continue to be guided by deeply ingrained discriminatory customs.

- Personnel officers whose stereotyped beliefs about women and minorities justify hiring them for low level and low paying jobs exclusively, regardless of their potential experience or qualifications for higher level jobs.[10]
- Administrators, historically white males, who rely on "word-of-mouth" recruiting among their friends and colleagues, so that only their friends and protégés of the same race and sex learn of potential job openings.[11]
- Employers who hire women for their sexual attractiveness or potential sexual availability rather than their competence, and employers who engage in sexual harassment of their female employees.[12]
- Teachers who interpret linguistic and cultural differences as indications of low potential or lack of academic interest on the part of minority students.[13]
- Guidance counselors and teachers whose low expectations lead them to steer female and minority students away from "hard" subjects, such as mathematics and science, toward subjects that do not prepare them for higher paying jobs.[14]
- Real estate agents who show fewer homes to minority buyers and steer them to minority or mixed neighborhoods because they believe white residents would oppose the presence of black neighbors.[15]
- Families who assume that property values inevitably decrease when minorities move in and therefore move out of their neighborhoods if minorities do move in.[16]
- Parole boards that assume minority offenders to be more dangerous or more

unreliable than white offenders and consequently more frequently deny parole to minorities than to whites convicted of equally serious crimes.[17]

These contemporary examples of discrimination may not be motivated by conscious prejudice. The personnel manager is likely to deny believing that minorities and women can only perform satisfactorily in low level jobs and at the same time allege that other executives and decisionmakers would not consider them for higher level positions. In some cases, the minority or female applicants may not be aware that they have been discriminated against—the personnel manager may inform them that they are deficient in experience while rejecting their applications because of prejudice; the white male administrator who recruits by word-of-mouth from his friends or white male work force excludes minorities and women who never learn of the available positions. The discriminatory results these activities cause may not even be desired. The guidance counselor may honestly believe there are no other realistic alternatives for minority and female students.

Whether conscious or not, open or hidden, desired or undesired, these acts build on and support prejudicial stereotypes, deny their victims opportunities provided to others, and perpetuate discrimination, regardless of intent.

Organizational Discrimination

Discrimination, though practiced by individuals, is often reinforced by the well-established rules, policies, and practices of organizations. These actions are often regarded simply as part of the organization's way of doing business and are carried out by individuals as just part of their day's work.

Discrimination at the organizational level takes forms that are similar to those on the individual level. For example:

- Height and weight requirements that are unnecessarily geared to the physical proportions of white males and, therefore, exclude females and some minorities from certain jobs.[18]
- Seniority rules, when applied to jobs historically held only by white males, make more recently hired minorities and females more subject to layoff—the "last hired, first fired" employee—and less eligible for advancement.[19]
- Nepotistic membership policies of some referral unions that exclude those who are not relatives of members who, because of past employment practices, are usually white.[20]
- Restrictive employment leave policies, coupled with prohibitions on part-time work or denials of fringe benefits to part-time workers, that make it difficult for the heads of single parent families, most of whom are women, to get and keep jobs and meet the needs of their families.[21]
- The use of standardized academic tests or criteria, geared to the cultural and

educational norms of the middle-class or white males, that are not relevant indicators of successful job performance. [22]

- Preferences shown by many law and medical schools in the admission of children of wealthy and influential alumni, nearly all of whom are white. [23]
- Credit policies of banks and lending institutions that prevent the granting of mortgage monies and loans in minority neighborhoods, or prevent the granting of credit to married women and others who have previously been denied the opportunity to build good credit histories in their own names. [24]

Superficially "color blind" or "gender neutral," these organizational practices have an adverse effect on minorities and women. As with individual actions, these organizational actions favor white males, even when taken with no conscious intent to affect minorities and women adversely, by protecting and promoting the status quo arising from the racism and sexism of the past. If, for example, the jobs now protected by "last hired, first fired" provisions had always been integrated, seniority would not operate to disadvantage minorities and women. If educational systems from kindergarten through college had not historically favored white males, many more minorities and women would hold advanced degrees and thereby be included among those involved in deciding what academic tests should test for. If minorities had lived in the same neighborhoods as whites, there would be no minority neighborhoods to which mortgage money could be denied on the basis of their being minority neighborhoods.

In addition, these barriers to minorities and women too often do not fulfill legitimate needs of the organization, or these needs can be met through other means that adequately maintain the organization without discriminating. Instead of excluding all women on the assumption that they are too weak or should be protected from strenuous work, the organization can implement a reasonable test that measures the strength actually needed to perform the job or, where possible, develop ways of doing the work that require less physical effort. Admissions to academic and professional schools can be decided not only on the basis of grades, standardized test scores, and the prestige of the high school or college from which the applicant graduated, but also on the basis of community service, work experience, and letters of recommendation. Lending institutions can look at the individual and his or her financial ability rather than the neighborhood or marital status of the prospective borrower.

Some practices that disadvantage minorities and women are readily accepted aspects of everyday behavior. Consider the "old boy" network in business and education built on years of friendship and social contact among white males, or the exchanges of information and corporate strategies by business acquaintances in racially or sexually exclusive country clubs and locker rooms paid for by the employer. [25] These actions, all of which have a discriminatory impact on minorities and women, are not necessarily acts of conscious prejudice. Because such actions are so often considered part of the "normal" way of doing things, people have difficulty recognizing that they are discriminating and therefore resist abandoning these practices despite the clearly discriminatory results. Consequently, many decision-makers have difficulty considering, much less accepting, nondiscriminatory alternatives that may work just as well or better to advance legitimate organizational interests but without systematically disadvantaging minorities and women.

This is not to suggest that all such discriminatory organizational actions are spurious or arbitrary. Many may serve the actual needs of the organization. Physical size or strength at times may be a legitimate job requirement; sick leave and insurance policies must be reasonably restricted; educational qualifications are needed for many jobs; lending institutions cannot lend to people who cannot reasonably demonstrate an ability to repay loans. Unless carefully examined and then modified or eliminated, however, these apparently neutral rules, policies, and practices will continue to perpetuate age-old discriminatory patterns into the structure of today's society.

Whatever the motivation behind such organizational acts, a process is occurring, the common denominator of which is unequal results on a very large scale.[26] When unequal outcomes are repeated over time and in numerous societal and geographical areas, it is a clear signal that a discriminatory process is at work.

Such discrimination is not a static, one-time phenomenon that has a clearly limited effect. Discrimination can feed on discrimination in self-perpetuating cycles.[27]

- The employer who recruits job applicants by word-of-mouth within a predominantly white male work force reduces the chances of receiving applications from minorities and females for open positions. Since they do not apply, they are not hired. Since they are not hired, they are not present when new jobs become available. Since they are not aware of new jobs, they cannot recruit other minority or female applicants. Because there are no minority or female employees to recruit others, the employer is left to recruit on his own from among his predominantly white and male work force.[28]
- The teacher who expects poor academic performance from minority and female students may not become greatly concerned when their grades are low. The acceptance of their low grades removes incentives to improve. Without incentives to improve, their grades remain low. Their low grades reduce their expectations, and the teacher has no basis for expecting more of them.[29]
- The realtor who assumes that white home owners do not want minority neighbors "steers" minorities to minority neighborhoods. Those steered to minority neighborhoods tend to live in minority neighborhoods. White neighborhoods then remain white, and realtors tend to assume that whites do not want minority neighbors.[30]
- Elected officials appoint voting registrars who impose linguistic, geographic, and other barriers to minority voter registration. Lack of minority registration leads to low voting rates. Lower minority voting rates lead to the election of fewer minorities. Fewer elected minorities leads to the appointment of voting registrars who maintain the same barriers.[31]

Structural Discrimination

Such self-sustaining discriminatory processes occur not only within the fields of employment, education, housing, and government but also between these structural areas. There is a classic cycle of structural discrimination that reproduces itself. Discrimination in education denies the credentials to get good jobs. Discrimination in employment denies the economic resources to buy good housing. Discrimination in housing confines minorities to school districts providing inferior education, closing the cycle in a classic form.[32]

With regard to white women, the cycle is not as tightly closed. To the extent they are raised in families headed by white males, and are married to or live with white males, white women will enjoy the advantages in housing and other areas that such relationships to white men can confer. White women lacking the sponsorship of white men, however, will be unable to avoid gender-based discrimination in housing, education, and employment. White women can thus be the victims of discrimination produced by social structures that is comparable in form to that experienced by minorities.

This perspective is not intended to imply that either the dynamics of discrimination or its nature and degree are identical for women and minorities. But when a woman of any background seeks to compete with men of any group, she finds herself the victim of a discriminatory process. Regarding the similarities and differences between the discrimination experienced by women and minorities, one author has aptly stated:

> [W]hen two groups exist in a situation of inequality, it may be self-defeating to become embroiled in a quarrel over which is more unequal or the victim of greater oppression. The more salient question is how a condition of inequality for both is maintained and perpetuated—through what means is it reinforced?[33]

The following are additional examples of the interaction between social structures that affect minorities and women:

- The absence of minorities and women from executive, writing, directing, news reporting, and acting positions in television contributes to unfavorable stereotyping on the screen, which in turn reinforces existing stereotypes among the public and creates psychological roadblocks to progress in employment, education, and housing.[34]
- Living in inner-city high crime areas in disproportionate numbers, minorities, particularly minority youth, are more likely to be arrested and are more likely to go to jail than whites accused of similar offenses, and their arrest and conviction records are then often used as bars to employment.[35]
- Because of past discrimination against minorities and women, female and minority-headed businesses are often small and relatively new. Further disadvantaged by contemporary credit and lending practices, they are more likely

than white male-owned businesses to remain small and be less able to employ full-time specialists in applying for government contracts. Because they cannot monitor the availability of government contracts, they do not receive such contracts. Because they cannot demonstrate success with government contracts, contracting officers tend to favor other firms that have more experience with government contracts.[36]

Discriminatory actions by individuals and organizations are not only pervasive, occurring in every sector of society, but also cumulative with effects limited neither to the time nor the particular structural area in which they occur. This process of discrimination, therefore, extends across generations, across organizations, and across social structures in self-reinforcing cycles, passing the disadvantages incurred by one generation in one area to future generations in many related areas.[37]

These interrelated components of the discriminatory process share one basic result: the persistent gaps seen in the status of women and minorities relative to that of white males. These unequal results themselves have real consequences. The employer who wishes to hire more minorities and women may be bewildered by charges of racism and sexism when confronted by what appears to be a genuine shortage of qualified minority and female applicants. The guidance counselor who sees one promising minority student after another drop out of school or give up in despair may be resentful of allegations of racism when there is little he or she alone can do for the student. The banker who denies a loan to a female single parent may wish to do differently, but believes that prudent fiscal judgment requires taking into account her lack of financial history and inability to prove that she is a good credit risk. These and other decisionmakers see the results of a discriminatory process repeated over and over again, and those results provide a basis for rationalizing their own actions, which then feed into that same process.

When seen outside the context of the interlocking and intertwined effects of discrimination, complaints that many women and minorities are absent from the ranks of qualified job applicants, academically inferior and unmotivated, poor credit risks, and so forth, may appear to be justified. Decisionmakers like those described above are reacting to real social problems stemming from the process of discrimination. But many too easily fall prey to stereotyping and consequently disregard those minorities and women who have the necessary skills or qualifications. And they erroneously "blame the victims" of discrimination,[38] instead of examining the past and present context in which their own actions are taken and the multiple consequences of these actions on the lives of minorities and women.

The Process of Discrimination

Although discrimination is maintained through individual actions, neither individual prejudices nor random chance can fully explain the persistent national patterns of inequality and underrepresentation. Nor can these patterns be blamed on the persons who are at the bottom of our economic, political, and social order. Overt racism and sexism as embodied in popular notions of white and male supremacy have been widely repudiated, but our history of discrimination based on race, sex, and national origin has not been readily put aside. Past discrimination continues to have present effects. The task today is to identify those effects and the forms and dynamics of the discrimination that produced them.

Discrimination against minorities and women must now be viewed as an inter-locking process involving the attitudes and actions of individuals and the organizations and social structures that guide individual behavior. That process, started by past events, now routinely bestows privileges, favors, and advantages on white males and imposes disadvantages and penalties on minorities and women. This process is also self-perpetuating. Many normal, seemingly neutral, operations of our society create stereotyped expectations that justify unequal results; unequal results in one area foster inequalities in opportunity and accomplishment in others; the lack of opportunity and accomplishment confirm the original prejudices or engender new ones that fuel the normal operations generating unequal results.

As we have shown, the process of discrimination involves many aspects of our society. No single factor sufficiently explains it, and no single means will suffice to eliminate it. Such elements of our society as our history of *de jure* discrimination, deeply ingrained prejudices,[39] inequities based on economic and social class,[40] and the structure and function of all our economic, social, and political institutions[41] must be continually examined in order to understand their part in shaping today's decisions that will either maintain or counter the current process of discrimination.

It may be difficult to identify precisely all aspects of the discriminatory process and assign those parts their appropriate importance. But understanding discrimination starts with an awareness that such a process exists and that to avoid perpetuating it, we must carefully assess the context and consequences of our everyday actions . . . .

NOTES

1. Dred Scott v. Sandford, 60 U.S. (19 How.) 393, 408 (1857).

2. For a concise summary of this history, see U.S., Commission on Civil Rights, *Twenty Years After Brown*, pp. 4–29 (1975); *Freedom to the Free: 1863, Century of Emancipation* (1963).

3. The discriminatory conditions experienced by these minority groups have been documented in the following publications by the U.S. Commission on Civil Rights: *The Navajo Nation: An American Colony* (1975); *The Southwest Indian Report* (1973); *The Forgotten Minority: Asian Americans in New York City* (State Advisory Committee Report 1977); *Success of Asian Americans: Fact or Fiction?* (1980); *Stranger in One's Land* (1970); *Toward Quality Education for Mexican Americans* (1974); *Puerto Ricans in the Continental United States: An Uncertain Future* (1976).

4. Frontiero v. Richardson, 411 U.S. 677, 684–86 (1973), citing L. Kanowitz, *Women and the Law: The Unfinished Revolution*, pp. 5–6 (1970), and G. Myrdal, *An American*

Dilemma 1073 (20th Anniversary Ed., 1962). Justice Brennan wrote the opinion of the Court, joined by Justices Douglas, White, and Marshall. Justice Stewart concurred in the judgment. Justice Powell, joined by Chief Justice Burger and Justice Blackmun, wrote a separate concurring opinion. Justice Rehnquist dissented. See also H. M. Hacker, "Women as a Minority Group," *Social Forces*, vol. 30 (1951), pp. 60–69; W. Chafe, *Women and Equality: Changing Patterns in American Culture* (New York: Oxford University Press, 1977).

  5. Bradwell v. State, 83 U.S. (16 Wall) 130, 141 (1873) (Bradley, J., concurring), quoted in *Frontiero, supra* note 4.

  6. U.S. Const. amend. XIX.

  7. See U.S., Commission on Civil Rights, *Statement on the Equal Rights Amendment* (December 1978).

  8. See note 4, Introduction.

  9. See, e.g., R. K. Merton, "Discrimination and the American Creed," in R. K. Merton, *Sociological Ambivalence and Other Essays* (New York: The Free Press, 1976), pp. 189–216. In this essay on racism, published for the first time more than 30 years ago, Merton presented a typology which introduced the notion that discriminatory actions are not always directly related to individual attitudes of prejudice. Merton's typology consisted of the following: Type I—the unprejudiced nondiscriminator; Type II—the unprejudiced discriminator; Type III—the prejudiced nondiscriminator; Type IV—the prejudiced discriminator. In the present context, Type II is crucial in its observation that discrimination is often practiced by persons who are not themselves prejudiced, but who respond to, or do not oppose, the actions of those who discriminate because of prejudiced attitudes (Type IV). See also D. C. Reitzes, "Prejudice and Discrimination: A Study in Contradictions," in *Racial and Ethnic Relations*, ed. H. M. Hughes (Boston: Allyn and Bacon, 1970), pp. 56–65.

  10. See R. M. Kanter and B. A. Stein, "Making a Life at the Bottom," in *Life in Organizations, Workplaces as People Experience Them*, ed. Kanter and Stein (New York: Basic Books, 1976), pp. 176–90; also L. K. Howe, "Retail Sales Worker," ibid., pp. 248–51; also R. M. Kanter, *Men and Women of the Corporation* (New York: Basic Books, 1977).

  11. See M. S. Granovetter, *Getting A Job: A Study of Contract and Careers* (Cambridge: Harvard University Press, 1974), pp. 6–11; also A. W. Blumrosen, *Black Employment and the Law* (New Brunswick, N.J.: Rutgers University Press, 1971), p. 232.

  12. See U.S., Equal Employment Opportunity Commission, "Guidelines on Discrimination Because of Sex," 29 C.F.R. §1604.4 (1979); L. Farley, *Sexual Shakedown: The Sexual Harassment of Women on the Job* (New York: McGraw-Hill, 1978), pp. 92–96, 176–79; C. A. Mackinnon, *Sexual Harassment of Working Women* (New Haven: Yale University Press, 1979), pp. 25–55.

  13. See R. Rosenthal and L. F. Jacobson, "Teacher Expectations for the Disadvantaged," *Scientific American*, 1968 (b) 218, 219–23; also, D. Bar Tal, "Interactions of Teachers and Pupils," in *New Approaches to Social Problems* ed. I. H. Frieze, D. Bar Tal, and J. S. Carrol (San Francisco: Jossey Bass, 1979), pp. 337–58; also, U.S., Commission on Civil Rights, *Teachers and Students, Report V: Mexican American Education Study. Differences in Teacher Interaction With Mexican American and Anglo Students* (1973), pp. 22–23.

  14. Ibid.

  15. U.S., Department of Housing and Urban Development, Measuring Racial Discrimination in American Housing Markets: The Housing Market Practices Survey (1979); D. M. Pearce, "Gatekeepers and Home Seekers: Institutional Patterns in Racial Steering," in *Social*

Problems, vol. 26 (1979) pp. 325–42; "Benign Steering and Benign Quotas: The Validity of Race Conscious Government Policies to Promote Residential Integration," 93 *Harv. L. Rev.* 938, 944 (1980).

16. See M. N. Danielson, *The Politics of Exclusion* (New York: Columbia University Press, 1976), pp. 11–12; U.S., Commission on Civil Rights, *Equal Opportunity in Suburbia* (1974).

17. See L. L. Knowles and K. Prewitt, eds., *Institutional Racism in America* (Englewood Cliffs, N.J.: Prentice Hall, 1969) pp. 58–77, and E. D. Wright, *The Politics of Punishment* (New York: Harper and Row, 1973). Also, S. V. Brown, "Race and Parole Hearing Outcomes," in *Discrimination in Organizations*, ed. R. Alvarez and K. G. Lutterman (San Francisco: Jossey Bass, 1979), pp. 355–74.

18. Height and weight minimums that disproportionately exclude women without a showing of legitimate job requirement constitute unlawful sex discrimination. *See* Dothard v. Rawlinson, 433 U.S. 321 (1977); Bowe v. Colgate Palmolive Co., 416 F.2d 711 (7th Cir. 1969). Minimum height requirements used in screening applicants for employment have also been held to be unlawful where such a requirement excludes a significantly higher percentage of Hispanics than other national origin groups in the labor market and no job relatedness is shown. See Smith v. City of East Cleveland, 520 F.2d 492 (6th Cir. 1975).

19. U.S., Commission on Civil Rights, *Last Hired, First Fired* (1976); Tangren v. Wackenhut Servs., Inc., 480 F. Supp. 539 (D. Nev. 1979).

20. U.S., Commission on Civil Rights, *The Challenge Ahead, Equal Opportunity in Referral Unions* (1977), pp. 84–89.

21. A. Pifer, "Women Working: Toward a New Society," pp. 13–34, and D. Pearce, "Women, Work and Welfare: The Feminization of Poverty," pp. 103–24, both in K. A. Fernstein, ed., *Working Women and Families* (Beverly Hills: Sage Publications, 1979). Disproportionate numbers of single-parent families are minorities.

22. See Griggs v. Duke Power Company, 401 U.S. 424 (1971); U.S., Commission on Civil Rights, *Toward Equal Educational Opportunity: Affirmative Admissions Programs at Law and Medical Schools* (1978), pp. 10–12; I. Berg, *Education and Jobs: The Great Training Robbery* (Boston: Beacon Press, 1971), pp. 58–60.

22. See U.S., Commission on Civil Rights, *Toward Equal Educational Opportunity: Affirmative Admissions Programs at Law and Medical Schools* (1978), pp. 14–15.

24. See U.S., Commission on Civil Rights, *Mortgage Money: Who Gets It? A Case Study in Mortgage Lending Discrimination in Hartford, Conn.* (1974); J. Feagin and C. B. Feagin, *Discrimination American Style, Institutional Racism and Sexism* (Englewood Cliffs, N.J.: Prentice Hall, 1976), pp. 78–79.

25. See *Club Membership Practices by Financial Institutions: Hearing Before the Comm. on Banking, Housing and Urban Affairs, United States Senate*, 96th Cong., 1st Sess. (1979). The Office of Federal Contract Compliance Programs of the Department of Labor has proposed a rule that would make the payment or reimbursement of membership fees in a private club that accepts or rejects persons on the basis of race, color, sex, religion, or national origin a prohibited discriminatory practice. 45 Fed. Reg. 4954 (1980) (to be codified in 41 C.F.R. §60–1.11).

26. See discussion of the courts' use of numerical evidence of unequal results in the text accompanying notes 4–21 in Part B of this statement.

27. See U.S., Commission on Civil Rights, *For All the People . . . By All the People* (1969), pp. 122–23.

28. See note 11.

29. See note 13.

30. See notes 15 and 16.

31. See Statement of Arthur S. Flemming, Chairman, U.S., Commission on Civil Rights, before the Subcommittee on Constitutional Rights of the Committee on the Judiciary of the U.S. Senate on S.407, S.903, and S.1279, Apr. 9, 1975, pp. 15–18, based on U.S., Commission on Civil Rights, *The Voting Rights Act: Ten Years After* (January 1975).

32. See, e.g., U.S., Commission on Civil Rights, *Equal Opportunity in Suburbia* (1974).

33. Chafe, *Women and Equality*, p. 78.

34. U.S., Commission on Civil Rights, *Window Dressing on the Set* (1977).

35. See note 17; Gregory v. Litton Systems, Inc., 472 F.2d 631 (9th Cir. 1972); Green v. Mo.-Pac. R.R., 523 F.2d 1290 (8th Cir. 1975).

36. See U.S., Commission on Civil Rights, *Minorities and Women as Government Contractors*, pp. 20, 27, 125 (1975).

37. See, e.g., A. Downs, *Racism in America and How to Combat It* (U.S., Commission on Civil Rights, 1970); "The Web of Urban Racism," in *Institutional Racism in America*, ed. Knowles and Prewitt (Englewood Cliffs, N.J.: Prentice Hall, 1969) pp. 134–76. Other factors in addition to race, sex, and national origin may contribute to these interlocking institutional patterns. In *Equal Opportunity in Suburbia* (1974), this Commission documented what it termed "the cycle of urban poverty" that confines minorities in central cities with declining tax bases, soaring educational and other public needs, and dwindling employment opportunities, surrounded by largely white, affluent suburbs. This cycle of poverty, however, started with and is fueled by discrimination against minorities. *See also* W. Taylor, *Hanging Together, Equality in an Urban Nation* (New York: Simon & Schuster, 1971).

38. The "self-fulfilling prophecy" is a well known phenomenon. "Blaming the victim" occurs when responses to discrimination are treated as though they were the causes rather than the results of discrimination. *See* Chafe, *Women and Equality* (New York: Oxford University Press, 1977) pp. 76–78; W. Ryan. *Blaming the Victim* (New York: Pantheon Books, 1971).

39. See, e.g., J. E. Simpson and J. M. Yinger, *Racial and Cultural Minorities* (New York: Harper and Row, 1965) pp. 49–79; J. M. Jones, *Prejudice and Racism* (Reading, Mass.: Addison Wesley, 1972) pp. 60–111; M. M. Tumin, "Who Is Against Desegregation?" in *Racial and Ethnic Relations*, ed. H. Hughes (Boston: Allyn and Bacon, 1970) pp. 76–85; D. M. Wellman, *Portraits of White Racism* (Cambridge: Cambridge University Press, 1977).

40. See, e.g., D. C. Cox, *Caste, Class and Race: A Study In Social Dynamics* (Garden City, N.Y.: Doubleday, 1948); W. J. Wilson, *Power, Racism and Privilege* (New York: MacMillan, 1973).

41. H. Hacker, "Women as a Minority Group," *Social Forces*, vol. 30 (1951) pp. 60–69; J. Feagin and C. B. Feagin, *Discrimination American Style*; Chafe, *Women and Equality*; J. Feagin, "Indirect Institutionalized Discrimination," *American Politics Quarterly*, vol. 5 (1977) pp. 177–200; M. A. Chesler, "Contemporary Sociological Theories of Racism," in *Towards the Elimination of Racism*, ed. P. Katz (New York: Pergamon Press, 1976); P. Van den Berghe, *Race and Racism: A Comparative Perspective* (New York: Wiley, 1967); S. Carmichael and C. Hamilton, *Black Power* (New York: Random House, 1967); Knowles and Prewitt, *Institutional Racism in America*; Downs, *Racism in America and How To Combat It* (1970).

2

Some Definitions of Racism and Sexism

Racism

Racism may be viewed as any attitude, action, or institutional structure which subordinates a person or group because of his or their color. . . . This is true of Negroes, Puerto Ricans, Mexican Americans, Chinese Americans and American Indians. Specifically, white racism subordinates members of all these other groups primarily because they are not white in color, even though some are technically considered to be members of the "white race" and even view themselves as "white."

> *Racism in America and How to Combat It*, United States Commission on Civil Rights, 1970.

Racism is the generalized and final assigning of values to real or imaginary differences, to the accuser's benefit and at his victim's expense, in order to justify the former's won privileges or aggression.

> Albert Memmi, *Dominated Man.*

A racist society is one in which social policies, procedures, decisions, habits and acts do in fact subjugate a race of people and permit another race to maintain control over them. . . . Racism may be expressed as an individual act or as an institutional practice.

> *Institutional Racism in American Society: A Primer*, Mid-Peninsula Christian Ministry.

Racism can mean culturally sanctioned beliefs which, regardless of the intentions involved, defend the advantages whites have because of the subordinated position of racial minorities.

> David T. Wellman: *Portraits of White Racism*, Cambridge University Press, 1977, p. xviii.

Sexism

Any attitude, action or institutional structure which subordinates a person or group because of their sex.

Any assignment of roles in society on the basis of sex.

Exploitation of females, individually or as a group, by males.
> *Fact Sheets on Institutional Sexism*, compiled by the Council on Interracial Books for Children, p. 1.

Sexism is a many-headed, ubiquitous monster that has manifested itself in different ways in different historical periods and in different cultures. It is a belief system based on the assumption that the physical differences between males and females are so *Biology* significant that they should determine virtually all social and economic roles of men *is :* and women. It holds that not just their reproductive functions are determined by sex, *destiny* but that sex is the factor that rules their entire lives, all their functions in society and the economy, and their relation to the state and all public institutions and especially to each other. Sexism is manifest in all forms of behavior from subtle gestures and language to exploitation and oppression, and in all human institutions from the family to the multinational corporation.
> Betty A. Reardon: *Sexism and the War System*, Teachers College Press, New York, 1985, p. 16.

The unconscious, taken-for-granted, unquestioned, unexamined, and unchallenged acceptance of the belief that the world as it looked to men was the only world, that the way of dealing with it that men had created was the only way, that the values men had evolved were the only ones, that the way sex looked to men was the only way it could look to anyone, that what men thought women were like was the only way to think about women.
> Jessie Bernard: *Women and the Public Interest*, Aldine, Chicago, 1971, p. 37.

3

The Ethics of Living Jim Crow:
An Autobiographical Sketch

Richard Wright

I

My first lesson in how to live as a Negro came when I was quite small. We were living in Arkansas. Our house stood behind the railroad tracks. Its skimpy yard was paved with black cinders. Nothing green ever grew in that yard. The only touch of green we could see was far away, beyond the tracks, over where the white folks lived. But cinders were good enough for me and I never missed the green growing things. And anyhow cinders were fine weapons. You could always have a nice hot war with huge black cinders. All you had to do was crouch behind the brick pillars of a house with your hands full of gritty ammunition. And the first woolly black head you saw pop out from behind another row of pillars was your target. You tried your very best to knock it off. It was great fun.

I never fully realized the appalling disadvantages of a cinder environment till one day the gang to which I belonged found itself engaged in a war with the white boys who lived beyond the tracks. As usual we laid down our cinder barrage, thinking that this would wipe the white boys out. But they replied with a steady bombardment of broken bottles. We doubled our cinder barrage, but they hid behind trees, hedges, and the sloping embankments of their lawns. Having no such fortifications, we retreated to the brick pillars of our homes. During the retreat a broken milk bottle caught me behind the ear, opening a deep gash which bled profusely. The sight of blood pouring over my face completely demoralized our ranks. My fellow-combatants left me standing paralyzed in the center of the yard, and scurried for their homes. A kind neighbor saw me and rushed me to a doctor, who took three stitches in my neck.

I sat brooding on my front steps, nursing my wound and waiting for my mother to come from work. I felt that a grave injustice had been done me. It was all right to throw cinders. The greatest harm a cinder could do was leave a bruise. But broken bottles were dangerous; they left you cut, bleeding, and helpless.

When night fell, my mother came from the white folks' kitchen. I raced down the street to meet her. I could just feel in my bones that she would understand. I knew she would tell me exactly what to do next time. I grabbed her hand and babbled out the whole story. She examined my wound, then slapped me.

"How come yuh didn't hide?" she asked me. "How come yuh awways fightin'?"

I was outraged, and bawled. Between sobs I told her that I didn't have any trees or hedges to hide behind. There wasn't a thing I could have used as a trench. And you couldn't throw very far when you were hiding behind the brick pillars of a house. She grabbed a barrel stave, dragged me home, stripped me naked, and beat me till I had a fever of one hundred and two. She would smack my rump with the stave, and, while the skin was still smarting, impart to me gems of Jim Crow wisdom. I was never to throw cinders any more. I was never to fight any more wars. I was never, never, under any conditions, to fight *white* folks again. And they were absolutely right in clouting me with the broken milk bottle. Didn't I know she was working hard every day in the hot kitchens of the white folks to make money to take care of me? When was I ever going to learn to be a good boy? She couldn't be bothered with my fights. She finished by telling me that I ought to be thankful to God as long as I lived that they didn't kill me.

All that night I was delirious and could not sleep. Each time I closed my eyes I saw monstrous white faces suspended from the ceiling, leering at me.

From that time on, the charm of my cinder yard was gone. The green trees, the trimmed hedges, the cropped lawns grew very meaningful, became a symbol. Even today when I think of white folks, the hard, sharp outlines of white houses surrounded by trees, lawns, and hedges are present somewhere in the background of my mind. Through the years they grew into an overreaching symbol of fear.

It was a long time before I came in close contact with white folks again. We moved from Arkansas to Mississippi. Here we had the good fortune not to live behind the railroad tracks, or close to white neighborhoods. We lived in the very heart of the local Black Belt. There were black churches and black preachers; there were black schools and black teachers; black groceries and black clerks. In fact, everything was so solidly black that for a long time I did not even think of white folks, save in remote and vague terms. But this could not last forever. As one grows older one eats more. One's clothing costs more. When I finished grammar school I had to go to work. My mother could no longer feed and clothe me on her cooking job.

There is but one place where a black boy who knows no trade can get a job, and that's where the houses and faces are white, where the trees, lawns, and hedges are green. My first job was with an optical company in Jackson, Mississippi. The morning I applied I stood straight and neat before the boss, answering all his questions with sharp yessirs and nosirs. I was very careful to pronounce my *sirs* distinctly, in order that he might know that I was polite, that I knew where I was, and that I knew he was a *white* man. I wanted that job badly.

He looked me over as though he were examining a prize poodle. He questioned me closely about my schooling, being particularly insistent about how much mathematics I had had. He seemed very pleased when I told him I had had two years of algebra.

"Boy, how would you like to try to learn something around here?" he asked me.

"I'd like it fine, sir," I said, happy. I had visions of "working my way up." Even Negroes have those visions.

"All right," he said. "Come on."

I followed him to the small factory.

"Pease," he said to a white man of about thirty-five, "this is Richard. He's going to work for us."

Pease looked at me and nodded.

I was then taken to a white boy of about seventeen.

"Morrie, this is Richard, who's going to work for us."

"Whut yuh sayin' there, boy!" Morrie boomed at me.

"Fine!" I answered.

The boss instructed these two to help me, teach me, give me jobs to do, and let me learn what I could in my spare time.

My wages were five dollars a week.

I worked hard, trying to please. For the first month I got along O.K. Both Pease and Morrie seemed to like me. But one thing was missing. And I kept thinking about it. I was not learning anything and nobody was volunteering to help me. Thinking they had forgotten that I was to learn something about the mechanics of grinding lenses, I asked Morrie one day to tell me about the work. He grew red.

"Whut yuh tryin' t' do, nigger, get smart?" he asked.

"Naw; I ain' tryin' t' git smart," I said.

"Well, don't, if yuh know whut's good for yuh!"

I was puzzled. Maybe he just doesn't want to help me, I thought. I went to Pease.

"Say, are yuh crazy, you black bastard?" Pease asked me, his gray eyes growing hard.

I spoke out, reminding him that the boss had said I was to be given a chance to learn something.

"Nigger, you think you're *white*, don't you?"

"Naw, sir!"

"Well, you're acting mighty like it!"

"But, Mr. Pease, the boss said. . . ."

Pease shook his fist in my face.

"This is a *white* man's work around here, and you better watch yourself!"

From then on they changed toward me. They said good-morning no more. When I was just a bit slow in performing some duty, I was called a lazy black son-of-a-bitch.

Once I thought of reporting all this to the boss. But the mere idea of what would happen to me if Pease and Morrie should learn that I had "snitched" stopped me. And after all the boss was a white man, too. What was the use?

The climax came at noon one summer day. Pease called me to his work-bench. To get to him I had to go between two narrow benches and stand with my back against a wall.

"Yes, sir," I said.

"Richard, I want to ask you something," Pease began pleasantly, not looking up from his work.

"Yes, sir," I said again.

Morrie came over, blocking the narrow passage between the benches. He folded his arms, staring at me solemnly.

I looked from one to the other, sensing that something was coming.

"Yes, sir," I said for the third time.

Pease looked up and spoke very slowly.

"Richard, *Mr.* Morrie here tells me you called me *Pease.*"

I stiffened. A void seemed to open up in me. I knew this was the show-down.

He meant that I had failed to call him Mr. Pease. I looked at Morrie. He was gripping a steel bar in his hands. I opened my mouth to speak, to protest, to assure Pease that I had never called him simply *Pease*, and that I had never had any intentions of doing so, when Morrie grabbed me by the collar, ramming my head against the wall.

"Now, be careful, nigger!" snarled Morrie, baring his teeth. "I heard yuh call 'im *Pease!* 'N' if yuh say yuh didn't, yuh're callin' me a *lie*, see?" He waved the steel bar threateningly.

If I had said: No, sir Mr. Pease, I never called you *Pease*, I would have been automatically calling Morrie a liar. And if I had said: Yes, sir, Mr. Pease, I called you *Pease*, I would have been pleading guilty to having uttered the worst insult that a Negro can utter to a southern white man. I stood hesitating, trying to frame a neutral reply.

"Richard, I asked you a question!" said Pease. Anger was creeping into his voice.

"I don't remember calling you *Pease*, Mr. Pease," I said cautiously. "And if I did, I sure didn't mean. . . ."

"You black son-of-a-bitch! You called me *Pease*, then!" he spat, slapping me till I bent sideways over a bench. Morrie was on top of me, demanding:

"Didn't yuh call 'im *Pease*? If yuh say yuh didn't, I'll rip yo'gut string loose with this bar, yuh black granny dodger! Yuh can't call a white man a lie 'n' git erway with it, you black son-of-a-bitch!"

I wilted. I begged them not to bother me. I knew what they wanted. They wanted me to leave.

"I'll leave," I promised. "I'll leave right *now*."

They gave me a minute to get out of the factory. I was warned not to show up again, or tell the boss.

I went.

When I told the folks at home what had happened, they called me a fool. They told me that I must never again attempt to exceed my boundaries. When you are working for white folks, they said, you got to "stay in your place" if you want to keep working.

II

My Jim Crow education continued on my next job, which was portering in a clothing store. One morning, while polishing brass out front, the boss and his twenty-year-old son got out of their car and half dragged and half kicked a Negro woman into the store. A policeman standing at the corner looked on, twirling his night-stick. I watched out of the corner of my eye, never slackening the strokes of my chamois upon the brass. After a few minutes, I heard shrill screams coming from the rear of the store. Later the woman stumbled out, bleeding, crying, and holding her stomach. When she reached the end of the block, the policeman grabbed her and accused her of being drunk. Silently, I watched him throw her into a patrol wagon.

When I went to the rear of the store, the boss and his son were washing their hands at the sink. They were chuckling. The floor was bloody and strewn with wisps of hair and clothing. No doubt I must have appeared pretty shocked, for the boss slapped me reassuringly on the back.

"Boy, that's what we do to niggers when they don't want to pay their bills," he said, laughing.

His son looked at me and grinned.

"Here, hava cigarette," he said.

Not knowing what to do, I took it. He lit his and held the match for me. This was a gesture of kindness, indicating that even if they had beaten the poor old woman, they would not beat me if I knew enough to keep my mouth shut.

"Yes, sir," I said, and asked no questions.

After they had gone, I sat on the edge of a packing box and stared at the bloody floor till the cigarette went out.

That day at noon, while eating in a hamburger joint, I told my fellow Negro porters what had happened. No one seemed surprised. One fellow, after swallowing a huge bite, turned to me and asked:

"Huh! Is tha' all they did t' her?"

"Yeah. Wasn't tha' enough?" I asked.

"Shucks! Man, she's a lucky bitch!" he said, burying his lips deep into a juicy hamburger. "Hell, it's a wonder they didn't lay her when they got through."

III

I was learning fast, but not quite fast enough. One day, while I was delivering packages in the suburbs, my bicycle tire was punctured. I walked along the hot, dusty road, sweating and leading my bicycle by the handle-bars.

A car slowed at my side.

"What's the matter, boy?" a white man called.

I told him my bicycle was broken and I was walking back to town.

"That's too bad," he said, "Hop on the running board."

He stopped the car. I clutched hard at my bicycle with one hand and clung to the side of the car with the other.

"All set?"

"Yes, sir," I answered. The car started.

It was full of young white men. They were drinking. I watched the flask pass from mouth to mouth.

"Wanna drink, boy?" one asked.

I laughed as the wind whipped my face. Instinctively obeying the freshly planted precepts of my mother, I said:

"Oh, no!"

The words were hardly out of my mouth before I felt something hard and cold smash me between the eyes. It was an empty whisky bottle. I saw stars, and fell backwards from the speeding car into the dust of the road, my feet becoming entangled in the steel spokes of my bicycle. The white men piled out and stood over me.

"Nigger, ain' yuh learned no better sense'n tha' yet?" asked the man who hit me. "Ain' yuh learned t' say *sir* t' a white man yet?"

Dazed, I pulled to my feet. My elbows and legs were bleeding. Fists doubled, the white man advanced, kicking my bicycle out of the way.

"Aw, leave the bastard alone. He's got enough," said one.

They stood looking at me. I rubbed my shins, trying to stop the flow of blood. No doubt they felt a sort of contemptuous pity, for one asked:

"Yuh wanna ride t' town now, nigger? Yuh reckon yuh know enough t' ride now?"

"I wanna walk," I said, simply.

Maybe it sounded funny. They laughed.

"Well, walk, yuh black son-of-a-bitch!"

When they left they comforted me with:

"Nigger, yuh sho better be damn glad it wuz us yuh talked t' tha' way. Yuh're a lucky bastard, 'cause if yuh'd said tha' t' somebody else, yuh might've been a dead nigger now."

IV

Negroes who have lived South know the dread of being caught alone upon the streets in white neighborhoods after the sun has set. In such a simple situation as this the plight of the Negro in America is graphically symbolized. While white strangers may be in these neighborhoods trying to get home, they can pass unmolested. But the color of a Negro's skin makes him easily recognizable, makes him suspect, converts him into a defenseless target.

Late one Saturday night I made some deliveries in a white neighborhood. I was pedaling my bicycle back to the store as fast as I could, when a police car, swerving toward me, jammed me into the curbing.

"Get down and put up your hands!" the policemen ordered.

I did. They climbed out of the car, guns drawn, faces set, and advanced slowly.

"Keep still!" they ordered.

I reached my hands higher. They searched my pockets and packages. They seemed dissatisfied when they could find nothing incriminating. Finally, one of them said:

"Boy, tell your boss not to send you out in white neighborhoods after sundown."

As usual, I said:

"Yes, sir."

V

My next job was a hall-boy in a hotel. Here my Jim Crow education broadened and deepened. When the bell-boys were busy, I was often called to assist them. As many of the rooms in the hotel were occupied by prostitutes, I was constantly called to carry them liquor and cigarettes. These women were nude most of the time. They did not bother about clothing, even for bell-boys. When you went into their rooms, you were supposed to take their nakedness for granted, as though it startled you no more than a blue vase or a red rug. Your presence awoke in them no sense of shame, for you were not regarded as human. If they were alone, you could steal sidelong glimpses at them. But if they were receiving men, not a flicker of your eyelids could show. I remember one incident vividly. A new woman, a huge, snowy-skinned blonde, took a room on my floor. I was sent to wait upon her. She was in bed with a thick-set man; both were nude and uncovered. She said she wanted some liquor and slid out of bed and waddled across the floor to get her money from a dresser drawer. I watched her.

"Nigger, what in hell you looking at?" the white man asked me, raising himself upon his elbows.

"Nothing," I answered, looking miles deep into the blank wall of the room.

"Keep your eyes where they belong, if you want to be healthy!" he said.

"Yes, sir."

VI

One of the bell-boys I knew in this hotel was keeping steady company with one of the Negro maids. Out of a clear sky the police descended upon his home and arrested him, accusing him of bastardy. The poor boy swore he had had no intimate relations with the girl. Nevertheless, they forced him to marry her. When the child arrived, it was found to be much lighter in complexion than either of the two supposedly legal parents. The white men around the hotel made a great joke of it. They spread the rumor that some white cow must have scared the poor girl while she was carrying the baby. If you were in their presence when this explanation was offered, you were supposed to laugh.

VII

One of the bell-boys was caught in bed with a white prostitute. He was castrated and run out of town. Immediately after this all the bell-boys and hall-boys were called together and warned. We were given to understand that the boy who had been castrated was a "mighty, mighty lucky bastard." We were impressed with the fact that next time the management of the hotel would not be responsible for the lives of "trouble-makin' niggers." We were silent.

VIII

One night, just as I was about to go home, I met one of the Negro maids. She lived in my direction, and we fell in to walk part of the way home together. As we passed the white night-watchman, he slapped the maid on her buttock. I turned around, amazed. The watchman looked at me with a long, hard, fixed-under stare. Suddenly he pulled his gun and asked:

"Nigger, don't yuh like it?"

I hesitated.

"I asked yuh don't yuh like it?" he asked again, stepping forward.

"Yes, sir," I mumbled.

"Talk like it, then!"

"Oh, yes sir!" I said with as much heartiness as I could muster.

Outside, I walked ahead of the girl, ashamed to face her. She caught up with me and said:

"Don't be a fool! Yuh couldn't help it!"

This watchman boasted of having killed two Negroes in self-defense.

Yet, in spite of all this, the life of the hotel ran with an amazing smoothness. It would have been impossible for a stranger to detect anything. The maids, the hall-boys, and the bell-boys were all smiles. They had to be.

IX

I had learned my Jim Crow lessons so thoroughly that I kept the hotel job till I left Jackson for Memphis. It so happened that while in Memphis I applied for a job at a branch of the optical company. I was hired. And for some reason, as long as I worked there, they never brought my past against me.

Here my Jim Crow education assumed quite a different form. It was no longer brutally cruel, but subtly cruel. Here I learned to lie, to steal, to dissemble. I learned to play that dual role which every Negro must play if he wants to eat and live.

For example, it was almost impossible to get a book to read. It was assumed that after a Negro had imbibed what scanty schooling the state furnished he had no further need for books. I was always borrowing books from men on the job. One day I mustered enough courage to ask one of the men to let me get books from the library in his name. Surprisingly, he consented. I cannot help but think that he consented because he was a Roman Catholic and felt a vague sympathy for Negroes, being himself an object of hatred. Armed with a library card, I obtained books in the following manner: I would write a note to the librarian, saying: "Please let this nigger boy have the following books." I would then sign it with the white man's name.

When I went to the library, I would stand at the desk, hat in hand, looking as unbookish as possible. When I received the books desired I would take them home. If the books listed in the note happened to be out, I would sneak into the lobby and forge a new one. I never took any chances guessing with the white librarian about what the fictious white man would want to read. No doubt if any of the white patrons had suspected that some of the volumes they enjoyed had been in the home of a Negro, they would not have tolerated it for an instant.

The factory force of the optical company in Memphis was much larger than that in Jackson, and more urbanized. At least they liked to talk, and would engage the Negro help in conversation whenever possible. By this means I found that many subjects were taboo from the white man's point of view. Among the topics they did not like to discuss with Negroes were the following: American white women; the Ku Klux Klan; France, and how Negro soldiers fared while there; French women; Jack Johnson; the entire northern part of the United States; the Civil War; Abraham Lincoln; U. S. Grant; General Sherman; Catholics; the Pope; Jews; the Republican Party; slavery; social equality; Communism; Socialism; the 13th and 14th Amendments to the Constitution; or any topic calling for positive knowledge or manly self-assertion on the part of the Negro. The most accepted topics were sex and religion.

There were many times when I had to exercise a great deal of ingenuity to keep out of trouble. It is a southern custom that all men must take off their hats when they enter an elevator. And especially did this apply to us blacks with rigid force. One day I stepped into an elevator with my arms full of packages. I was forced to ride with my hat on. Two white men stared at me coldly. Then one of them very kindly lifted my hat and placed it upon my armful of packages. Now the most accepted response for a Negro to make under such circumstances is to look at the white man out of the corner of his eye and grin. To have said: "Thank you!" would have made the white man *think* that you *thought* you were receiving from him a personal service. For such an act I have seen Negroes take a blow in the mouth. Finding the first alternative distasteful, and the second dangerous, I hit upon an acceptable course of action which fell safely between these two poles. I immediately—no sooner than my hat was lifted—pretended that my packages were about to spill, and appeared deeply distressed with keeping them in my arms. In this fashion I evaded having to acknowledge his service, and, in spite of adverse circumstances, salvaged a slender shred of personal pride.

How do Negroes feel about the way they have to live? How do they discuss it when alone almost themselves? I think this question can be answered in a single sentence. A friend of mine who ran an elevator once told me:

"Lawd, man! Ef it wuzn't fer them polices 'n' them ol' lynch-mobs, there wouldn't be nothin' but uproar down here!"

"Bias Incident" at Staten Island's Miller Field:

A Tale of Two Neighborhoods

Howard Blum

The selection that follows is a newspaper account of an incident that occurred in New York City in August 1983.

Gregory Cotton had adjusted the tan leather cap on his head to a jaunty angle and was returning to the punchball game when he found his path blocked by two husky teen-agers.

"This field is for white people only," Gregory, a sixth grader, remembers one of the youths calling to him. The other motioned with a can of beer as if to underline the threat.

Some of Gregory's classmates saw the confrontation by the water fountain and walked across Staten Island's Miller Field to intervene.

There were more threats. A punch was thrown. And then another. And suddenly the Public School 139 graduation picnic had turned into what the New York City police would later call "a confirmed bias incident."

All this happened on June 17, but weeks later it still affects the lives of those involved, young and old. The children from Flatbush certainly remember it. So do the teen-agers from Staten Island. One of them was sentenced on July 19 to perform 70 hours of community service for his actions that afternoon on Miller Field.

"Our reports show there was a racial incident that afternoon," said Lieut. James I. Radney of the Federal park police, which patrols the field, part of the Federal Gateway National Recreation Area.

It was only one racial incident in a city where, according to the Police Department, there were 71 "confirmed bias incidents" in the first six months of this year.

But what happened that afternoon remains a jumble of frightening images to the 12-year-olds from the Brooklyn school: a group of perhaps 15 white teen-agers throwing rocks and shouting racial epithets as they chased them across the field; cries of "Go back to where you belong"; a teacher swinging a bat frantically as he tried to defend his pupils, and rocks and bottles flying through the air, hitting children, crashing through school bus windows.

The sixth grade of P. S. 139 left the picnic on Staten Island under a police escort. The pupils made the trip back to Brooklyn in different buses from those in which they had arrived; the original school buses, their windows shattered, were littered with shards of glass. Six of the pupils—one Hispanic youth and five blacks—were treated in the emergency room of Staten Island Hospital for minor cuts and bruises.

Their class picnic had become a racial incident. And it had become the story of two divergent communities and a generation coming of age on the issue of race.

"A Neighborhood to Protect"

The bungalows at New Dorp Beach on Staten Island were built after World War II as summer getaway homes. As the completion of the Verrazano-Narrows Bridge made Staten Island more accessible to the rest of the city and the economy made second homes less accessible to many, these bungalows, with some insulation, gradually became year-round residences.

It was not long before developers moved in to plow dusty roads through the woods and erect rows of adjoining red-brick town houses and clapboard houses with neat front lawns. A community, just a stone's throw from the Atlantic Ocean, evolved.

Many of the second generation of New Dorp Beach residents—the teenage children of Civil Service and other middle-class workers—hang out on summer nights at the General Store on Topping Street, across from a strip of dunes leading to a rocky beach. Seated on a low fence near the store is a row of teen-agers, boys and girls, in an orderly line like birds perched on a wire.

Two antiquated gas pumps stand in front and the inside is crowded with a haphazard assortment of food and soda. A video game across from the front door is surrounded by youngsters; the machine fills the store with a steady background of shrill, high-pitched noises. About a block away is Miller Field.

"We got a neighborhood to protect," explains Ralph Fellini, 31, the owner of the General Store and the only one in the crowd outside willing to answer questions. "That's really what the whole thing on Miller Field was about."

"Hey, you guys know what went down at the field that day," he says to a group of uncommunicative youths. "You got nothing to be ashamed of. Tell the man."

"Well, if Ralphie says it's all right," decides a youth who had moments before denied even knowing the location of Miller Field.

"This is our neighorhood," says Darren Scaffidi, 15. "You let in one colored, you gotta let in a thousand."

"They don't have to come to Staten Island," says Petey Smith, 14. "Couldn't they go to Prospect Park in Brooklyn or some place like that?"

"I mean what would happen if we went up to Harlem?" asks Mike Cumminsky, 17.

"Look," says Charles Trainer, 17, "sure black people got a right to come to the field. It's public property. But they should know they don't belong here. The teachers who took them here are to blame."

The specifics of the incident have also taken on a reality unique to the logic of the neighborhood: A half-dozen voices insist that it could not have been a sixth-grade class that was attacked.

"They were really big dudes—huge," John Coe argues.

"Oh, maybe there were some little kids," Kevin McCarthy Jr., 15, finally agrees. "But they were day-care center kids. They should know better than to bus day-care center kids out here."

Mr. Fellini, a parent himself, sums it up: "These are good kids. They're not troublemakers. They're like I was when I was growing up in this neighborhood. They're just trying to make sure New Dorp Beach stays the kind of place where they'll want to raise their kids someday."

"The Racial Mix of the Real World"

P.S. 139 on Cortelyou Road in the Flatbush section of Brooklyn is on the fringe of a neighborhood of grand Victorian homes that seem out of place in Brooklyn. Tiled fireplaces, paneled rooms, wainscoting, parquet floors—all are common amenities surviving from a more comfortable era. Even the street names—Buckingham, Marlborough, Rugby—suggest the sort of gracious and static vision of Britannia that fuels romantic imaginations.

Yet Flatbush is a neighborhood hectic with modern-day problems and transition. Signs on the streets announce the private security police patrol the neighborhood. It is not an unrealistic precaution: in the 70th Precinct, which includes P.S. 139, the police report there were 3,534 burglaries in 1982.

And although the people whose children were attacked on Staten Island talk as though it could not happen here, there were also, police records show, four "confirmed bias incidents" in the precinct during that year. The incidents involved anti-Semitic actions and resulted in the arrests of youths aged 10 to 17.

From a population that was heavily Jewish and white in 1970, the 1980 census found Flatbush 30 percent white, 50 percent black, 13 percent Hispanic and 7 percent Asian.

P.S. 139 also reflects the changing character of the neighborhood. According to Lawrence Levy, the school's principal, 70 percent of the school's 1,500 pupils are black, Hispanic or Asian.

It was this racial cross-section of students that the principal addressed at a special assembly two days after the events in Staten Island.

"I simply told the children," Mr. Levy recalled, "that there are some people in this world who are determined to hate other people because of their race or religion. This is not the way things are at P.S. 139, but we can't ignore that such hatred exists elsewhere."

"Part of the strength of P.S. 139 is that it reflects the racial mix of the real world," said Jackie Lieberman, whose sixth-grade child had been at the picnic. "And it would be wrong for our children simply to forget what happened that day. They should remember so that they can someday do something about the hatred which exists in this very imperfect but very real world."

So one day, a group of sixth graders gathered in a shady corner planted with day lilies across from the school's playground to discuss how they felt about what happened at Miller Field.

"They think we're still going to be slaves," says Bruce Johnston, 11. "I was scared, but I'd rather be scared than a racist."

"I was angry," says Charlene Ohayon, 11. "This is a free country, and we got a right to play anywhere."

"They could come here if they want," says Stephen Delabstide, 12. "Maybe they should. Those kids from Staten Island in their punk rock T-shirts should see that all kinds of kids can get along out here."

"Yeah," says Tricia Moretti, 11. "They grow up in that neighborhood hating people who are strange to them. It's their parents who teach them that. Their parents taught them to hate people who are different, and now it's too late. Their parents are to blame."

"We Don't Want All This Destroyed"

Rose Lanza's 16-year-old son, Nicholas, was arrested and charged with six counts of second-degree assault, reckless endangerment, criminal mischief and resisting arrest for his purported role in the incident on Miller Field. On July 19, after plea bargaining, Nicholas was sentenced to perform 70 hours of community service.

The boy's lawyer, Dennis M. Karsch, contends that his client is not guilty. "Nicholas Lanza did nothing wrong," says Mr. Karsch. "He was just walking up the street when he was arrested. He didn't call any names or throw any rocks. He didn't do anything."

"What really bothers me," Mr. Karsch continues as he sits in his Staten Island office, "is the way some people have thrown racism into this. There's no proof. Some people are just trying to fire things up by calling this a racial issue. I think it was just a group of kids who had an argument that led to a fight with another group of kids."

Mrs. Lanza, a school crossing guard, breaks into tears when she discusses her son. In the living room of her brick town house, there are plastic seat covers on the blue couch and a wedding picture of her and her husband on a wooden coffee table.

"I'm a widow," she manages to say through her tears, "and I have to raise Nick all by myself. Now look what they done to him. They kept him in jail overnight. Jail in Brooklyn. They made him drink coffee. I never let my son drink coffee. He's just a boy. A good boy. How could they do that to him?

"And now what's going to happen to us? If our name is in the paper, they'll come back here and rob us. Those kids from Brooklyn have relatives. Uncles. Brothers. What if those people from Brooklyn come after us? I was robbed last winter. I couldn't live through another robbery. Why did they have to pick on my son?"

Esther Scaffidi's son Kevin, 15, was also arrested by the park police after the incident at Miller Field. Kevin was arrested in front of the General Store while he was trying to prevent the park police from arresting a friend who he said was innocent.

The authorities agreed that Kevin had not been at Miller Field that afternoon, and he was released after his mother paid a $25 fine and he promised to buy a new pair of sunglasses for a park police officer who had his broken in the scuffle.

Mrs. Scaffidi is disabled. She sits in the living room of her bungalow in New Dorp Beach while her son and Ralph Fellini listen.

"I don't know the Lanza boy," she says, "but I'm sure he's a good kid like all the other kids in the neighborhood. It isn't that we're prejudiced. People out here just work hard. We don't want all this destroyed. It's wrong for black people to yell prejudice. We're not racists."

5

Hidden Lessons:
Do Little Boys Get a Better Education Than Little Girls?

Claire Safran

Our public school teachers are targets once again of the researchers. This time, they have been charged with sex-biased instructional methods.

Drs. David and Myra Sadker of American University in Washington, D.C., sent observers to 100 classrooms in five states to sit in on teaching sessions. The Sadkers' researchers cited instances of boys being taught differently from girls in elementary schools, where women teachers far outnumber men, through secondary schools, where more than half the teachers are male.

The bias generally is unintentional and unconscious, says Myra Sadker, dean of the School of Education at American University. She notes: "We've met teachers who call themselves feminists. They show me their nonsexist textbooks and non-sexist bulletin boards. They insist there is equity in their classrooms. Then," she continues, "I videotape them as they're teaching—and they're amazed. If they hadn't seen themselves at work on film, they'd never have believed that they were treating boys and girls so differently."

Such videotaping of teachers is among the functions of 12 U.S. Department of Education Centers for Sex Equity in educational districts across the country.

From nursery school to beyond graduate school, studies show that teachers call on male students in class far more often then they call on female students. That difference in involvement in the learning process is crucial, say educators, who add that the students who are active in class are the ones who go on to higher achievement and a more positive attitude.

Many teachers unwittingly hinder girls from being active in class. Dr. Lisa Serbin of Concordia University in Montreal studied nursery schools in Suffolk County, N.Y. She tells how a teacher poured water into containers of different heights and widths, then told a little boy to try it—to learn for himself how water can change its shape without changing its amount.

"Can I do it?" a little girl asked.

"You'll have to wait your turn," the teacher replied, giving the pitcher to a second boy. The girl asked again, but it was time to put the materials away.

"You can help me to do that," the teacher offered.

Who gets to pour the water is important. Learning is connected to instruction and direction, and boys get more of that than girls do all through school. Why? Partly because teachers tend to question the students they expect will have the answers. Since girls traditionally don't do so well as boys in such "masculine" subjects as math and science, they're called on least in those classes. But girls are called on most in verbal and reading classes, where boys are expected to have the trouble. The trouble is in our culture, not in our chromosomes. In Germany, everything academic is considered masculine, most teachers are men, and girls have the reading problems. In Japan, there's no sex bias about reading, and neither sex has special problems with it.

In most U.S. schools, there are remedial classes for reading—the "boys' problem"—and boys quickly catch up to the girls. But there are very few remedial classes in math and science—the "girls' problems." Thus boys have the most skill in these subjects, which can lead to better-paying jobs later.

According to the National Assessment of Educational Progress, an organization in Denver that surveys both public and private schools nationally, girls get better math grades than boys do at age 9, but their scores decline as they progress while boys' math scores rise. Researchers say such things happen because boys are taught to take a more active part in learning than girls.

This differing of the educational process for the sexes starts at home. For example, in one study, preschool youngsters were shown a drawing of a house and asked, "How far can you go from your own house?" Most girls pointed to an area quite near the house and said that was how far their parents permitted them to go and how far they actually went. Most boys pointed to a much wider perimeter of permission and generally said they exceeded it. In the classroom, unconscious sex bias takes various forms:

- Girls tend to be called on if they sit close to the teacher—first row—right under his or her nose. Boys tend to be called on wherever they sit. (*Girls' Lesson:* Be dependent—stay close to the teacher, and you'll be rewarded. *Boys' Lesson:* Be independent—sit anywhere; you'll be rewarded.)
- The Sadkers report this interchange. Fourth-grade teacher to a girl: "That's a neat paper. The margins are just right." To a boy: "That's a good analysis of the cause of the Civil War." (*Girl's Lesson:* Form, not content, is all that's expected of you. *Boy's Lesson:* Analytical thinking is what's expected of you.)
- Dr. Carol Dweck, professor of education at Harvard University, cites these comments by a teacher to students who have given incorrect answers. To a girl: "That's wrong." To a boy: "You'd know the right answer if you'd done your homework." (*Girl's Lesson:* The failure may be due to your own lack of ability. *Boy's Lesson:* You can do better if you make the effort.) Told that effort brings success, both sexes try—and succeed. Otherwise, both stop trying. Educators call this concept "attribution to effort."

Some teachers are learning to recognize—and then change—their methods. And small changes can make large differences. The Sadkers, for example, found that if teachers wait a few seconds after asking a question before they call on a student, more students will participate and their answers will be more complete.

Parents disturbed by sex bias in classrooms might first test themselves for it at home. Those who want to help combat teachers' sex bias might arrange to observe classes in their children's schools, and they might discuss sex bias at PTA meetings. On this issue, awareness is the first step.

Oppression

Marilyn Frye

It is a fundamental claim of feminism that women are oppressed. The word "oppression" is a strong word. It repels and attracts. It is dangerous and dangerously fashionable and endangered. It is much misused, and sometimes not innocently.

The statement that women are oppressed is frequently met with the claim that men are oppressed too. We hear that oppressing is oppressive to those who oppress as well as to those they oppress. Some men cite as evidence of their oppression their much-advertised inability to cry. It is tough, we are told, to be masculine. When the stresses and frustrations of being a man are cited as evidence that oppressors are oppressed by their oppressing, the word "oppression" is being stretched to meaninglessness; it is treated as though its scope includes any and all human experience of limitation or suffering, no matter the cause, degree or consequence. Once such usage has been put over on us, then if ever we deny that any person or group is oppressed, we seem to imply that we think they never suffer and have no feelings. We are accused of insensitivity, even of bigotry. For women, such accusation is particularly intimidating, since sensitivity is one of the few virtues that has been assigned to us. If we are found insensitive, we may fear we have no redeeming traits at all and perhaps are not real women. Thus are we silenced before we begin: the name of our situation drained of meaning and our guilt mechanisms tripped.

But this is nonsense. Human beings can be miserable without being oppressed, and it is perfectly consistent to deny that a person or group is oppressed without denying that they have feelings or that they suffer.

We need to think clearly about oppression, and there is much that mitigates against this. I do not want to undertake to prove that women are oppressed (or that men are not), but I want to make clear what is being said when we say it. We need this word, this concept, and we need it to be sharp and sure.

The root of the word "oppression" is the element "press." *The press of the crowd; pressed into military service; to press a pair of pants; printing press; press the button.* Presses are used to mold things or flatten them or reduce them in bulk, sometimes to reduce them by squeezing out the gasses or liquids in them. Something pressed is something caught between or among forces and barriers which are so related to each other that jointly they restrain, restrict or prevent the thing's motion or mobility. Mold. Immobilize. Reduce.

The mundane experience of the oppressed provides another clue. One of the most characteristic and ubiquitous features of the world as experienced by oppressed people is the double bind—situations in which options are reduced to a very few and all of them expose one to penalty, censure or deprivation. For example, it is often a requirement upon oppressed people that we smile and be cheerful. If we comply, we signal our docility and our acquiescence in our situation. We need not, then, be taken note of. We acquiesce in being made invisible, in our occupying no space. We participate in our own erasure. On the other hand, anything but the sunniest countenance exposes us to being perceived as mean, bitter, angry or dangerous. This means, at the least, that we may be found "difficult" or unpleasant to work with, which is enough to cost one one's livelihood; at worst, being seen as mean, bitter, angry or dangerous has been known to result in rape, arrest, beating and murder. One can only choose to risk one's preferred form and rate of annihilation.

Another example: It is common in the United States that women, especially younger women, are in a bind where neither sexual activity nor sexual inactivity is all right. If she is heterosexually active, a woman is open to censure and punishment for being loose, unprincipled or a whore. The "punishment" comes in the form of criticism, snide and embarrassing remarks, being treated as an easy lay by men, scorn from her more restrained female friends. She may have to lie and hide her behavior from her parents. She must juggle the risks of unwanted pregnancy and dangerous contraceptives. On the other hand, if she refrains from heterosexual activity, she is fairly constantly harassed by men who try to persuade her into it and pressure her to "relax" and "let her hair down"; she is threatened with labels like "frigid," "uptight," "man-hater," "bitch" and "cocktease." The same parents who would be disapproving of her sexual activity may be worried by her inactivity because it suggests she is not or will not be popular, or is not sexually normal. She may be charged with lesbianism. If a woman is raped, then if she has been heterosexually active she is subject to the presumption that she liked it (since her activity is presumed to show that she likes sex), and if she has not been heterosexually active, she is subject to the presumption that she liked it (since she is supposedly "repressed and frustrated"). Both heterosexual activity and heterosexual nonactivity are likely to be taken as proof that you wanted to be raped, and hence, of course, weren't *really* raped at all. You can't win. You are caught in a bind, caught between systematically related pressures.

Women are caught like this, too, by networks of forces and barriers that expose one to penalty, loss or contempt whether one works outside the home or not, is on welfare or not, bears children or not, raises children or not, marries or not, stays married or not, is heterosexual, lesbian, both or neither. Economic necessity; confinement to racial and/or sexual job ghettos; sexual harassment; sex discrimination; pressures of competing expectations and judgments about *women, wives* and *mothers* (in the society at large, in racial and ethnic subcultures and in one's own mind); dependence (full or partial) on husbands, parents or the state; commitment to political ideas; loyalties to racial or ethnic or other "minority" groups; the demands of self-respect and responsibilities to others. Each of these factors exists in complex tension with every other, penalizing or prohibiting all of the apparently available options. And nipping at one's heels, always, is the endless pack of little things. If one dresses one way, one is subject to the assumption that one is advertising one's sexual availability; if one dresses another way, one appears to "not care about oneself" or to be "unfeminine." If one uses "strong language," one invites categorization as a whore or slut; if one does not, one invites categorization as a "lady"—one too delicately constituted to cope with robust speech or the realities to which it presumably refers.

The experience of oppressed people is that the living of one's life is confined and shaped by forces and barriers which are not accidental or occasional and hence avoidable, but are systematically related to each other in such a way as to catch one between and among them and restrict or penalize motion in any direction. It is the experience of being caged in: all avenues, in every direction, are blocked or booby-trapped.

Cages. Consider a birdcage. If you look very closely at just one wire in the cage, you cannot see the other wires. If your conception of what is before you is determined by this myopic focus, you could look at that one wire, up and down the length of it, and be unable to see why a bird would not just fly around the wire any time it wanted to go somewhere. Furthermore, even if, one day at a time, you myopically inspected each wire, you still could not see why a bird would have trouble going past the wires to get anywhere. There is no physical property of any one wire, *nothing* that the closest scrutiny could discover, that will reveal how a bird could be inhibited or harmed by it except in the most accidental way. It is only when you step back, stop looking at the wires one by one, microscopically, and take a macroscopic view of the whole cage, that you can see why the bird does not go anywhere; and then you will see it in a moment. It will require no great subtlety of mental powers. It is perfectly *obvious* that the bird is surrounded by a network of systematically related barriers, no one of which would be the least hindrance to its flight, but which, by their relations to each other, are as confining as the solid walls of a dungeon.

It is now possible to grasp one of the reasons why oppression can be hard to see and recognize: one can study the elements of an oppressive structure with great care and some good will without seeing the structure as a whole, and hence without seeing or being able to understand that one is looking at a cage and that there are people there who are caged, whose motion and mobility are restricted, whose lives are shaped and reduced.

The arresting of vision at a microscopic level yields such common confusion as that about the male door-opening ritual. This ritual, which is remarkably widespread across classes and races, puzzles many people, some of whom do and some of whom do not find it offensive. Look at the scene of the two people approaching a door. The male steps slightly ahead and opens the door. The male holds the door open while the female glides through. Then the male goes through. The door closes after them. "Now how," one innocently asks, "can those crazy womenslibbers say that is oppressive? The guy *removed* a barrier to the lady's smooth and unruffled progress." But each repetition of this ritual has a place in a pattern, in fact in several patterns. One has to shift the level of one's perception in order to see the whole picture.

The door-opening pretends to be a helpful service, but the helpfulness is false. This can be seen by noting that it will be done whether or not it makes any practical sense. Infirm men and men burdened with packages will open doors for able-bodied women who are free of physical burdens. Men will impose themselves awkwardly and jostle everyone in order to get to the door first. The act is not determined by convenience or grace. Furthermore, these very numerous acts of unneeded or even noisome "help" occur in counterpoint to a pattern of men not being helpful in many practical ways in which women might welcome help. What *women* experience is a world in which gallant princes charming commonly make a fuss about being helpful and providing small services when help and services are of little or no use, but in which there are rarely ingenious and adroit princes at hand when substantial assistance is really wanted either in mundane affairs or in situations of threat, assault or terror. There is no help with the (his) laundry; no help typing a report at 4:00 A.M.; no help in mediating disputes among relatives or children. There is nothing but advice that women should stay indoors after dark, be chaperoned by a man, or when it comes down to it, "lie back and enjoy it."

The gallant gestures have no practical meaning. Their meaning is symbolic. The door-opening and similar services provided are services which really are needed by people who are for one reason or another incapacitated—unwell, burdened with parcels, etc. So the message is that women are incapable. The detachment of the acts from the concrete realities of what women need and do not need is a vehicle for the message that women's actual needs and interests are unimportant or irrelevant. Finally, these gestures imitate the behavior of servants toward masters and thus mock women, who are in most respects the servants and caretakers of men. The message of the false helpfulness of male gallantry is female dependence, the invisibility or insignificance of women, and contempt for women.

One cannot see the meanings of these rituals if one's focus is riveted upon the individual event in all its particularity, including the particularity of the individual man's present conscious intentions and motives and the individual woman's conscious perception of the event in the moment. It seems sometimes that people take a deliberately myopic view and fill their eyes with things seen microscopically in order not to see macroscopically. At any rate, whether it is deliberate or not, people can and do fail to see the oppression of women because they fail to see macroscopically and hence fail to see the various elements of the situation as systematically related in larger schemes.

As the cageness of the birdcage is a macroscopic phenomenon, the oppressiveness of the situations in which women live our various and different lives is a macroscopic phenomenon. Neither can be *seen* from a microscopic perspective. But when you look macroscopically you can see it—a network of forces and barriers which are systematically related and which conspire to the immobilization, reduction and molding of women and the lives we live.

7

Theories of Discrimination

Joe R. Feagin and Clairece Booher Feagin

Traditionally discrimination has been viewed as a creature of prejudice.* Until the late 1960s the dominant perspective among popular and social science analysts of discrimination underscored prejudice and intolerance as the causes underlying discriminatory actions. Some analysts have focused on individual racists and sexists, viewing the fundamental problem as the individual motivated by hatred of a given

---

*For the moment, *discriminatory acts* can be viewed as acts that have a negative impact on minorities or women. *Prejudices* will be taken to mean negative and/or hostile attitudes toward a sexual or race/ethnic outgroup.

"outgroup." For others operating within the traditional perspective this emphasis on the individual has been coupled with a concern for patterns of segregation in the form of community practices, particularly racial practices—usually in the American South. Here prejudice, manifested in the guise of numerous racist (or sexist) individuals, is perceived as the motivation for both the origin and continuation of these patterns. The prevailing model has thus been a prejudice-causes-discrimination model.

In addition, much traditional analysis before the late 1960s and early 1970s was optimistic, although sometimes cautiously so, tending to view prejudice as an archaic survival of an irrational past which could and would disappear as this society became more industrialized, rational, and progressive. This view has been coupled with the commonplace idea that the eradication of prejudice will lead to the progressive eradication of discrimination. . . .

It is not surprising that prejudice has received so much emphasis in conventional assessments of discrimination, particularly race discrimination, for such attitudes have been both blatant and conspicuous in the United States. The negative racist and sexist attitudes of individuals and the consequent prejudice-generated discrimination have long been very serious societal problems. Yet numerous recent public opinion polls have shown a sharp decline in, for example, white prejudice and stereotypes concerning blacks (and to some extent other nonwhites) compared to opinions several decades ago.[1] While this decline in prejudice may to some extent reflect a subtle concealment of rank-and-file attitudes from interviewers, it is so steep a decline that it almost certainly reflects some change from the blatantly racist and nearly universally hostile white prejudices of the recent past. Over the same period the economic, social, and political positions of nonwhites have improved much more slowly. Prejudiced attitudes of whites seem to have lessened substantially more rapidly than discrimination has declined. Such conflicting trends also seem to be the case for women, although the limited data we have on the decline in prejudice are impressionistic. In addition, the growing view among white males that they are not prejudiced, that they are not intolerant "Archie Bunker" types, supports the contention that they are no longer responsible for the oppressive subordinate conditions of women or nonwhites. From the vantage point of the conventional prejudice→discrimination model, most rank-and-file whites (or white males) can argue that they are not prejudiced and, therefore, that their actions are no longer discriminatory. This points up the critical policy implications of one's view of discrimination—a point we will return to later.

Primarily since the 1960s three formidable streams of thought relevant to a systematic rethinking of discrimination have emerged in the literature. All point to the importance of the social and organizational environment. One stream can be termed the *interest theory* of discrimination; the second is usually called *internal colonialism;* the third stream has been termed *institutional racism* (or *institutional sexism*). All three streams will here be drawn on to flesh out a more adequate conceptualization of discrimination. All three raise questions as to whether subordinate groups can be viewed simply in terms of a model which assumes a progressive, gradual process of inclusion into the dominant society and as to whether a prejudice→discrimination model is adequate for a thorough analysis of discrimination patterns. Let us briefly examine the contributions of these three perspectives.

First, we can note the development of an *interest theory of discrimination*. The basic idea here is that the motivating force behind discrimination can be the desire to protect one's own privilege and power. . . .

Very important in the development of this interest (intent-to-harm) perspective have been authors such as Herbert Blumer, Robin Williams, and David Wellman. In the late 1950s Blumer argued that race prejudice was better viewed as a "sense of group position" rather than as a set of hostile feelings toward an outgroup. In his view the dominant group's race prejudice is but a mask, or rationalization, for protecting the dominant group's position.[2] In the mid-1960s Robin Williams pointed up the importance of race discrimination as a way of perpetuating a white group's current privileges. In a fashion similar to that of the internal colonialism analysts we will examine in a moment, Williams has argued that the colonial expansion of mercantilist European powers overseas created the great racial inequality in North America. Racial ideologies developed to rationalize the social, economic, and political domination initially developed to enhance the resources and privileges of white Europeans. This colonial expansion established structured-in privileges persisting to the present day. Protection of white privilege is critical to patterns of discrimination: "Whenever a number of persons within a society have enjoyed for a considerable period of time certain opportunities for getting wealth, for exercising power and authority, and for successfully claiming prestige and social deference, there is a strong tendency for these people to feel that these benefits are theirs 'by right.' " Those who have greater privilege will vigorously defend "their established system of vested interests."[3]

More recently, Wellman has cogently argued that discrimination against nonwhites is a "rational response to struggles over scarce resources.[4] Racial stratification is a critical feature in the operation of American society. In the struggle over resources a system of stratification was established in which whites benefited economically, politically, socially, and psychologically. Indeed, "without the notion of privilege, the concept of discrimination is static; it just refers to blocked access. When you introduce the idea of privilege you have a much more dynamic relationship involved: one group is 'fat' because the other is 'skinny.' "[5] Discrimination is more than the imposition of barriers at a given point in time; it entails a process of constantly defending one group's privileges gained at the expense of another. Thus race discrimination (and by extension sex discrimination, although this view has yet to be systematically developed) can be seen as behavioral processes aimed at maintaining the privileges of the dominant group. There may be a social "law of inertia" here—a "law of inertia of privilege"—guaranteeing that the privileges or resources gained at the expense of another group remain massed in the hands of the dominant group unless acted on by that other group. In the world of race and sex privilege, as well as in the world of physics, there is a tendency for things to stay the same without outside pressure. Moreover, actions are taken to protect that privilege, actions falling under the rubric of discrimination.

A closely related perspective, the *internal colonialism* interpretation of privilege, has been persuasively argued in recent years. Internal colonialism theorists have placed less emphasis on prejudiced individuals; they have underscored the way in which privilege was created in the process of white European groups taking by force resources such as land (for example, of Native Americans) and labor (for example, of African Americans) and using those resources for their own advantage. Unequal life chances by race in the Americas (and elsewhere) originated in the European colonization beginning in the fifteenth century. The uneven spread of technological development and industrialization resulted in technologically advanced and less advanced groups, particularly in the sphere of military technology and firepower. This in turn created critical power imbalances. In newly colonized societies the unequal distribution and control of economic and political resources, initially established by force, was institutionalized: "The super-ordinate group, now ensconced as the core, seeks to stabilize and monopolize its advantages through policies aiming at the institutionalization and perpetuation of the existing stratification system."[6] The historical conquest or enslavement of predominantly non-European groups such as blacks, Mexican Americans, and Native Americans ("Indians") provided the underpinning for institutionalized arrangements that became a structure of *internal* colonialism. Nonwhite workers were brought in as cheap labor, or their land was stolen. Industrialization in the late nineteenth and early twentieth centuries saw the incorporation of racial discrimination into a sophisticated economic system. A critical, persisting racial division of labor, labor colonialism, was set up, at first by force, then by law and more informal mechanisms. This situation is one of internal colonialism. From this perspective, racial stratification can exist where there are currently few prejudiced people because "the processes that maintain domination—control of whites over nonwhites—are built into the major social institutions."[7] Subordination is built into the warp and woof of the societal fabric.

Only a few analysts have begun the potentially fruitful assessment of sexual colonialism in analogous terms. Millett has noted that "what goes largely unexamined, often even unacknowledged (yet is institutionalized nonetheless) in our social order, is the birthright priority whereby males rule females." She further notes that "through this system a most ingenious form of 'interior colonization' has been achieved."[8] The exact origin of this ancient type of internal colonialism is apparently lost in the distant past, but a rigid form of sex subordination, the patriarchal family structure, characterized the North American colonies from the earliest decades. In an earlier stage of European society the concentration of subsistence activities in a larger household or clan and the relative absence of individually controlled private property seem to have made the work of women considerably more important than in later periods. Engels and neo-Marxist writers in his tradition have argued that the emergence of commercial and industrial capitalism in the Western world actually made for a *worsening* of the subordinate situation of women.[9]

Yet most would argue that women were never equal. Nevertheless, changes in resources, private property, and capitalist technology in the eighteenth and nineteenth centuries did bring changes in the hierarchical nature of the household and the significance of men's and women's work. Increasingly, women in nuclear families were more subordinated than before; they now worked specifically for their employed husbands rather than for the larger extended family group.[10] A rigid sexual division of labor developed, a familial colonialism of the most intimate, internal type. Men went into higher-status, socially "productive" work. Responsibility for low-status, and private, domestic work became the material basis of female subordination both in Europe and the far-flung North American colonies. A man's home became *his* castle. Moreover, in the ever-increasing industrialization process both male employers and male workers shaped sex segregation outside the home in the labor market, utilizing both traditional patriarchal family techniques and the new techniques of bureaucratic organization to keep women in a subordinate position outside the home. "Thus, the hierarchical domestic division of labor is perpetuated by the labor market and this domestic division of labor, in turn, acts to weaken women's position in the labor market."[11] Since working women had been relegated to domestic work and childrearing, when they entered the larger labor market they did so with handicaps which made competition with men difficult. Male-dominated workers' movements and unions also kept women down. The hierarchical system favored by employers, the patriarchal family, and male-dominated unions reinforced one another.[12] Labor market colonialism and familial colonialism became twin burdens for women.

Sexual colonialism in the United States is similar in many—*although by no means all*—important ways to race colonialism, for both involve control defined by birth. In both cases the relationship is one of dominance and subordination. Today the hierarchy in the typical sexual division of labor indicates that this type of internal colonialism is still similar to that of racial minorities. Racial and sexual hierarchies both have a *material* basis, the former in the sexual division of labor in the family and in the economy, the latter in the racial division of labor in the economy. Homemaking, in which a large proportion of adult females are still engaged full-time or part-time, is unpaid, although economically essential. Outside the home women workers still are typically in domestic, clerical, and other service positions that confer relatively low status and pay.[13] Basic to patriarchal stratification is family subordination, and this distinguishes sex from race subordination, but the broader economic and political situations of women and minorities are strikingly similar. Indeed, sexual colonialism in the family may be the most ancient prototype of internal colonialism. Even such Marxist analysts as Friedrich Engels have underscored the point that historically the "first class oppression" was that of "the female by the male sex."[14]

We can now turn to the third important perspective enlarging our understanding of discrimination—that of *institutional racism/institutional sexism*. As we have seen, once a colonial system is established historically, those in the superior position seek to monopolize basic resources. In this process, privilege becomes institutionalized, that is, it becomes imbedded in the norms (regulations and informal rules) and roles (social positions and their attendant duties and rights) in a variety of social, economic, and political organizations. We should note here that *institution* is a word used in several different senses. One common usage is in regard to specific organizations such as a business, a corporation, a union, a school, a hospital, and so on. These are formally, legally constituted organizations, and written and unwritten rules governing the conduct of those who fill positions therein, such as supervisor or teacher. *Institution* is also a term used for larger sets or combinations of organizations such as "the economy" or "the family." In institutionalized racism and sexism the concept can be applied in both senses. Just how the imbalance in privilege gets incorporated in the first place is a major concern of internal colonialism theorists. Note too that a major concern in much institutional analysis is with the effects and mechanisms (methods) of contemporary discrimination, an emphasis more on different *types* of discrimination than on the *origins* of discrimination.

Writing in the mid-1960s, Charles Hamilton and Stokeley Carmichael were apparently the first to systematically probe the concept of institutional racism. Contrasting "individual racism"—illustrated, for example, by the actions of a small band of white terrorists bombing a black church—with "institutional racism"— illustrated by the practices which lead to many black children dying each year because of inadequate food, medical facilities, and shelter—Hamilton and Carmichael attempted to move beyond a focus on prejudiced white bigots acting out racist attitudes.[15] Yet even for them prejudiced attitudes ultimately underlay institutions. They were among the first to link institutional racism, seen as discriminatory mechanisms and effects, to the concept of internal colonialism: "Black people in the United States have a colonial relationship to the larger society, a relationship characterized by institutional racism."[16] In a 1969 book Knowles and Prewitt (and their associates) utilized institutional racism for their conceptual framework. In their view individual acts of racism and racist institutional policies can "occur without the presence of conscious bigotry, and both may be masked intentionally or innocently."[17] Here was the suggestion that institutional mechanisms need not be intentional, although this important point was not developed. Their subsequent analysis of institutional areas such as the economy and housing combined many examples of the effects of intentional discrimination with a few examples of the effects of unintentional discrimination. Their major emphasis was on racial differentials in the *effects* of societal operations. . . .

Social scientists are not the only ones who have contributed to broadening the concept of discrimination in the institutional direction. By the late 1960s legal researchers and practicing lawyers, such as those in the federal government's Equal Employment Opportunity Commission (EEOC), were pressing to extend the traditional prejudice→discrimination concept of discrimination underlying earlier court decisions. These developments, which focused primarily on discrimination in employment practices, were apparently independent of social science analysis. Blumrosen has charted this shift from a concern with what lawyers quaintly term "evil-motive" discrimination (actions which are intended to have a harmful effect on minority group members) to "effects" discrimination (actions which have a harmful effect whatever their motivation).[18] The EEOC view emphasizing "effects" discrimination was accepted by several federal judges in the late 1960s and early 1970s. Increasingly, until about 1974, employment discrimination decisions in the federal courts frequently emphasized the *consequences* of employment practices, rather than the motivation lying behind those practices. Here was a practical application of a concept of institutional discrimination which stresses the "effects" aspect. More recently, however, the Supreme Court has been moving back to a position recognizing "evil-motive" (intentional) discrimination as the only type prohibited by law.

As for institutional sexism, social science analysts have done little more than use the concept occasionally in sorting out empirical analyses of the situation of women in the United States. None has developed a systematic conceptual analysis. Like a growing number of authors, Amundsen has explicitly used the concept and term *institutional sexism* to refer both to intentional and unintentional discrimination against women, with a particular emphasis on intentional discrimination.[19] Her analysis relies heavily on, and is thus limited by, earlier interpretations of institutional racism. Moreover, the legal development of the "effects" concept of discrimination in certain federal court cases (noted in the previous paragraph) has covered the situation of women—again, mainly in regard to employment. Nonetheless, the basic ideas of discriminatory effects and mechanisms suggested by the institutional racism arguments seem relevant to the situation of women. . . .

NOTES

1. See Paul B. Sheatsley, "White Attitudes Toward the Negro," in Parsons and Clark, *The Negro American*, pp. 303–324; Herbert H. Hyman and Paul B. Sheatsley, "Attitudes Toward Desegregation," *Scientific American* 211 (July 1964): 16–23; Andrew Greeley and Paul B. Sheatsley, "Attitudes Toward Racial Integration," *Scientific American* 225 (December 1971): pp. 14ff.

2. Herbert Blumer, "Race Prejudice as a Sense of Group Position," *Pacific Sociological Review* 1 (Spring 1960): 3–5.

3. Robin M. Williams, Jr., "Prejudice and Society," in *The American Negro Reference Book*, edited by J.P. Davis (Englewood Cliffs, N.J.: Prentice-Hall, 1966), pp. 727–30. Others emphasizing a structural perspective include: Pierre L. van den Berghe, *Race and Racism* (New York: Wiley, 1967), and R. A. Schermerhorn, *Comparative Ethnic Relations* (New York: Random House, 1970).

4. David M. Wellman, *Portraits of White Racism* (Cambridge: Cambridge University Press, 1977).

5. Personal correspondence to senior author, 1975.

6. Michael Hechter, *Internal Colonialism* (Berkeley: University of California Press, 1975), p. 39.

7. Blauner, *Racial Oppression in America*, pp. 9–10. On Mexican Americans and colonialism, see Joan W. Moore, "Colonialism: The Case of the Mexican Americans," *Social Problems* 17 (Spring 1970): 436–72.

8. Kate Millett, *Sexual Politics* (New York: Avon Books, 1969), p. 25; also see pp. 40–42.

9. See Friedrich Engels, *The Origins of the Family, Private Property, and the State* (Chicago: Charles H. Kerr, 1902).

10. Karen Sacks, "Engels Revisited: Women, the Organization of Production, and Private Property," in *Woman, Culture, and Society,* edited by Michelle Zimbalist Rosaldo and Louise Lamphere (Stanford, Calif.: Stanford University Press, 1974), pp. 209, 220–21.

11. Heidi Hartmann, "Historical Perspectives on Job Segregation by Sex; or, the Fruits of Patriarchy," paper presented at Conference on Occupational Segregation, Wellesley College, May 1975, p. 3. I am drawing on Hartmann throughout this paragraph.

12. Ibid., pp. 1–10; see the similar paper by Hartmann, "Capitalism, Patriarchy, and Job Segregation," in *Signs* 1 (Spring 1976): 137–69.

13. Millett, *Sexual Politics,* pp. 24, 40–42.

14. Friedrich Engels, "The Origin of the Status of Women," in *Woman in a Man-made World,* edited by Nona Glaser and Helen Youngelson Waehrer (Chicago: Rand McNally, 1977), p. 151.

15. Charles Hamilton and Stokeley Carmichael, *Black Power* (New York: Random House, 1967), p. 4.

16. Ibid., p. 6.

17. Louis L. Knowles and Kenneth Prewitt (eds.), *Institutional Racism in America* (Englewood Cliffs, N.J.: Prentice-Hall, 1969), p. 5.

18. Blumrosen distinguishes three stages in the evolution of the concept. See Alfred W. Blumrosen, "Strangers in Paradise: *Griggs* v. *Duke Power Co.* and the Concept of Employment Discrimination," *Michigan Law Review* 71 (November 1972): 67–71; see also Alfred W. Blumrosen, *Black Employment and the Law* (New Brunswick, N.J.: Rutgers University Press, 1971), p. 232.

19. Kirsten Amundsen, *The Silenced Majority* (Englewood Cliffs, N.J.: Prentice-Hall, 1971), pp. 42–61.

Suggestions for Further Reading

Andreas, Carol: *Sex and Caste in America,* Prentice-Hall, Englewood Cliffs, NJ, 1971.

De Beauvoir, Simone: *The Second Sex,* Alfred A. Knopf, New York, 1952.

Lipman-Blumen, Jean: *Gender Roles and Power,* Prentice-Hall, Englewood Cliffs, NJ, 1984.

Memmi, Albert: *Dominated Man,* Boston, Beacon Press, 1969.

Knowles, Louis L., and Kenneth Prewitt (eds.): *Institutional Racism in America,* Prentice-Hall, Englewood Cliffs, NJ, 1969.

United States Commission on Civil Rights: *Racism in America and How to Combat It,* Washington, DC, 1970.

Wellman, David T: *Portraits of White Racism,* Cambridge University Press, Cambridge, 1977.

PART II

The Economics of Race, Class, and Gender in the United States: A Statistical Portrait

In an ideal world, every child born would have the same opportunity to realize his or her potential. In the real world, this is not yet the case. Although many factors play a role in defining and limiting opportunity, three factors are of primary importance: *race, class,* and *gender.* We have already begun to look at some ways in which our race and gender affect how others treat us and how we come to think of ourselves. In Part II, we continue our examination of race and gender but add to it the additional variable of class.

Most Americans dislike talking about class. It is fashionable to deny the existence of rich and poor and to proclaim us all as "middle class." However, class divisions are real, and recent economic data show that the gap between rich and poor in this country is growing larger. Current estimates suggest that while the bottom 60 percent of the population controls less than 10 percent of the wealth in this country, the wealthiest 0.5 percent holds 19% of all personal wealth.[1] Being born to the upper class, the middle class, or the lower class in the United States has repercussions that affect every aspect of a person's life. Furthermore, our class position affects our relation to others of our gender and race, as well as our relations with people of a different gender or race. For example, all women earn less than do all men, but white women earn more and experience less unemployment than do women of color. In assessing the privileges or lack of them of any particular individual in relation to any other, it is important to analyze the impact of race, class, and gender simultaneously.

Some people find this difficult. They are uncomfortable noticing a person's race or gender and believe that to do so is somehow racist or sexist. They prefer to treat people as people and to ignore or deny differences. But failing to notice differences that significantly affect people's lives does not make the differences go away; rather, it produces a distorted or false picture of reality. Perhaps an example will be helpful. Infant mortality rates are a good indicator of how well a society provides basic services to its population. If we look at the infant mortality rate in the United States, we see that it has been declining in recent years. For example, infant mortality declined from 14.1 deaths per 1000 live births in 1977 to 11.2 in 1983. However, if we break down these figures by race, we find dramatic and disturbing differences in the quality of life enjoyed by people in the United States. The infant mortality rate of white infants was 9.7 per 1000 live births, while the rate for Black infants was 19.2.[2] In short, Black infants were dying at nearly twice the rate of white infants, and minority children had a 30 percent higher chance of dying before their fourteenth birthday than did white children.[3] The figures on maternal death rates per 100,000 live births were equally revealing. While the overall figure was 9.6 percent, the figure for white women was 6.4 percent and the total for all minorities was 22.7 percent. The figure for Black women was even higher: 25.1 percent. Indian mothers faced a maternal death rate 20 percent higher than the national rate.[4] In light of statistics like these, it is clear that failing to notice a person's race or gender or class position will give us an incorrect understanding of the factors that shape people's lives.

In addition to denying the existence or importance of class divisions in the United States, it is very much in fashion to say that racism and sexism existed in the past but have now been replaced by "reverse discrimination," a kind of preferential treatment afforded women and people of color to the detriment of white males. This belief is created and reinforced by advertising, by the media, and even by statements of misinformation from people in high places. The overused but still widely believed assurance that "You've Come a Long Way, Baby," accompanied by photographs of models representing women who clearly travel in the "fast lane," creates an impression that some find hard to shake. Magazine covers displaying female and Black and Asian male astronauts, female jockeys, and Black business executives would have us believe that women and people of color have been fully integrated into society. But is this the case? Do these highly touted "firsts" indicate profound and fundamental changes in the distribution of wealth and opportunity in society, or do they merely serve to distract our attention from the reality of most people's lives?

In Part II, we attempt to answer these critical questions about the impact of race, class, and gender by turning our attention from magazine covers and sports stars' salaries to statistics that reveal the economic realities that confront ordinary people. Most of the statistics cited here are drawn from United States government publications. It is important to understand that a gap exists between the time these statistics were collected and the time they were published. For the most part, however, it is reasonable to regard figures gathered within the past ten years as current.

Another concern that arises is the accuracy of statistics. For example, according to figures for 1983 published by the United States Census Bureau, the population of the United States breaks down into the following percentages: non-Hispanic whites made up 78.7 percent of the population; Blacks, 12.0 percent; Hispanics, 6.7 percent; and others, 2.6 percent. In reporting these statistics, The Council on Interracial Books for Children, an important source of data analyzed in terms of race and gender, offered the following qualifications on its accuracy:

> It is also important to note that the Census acknowledges serious undercounts of the Black and Hispanic populations, so that the actual statistics for U.S. minorities is likely to be almost 25% of all U.S. residents, counting undocumented workers and people who are not located by the Census. For example, according to the *New York Times*, 5/11/84, the census undercount of working age Black men is more than 10% compared to less than 1% for working age White men. [5]

Although no statistic should be treated as literally true, statistics are enormously useful for gaining a general picture of conditions in a society. In addition, they allow us to make reasonably accurate judgments about the relative position of various groups in the work force and economy over a period of years.

Another problem that we should remember is that statistics are not always available in the form we might wish. For example, although it is now possible to obtain data that compare the situation of women and men with regard to a whole series of concerns, it is not always possible to get data that break down "male" and "female" into such other categories as Blacks, Hispanics, and Asians. Obtaining statistics on each specific group included under the catchall heading "Hispanics" is often difficult, and getting any statistics at all for other groups—for example, American Indians and Alaskan natives—can be impossible.

Finally, what statistics shall we examine? If we want to learn something about the economic realities of daily life, where should we look? Should we look at the Dow-Jones average and the gross national product, or should we look at take-home pay, infant mortality, and the cost-of-living index? The Dow-Jones average tells us something about the level of activity in the stock market and gives us an idea of how investors view the overall health of the economy, while the GNP tells us something about productivity levels in the society. However, it is difficult to make direct inferences from such figures to the actual economic well-being of individuals. To draw conclusions about the latter, it is obviously more relevant to look, for example, at statistics on mean earnings of full- and part-time workers that are broken down by race and gender or at poverty figures for families broken down along similar lines as well as age and marital status. If our concern is with determining whether race and gender discrimination continue to play an important role in determining people's opportunities and realities, then it will be necessary to make comparisons between past and present statistics in these and related areas.

The first two selections in Part II analyze the importance of class in determining life choices. The first selection summarizes Richard de Lone's book *Small Changes*, in which he offers persuasive evidence that "status," rather than ability, is the primary determinant of success. Unfortunately, the author chooses to frame his central thesis in narrow terms by saying, "Only one man in five exceeds his father's social status." Although he is clearly sensitive to the injustice of having factors other than ability determine opportunity, he inadvertently renders women invisible by this use of language. Richard de Lone's thesis is developed further in the second selection, which explores the many myths about opportunity in the United States and concludes that class plays a crucial role in shaping opportunity and determining life choices.

The next three selections include a myriad of statistics about women, work, and poverty. In 1954, the median earnings of women as a percentage of men's earnings stood at 64 percent. By 1980, after the contemporary women's movement had peaked, 19 years after the signing of the Federal Equal Pay Act, and 18 years after the establishment of the Equal Employment Opportunities Commission, that figure had dropped to 60.2 percent. The selection on pay equity examines the various explanations commonly offered for this discrepancy and concludes that sexism, not ability or qualifications, has determined what jobs women and men do and how much worth is attached to their work.

While the selection on pay equity includes some statistics on women that are broken down by race, discussions of "women's work" have often focused exclusively on the experiences of white women, just as women's history and literature have often been the history and writings of white, middle-class women. The fourth selection, "Ain't I a Woman," highlights these omissions. In this piece, Julianne Malveaux examines the conditions that face Black women in the labor market and explores the similarities and differences between Black and white women workers.

Statistics show that almost 25 percent of all American children under 6 live in poverty, with the figure for Black children under 6 at 50 percent and the figure for Hispanic children at more than 40 percent.[6] The 1980 poverty rate as reported by the United States Department of Commerce was 17.4 percent for males and 27.4 percent for females. Approximately two-thirds of those currently living in poverty are employed, and roughly 1 of every 4 women working today can expect to be poor in her old age.[7] "The Feminization of Poverty" looks at the dramatic and ominous trend, which many claim is turning the area below the poverty line into a female ghetto. One of the most revealing statistics reported in this selection is that "the poverty rate of black mothers working full-time is the same experienced by white men who do not work at all." This fact can be explained only be recognizing that the realities women of color often confront are the end result of racism, sexism, and class position operating together. While the concept of the "feminization of poverty" is important because it dramatically highlights one aspect of the increasing plight of women in the economy, we must guard against its potential to blunt our awareness of the extraordinary levels of poverty and unemployment experienced by Black men in the United States. These realities are reflected in some of the data that follow.

Comparisons of median family incomes with regard to race shows that in January 1960 the median income of Black families stood at 56 percent of the median income of white families. In 1984, twenty-four years later, the figure remained the same, that is, Black families still had a median income of 56 percent of that of whites, despite the gains resulting from the Civil Rights Movement and the Black Power Movement. How can this persistent gap be explained? Part II concludes with a chart comparing the gains made by Black Americans in certain areas with their lack of gains in others. The chart suggests that Black Americans as a group have made significant gains in political representation, education, and employment—areas that are supposed to assure success in the United States—without experiencing the income, employment, and life-style benefits that one would expect. This implies that some other factor prevents Black people (and people of color in general) from enjoying the same benefits that many white Americans do. This factor would appear to be racism.

All of us would like to live in a world where race, class, and gender are unimportant in determining the opportunities in life, but the statistics presented in Part II make it clear that, in the United States, this is not yet the case. One's race, class, and gender affect life expectancy, standard of living, health care, education, and every other aspect of the quality of life we can expect to enjoy. The way to create a society of equals is to abolish those differences, not deny them.

NOTES

1. Beth B. Hess et al. (eds.): *Sociology* (2nd ed.), p. 169. Macmillan, New York, 1985.
2. Reported in the *New York Times*, 10/24/85.
3. Reported in the *New York Times*, 2/29/84.
4. *Fact Sheets on Institutional Racism*, The Council on Interracial Books for Children, Inc., November 1984, p. 18.
5. Ibid, p. 1.
6. Reported in the *New York Times*, 9/85.
7. Reported in the *New York Times*, 1980.

Carnegie Study Finds Status, Not Brains, Makes a Child's Future

Leslie Bennets

Jimmy is in the second grade and he likes school. He pays attention in class and does well. He has an above average I.Q. and is reading slightly above grade level. Bobby is a second grader too. Like Jimmy, he is attentive in class, which he enjoys. His I.Q. and reading skills are comparable to Jimmy's.

But Bobby is the son of a successful lawyer whose annual salary of more than $35,000 puts him within the top percentages of income distribution in this country. Jimmy's father, on the other hand, works from time to time as a messenger or a custodial assistant, and earns $4,800 a year.

Despite the similarities in ability between the two boys, the difference in the circumstances to which they were born makes it 27 times more likely that Bobby will get a job that, by the time he is in his late 40's, will pay him an income in the top tenth of all incomes in this country. Jimmy has only about one chance in eight of earning even a median income. And Bobby will probably have at least four years more schooling than Jimmy.

These odds . . . are "the arithmetic of inequality in America." In "Small Futures: Children, Inequality, and the Limits of Liberal Reform," a report to the Carnegie Council on Children, Richard de Lone challenges the traditional American view that a child's future in our society is determined by ability, early childhood training, education or drive. To the contrary, says Mr. de Lone, a former policy analyst for the Carnegie Council who is now executive vice president of the Corporation for Public/Private Ventures in Philadelphia.

Although being born poor does not guarantee that one will remain poor, it makes it far more likely, Mr. de Lone says. In his view, "Class, race and sex are the most important factors in determining a child's future"—Horatio Alger notwithstanding. Given the compounding penalties of being born poor, or a member of a racial minority, or to parents with little education and with intermittent or dead-end employment, or—a further disadvantage—female, a particular child will be unlikely to advance significantly above the socioeconomic status of his parents.

The report, published . . . by Harcourt Brace Jovanovich, was originated by the Carnegie Commission, a study group established in 1972 by the Carnegie Corporation of New York. "Small Futures" surveys the history of social reform movements in this country and brands them a failure, from the Jacksonian era to the Great Society of the 1960's. Although the standard of living for all Americans, including the poor, has risen during the last generation, Mr. de Lone charges that the distributional inequities in American society—and hence the opportunities for those at the bottom of the scale—have changed little throughout American history. "People born in the 1830's faced about the same mobility possibilities as people born in the 1970's," he says. And so, even with an expanding economy, Mr. de Lone says, "When the distribution is consistently unequal . . . no matter how fast the engine proceeds, the caboose never catches up."

In his view, one conceptual flaw that has helped perpetuate those inequities is the emphasis on programs predicated on the mistaken assumption that helping children today will equalize their opportunities in the future. Without equality in the present, Mr. de Lone says, that is simply not true. "Confronted with unacceptable economic and social inequalities, we Americans have reflexively channeled our moral indignation into efforts to improve the morality, character, skills and intelligence of children—especially those who are poor, immigrant or nonwhite."

Such attempts not only demand that children carry a grossly unfair burden, Mr. de Lone believes, but they have also proved ineffective. "The dynamics of our social structure are not likely to produce more equality of opportunity unless there is more equality to begin with," he says.

Creating such equality, Mr. de Lone acknowledges, is a formidable task. The top 20 percent of American families [as of the date of this article] receive over 40 percent of the country's net income, and families in the bottom 20 percent receive less than 6 percent. The top 4 percent of families own 37 percent of personal wealth, while the net worth of the average family in the bottom 20 percent is zero. Only one man in five exceeds his father's social status through individual effort and achievement—and that figure may drop as the post–World War II boom years dissolve into the shrinking economy forecast for the coming decades. And finally, according to Mr. de Lone, the employment, earnings and social mobility gaps separating blacks and whites in this country have scarcely changed in a century.

The report, which traces the sources of inequality to a "basic tension between the democratic and capitalist strands of our heritage," argues that Americans have generally failed to perceive that the ultimate penalty of poverty is the pervasive influence on one's adult future of "growing up unequal," with all the developmental limits that may entail. The material hardships of poverty may finally be less damaging than the permanent narrowing of a child's sense of possibilities in the world.

Each child, according to Mr. de Lone, forms a personal "theory of social reality" that influences development and shapes his or her aspirations. He cites another Carnegie Council study, John Ogbu's "Minority Education and Caste," in arguing that much of what looks like bad study habits, disruptive behavior or poor school performance among black children in the United States may be better understood as "a perfectly accurate assessment of the unimportance of school performance in their subordinate caste, where the payoff from school is systematically lower than for whites."

Mr. de Lone quotes one child of a migrant worker as saying, "Once a policeman asked me if I liked school and I said sometimes I did and then he said I was wasting my time there, because you don't need a lot of reading and writing to pick the crops, and if you get too much of schooling, he said, you start getting too big for your shoes, and cause a lot of trouble, and then you'll end up in jail pretty fast and never get out if you don't watch your step—never get out."

Having reviewed the impact of such attempts at reform as Aid to Families with Dependent Children (commonly known as welfare), the child welfare system (including foster care and the family court system) and juvenile justice, Mr. de Lone cautions that despite their failings, "simply eliminating those systems would be irresponsible. Half a loaf is better than none."

What is needed, he suggests, are far deeper structural changes to reduce economic distance between classes, including public policies of full employment, targeted economic and investment development, aggressive affirmative action and income-tax reform to lighten tax burdens on the poor and transfer them to the wealthy.

In an interview this week, Mr. de Lone said that Americans might be more comfortable continuing to pay lip service to equality rather than actually achieving it. "Equality of assets has been an important strand in rhetoric, but not in reality," he said. "As for whether it's politically feasible to have massive redistribution of anything . . . well, you've got to be pretty pessimistic about it. But I can't imagine a more important goal for a society than the well-being of its members. It seems to me that's ethically self-evident. I never said it was easy."

Class in America:
Myths and Realities

Gregory Mantsios*

People in the United States don't like to talk about class. Or so it would seem. We don't speak about class privileges, or class oppression, or the class nature of society. These terms are not part of our everyday vocabulary, and in most circles they are associated with the language of the rhetorical fringe. Unlike people in most other

*The author wishes to thank Vincent Serravallo for his assistance in preparing this selection.

parts of the world, we shrink from using words that classify along economic lines or that point to class distinctions: phrases like *working class, upper class*, and *ruling class* are rarely uttered by Americans.

For the most part, avoidance of class-laden vocabulary crosses class boundaries. There are few among the poor who speak of themselves as lower class; they identify, rather, with their race, ethnic group, or geographic location. Workers are more likely to identify with their employer, industry, or occupational group than with other workers, or with the working class.[1]

Neither are those at the other end of the economic spectrum likely to identify with the word *class*. In her study of 38 wealthy and socially prominent women, Susan Ostrander asked participants if they considered themselves members of the upper class. One participant responded,

> I hate to use the word 'class.' We are responsible, fortunate people, old families, the people who have something.

Another said,

> I hate [the term] upper class. It is so non–upper class to use it. I just call it 'all of us,' those who are wellborn.[2]

It is not that Americans, rich or poor, aren't keenly aware of class differences—those quoted above obviously are—it is that class is not in the domain of public discourse. Class is not discussed or debated in public because class identity has been stripped from popular culture. The institutions that shape mass culture and define the parameters of public debate have avoided class issues. In politics, in primary and secondary education, and in the mass media, formulating issues in terms of class is unacceptable, perhaps even un-American.

There are, however, two notable exceptions to this phenomenon. First, it is acceptable in the United States to talk about "the middle class." Interestingly enough, such references appear to be acceptable precisely because they mute class differences. References to the middle class by politicians, for example, are designed to encompass and attract the broadest possible constituency. Not only do references to the middle class gloss over differences, but also these references avoid any suggestion of conflict or exploitation.

This leads us to the second exception to the class avoidance phenomenon. We are, on occasion, presented with glimpses of the upper class and the lower class (the language used is "the wealthy" and "the poor"). In the media, these presentations are designed to satisfy some real or imagined voyeuristic need of "the ordinary person." As curiosities, the ground-level view of street life and the inside look at the rich and the famous serve as unique models, one to avoid and one to aspire to. In either case, the two models are presented without causal relation to each other: One is not rich because the other is poor. Similarly, when social commentators or liberal politicians draw attention to the plight of the poor, they do so in a manner that obscures the class structure and denies class exploitation. Wealth and poverty are viewed as one of several natural and inevitable states of being: Differences are only differences. One may even say differences are the American way, a reflection of American social diversity.

We are left with one of two possibilities: Either talking about class and recognizing class distinctions are not relevant to U.S. society, or we mistakenly hold a set of beliefs that obscure the reality of class differences and their impact on people's lives.

Let us look at four common, albeit contradictory, beliefs about the United States.

Myth Number 1:   The United States is fundamentally a classless society. Class distinctions are largely irrelevant today, and whatever differences do exist in economic standing are, for the most part, insignificant. Rich or poor, we are all equal in the eyes of the law, and such basic needs as health care and education are provided to all regardless of economic standing.

Myth Number 2:   We are, essentially, a middle-class nation. Despite some variations in economic status, most Americans have achieved relative affluence in what is widely recognized as a consumer society.

Myth Number 3:   We are all getting richer. The American public as a whole is steadily moving up the economic ladder, and each generation propels itself to greater economic well-being. Despite some fluctuations, the United States position in the global economy has brought previously unknown prosperity to most, if not all, North Americans.

Myth Number 4:   Everyone has an equal chance to succeed. Success in the United States requires no more than hard work, sacrifice, and perseverance: "In America, anyone can be president." And with a little luck (a clever invention or a winning lottery ticket), there are opportunities for the easygoing as well. "In America, anyone can become a millionaire"; it's just a matter of being in the right place at the right time."

In trying to assess the legitimacy of these beliefs, we want to ask several important questions. Are there significant class differences among Americans? If these differences do exist, are they getting bigger or smaller, and do these differences have a significant impact on the way we live? Finally, does everyone in the United States really have an equal opportunity to succeed?

The Economic Spectrum

We will begin by looking at differences. An examination of official census material reveals that variations in economic well-being are in fact immense. Consider the following:

- The wealthiest 15 percent of the American population holds nearly 75 percent of the total household wealth in the country. That is, they own three-quarters of all the consumer durables (such as houses, cars, and stereos) and financial assets (such as stocks, bonds, property, and savings accounts).[3]

- Approximately 17,000 Americans declared more than $1 million of *annual* income on their 1985 tax returns; that is more money than most Americans expect to earn in an entire lifetime.[4]

Affluence and prosperity are clearly alive and well in certain segments of the United States population. However, this abundance is in contrast to the poverty and despair that is also prevalent in the United States. At the other end of the spectrum:

- A total of 15 percent of the American population—that is, one of every seven—live below the government's official poverty line (calculated in 1984 at $5,278 for an individual and $10,600 for a family of four).[5] These poor include a significant number of homeless people—approximately three million Americans.[6]
- Nearly a quarter of all the children in the United States under the age of six live in poverty.[7]

The contrast between rich and poor is sharp, and with nearly one-third of the American population living at one extreme or the other, it is difficult to argue that we live in a classless society. The income gap between rich and poor in the United States (measured as the percentage of total income held by the wealthiest 20 percent of the population versus the poorest 20 percent is approximately 11 to 1, one of the highest ratios in the industrialized world.[8] (For example, the ratio in Great Britain is 7 to 1; in Japan, it is 4 to 1.)

Reality 1: There are enormous differences in the economic status of American citizens. A sizable proportion of the United States population occupies opposite ends of the economic spectrum.

Nor can it be said that the majority of the American population fairs very well. In the middle range of the economic spectrum:

- 50 percent of the American population holds less than 3.5 percent of the nation's wealth.[9]
- The median household income (that is, half the American population made more and the other half made less) was $22,420 in 1984. This is a margin of approximately $225 per week above the poverty level.[10]

The level of inequality is sometimes difficult to comprehend fully with dollar figures and percentages. To help his students visualize the distribution of income, the well-known economist Paul Samuelson asked them to picture an income pyramid made of children's blocks, with each layer of blocks representing $1000. If we were to construct Samuelson's pyramid today, the peak of the pyramid would be much higher than the Eiffel Tower, yet almost all of us would be within six feet of the ground.[11] In other words, the distribution of income is heavily skewed; a small minority of families take the lion's share of national income, and the remaining income is distributed among the vast majority of middle-income and low-income families. Keep in mind that Samuelson's pyramid represents the distribution of income, not wealth. The distribution of wealth is skewed even further.

Reality 2:   The middle class in the United States holds a very small share of the nation's wealth.

Lottery millionaires and Horatio Alger stories notwithstanding, evidence suggests that the level of inequality in the United States is getting higher. Statistically, it is getting harder to make it big and more difficult to even stay in the middle-income level. Census data show the gap between the rich and the poor to be the widest since the government began collecting information in 1947. Furthermore, the percentage of households earning at a middle-income level (that is, between 75% and 125% of the median income) has been falling steadily since 1967.[12] Most of those who disappeared from the middle-income level moved downward, not upward. And economic polarization is expected to increase over the next several decades.[13]

Reality 3:   The middle class is shrinking in size, and most of those leaving the ranks of the middle class are falling to a lower economic standing.

AMERICAN LIFE-STYLES   At last count, approximately 35 million Americans across the nation lived in unrelenting poverty. Yet, as political scientist Michael Harrington once commented, "America has the best dressed poverty the world has ever known."[14] Clothing disguises much of the poverty in the United States, and this may explain, in part, its middle-class image. With increased mass marketing of "designer" clothing and with shifts in the nation's economy from blue-collar (and often better-paying) manufacturing jobs to white-collar and pink-collar jobs in the service sector, it is becoming increasingly difficult to distinguish class differences based on appearance.[15]

Beneath the surface, there is another reality. Let us look at some "typical" and not-so-typical life-styles.

AMERICAN PROFILE NO. 1

Name: Harold S. Browning.
Father: manufacturer, industrialist.
Mother: prominent social figure in the community.
Principal child-rearer: governess.
Primary education: an exclusive private school, Manhattan's Upper East Side.
  Notes: a small, well-respected primary school where teachers and administrators have a reputation for nurturing student creativity and for providing the finest educational preparation.
  Student's ambition: "to become president."
Supplemental tutoring: tutors in French and math.
Summer camp: a sleepaway camp in northern Connecticut.
  Notes: camp provides instruction in the creative arts, athletics, and the natural sciences.

Secondary education: a prestigious preparatory school, Westchester County.

> Notes: classmates included the sons of ambassadors, doctors, attorneys, television personalities, and well-known business leaders.
>
> After-school activities: private riding lessons.
>
> Student's ambition: "to take over my father's business."
>
> High-school graduation gift: BMW.

Family activities: theater, recitals, museums, summer vacations in Europe, occasional winter trips to the Caribbean.

> Notes: as members and donors of the local art museum, the Brownings and their children attend private receptions and exhibit openings at the invitation of the museum director.

Higher education: an Ivy League liberal arts college, Massachusetts.

> Major: economics and political science.
>
> After-class activities: debating club, college newspaper, swim team.
>
> Ambition: "to become a leader in business."

First full-time job (age 23): assistant manager of operations, Browning Tool and Dye, Inc. (family enterprise).

Subsequent employment:

> 3 years—Executive Assistant to the President, Browning Tool and Dye.
>
> > Responsibilities included: purchasing (materials and equipment), personnel, and distribution networks.
>
> 4 years—Advertising Manager, Lackheed Manufacturing (home appliances).
>
> 3 years—Director of Marketing and Sales, Comerex Inc. (business machines).

Present Employment (age 38):

> Executive Vice President, SmithBond and Co. (digital instruments).
>
> Typical daily activities: review financial reports and computer printouts, dictate memorandam, lunch with clients, initiate conference call, meet with assistants, plan business trips, meet with associates.
>
> Transportation to and from work: chauffeured company limousine.
>
> Annual salary: $215,000.
>
> Ambition: "to become chief executive officer of the firm, or one like it, within the next 5 to 10 years."

Present residence: 18th-floor condominium in Manhattan's Upper West Side, 11 rooms, including 5 spacious bedrooms and terrace overlooking river.

> Interior: professionally designed and accented with elegant furnishings, valuable antiques, and expensive artwork.
>
> Notes: building management provides doorman and elevator attendant. Family employs au pair for children and maid for other domestic chores.

Second residence: Farm in northwestern Connecticut, used for weekend retreats and for horse breeding (investment/hobby).

> Notes: to maintain the farm and cater to their needs when they are there, the Brownings employ a part-time maid, groundskeeper, and horse breeder.

Harold Browning was born into a world of nurses, maids, and governesses. His world today is one of airplanes and limousines, five-star restaurants, and luxurious living accommodations. The life and life-style of Harold S. Browning is in sharp contrast to that of Bob Farrell.

AMERICAN PROFILE NO. 2

Name: Bob Farrell.
Mother: Retail clerk.
Father: Machinist.
Principal child-rearer: mother and sitter.
Early education: a medium-sized public school in Queens, New York.
   Notes: school characterized by large class size, outmoded physical facilities, and
   an educational philosophy emphasizing basic skills and student discipline.
   Student's ambition: "to become president."
Supplemental tutoring: none.
Summer camp: YMCA day camp.
   Notes: emphasis on team sports, arts and crafts.
Secondary education: large regional high school in Queens.
   Notes: classmates included the sons and daughters of carpenters, postal clerks,
   teachers, nurses, shopkeepers, mechanics, bus drivers, police officers, salesmen.
   After-school activities: basketball and handball in school park.
   High-school graduation gift: $500 savings bond.
   Student's ambition: "to make it through college."
Family activities: family gatherings around television set, bowling, an occasional trip
   to the movie theater, summer Sundays at the public beach.
Higher education: a two-year community college with a technical orientation.
   Major: electrical technology.
   After-school activities: employed as a part-time bagger in local supermarket.
   Student's ambition: "to become an electrical engineer."
First full-time job (age 19): service-station attendant.
   Notes: continued to take college classes in the evening.
Subsequent employment:
   Mail clerk at large insurance firm.
   Manager trainee, large retail chain.
Present employment:
   Assistant Sales Manager, building supply firm.
   Typical daily activities: demonstrate products, write up product orders, handle
   customer complaints, check inventory.
   Means of transportation to and from work: city subway.
   Annual salary: $20,000.
   Ambition: "to open up my own business."
Additional income: $4,100 in commissions from evening and weekend work as
   salesman in local men's clothing store.
Present residence: the Farrells own their own home in a working-class suburb in
   Queens.

Bob Farrell and Harold Browning live very differently: the life-style of one is
privileged; the other is not so privileged. The differences are class differences, and
these differences have a profound impact on the way they live. They are differences
between playing a game of handball in the park and taking riding lessons at a private
stable, watching a movie on television and going to the theater, and taking the

subway to work and being driven in a limousine. More important, the difference in class determines where they live, who their friends are, how well they are educated, what they do for a living, and what they come to expect from life.

Yet, as dissimilar as their life-styles are, Harold Browning and Bob Farrell have some things in common. They live in the same city, they work long hours, and they are highly motivated. More important, they are both white males.

Let us look at someone else who works long and hard and is highly motivated. This person, however, is black and female.

AMERICAN PROFILE NO. 3

Name: Cheryl Mitchell.
Father: Janitor.
Mother: Waitress.
Principal child-rearer: grandmother.
Primary education: large public school in Ocean Hill-Brownsville, Brooklyn, New York
    Notes: rote teaching of basic skills and emphasis on conveying the importance of good attendance, good manners, and good work habits. School patrolled by security guards.
    Student's ambition: "to be a teacher."
Supplemental tutoring: none.
Summer camp: none.
Secondary education: large public school in Ocean Hill-Brownsville.
    Notes: classmates included sons and daughters of hairdressers, groundskeepers, painters, dressmakers, dishwashers, domestics.
    After-school activities: domestic chores, part-time employment as babysitter and housekeeper.
    Student's ambition: "to be a social worker."
    High-school graduation gift: corsage.
Family activities: church-sponsored socials.
Higher education: one semester of local community college.
    Note: student dropped out of school for financial reasons.
First full-time job (age 17): counter clerk, local bakery.
Subsequent employment: file clerk with temporary service agency, supermarket checker.
Present employment: nurse's aide, municipal hospital.
    Typical daily activities: make up hospital beds, clean out bedpans, weigh patients and assist them to the bathroom, take temperature readings, pass out and collect food trays, feed patients who need help, bathe patients, and change dressings.
    Annual salary: $11,200.
    Ambition: "to get out of the ghetto."
Present residence: three-room apartment in the South Bronx, needs painting, has poor ventilation, is in a high-crime area.
    Notes: Cheryl Mitchell lives with her two children and her elderly mother.

When we look at the lives of Cheryl Mitchell, Bob Farrell, and Harold Browning, we see life-styles that are very different. We are not looking, however, at economic extremes. Cheryl Mitchell's income as a nurse's aide puts her above the government's official poverty line. Below her on the income pyramid are 35 million poverty-stricken Americans. Far from being poor, Bob Farrell's annual income as an assistant sales manager puts him in the 52nd percentile of the income distribution. More than 50 percent of the United States population earns less money than Bob Farrell. And while Harold Browning's income puts him in a high-income bracket, he stands only a fraction of the way up Samuelson's income pyramid. Well above him are the 17,000 individuals whose annual salary exceeds $1 million. Yet, Harold S. Browning spends more money on his horses than Cheryl Mitchell earns in a year.

Reality 4:   Even ignoring the extreme poles of the economic spectrum, we find enormous class differences in the life-styles among the haves, the have-nots, and the have-littles.

Class affects more than life-style and material well-being. It has a significant impact on our physical and mental well-being as well.

Researchers have found an inverse relation between social class and health. Lower-class standing is correlated to higher rates of infant mortality, [16] eye and ear disease, arthritis, physical disability, diabetes, nutritional deficiency, [17] respiratory disease, [18] mental illness, [19] and heart disease. [20] In all areas of health, poor people do not share the same life chances as those in the social class above them. Furthermore, lower-class standing is correlated to a lower quality of treatment for illness and disease. The results of poor health and poor treatment are born out in the life expectancy rates within each class. Aaron Antonovsky found that the higher your class standing, the higher your life expectancy. [21] Conversely, Lillian Guralnick studied the relationship between class and the death rate per 1000 in each of six age categories. Within each age group, she found that the lower one's class standing, the higher the death rate; in some age groups, the figures were as much as two and three times as high. [22]

Reality 5:   From cradle to grave, class standing has a significant impact on our chances for survival.

The lower one's class standing, the more difficult it is to secure appropriate housing, the more time is spent on the routine tasks of everyday life, the greater is the percentage of income that goes to pay for food and other basic necessities, [23] and the greater is the likelihood of crime victimization. [24] Class can predict changes for both survival and success.

CLASS AND EDUCATIONAL ATTAINMENT   In his study for the Carnegie Council on Children, Richard de Lone correlates school performance—i.e., grades and test scores—with the economic status of the student's family. After looking at the test scores of 647,031 students who took the College Board exams (SATs), he concluded that "the higher the student's social status, the higher the probability that he or she will get higher grades."

Relation of SAT Scores to Family Income[25]

Student's Scores	Student's Mean Family Income
750–800	$24,124
700–750	21,980
650–700	21,292
600–650	20,330
550–600	19,481
500–550	18,824
450–500	18,122
400–450	17,387
350–400	16,182
300–350	14,355
250–300	11,428
200–250	8,369

De Lone's findings were consistent with earlier studies that showed a direct relation between class and scores on standardized tests.[26]

Another researcher, William Sewell, showed a positive correlation between class and overall educational achievement. In comparing the top 25 percent of his sample to the bottom 25 percent, he found that students from upper-class families were: twice as likely to obtain training beyond high school, four times as likely to go to college, six times as likely to graduate from college, and nine times as likely to attain a postgraduate degree. Sewell concluded, "Socio-economic background . . . operates independently of academic ability at every stage in the process of educational attainment."[27]

Reality 6: Class standing has a significant impact on chances for educational attainment.

Class standing and consequently life chances are largely determined at birth. Although examples of individuals who have gone from rags to riches abound in the mass media, statistics on class mobility show these leaps to be extremely rare. In fact, less dramatic advances in class standing are relatively few. One study showed that fewer than one in five men surpass the economic status of their fathers.[28] For those whose annual income is in six figures, economic success is due in large part to the wealth and privileges bestowed upon them at birth. Over 66 percent of the consumer units with incomes of $100,000 or more have some inherited assets. Of these units, over 86 percent reported that inheritances constituted a substantial portion of their total assets.[29]

Economist Harold Wachtel likens inheritance to a series of Monopoly games in which the winner of the first game refuses to relinquish his cash and commercial property for the second game. "After all," argues the winner, "I accumulated my wealth and income by the strength of my own wits." With such an arrangement, it is not difficult to predict the outcome of subsequent games. [30]

Reality 7:   All Americans do not have an equal opportunity to succeed. Inheritance laws assure a greater likelihood of success for the offspring of the wealthy.

Spheres of Power and Oppression

When we look at society and try to determine what it is that keeps most people down—what holds them back from realizing their potential as healthy, creative, productive individuals—we find institutionally oppressive forces that are largely beyond their individual control. Class domination is one of these forces. People do not choose to be poor or working class; instead, they are limited and confined by the opportunities afforded or denied them by a social system. The class structure in the United States is a function of its economic system—capitalism, a system that is based on private rather than public ownership and control of commercial enterprises, and on the class division between those who own and control and those who do not. Under capitalism, these enterprises are governed by the need to produce a profit for the owners, rather than to fulfill collective needs.

Racial and gender domination are other such forces that hold people down. Although there are significant differences in the way capitalism, racism, and sexism affect our lives, there are also a multitude of parallels. And although race, class, and gender act independently of each other, they are at the same time very much interrelated.

On the one hand, issues of race and gender oppression cut across class lines. Women experience the effects of sexism whether they are well-paid professionals or poorly paid clerks. As women, they face discrimination and male domination, as well as catcalls and stereotyping. Similarly, a black man faces racial oppression whether he is an executive, an auto worker, or a tenant farmer. As a black, he will be subjected to racial slurs and be denied opportunities because of his color. Regardless of their class standing, women and members of minority races are confronted with oppressive forces precisely because of their gender, color, or both.

On the other hand, class oppression permeates other spheres of power and oppression, so that the oppression experienced by women and minorities is also differentiated along class lines. Although women and minorities find themselves in subordinate positions vis-à-vis white men, the particular issues they confront may be quite different depending on their position in the class structure. Inequalities in the class structure distinguish social functions and individual power, and these distinctions carry over to race and gender categories.

Power is incremental and class privileges can accrue to individual women and to individual members of a racial minority. At the same time, class-oppressed men, whether they are white or black, have privileges afforded them as men in a sexist society. Similarly, class-oppressed whites, whether they are men or women, have privileges afforded them as whites in a racist society. Spheres of power and oppres-

Chances of Being Poor in America[31]

	White male & female	White female head*	Black male & female	Black female head
Poverty	1 in 9	1 in 4	1 in 3	1 in 2
Near Poverty	1 in 6	1 in 3	1 in 2	2 in 3

*Persons in families with female householder, no husband present

sion divide us deeply in our society, and the schisms between us are often difficult to bridge.

Whereas power is incremental, oppression is cumulative, and those who are poor, black, and female have all of the forces of classism, racism, and sexism bearing down on them. This cumulative oppression is what is meant by the double and triple jeopardy of women and minorities. †

Furthermore, oppression in one sphere is related to the likelihood of oppression in another. If you are black and female, for example, you are much more likely to be poor or working class than you would be as a white male. Census figures show that the incidence of poverty and near-poverty (calculated as 125% of the poverty line) varies greatly by race and gender.

In other words, being female and being nonwhite are attributes in our society that increase the chances of poverty and of lower-class standing.

Reality 8:   Racism and sexism compound the effects of classism in society.

NOTES

1. See Oscar Glantz, "Class Consciousness and Political Solidarity," *American Sociological Review*, vol. 23, August 1958, pp. 375–382; Robert Nisbet, "The Decline and Fall of Social Class," *Pacific Sociological Review*, vol. 2, Spring 1959, pp. 11–17; Charles W. Tucker, "A Comparative Analysis of Subjective Social Class: 1945–1963," *Social Forces*, no. 46, June 1968, pp. 508–514; and Ira Katznelson, *City Trenches: Urban Politics and Patterning of Class in the United States*, New York, Pantheon Books, 1981.

2. Susan Ostander, "Upper-Class Women: Class Consciousness as Conduct and Meaning," in *Power Structure Research* by G. William Domhoff, Beverly Hills, California, Sage Productions, 1980, pp. 78–79.

3. Steven Rose, *The American Profile Poster*, New York, Pantheon Books, 1986, p. 31.

4. Barbara Kallen, "Getting By on $1 Million a Year," *Forbes*, October 27, 1986, p. 48.

5. "Characteristics of the Population Below the Poverty Level: 1984," from *Current*

†Gloria Steinem offers an opposing view, arguing that class acts in reverse for women and that power relations between wealthy men and their dependent wives are such that upper-class women are even more powerless than poor and working-class women vis-à-vis men.[32]

Population Reports, Consumer Income Series P-60, No. 152, Washington, D.C., U.S. Department of Commerce, Bureau of the Census, June 1986.

6. Constance Holden, "Homelessness: Experts Differ on Root Causes," *Science*, May 2, 1986, pp. 569–570.

7. "New Class of Children Is Poorer and the Prospects of Advancement Are Dim," *New York Times*, October 20, 1985, p. 56.

8. "United Nations National Accounts Statistics," *Statistical Papers, Series M no. 79*, New York, United Nations, 1985, pp. 1–11. See also Ira C. Magaziner and Robert B. Reich, *Minding America's Business: The Decline and Rise of the American Political Economy*," New York, Vintage, 1983, p. 23.

9. Steven Rose, *The American Profile Poster*, p. 31.

10. "Money Income of Households, Families, and Persons in the United States: 1984," *Current Population Reports P-60, no. 151*, Washington D.C., Department of Commerce, Bureau of Census, 1986, p. 1.

11. Paul Samuelson, *Economics*, 10th ed., New York, McGraw-Hill, 1976, p. 84.

12. Chris Tilly, "U-Turn on Equality," *Dollars and Sense*, May 1986, p. 11.

13. Paul Blumberg, *Inequality in an Age of Decline*, Oxford University Press, 1980.

14. Michael Harrington, *The Other America*, New York, Macmillan, 1962, pp. 12–13.

15. Stuart Ewen and Elizabeth Ewen, *Channels of Desire: Mass Images and the Shaping of American Consciousness*, New York, McGraw-Hill, 1982.

16. Kyriakos S. Markides and Connie McFarland, "A Note on Recent Trends in the Infant Mortality–Socioeconomic Status Relationship," *Social Forces*, 61:1, September 1982, pp. 268–276.

17. Stanley D. Eitzen, *In Conflict and Order: Understanding Society*, Boston, Allyn and Bacon, 1985, p. 265. Lucile Duberman, *Social Inequality: Class and Caste in America*, New York, J. B. Lippincott, 1976, p. 200.

18. *Statistical Abstracts of the U.S.*, 1986, p. 116.

19. August Hollingshead and Frederick Redlick, *Social Class and Mental Illness: A Community Study*, New York, John Wiley, 1958. Also Leo Srole, *Mental Health in the Metropolis: The Midtown Manhattan Study*, New York, McGraw-Hill, 1962.

20. U. S. Bureau of the Census, *Social Indicators III*, Washington D.C., U.S. Government Printing Office, 1980, p. 101.

21. Aaron Antonovsky, "Social Class, Life Expectancy and Overall Mortality," *The Impact of Social Class*, New York, Thomas Crowell, 1972, pp. 467–491.

22. Lillian Guralnick, "Socioeconomic Differences in Mortality by Cause of Death," in *International Population Conference, Ottawa, 1963*, Liège, International Union for the Scientific Study of Population, 1964, p. 298, quoted in Antonovsky, op. cit. See also Steven Caldwell and Theodore Diamond, "Income Differentials in Mortality" in Linda Del Bene and Fritz Scheuren, eds. *Statistical Uses of Administrative Records*, Washington, D.C., United States Social Security Administration, 1979, p. 58. Harriet Duleep, "Measuring the Effect of Income on Adult Mortality Using Longitudinal Administrative Record Data," *Journal of Human Resources*, vol. 21, no. 2, Spring 1986.

23. Paul Jacobs, "Keeping the Poor, Poor?" in Jerome H. Skolnick and Elliot Currie, *Crisis in American Institutions*, Boston, Little, Brown and Company, 1982, pp. 104–114.

24. Dennis W. Roncek, "Dangerous Places: Crime and Residential Environment," *Social Forces*, 60:1, September 1981, pp. 74–96.

25. Richard de Lone, *Small Futures*, New York: Harcourt Brace Jovanovich, 1978, p. 102.

26. Kenneth Eells and Allison Davis, *Intelligence and Cultural Differences: A Study of Cultural Learning and Problem Solving*, Chicago, University of Chicago Press, 1951.

27. William H. Sewell, "Inequality of Opportunity for Higher Education," *American Sociological Review*, vol. 36, no. 5, 1971, pp. 793–809.

28. Richard de Lone, *Small Futures*, New York: Harcourt Brace Jovanovich, 1978, pp. 14–19.

29. Howard Tuchman, *Economics of the Rich*, New York, Random House, 1973, p. 15.

30. Howard Wachtel, *Labor and the Economy*, Orlando Florida, Academic Press, 1984, pp. 161–162.

31. "Characteristics of the Population Below the Poverty Level: 1984," pp. 5–9.

32. Gloria Steinem, "The Trouble with Rich Women," *Ms.*, June 1986, p. 41.

3

The Wage Gap:
Myths and Facts

National Committee on Pay Equity

1. The United States Labor Force Is Occupationally Segregated by Race and Sex.

- In 1986, women constituted 44.5 percent of all workers in the civilian labor force (over 6 million women).[1]
- People of Color constituted 20 percent of all workers.[2]
- Labor force participation is almost equal among white women, Black women and women of Hispanic origin. In 1985, 57 percent (6.1 million) of Black women, 54 percent (43.5 million) of white women and 49 percent (2.9 million) of Hispanic women were in the paid labor force.[3]
- In 1986, women were:
    99 percent of all clericals
    94.3 percent of all registered nurses
    96.5 percent of all child care workers
    87.9 percent of all telephone operators
    85.2 percent of all teachers (excluding colleges and universities)
    91.1 percent of all data entry operators

Women were only:
4.4 percent of all dentists
6.0 percent of all engineers
18.1 percent of all lawyers and judges
4.8 percent of all police and detectives
8.6 percent of all precision, production, craft and repair workers
17.6 percent of all physicians[4]

The U.S. Labor force is segregated by sex and race:

Occupations with the Highest Concentration by Race/Ethnicity/Sex

Black women:	Private household workers, cooks, housekeepers, welfare aides
Black men:	Stevedores, garbage collectors, longshore equipment operators, baggage porters
Hispanic women:	Graders and agricultural workers, housekeepers, electrical assemblers, sewing machine operators
Hispanic men:	Farm workers, farm supervisors, elevator operators, concrete finishers
Asian women:	Marine life workers, electrical assemblers, dressmakers, launderers
Asian men:	Physicians, engineers, professors, technicians, baggage porters, cooks, launderers, longshore equipment operators
Native American women:	Welfare aides, child care workers, teacher's aides, forestry (except logging)
Native American men:	Marine life workers, hunters, forestry (except logging), fishers
White women:	Dental hygienists, secretaries, dental assistants, occupational therapists[5]

2. Economic Status.

- In 1985, two-thirds of all women were either the sole supporter of their families or their husbands earned $15,000 or less per year.[6] (Source: *20 Facts*)
- Over 2 million women work full time in jobs which pay wages below the poverty line (in 1985 for a family of three the poverty line was $8,741 per year). They work in jobs such as day care, food counter, and many service jobs. Many more women than men are part of the working poor (125 percent of the poverty level) and work in jobs such as clerical, blue collar, and sales jobs.[7]

Women of color are in the lowest paid jobs.

Occupations and Average Salaries of Occupations with a High Percentage of Women of Color[8]

Occupation	Annual Salary	Percentage of Women of Color*
Child care worker	$7,119	26.4
Sewing machine operator	7,568	29.6
Maids and housemen	7,945	35.5
Nursing aides	8,778	29.6
Health aides	9,489	19.5
Food preparation workers	7,132	18.9

*Women of color represented 7.59 percent of the United States workforce in the 1979 Census data.

The majority of women, just as the majority of men, work out of economic necessity to support their families. Women do not work for "pin money."

3. The Wage Gap Is One of the Major Causes of Economic Inequality in the United States Today.

- In 1985, all men, working year-round full-time, were paid a median salary of $24,195 per year.
- All women, working year-round full-time, were paid a median salary of $15,624 per year.
- Therefore, women were paid 64.5 cents compared to each dollar paid to men.

The breakdown by race shows the double burden that women of color face because of race and sex discrimination.

Year-Round Full-Time Earnings for 1985[9]

Race/Sex	Earnings	Earnings as a Percent of White Men's
White men	$25,062	100
Black men	17,479	69.7
Hispanic men	17,479	68.0
White women	15,796	63.0
Black women	14,308	57.1
Hispanic women	13,066	52.1

• In 1980 according to the United States Census Bureau, workers were paid the following average annual salaries based on race and sex:

Race/Sex	1980 Earnings	Earnings as a Percent of White Men's
White men	$20,335	100
Asian men	20,148	99.1
Native American men	16,019	78.8
Hispanic men	14,935	73.4
Black men	14,372	70.7
Asian women	12,432	60.0
White women	11,213	55.1
Black women	10,429	51.3
Native American women	10,052	49.4
Hispanic women	9,725	47.8

4. The Wage Gap Has Fluctuated, But Has Not Disappeared in the Last Several Decades.

Comparison of Median Earnings of Year-Round Full-Time Workers, by Sex, Selected Years

Year	Median Earnings		Women's Earnings as a Percent of Men's	Year	Median Earnings		Women's Earnings as a Percent of Men's
	WOMEN	MEN			WOMEN	MEN	
1985	$15,624	$24,195	64.5				
1984	14,780	23,218	63.7				
1983	13,915	21,881	63.6				
1982	13,014	21,077	61.7				
1981	12,001	20,260	59.2	1966	3,973	6,848	58.0
1980	11,197	18,612	60.2	1965	3,823	6,375	60.0
1979	10,151	17,014	59.7	1964	3,690	6,195	59.6
1978	9,350	15,730	59.4	1963	3,561	5,978	59.6
1977	8,618	14,626	58.9	1962	3,446	5,974	59.5
1976	8,099	13,455	60.2	1961	3,351	5,644	59.4
1975	7,504	12,758	58.8	1960	3,293	5,317	60.8
1974	6,772	11,835	57.2	1959	3,193	5,209	61.3
1973	6,335	11,186	56.6	1958	3,102	4,927	63.0
1972	5,903	10,202	57.9	1957	3,008	4,713	63.8
1971	5,593	9,399	59.5	1956	2,827	4,466	63.3
1970	5,323	8,966	59.4	1955	2,719	4,252	63.9
1969	4,977	8,227	60.5	1946	1,710	2,588	66.1

5. The Cause of the Wage Gap Is Discrimination.

Differences in education, labor force experience, and commitment (years in the labor force) do not account for the entire wage gap.

- The National Academy of Sciences found in 1981 that usually less than a quarter (25 percent), and never more than half (50 percent), of the wage gap is due to differences in education, labor force experience, and commitment.
- According to the 1986 NAS study, entitled *Women's Work, Men's Work,* "each additional percentage point female in an occupation was associated with $42 less in median annual earnings."
- According to the 1987 NCPE study, in New York State, for every 5 to 6 percent increase in Black and Hispanic representation in a job there is a one salary grade decrease. (A one salary grade decrease amounts to a 5 percent salary decrease.)
- In 1985, both women and men had a median educational level of 12.8 years.
- In 1985, the United States Bureau of the Census reported that differences in education, labor force experience, and commitment account for only 14.6% of the wage gap between women and men.

White Vs. Minority Wage Inequity By Education for Entry Level Jobs

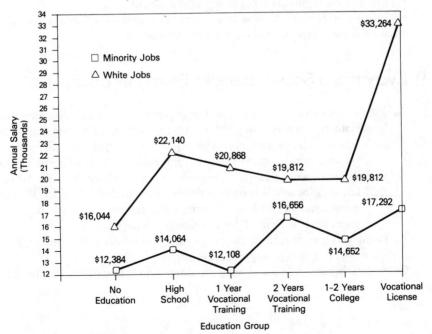

6. Employers Are Always Comparing Different Jobs in Order to Set Wages.

- Two-thirds (⅔) of employees are paid according to a formal job evaluation system

7. The Cost of Implementing Pay Equity.

- Achieving pay equity usually costs about 2 to 5 percent of an employer's pay roll budget.

For example, in the State of Minnesota, after conducting a job evaluation study, it was determined that there was a 20 percent gap between comparable male-dominated and female-dominated jobs. It cost the state 3.7 percent of the payroll budget to eliminate this inequity. The adjustments are being phased-in over a 4-year period.

8. Pay Equity Is Not a "Looney Tunes" Idea; It Is Being Addressed All Over the Country.

- All but 4 states have addressed the issue of pay equity
- 26 states and Washington, D.C. have conducted or are conducting job evaluation studies to determine if their wage setting systems are discriminatory
- 17 states have begun to make pay equity adjustments
- Three states (New York, New Jersey, and Wisconsin) and Washington, D.C. have addressed race in addition to sex discrimination

9. Everyone in Society Benefits From Pay Equity.

A. Men's wages will not be lowered. Employers cannot remedy discrimination by penalizing another group. Men who are working in predominantly female jobs will also be paid more if pay equity adjustments are made.

Everyone benefits from women being paid fairly. Whether it is your mother, sister, wife or daughter, wage discrimination hurts the entire family.

Men of color will benefit in additional ways to those listed for all men:
- elimination of race from the wage setting system.
- more likely to be in undervalued women's occupations.

B. Employers benefit because the employees' productivity will increase if there is a sense of fairness in how wages are set.

C. Society benefits because if wage discrimination is eliminated, the need for government subsidies for food stamps, health care, etc., will not be necessary. In addition when workers whose wages were lowered by discrimination are paid fairly, their pensions will be greater upon retirement.

Where We Get the Statistics

The U.S. Census Bureau collects wage data every 10 years. This data provides in-depth data for Blacks, whites, Hispanics, Asian Pacific Islanders and Native Americans.

The most recent salary data is from 1979. The United States Census Bureau also provides annual salary data for Blacks, whites, and Hispanics. They gather this information in March of the following year and release it in August. Therefore, the annual salary data for 1986 will not have been released until August of 1987.

The Bureau of Labor Statistics (BLS) provides quarterly reports each year on weekly salaries for Blacks, whites and Hispanics. They also provide an annual average of weekly wages.

The Women's Bureau releases "20 Facts on Working Women" on an annual basis.

The BLS and the Women's Bureau are part of the United States Department of Labor.

NOTES

1. *Employment and Earnings*, Bureau of Labor, vol. 34.1, Jan., 1987.
2. U.S. Census Bureau.
3. *20 Facts on Working Women*, Women's Bureau, 1986.
4. *Employment and Earnings*.
5. *Pay Equity: An Issue of Race, Ethnicity and Sex*, by the NCPE, February, 1987.
6. *20 Facts*.
7. Women's Bureau, unpublished.
8. *Pay Equity: An Issue of Race, Ethnicity and Sex*.
9. U.S. Census Bureau, Current Population Series P-60 #154, most recent annual data available.

4

Ain't I a Woman:
Differences in the Labor Market Status of Black and White Women*

Julianne Malveaux

"Ain't I A Woman." That statement symbolizes some of the differences between black and white women from the standpoint of foremother and freedom fighter Sojourner Truth. In many ways the similarities and differences between black and white women in the labor market can be dealt with from the standpoint of Sojourner's statement. For, while black women experience some of the same labor market problems as do white women, they are far more disadvantaged in terms of occupational status, in terms of unemployment, and in terms of pay.

Labor Market Trends

The most marked change in the labor force in the past twenty years has been the increase in the labor force participation of women. Most of this increase, though, has been an increase in the proportion of white women working. In 1960 just a third of all white women participated in the labor force (meaning they either worked or looked for work). By January 1983, 52% participated in the labor force, a proportional increase of over 50%.

On the other hand, black women have always worked proportionately more than white women have. Historical data show that in 1890 20% of all black *girls* between ages ten and fourteen worked. Data collected in 1890 and 1910 show black women

*Data came from published and unpublished Bureau of Labor Statistics sources, especially the February, 1983 issue of "Employment and Earnings," the 1981 issue of "The Employment and Training Report of the President," and unpublished tables.

working more than white women, with the notable difference being that white women's participation fell off markedly after age 25, while black women's participation remained level until age 65.

In the recent period where the participation of white women rose by more than 50%, black women's participation rose more slowly. Nearly half of all black women (48%) worked in 1960; this number rose to 57% by January, 1983, an increase of 18%. So while black women's participation did not rise as rapidly as did white women's, it continues to exceed the participation of white women.

The media gives us a perception of work that is very different from fact. The notion that women have "come a long way, baby" is not borne out by much of the labor market data. Women tend to work in the market in many of the same ways that they work in the home: as helpers or nurturers, with children, food, clothing or cleaning. This has changed a little bit in the past few years, but not a lot. Importantly, the increase in women's labor force participation has not changed, in great measure, the kind of work they do. The fact that black women participate more in the labor market than do white women has not given them an advantaged position occupationally; in fact, the opposite. It is important to understand that women, black and white, work out of economic necessity in jobs that tend to be low paying.

Occupational Segregation

Occupational segregation is a fact of the work world for both black and white women. Most women work in jobs that are "crowded" with other women. In viewing the range of jobs in the labor market, and looking at the percentages of men and women in these jobs, it is clear that most jobs are stratified by sex. Thirty percent of all women work in jobs that are more than 90% female. Sixty percent work in jobs that are more than 70% female.

Occupational segregation wouldn't matter so much if it weren't for the reality of unequal pay. The "women's jobs" are much less well paid than "men's jobs." For example, median weekly pay for a clerical worker (a job category that is overwhelmingly female) was $201 in 1980, while median weekly pay for a crafts worker (a male job category) was $333.

Black and white women experience a different kind of job segregation. Black women's work experiences are historically rooted in the work they did as slaves. In 1940, the majority of black women who worked were private household workers. Fewer than 5% worked in "white collar" jobs. By 1960, that situation was little changed, with fully half of all black women working as domestic workers. Differences between black and white women in the workplace are ironically illustrated by the fact that Lyndon Johnson's Commission on the Status of Women expressed concern that the number of domestic servants was declining at that time. As a result of this concern, there was some effort to upgrade household employment. As one writer noted at the time, the best way to upgrade the status of women in private household work is to "help them escape such employment."

Black women have escaped household employment in the past twenty years. Where half of all black women were household workers in 1960, just 6% of black women worked in that occupation by 1981. But black women left that occupation to enter "substitute" service occupations where the work is similar but pay is more regular.

"Typically female" jobs, those with high female concentrations, can be defined as health professionals, non-college teachers, retail sales workers, clerical workers, non-durable goods operatives, private household workers, and service workers, except protective service workers. More than three-quarters of black women worked in these jobs in 1981. About 70% of all white women worked in these same jobs. There were differences in the types of jobs black and white women held, though. Two-thirds of the white women in typically female jobs worked in "white collar" jobs. These included health professionals, non-college teachers, retail sales workers, and clerical workers, with the bulk of women working as clerical workers. Slightly more than half of the black women worked in "white collar," typically female jobs with proportionately more of them working in the "blue collar" (non-durable goods operatives, private household workers, service workers).

The historical position of black women changed somewhat since 1968, when most of them worked in blue collar, typically female jobs. There have been two changes. Firstly, the degree of concentration in typically female jobs dropped by about 4%. Secondly, black women moved out of blue collar, typically female jobs, especially the private household job, and into white collar, typically female jobs, especially the clerical job. White women's concentration in typically female jobs declined, too. But white women left blue collar jobs and maintained their concentration in typically female white collar jobs.

Age Patterns

When we look at age patterns, we note white women between 25 and 44 experiencing less occupational segregation than do younger or older white women. This makes sense because young (i.e. 16–24) women are often employed on a temporary basis in the jobs traditionally available to them, while older women are skill-locked into typically female jobs. The pattern among black women is similar, but there are two striking trends to note. Firstly, older black women are overwhelmingly concentrated in typically female, blue collar jobs. Secondly, at every age level except for among teens, black women are more concentrated in typically female jobs than are white women.

Among young black women (16–21), patterns are somewhat disturbing. These black women are less frequently participants in the labor force than are young black men, white women, or white men. Just a third of them work or are looking for work, compared with almost half of the black men in this age group, and nearly 60% of the white men and women in this age group. Thus, for the majority of young black women, work is the exception rather than the rule.

Teen unemployment and labor force participation are not major problems when youth plan to attend college. But when youth terminate education with high school and some vocational training, youth unemployment may have long-term effects on the ability to find a job and to have earnings as an adult. This is especially important for young black women, who increasingly head families, nearly all of whom are in poverty.

Future Projections

The industrial structure of the United States is changing. The jobs projected to experience most growth in the next three years or so are typically female jobs, the health professions and clerical work. The dimensions of these jobs will change somewhat, especially the dimensions of the clerical job which will become more computerized, and more skilled. What this means for women in the future is that they are likely to remain as stratified in the labor market as they are now.

Economic competition has prevented smooth entry of young black women into the labor market. The fact that so few of them work now has negative implications for the future status of black women in the workplace. However, the lower economic status that black women are likely to have because of their workplace experience points up the many issues of concern for black women. These are the bread-and-butter issues of access to jobs, access to childcare (because of their high incidence of female headship), access to affordable housing and to equal pay. Issues also include the availability of non-college job training.

Summary

Black women have consistently participated in the labor market, though in the lowest-paying jobs in the occupational strata. In fact, most labor market statistics point to the disadvantaged status of black women in the labor market. Though the occupational position of black women has its roots in slavery, black women have continued to be segregated occupationally and in different ways than are white women. Labor market trends suggest that the relative labor market position of most black women will not improve considerably in the near future.

The differential labor market status of black women as well as the differential economic status of black men and women is a critical factor determining the issues focus of many black women. These issues are the key issues facing people of color since work and economic status affect survival. Thus, those concerned with organizing black women (and by extension, other women of color who experience similar labor market problems), might use labor market problems as an organizing focus.

5

The Feminization of Poverty

The Women's Economic Agenda Working Group of the Institute for Policy Studies

In the 1960s, at the time of the revival of the women's movement, many assumed that the entry of women into the workforce would automatically result in their independence and self-respect. But today, while over one-half of American women are in the labor force, the majority of American women are still economically disadvantaged: Over 3.5 million women head households in poverty,[1] while many married women find themselves working desperately to keep their families above subsistence level. . . .

The "other America" is a changing neighborhood: Men have been moving out and women, many with children, are moving in. In the last decade, the proportion of families in poverty who were maintained by women alone rose from 36 to 50 percent[2]—a net increase each year of approximately 100,000 poor families headed by women alone.[3] If this trend persisted, and other factors remained unchanged, by the year 2000 all those in poverty would be women and their children.[4]

This trend towards the feminization of poverty does not counter, but rather reinforces, the greater poverty traditionally experienced by black Americans and other racial/ethnic minority peoples. But there has been a change: The burden of poverty has shifted from two-parent black or Hispanic families to families sustained by women alone, so that now almost three-fourths of poor minority families are headed by women.[5] Because the economic status and opportunities of minority women (black, Hispanic, Asian/Pacific, native American) are even more dismal than those of majority women, the trend towards the feminization of poverty has increased minority poverty and exacerbated racial inequality.

Women are not only more of the poor, but they are getting poorer. The relative economic status of families headed by women alone has declined over the last two decades, with average income falling from 51 to 46 percent of the average income of male householder families (including married couples as well as male householders alone).[6] And once poor, women and their families are much more likely to stay poor.[7] While many women are poor for some of the same reasons that men are poor (such as low skills, location in a job-poor area), much of women's poverty can be traced to two distinctly female factors: women's disadvantaged position in the labor market, and the economic burden of children.

Women's disadvantaged position in the labor market is attributable in part to the unequal income women earn, the now familiar 59 cents (current estimates range between 61 and 64 cents) on the average dollar earned by men. But it also stems from the fact that many women have not yet achieved full-time year-round jobs. While 63 percent of male householders work full-time, year-round only 36 percent of women maintaining households do so.[8] Furthermore, women must work much harder to stay out of poverty. The poverty rate of black mothers working full-time, year-round is 13 percent, the same rate experienced by white men who do not work at all.[9] Because of these disadvantages, a job is a much less certain route out of poverty for women heading families than for male householders. About one-fourth of the families headed by working women are poor, compared to only one-twentieth of families with an employed adult male.[10]

Women must often bear the economic burden of raising children alone or with little help. Of families with children, 43 percent of those maintained by a woman alone live in poverty, compared to 8 percent of those maintained by a man, alone or in a married couple.[11] This high rate of poverty is the result, in part, of the failure of fathers, and/or the larger society, to adequately support children. Child support from absent parents (almost all fathers) as of 1981 averaged about $2,100 per family, not per child, a decline in real terms of 16 percent in three years.[12] The society at large provides support for dependent children through welfare (AFDC—Aid to Families with Dependent Children). While the average payment to a family of four rose between 1974 and 1982 from $248 to $356, an increase of 43 percent, prices almost doubled over the same period. Due to inflation, these children have experienced a real decline of more than 25 percent in their financial resources.[13]

NOTES

1. U.S. Bureau of the Census, *Money, Income and Poverty Status of Families in the United States: 1983* (hereinafter referred to as *Income and Poverty Statistics, 1983*) Series P-60, No. 145. Washington, D.C.: Government Printing Office, August 1984, Table 18.

2. National Advisory Council on Economic Opportunity, *Final Report: The American Promise: Equal Justice and Economic Opportunity.* Washington, D.C.: Government Printing Office, August 1981.

3. Income and Poverty Statistics, 1983, Table 18.

4. U.S. Bureau of the Census, *Money Income of Households, Families and Persons in the United States: 1960 and 1983*, Series P-60. Washington, D.C.: Government Printing Office, 1961 and 1984 respectively.

5. Greg J. Duncan, *Years of Poverty, Years of Plenty: The Changing Economic Fortunes of American Workers and Families.* Ann Arbor, Michigan: University of Michigan, Institute for Social Research, 1984, p. 63.

6. *Income and Poverty Statistics, 1983*, Table 18.

7. *Poverty Characteristics, 1983*, Table 26.

8. Ibid., Table 5.

9. Ibid., Table 18.

10. U.S. Bureau of the Census, *Child Support and Alimony: 1981* (Advance Report) Series P-23, No. 124. Washington, D.C.: Government Printing Office, 1983.

11. Diana M. Pearce, Statement before the Select Committee on Children, Youth and Families, U.S. House of Representatives, July 18, 1983.

6 Blacks in America: A Statistical Profile

Blacks Have Gained in Education . . .

Median years of school completed by those over 25 years old in each group.

WHITE

BLACK

*Figures for blacks include all other nonwhites.

Source: Census Bureau

15 — 10 — 5 — 0

'62* '65 '70 '75 '80 '82

. . . In Political Representation . . .

In 1965, there were an estimated 300 black elected officials in the nation. 1970 is the first year the Joint Center for Economic Studies began compiling data on this issue.

	1970	1982
Federal	10	18
State and regional	169	397
County	92	465
Municipal	623	2,451
Judicial and law enforcement	213	583
Education	362	1,266
TOTAL:	1,469	5,160

. . . And in White-Collar Employment . . .

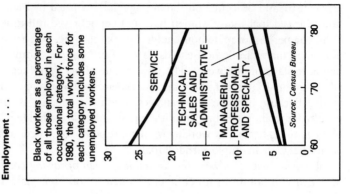

Black workers as a percentage of all those employed in each occupational category. For 1980, the total work force for each category includes some unemployed workers.

SERVICE

TECHNICAL, SALES AND ADMINISTRATIVE

MANAGERIAL, PROFESSIONAL AND SPECIALTY

Source: Census Bureau

30 — 25 — 20 — 15 — 10 — 5 — 0

'60 '70 '80

. . . And the Poverty Gap Persists

Percentage of the population living below poverty level, which now stands at $9,862 for an urban family of four.

*Figures for blacks include all other nonwhites.

Source: Census Bureau

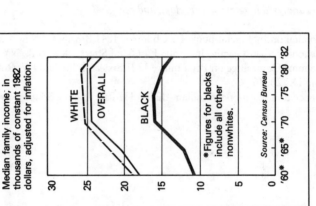

. . . Or Income . . .

Median family income, in thousands of constant 1982 dollars, adjusted for inflation.

*Figures for blacks include all other nonwhites.

Source: Census Bureau

. . . But Not in Overall Jobs . . .

Employed percentage of the labor force 16 years old and older. Figures for 1983 are as of July.

*Figures for blacks include all other nonwhites.

Source: Bureau of Labor Statistics

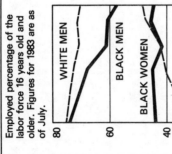

Source: The *New York Times*, 8/28/83.

Suggestions for Further Reading

Blumberg, Paul: *Inequality in an Age of Decline*, Oxford University Press, Oxford, 1980.

Domhoff, G. William: *Who Rules America Now?* Simon and Schuster, New York, 1983.

Hacker, Andrew: *U/S A Statistical Portrait of the American People*, Viking Press, New York, 1983.

Horwitz, Lucy and Lou Ferleger: *Statistics for Social Change*, South End Press, Boston, 1980.

Sennett, Richard and Cobb, Jonathan: *The Hidden Injuries of Class*, Vintage Books, New York, 1973.

In addition to these books, the following organizations are good sources for obtaining current statistics analyzed in terms of race, class, and gender:

The Council on Interracial Books for Children, 1841 Broadway, New York, NY 10023.

The National Urban League, Inc., 500 East 62nd Street, New York, NY 10021.

The National Committee on Pay Equity, 1201 Sixteenth Street, NW, Room 422, Washington, DC 20036.

The Association of American Indian Affairs, 432 Park Avenue South, New York, NY 10016.

PART III

Paying the Price: Some Consequences of Racial, Gender, and Class Inequality

Statistics can tell us a great deal about living conditions in a given society, but they paint only part of the picture. They can tell us that more and more women and children are living in poverty, but they cannot make that poverty real to us. They can tell us that a woman is raped in the United States at least as often as every two minutes, but they cannot help us share her pain, anger, or terror.[1] They can tell us that one-third of the adult population in this country cannot read well enough to get through the front page of a daily newspaper, but they cannot translate those numbers into lived experience.[2] For that, we must turn to stories about people's lives.

Who will tell these stories? For many years, it was difficult to find books about the experiences of women and minorities. Even books about breast-feeding and childbirth were authored almost exclusively by male "experts," who described and defined a reality that they had never known. White sociologists and anthropologists set themselves up as experts on Black, Hispanic, and American Indian experiences and offered elaborate, critical accounts of the family structure and life-style of each. Novels chronicling the growth to manhood of young white males from the upper or upper-middle class were routinely assigned in high-school and college English courses and examined for "universal themes," while novels about women's lives or the experiences of minorities or working people were relegated to "special-interest" courses and treated as marginal. In short, by definition, great literature has been that which was by well-to-do white males and about their experiences; accounts of the lives of other groups, if available at all, were rarely written by members of these groups.

During the recent past, more accounts of the lives of ordinary people have become available, thus bridging some of the gaps in the limited experience each of us brings to our study of race, class, and gender. The selections in Part III are offered as a way of putting flesh and blood around the bare-bones facts provided in Part II. Some of the selections are excerpts from novels; others are nonfiction pieces drawn from magazines and books. All of them are offered as a vehicle for shedding our own particular identity, at least for a few minutes, and finding out what it is like to live as someone who is of a different gender or is from another race or class or who lives a different life-style. They can begin to suggest to us something of the terrible price that is paid in the destruction of human lives by the racism, sexism, and class differences that define our world.

While race, class, and gender are the primary factors that define opportunity and limit possibility for people in the United States at this time, other factors can also have a significant impact on life choices: among them are age, sexual preference, disability, and whether one lives in a rural or an urban area. Some of these factors are touched upon or highlighted in selections included in Part III. In some contexts, these factors play a major role in shaping the way others treat us and how we come to see ourselves. They determine the kinds of work offered to us, how much we are paid, what kinds of educational opportunities are available to us, and where and how we can live. In other contexts, these variables may well be irrelevant. Reading about them adds another dimension to our understanding of the complex set of additional factors that interact with issues of race, class, and gender.

There is much to learn from looking at the experiences of others, but there is also a danger in this project—the danger of overgeneralizing. It is easy to fall into the trap of stereotyping people and failing to remember that, for example, the experiences of one young Puerto Rican woman, such as those in the excerpt from *Nilda*, are not the experiences of *all* Hispanics or even of all Puerto Ricans. For the purposes of studying race, class, and gender, it is often necessary to generalize about "Asians" or "Chicanas" or "men" in order to highlight things that are more typical of the experiences of certain groups than of others. Yet, we must remember that every individual is just that, an individual person, and we must try to look beyond stereotypes and generalizations to find that person. On the other hand, as we have already seen, it is naive to think that the individual exists in a vacuum, untouched by the racism, sexism, and class bias of society. Unless we understand something about the way different groups experience life in the United States, we will never adequately understand the particular experiences of individual people.

The articles in this part then have been selected because they can give us some understanding of the consequences of the racial, gender, and class inequality documented in Part II, as well as a dramatic account of some of the other variables that affect people's lives. For the most part, these articles and essays need no introduction. They speak for themselves.

NOTES

1. The statistic on rape is drawn from the FBI's Uniform Crime Report for 1985.

2. The statistic on literacy is drawn from an article Jonathan Kozol wrote for the *New York Times* Book Review Section, March 3, 1985. There he writes: "Among adults, 16 percent of whites, 44 percent of blacks and 56 percent of Hispanic people are either total, functional or marginal nonreaders."

Racial and Ethnic Minorities:
An Overview

Beth Hess, Elizabeth W. Markson, and Peter J. Stein

The United States has been heavily populated only in the past two hundred years, primarily through the immigration of Europeans. These early immigrants displaced an estimated 2.5 million native people who had entered the continent at least twenty thousand years earlier across a land bridge from Asia. But it was not long before the Native American tribes were reduced to a racial and ethnic group "inferior" to the "more civilized" white newcomers. They were all categorized as "Indians," and their widely varying cultures were destroyed. Because white settlers thought of their culture as superior to that of other people, the physical characteristics of all other racial groups were taken as evidence of their biological inferiority. Thus, the white colonists rationalized their seizure of land and resources and the destruction of the Native American cultures.

Native Americans

A typical nineteenth-century view was expressed by President Andrew Jackson on signing the Indian Removal Act of 1830:

> What good man would prefer a country covered with forests and ranged by a few thousand savages to our . . . Republic; studded with cities . . . and prosperous farms, embellished with more than 12 million happy people, and filled with all the blessing of liberty, civilization, and religion? (Quoted in Pearce 1978)

Treaties with Native American tribes could be ignored on the grounds that Indians were not entitled to equal status with white Americans. Meanwhile, government policy supported the forceful removal of Indians from lands wanted by white settlers. Even lands set aside by the federal government for each Native American tribe eventually fell into the hands of non-Indians. By 1983, about fifty-three million acres, or 2.4 percent of United States land, was managed in trust by the Bureau of Indian Affairs. Because traditionally the Department of the Interior (in which the Bureau of Indian Affairs is located) has been interested in conservation rather than the economic development of the reservations, a self-fulfilling prophecy of economic backwardness has come about (Guillemin 1980).

In 1983, President Reagan announced a new Indian policy. Criticizing the reservations for fostering dependency, he stressed the need for the reservations to become economically self-sufficient, primarily through developing mineral resources and energy reserves. Yet, only 37 of the 283 tribes recognized by the federal government have energy or minerals on their land, and only 24 of these have large amounts (Winslow 1983). Moreover, most tribes own only a small part of their reservations. For example, although there is an estimated eleven billion tons of coal on the Crow reservation, the tribe owns only 22 percent of the land. Nor can self-determination and economic self-sufficiency be achieved easily when the most basic needs, such as adequate education, housing, and health care, have not yet been met.

Native Americans remain the poorest and the most disadvantaged of all racial or ethnic groups in the United States, as shown by death rates from a wide range of diseases far greater than those of the population as a whole. According to 1982 Senate hearings, mortality from alcohol-related causes among Native Americans is twenty-two times higher than the national average. Indians die from tuberculosis at six times the rate of non-Indians. Their suicide rate is twice the national average. Unemployment rates are high; housing is substandard; and nearly half the hospitals built by the Indian Health Service were built before 1940 and are both understaffed and in need of repairs.

According to the 1980 U.S. Census, there are about 1.4 million Native Americans. The states with the largest Indian population are California, Oklahoma, Arizona, New Mexico, and North Carolina. Contrary to popular belief, only slightly more than half of all Native Americans live on reservations. Many live in metropolitan areas such as Los Angeles, Chicago, Seattle, and Minneapolis–St. Paul. Others are farmers and migrant laborers in the southwest and the north-central regions, and many live in New York State and in New England.

Far from being on the verge of extinction, the Native American population has grown faster than the U.S. population as a whole. New births, however, can account for only a small percentage of the 72 percent increase in Native Americans between the 1970 Census and the 1980 Census. It seems likely that many people who had identified themselves as belonging to some other race or ethnicity in the 1970 Census decided to identify themselves as Native Americans in 1980.

Among Native Americans, a new militancy is evident. There has been a rising tide of political activity, illustrated by the American Indian Movement (AIM). Demonstrations and lawsuits have called attention to the treaties broken by the U.S. government and the unmet needs of the American Indian. Several of the lawsuits have resulted in a return of native lands and/or million-dollar reparation payments. In recent years, the courts have ordered that $106 million be paid to the Sioux for the Black Hills, $4.5 million to the Narragansetts for Rhode Island, and $81.5 million to three tribes for lands in Maine. But it has been difficult for Native Americans to create a unified political front because of the great variety among tribes. There is no typical Native American, no one Indian culture, language, religion, or physical type.

Blacks in America

Blacks and Stratification Hierarchies   In 1980, 26.5 million blacks accounted for almost 12 percent of the total population of the United States. To what extent have American blacks moved into and up the stratification system?

Power   Although all legal barriers to black voting have been removed, blacks are less likely to vote than whites, partly because of difficulties encountered in registering and voting in the South, but probably mostly because of lower income and education, which, in turn, are associated with lower voter turnout in general. Also, feelings of powerlessness and alienation reduce the motivation to vote ("What good would it do?").

The number of black elected officials rose dramatically from about one thousand five hundred in 1970 to more than five thousand in 1983. Over half are city or county officials, including the mayors of major cities such as Atlanta, Philadelphia, Los Angeles, and Chicago. An urban black political elite is beginning to emerge. But for such an elite to develop, political subdivisions must contain not only many blacks but also a secure and expanding black middle class with funds to contribute to political campaigns (Karnig and Welch 1981). Few blacks hold high positions in federal or state government, although the proportions have increased slowly. So have the number of judges, midlevel civil servants, and law-enforcement officers. At the moment, these officeholders represent considerably fewer than the 12 percent that would reflect the percentage of blacks in the population. Much of the mobility among blacks has been due to entrance into middle-management jobs in the government sector during the 1960s and 1970s (Oliver and Glick 1982), precisely the jobs currently being cut back at the federal and state levels.

Property   In terms of employment, occupation, income, and wealth, blacks remain disadvantaged compared to whites. Blacks are also likely to have less valuable homes and less housing equity (Parcel 1982), and to pay higher lending rates for home mortgages (Pol, Guy, and Bush 1982). As the last hired, blacks are also typically among the first fired when the economy turns downward. Thus, in 1983, annual unemployment rates were twice as high for blacks as for whites.

The incomes of black workers lag behind those of whites. Among families with a full-time worker, the median income for a black family is roughly three quarters of that for a white family. Overall, black incomes are about 56 percent of that for white families. In part, these figures reflect the high proportion of black families headed by females (41 percent vs. 12 percent for whites), many of whom are not in the labor force (Pear 1983). It is truly in the black female-headed family that we can see most clearly the "feminization of poverty" (Pearce 1978). In 1982, 36 percent of black families fell below the poverty level—nearly three times the rate for white families (Pear 1983).

High unemployment and economic tension have taken their toll among blacks. The suicide rate among young blacks has risen, and young men in their twenties without strong family and community ties are at the highest risk (Davis 1979). Divorce rates have also increased dramatically, often because of discrimination in the work force, racism, unemployment, and the stresses associated with trying to survive on very low incomes (Rule 1982). Because the last hired are also younger than those already established in jobs, most black unemployment occurs among young men who are in precisely the age group requiring the economic security to marry, raise families, and become attached to the labor force. In 1982, 48 percent of black teenagers were unemployed, as compared to 19 percent of white teenagers (*Statistical Abstract of the United States*, 1982–83). The long-term results of their unemployment cannot be calculated but will probably include social unrest in the years ahead. Yet, . . . whites in general believe that blacks are benefiting from reverse discrimination in employment, see blacks' opportunity as having greatly improved in recent years, and deny the structural limits on blacks' opportunities (Kluegel and Smith 1982).

Much has been written of the increasing numbers of black families that have moved into the middle class (Wilson 1980, 1981), but blacks still work harder for fewer rewards. At the same level of education and occupation, black wages are still lower than those of whites. In fact, a typical white male high-school dropout earns more than a college-educated black male, largely because of discrimination and the differing employment opportunities for the two races. Although 40 percent of black workers were in white-collar jobs in 1980, compared to 54 percent of white workers, blacks were still underrepresented in the best paying jobs. For example, black men and women make up between 3 and 7 percent of engineers, physicians, and lawyers (Reid 1982). Blacks have made occupational gains since 1960 but they have not been as significant as those of whites, particularly white males (Oliver and Glick 1982).

Prestige   Given the political, income, and occupational data just presented, it seems clear that many sources of personal and social prestige are denied to blacks. In education, advancement may be more apparent than real. By 1982, the college enrollment of blacks aged eighteen to twenty-four had nearly doubled since 1965—from 10 percent to 19 percent. However, whereas most white high-school graduates were at four-year colleges and universities, most blacks were at two-year colleges and trade schools. Only 8 percent of black adults, compared to 18 percent of whites, have a college degree—the admission ticket to advancement (Reid 1982). Furthermore, well-educated black males often go into jobs with moderate prestige but lower pay, such as education and social service (Hogan and Pazul 1981).

How have black executives fared? For them, corporate America may be what professional sports were for blacks before Jackie Robinson. They are underrepresented and unwanted and are made to feel uncomfortable (Davis and Watson 1982). Blacks have actually made smaller gains in businesses and corporations in the last few years than they did in the 1960s; even those in positions that pay well and sound prestigious have complained that they have been placed in highly visible but dead-end jobs (*Time*, December 6, 1982).

Caste or Class?   The evidence supports the *caste* model of black–white stratification, although debates over the relative importance of class and race continue. Some analysts (e.g., Wilson 1980) claim that the overwhelming effects of poverty have become more important than race in itself. Others cite continuing racism as a major factor in the persistence of poverty. That blacks have fared poorly seems evident. Over the last six decades, blacks have moved out of the rural South into urban areas; they have also increased their level of education and their political activity. Yet, they remain outside the mainstream stratification system. Their disadvantages have been built into the social structure (Pinkney 1975).

For generations, despite their familiarity with American customs and language, blacks were denied the right to vote, to be on juries, and even to be promoted in the military long after newer immigrant groups had achieved these goals (Steinberg 1981, Liberson 1981). Moreover, as the number of blacks has increased, they have tended to become more, not less, segregated by the white community, and this increased segregation has preserved occupational and economic advantages for whites (Liberson 1981). Residential segregation is but one example.

Recently, the trend toward political and economic gains for blacks has been halted and even reversed as the overall economic situation has grown worse. The costs of recession and inflation in the United States are disproportionately borne by the poor in general and by blacks in particular. Although affirmative-action programs have helped the better-trained and better-educated blacks, these programs have not improved the economic prospects for poor black men or women (Wilson 1981).

Asians in the United States

Like European-Americans, Asian-Americans come from different cultures and religious backgrounds and speak different languages. Yet, a tendency to classify all Asians together has dominated both immigration policy and popular attitudes. In this section, we describe some of the different Asian groups that have immigrated to the United States and the similar and dissimilar problems that they have experienced as a result of both race and ethnicity.

Chinese   In the mid-nineteenth century young Chinese males were imported to work on the transcontinental railroad. Unable to bring wives with them or to send for brides, those who remained in the United States formed an almost exclusively male community. Chinese men were victims of extreme prejudice, discrimination, and open violence until the outbreak of World War II in 1941, when suddenly they became the "good Asians," compared to the "evil" Japanese. Restrictive immigration laws were ended, and the Chinese-American population has grown rapidly over the past several decades. According to 1980 census data, there were over 800,000 Americans of Chinese ancestry, the largest single group of Asians in our country. Most Chinese live in seven states: the largest percentage in California, then in New York, then in Hawaii, Illinois, Texas, Massachusetts, and New Jersey.

The Chinese-American population is characterized by growing professionalization (for example, in medicine, scientific research, and engineering) and by high rates of upward mobility. Although residential discrimination still exists in some areas, it has been less difficult for Chinese than for blacks to assimilate culturally or to amalgamate, as seen in the relatively high rates of Chinese–white marriages.

Japanese   According to one social scientist (Kitano 1976), Japanese immigrants "came to the wrong country and the wrong state (California) at the wrong time (immediately after the Chinese) with the wrong race and skin color, with the wrong religion, and from the wrong country" (p. 31).

The first generation of Japanese-born immigrants who arrived in the early 20th century were called *Issei* and were not highly assimilated. Yet, their children, born in the United States and known as *Nisei*, were taught the value both of education and of conformity to the norms and expectations of the majority culture. After the outbreak of World War II, the Japanese in North America were forcibly moved from their homes and relocated. Inasmuch as hostility toward Japan was high in the U.S. during World War II, Japanese-Americans provided available visible targets for its expression. Their appearance, language, and culture were interpreted as indications of disloyalty to the U.S. Over 100,000 West Coast Japanese-Americans were placed in detention camps with guard towers and barbed-wire fences. Their property was confiscated, sold, or stolen. Among the long-term effects of relocation were a reduction in the relative power of men over women in the family, a weakening of control over offspring, and reinforcement of a sense of ethnic identity.

According to the 1980 census, almost 800,000 Japanese-Americans lived in the United States. Most live in five states: the largest percentage in California, then in Hawaii, then in Washington, New York, and Illinois. Third-generation Japanese-Americans rank highest among all nonwhite groups in educational attainment and income. Their occupational distribution is more varied than that of Chinese ethnics.

Has the pattern of Japanese-American assimilation been similar to that of other minority racial groups, or are they still excluded from the majority society? Although they have experienced rapid social mobility, a racial disadvantage remains (Woodrum 1981). The answer to this question is not clear-cut, however. The Japanese value system has promoted economic success, which has led to high rates of upward mobility (Montero 1980). Greater mobility, in turn, has been associated with a shift from employment in the ethnic community to the corporate economy, and to greater assimilation (Bonacich 1975). For example, third-generation Japanese-Americans have a higher percentage of non-Japanese friends than do first- or second-generation

Japanese-Americans. They are also more likely to have non-Japanese spouses, to live in a non-Japanese neighborhood, and to profess non-Japanese religious beliefs (Montero 1981).

In short, as occupational and financial mobility has occurred, greater cultural, structural, and marital assimilation has taken place.

Can the Japanese-American community remain intact or will it be amalgamated into the majority society? The answer will depend on whether Japanese-Americans develop a broader identity as Asian-Americans. But the most highly educated and most successful Japanese-Americans have become the most cut off from their ethnic background; for example, 40 percent have non-Japanese spouses (Montero 1980, 1981). The irony of this trend toward amalgamation is that the Japanese may lose their roots in the tradition that gave rise to their upward mobility.

Other Asians   In 1980, there were about 1.5 million people of other Asian ethnicities in the United States. Filipinos accounted for 52 percent, followed by Asian Indians, Koreans, and Vietnamese. Koreans showed the most remarkable growth, increasing from 69,999 in 1970 to 355,000 in 1980, a growth rate of 413 percent. Most of the 262,000 Vietnamese in America were refugees from the Vietnam war and other political unrest at home. The welcome given to the arrival of Asian-Americans, like that of most new immigrants who are not of northern European origin, has been mixed. However, Asians, whether from Korea, Vietnam, or elsewhere, may be the achievers of the future.

Hispanic Americans

Hispanic American is a category made up of many separate cultural and racial subgroups bound together by a common language, Spanish (although even language patterns vary by country of origin). In 1984, over fifteen million Spanish-speaking people were officially recorded as residing in the United States; and several million additional Hispanics are believed to have entered without official documents. Because of their generally younger ages and high birth rates, it is likely that Spanish-speaking Americans will soon outnumber blacks as the single largest minority group in the United States.

In 1984, the three major ethnic subdivisions within the Spanish-speaking population were Mexican-Americans (Chicanos), roughly 60 percent; Puerto Ricans, 14 percent; and Cubans, approximately 6 percent. The remainder were immigrants from other Central and South American countries, particularly the Dominican Republic, Colombia, and El Salvador. As Table 1 indicates, differences within the Spanish-speaking minority are striking, especially in terms of education, occupation, and income. There is a stratification system within the Hispanic population, based not only on these indicators of socioeconomic status but also on skin color. Thus, race and ethnicity combine to determine the relative status of Spanish-speaking Americans, both within the stratification system of the wider society and within the hierarchy of the Hispanic subculture. These divisions reduce the likeli-

TABLE 1.
Selected Characteristics of Persons of Mexican, Puerto
Rican, and Cuban Origins: 1980

Characteristics	Mexican	Puerto Rican	Cuban
Age			
Under 18	42.4%	44.3%	29.8%
65+	3.7%	2.7%	9.7%
Median age	21.4	20.7	33.5
Percent unemployed	9.4%	11.7%	5.0%
Median income (1979)	$15,171	$9,855	$17,538
Area of residence			
Metropolitan	79.0%	95.0%	97.0%
In central cities	43.0%	75.0%	40.0%
Outside central cities	36.0%	20.0%	57.0%
Nonmetropolitan areas	21.0%	5.0%	3.0%
Employment			
White collar	31.0%	35.0%	41.0%
Blue collar	48.0%	45.0%	48.0%
Service, farm	21.0%	20.0%	11.0%

Source: "Persons of Spanish Origin in the United States," *Current
Population Reports*, Series P20, No. 361 (May 1981), pp. 5–6.

hood of the development of shared interests necessary to build a unified Hispanic
power base.

Chicanos   When the United States acquired its territories in the Southwest,
these areas had already been settled by Mexican migrants. A gradual pattern of
economic and social subordination of the Mexicans, as well as Native Americans,
developed as white Americans ("Anglos") migrated west (Moore 1976).

Like many other ethnic groups who have not been accepted by the majority
group, Chicanos tend not only to live in particular geographic areas, such as
Southern California, South Texas, and New Mexico, but to live in distinctly Mexican neighborhoods, or *barrios*. However, depending on the community in which
they live, residential conditions range from highly segregated to almost completely
nonsegregated living patterns (Moore 1976).

Although the stereotype of the Mexican farm laborer persists, relatively few
Chicanos today work on farms, in contrast to the employment pattern of their
parents. This change, however, reflects the increasing industrialization of agricul-
ture rather than gains in job status or income. The occupational mobility of Chicanos has been horizontal rather than vertical. That is, the present generation has
moved from farm labor into other unskilled jobs, such as work in canning factories

(*ISR Newsletter,* Winter 1982). Relatively few have moved into semiskilled or higher-status occupations. Many undocumented workers from Mexico, sometimes called *illegal aliens,* have been employed in low-wage service and manufacturing jobs to keep labor costs low and to prevent unionization (Wilson 1981).

On various measures of social mobility, Chicanos rank below the average for the population as a whole. Chicanos in general have less education than do non-Hispanics or blacks. The differences in school achievement are primarily due to a conflict of cultures (and language) between home and school. Over time, many drop out of a punishing situation. Although most adults have very high goals for their children's education, their own lack of training locks them into low-paying, dead-end jobs.

The traditional Mexican family is an extended one, with the kinship group being both the main focus of obligation and the source of emotional and social support. Within Chicano families, gender roles are well defined. Both mothers and daughters are expected to be protected and submissive, and to dedicate themselves to caring for the males of the family. For the Mexican male, *machismo,* or the demonstration of physical and sexual powers, is basic to self-respect.

These traditional patterns protect Chicanos against the effects of prejudice and discrimination, but they also reinforce isolation from the majority culture. An upwardly mobile Chicano must choose between remaining locked into a semi-isolated ethnic world or becoming alienated from family, friends, and ethnic roots (Arce, 1981).

Puerto Ricans   Citizens of the United States since 1898 but relative newcomers to the mainland, Puerto Ricans began to arrive on the mainland in large numbers in the 1950s because of the collapse of the sugar industry on the island of Puerto Rico. One third of the world's Puerto Ricans now reside in the mainland United States. Of the two million mainland Puerto Ricans, 80 percent live in six states: New York, New Jersey, Connecticut, Illinois, Pennsylvania, and Massachusetts. Although about two fifths of the Puerto Ricans in the continental United States have incomes below the poverty level, their expectations of success are higher than the expectations of those who have remained in Puerto Rico, where the cost of living is about eight times that of Washington, D.C., and the income per person is only three fifths of that in Mississippi, our poorest state.

Although Puerto Ricans are often grouped with Chicanos, the two populations are very different in history, culture, and racial composition. Puerto Rico's culture is a blend of black and Spanish influences, with a heavy dose of American patterns. This pattern is in sharp contrast to Mexico, where the people and their culture combine Spanish and Native American elements.

The Puerto Rican experience on the mainland has included a continuing struggle for stability and achievement in education, politics, the arts, and community control. Puerto Ricans have been elected to the U.S. Congress, to state legislatures, and to city councils. In 1983, a Puerto Rican was appointed Chancellor of the New York City schools. Growing numbers of Puerto Ricans have moved from the inner city to middle-income, homeowner suburbs (*New York Times Magazine,* December

12, 1982, p. 59), and young Puerto Ricans are entering the fields of law, business, medicine, and teaching. Yet, others continue to have difficulty on standardized English and math tests, to drop out of school, and to face unemployment. Compared to other ethnic groups, more Puerto Rican families (about 44 percent) are likely to be headed by a woman with no husband present. Less than four in ten mainland Puerto Ricans of voting age are registered to vote, a circumstance that has limited their political influence. A national voter registration drive is currently under way. The island of Puerto Rico has been hit especially hard by the economic recession, and within the past few years, the arrival of people from Puerto Rico has increased threefold. A new wave of middle-class, professional, and skilled workers has come to the mainland. Many are settling *not* in the New York area, where 50 percent of the mainland Puerto Ricans lived in 1980, but in the Sunbelt and in Connecticut and Massachusetts (*New York Times*, June 3, 1983). At least 20 percent of the physicians who graduate from Puerto Rico's four medical schools leave to practice on the mainland. Recruitment of bilingual teachers, social workers, and health professionals by mainland employers may be creating a "brain drain" from the island (*New York Times*, December 12, 1983).

Cubans Cuban immigration to the United States began in large numbers when Fidel Castro came to power in the mid-1950s. Between 1954 and 1978, over 325,000 Cubans were admitted as permanent residents in the United States. In early 1980, an additional 115,000 Cuban refugees entered the country in a sudden, somewhat chaotic exodus. Although it is too early to determine how these new Cuban immigrants will fare in the United States, many earlier immigrants have achieved success operating small businesses within Cuban communities.

Of all Spanish-speaking subgroups, the Cubans are older and better educated; are more likely to live in metropolitan areas, though not the central city; and have the highest median income. Much of their success, however, can be attributed to the educational and occupational characteristics with which the first wave entered America; theirs was an upper- and middle-class emigration in contrast to that of the Cuban newcomers of 1980, who were, on the average, younger, less educated, and less skilled. Recent Cuban immigrants have also been received with greater hostility and fear, and they are experiencing barriers to mobility within the established Cuban communities as well as outside.

NOTES

Arce, Carlos, "A Reconsideration of Chicano Culture and Identity." *Daedalus*, 110(2) (Spring 1981):177–191.

Bonacich, Edna. "Advanced Capitalism and Black/White Relations in the U.S.: A Split Labor Market Interpretation." *American Sociological Review*, 41(1) (1975):34–51.

Davis, George, and Gregg Watson. *Black Life in Corporate America: Swimming in the Mainstream*. Garden City, N.Y.: Doubleday, 1982.

Davis, R. "Black Suicide in the Seventies: Current Trends." Paper presented at the annual meeting of the American Sociological Association, Boston, August 1979.

Guillemin, Jeanne. "Federal Policies and Indian Politics." *Society*, 17(4) (May–June 1980):29–34.

Hogan, Dennis P., and Michele Pazul. "The Career Strategies of Black Men." *Social Forces*, 59(1981):1217–1228.

ISR Newsletter. "Maintaining a Group Culture" (Winter 1982):7–8. Ann Arbor: Institute for Social Research, University of Michigan.

Karnig, Albert K., and Susan Welch. *Black Representation and Urban Policy*. Chicago: University of Chicago Press, 1981.

Kitano, Harry. *Japanese Americans*. Englewood Cliffs, N.J.: Prentice-Hall, 1976.

Kluegel, James R., and Eliot R. Smith. "Whites' Beliefs About Blacks' Opportunities." *American Sociological Review*, 47 (1982):518–532.

Liberson, Stanley. *A Piece of the Pie: Blacks and White Immigrants Since 1880*. Berkeley and Los Angeles: University of California Press, 1981.

Montero, Darrel. *Japanese Americans: Changing Patterns of Ethnic Affiliation over Three Generations*. Boulder, Colo.: Westview Press, 1980.

———. "The Japanese Americans: Changing Patterns of Assimilation over Three Generations." *American Sociological Review*, 46 (1981):829–839.

Moore, Joan. *Mexican Americans*. Englewood Cliffs, N.J.: Prentice-Hall, 1976.

Oliver, Melvin L., and Mark A. Glick. "An Analysis of the New Orthodoxy on Black Mobility." *Social Problems*, 29 (1982):511–523.

Parcel, Toby L. "Wealth Accumulation of Black and White Men: The Case of Housing Equity." *Social Problems*, 30(2) (December 1982):199–211.

Parrillo, Vincent N., John Stimson, and Ardyth Stimson. *Social Problems*. New York: John Wiley, 1985.

Pear, Robert. "U.S. Finds Black Economic Improvement Halted." *The New York Times*. August 22, 1983, p. A22.

Pearce, Diana. "The Feminization of Poverty: Women, Work and Welfare." *Urban and Social Change Review* (February 1978).

Pinkney, Alphonso. *The American Way of Violence*. New York: Vintage, 1972.

———. *Black Americans* (2nd ed.). Englewood Cliffs, N.J.: Prentice-Hall, 1975.

Pol, Louis G., Rebecca F. Guy, and Andrew J. Bush. "Discrimination in the Home Lending Market: A Macro Perspective." *Social Science Quarterly*, 63 (December 1982).

Reid, John. "Black America in the 1980s." *Population Bulletin*, 37(3) (1982).

Rule, Sheila. "Black Divorces Soar: Experts Cite Special Strains." *The New York Times*, May 24, 1982.

Steinberg, Stephen. *The Ethnic Myth*. New York: Atheneum, 1981.

United States Bureau of the Census. *Statistical Abstract of the U.S.* Washington, D.C.: United States Government Printing Office, 1982, 1983.

Time. "The Myth of the Black Executive." December 6, 1982, p. 53.

Wilson, William Julius. *The Declining Significance of Race: Blacks and Changing American Institutions*. Chicago: University of Chicago Press, 1980.

———. "The Black Community in the 1980s: Questions of Race, Class, and Public Policy." *Annals of the American Academy of Political and Social Science*, 454 (March 1981):26–41.

Winslow, Art. "Speaking with Forked Tongue." *The Nation*, February 12, 1983, pp. 177–179.

Woodrum, Eric. "An Assessment of Japanese American Assimilation, Pluralism, and Subordination." *American Journal of Sociology*, 87 (1981):157–169.

2

Sun Chief:
Autobiography of a Hopi Indian

Leo W. Simmons, Editor

I grew up believing that Whites are wicked, deceitful people. It seemed that most of them were soldiers, government agents, or missionaries, and that quite a few were Two-Hearts. The old people said that the Whites were tough, possessed dangerous weapons, and were better protected than we were from evil spirits and poison arrows. They were known to be big liars too. They sent Negro soldiers against us with cannons, tricked our war chiefs to surrender without fighting, and then broke their promises. Like Navahos, they were proud and domineering—and needed to be reminded daily to tell the truth. I was taught to mistrust them and to give warning whenever I saw one coming.

Our chief had to show respect to them and pretend to obey their orders, but we knew that he did it halfheartedly and that he put his trust in our Hopi gods. Our ancestors had predicted the coming of these Whites and said that they would cause us much trouble. But it was understood that we had to put up with them until our gods saw fit to recall our Great White Brother from the East to deliver us. Most people in Oraibi argued that we should have nothing to do with them, accept none of their gifts, and make no use of their building materials, medicine, food, tools, or clothing—but we did want their guns. Those who would have nothing to do with Whites were called "Hostiles" and those who would cooperate a little were called "Friendlies." These two groups were quarreling over the subject from my earliest memories and sometimes their arguments spoiled the ceremonies and offended the Six-Point-Cloud-People, our ancestral spirits, who held back the rain and sent droughts and disease. Finally the old chief, with my grandfather and a few others, became friendly with the Whites and accepted gifts, but warned that we would never give up our ceremonies or forsake our gods. But it seemed that fear of Whites, especially of what the United States Government could do, was one of the strongest powers that controlled us, and one of our greatest worries.

A few years before my birth the United States Government had built a boarding school at the Keams Canyon Agency. At first our chief, Lolulomai, had not wanted to send Oraibi children, but chiefs from other villages came and persuaded him to accept clothes, tools, and other supplies, and to let them go. Most of the people disliked this and refused to cooperate. Troops came to Oraibi several times to take the children by force and carry them off in wagons. The people said that it was a terrible sight to see Negro soldiers come and tear children from their parents. Some boys later escaped from Keams Canyon and returned home on foot, a distance of forty miles.

Some years later a day school was opened at the foot of the mesa in New Oraibi, where there were a trading post, a post office, and a few government buildings. Some parents were permitted to send their children to this school. When my sister started, the teacher cut her hair, burned all her clothes, and gave her a new outfit and a new name, Nellie. She did not like school, stopped going after a few weeks, and tried to keep out of sight of the Whites who might force her to return. About a year later she was sent to the New Oraibi spring to fetch water in a ceremonial gourd for the Ooqol society and was captured by the school principal who permitted her to take the water up to the village, but compelled her to return to school after the ceremony was over. The teachers had then forgotten her old name, Nellie, and called her Gladys. Although my brother was two years older than I, he had managed to keep out of school until about a year after I started, but he had to be careful not to be seen by Whites. When finally he did enter the day school at New Oraibi, they cut his hair, burned his clothes, and named him Ira. . . .

3

The Native American Experience*

Ann H. Beuf

From the outset, exploitation and cultural supremacy were the hallmarks of white attitudes toward Native Americans. Greeted with friendliness, the invaders, with their growing population, soon felt the need to expand westward and proceeded to do so, removing more and more land from the inhabitants. What Native Americans regarded as the wisdom of conservation and the coexistence of man and nature was

---

*Although the book from which this selection is taken was published in 1977, the conditions it describes remain essentially unchanged. Statistics on unemployment and education were virtually the same ten years later. New statistics on median family income and poverty have been added to the text in the form of an editor's note on page 102.

regarded as ignorance and wastefulness by the white settlers. With psyches dominated by the Protestant ethic, they rationalized and justified atrocities against Native Americans in terms of their belief that land and resources that were not being turned into something else were being improperly utilized. Thus they were not above rejoicing when disaster and plague struck the indigenous peoples, going so far as to thank God for sending smallpox to the Native Americans. These people considered the original inhabitants of the continent as somewhat lower than human beings, a species of animal. Had they known of evolution, they would doubtless have placed the Native American somewhere beneath *homo sapiens* on the evolutionary scale.[1]

Of course, white ethnocentrism is most evident in the concept of discovery itself. It is difficult to perceive how one can "discover" and lay claim to territory which is already inhabited. It is only if one considers one's own ethnic group to be the *only* human group that one can ignore over a million people and claim such territory. Yet, to this day, white and Native American children are taught in their schools that Columbus *discovered* America. . . .

The expedient nature of white policy towards Native Americans is apparent in the history of the colonial period and the time following independence. So long as other Europeans posed a threat to the settlers, care was taken to insure alliance with Native Americans. Promises were frequently made to tribes in exchange for their assistance in warfare. These promises were just as frequently left unfulfilled once hostilities ceased. After the colonies had gained independence, and prior to the Louisiana Purchase, fear of the French kept the colonists honest. To insure the borders, friendships with strong Native American groups were formed and supported by fur-trading posts, which paid fair to very good prices. As soon as the purchase had been made and there was no external threat on the border, the posts were closed, and traders who paid unfair prices for their furs were permitted to assume the Native American trade.

The desire for land was becoming more intense, and huge profits were realized as the government bought land from the Native Americans for a pittance and resold it to whites for handsome sums. Sometimes the government realized a profit amounting to ten times what it had paid for a piece of land. This type of exploitation continued throughout the early days of the nation, as Manifest Destiny took the white man's hunger for land and sanctimonious belief in his divine right to it across the continent. Indeed, we can see signs of Manifest Destiny still: in the government's attempt to make the sacred Blue Lake of the Taos people part of a national park; in the extensive strip-mining undertaken on many reservations by large corporations; and in the state of New York's "removal" of a large portion of the Tuscarora reservation to create a reservoir.

White desire for more land for cultivation brought about the first effort at "relocating" Native Americans. Despite protest from the Supreme Court, Andrew Jackson's administration began the process of moving all the Native Americans east of the Mississippi to the western side. This was accomplished under the Indian Removal Act of 1830, with the loss of many lives on the notorious Trail of Tears. There is a particular irony involved in this event which demonstrates the extent of white racism at that time. The groups most damaged by this treaty were those known as the "civilized tribes," tribes which had gone to great lengths to accommodate the invaders. They had become first-rate farmers, spoke English as well as their own tongues, read and wrote, dressed like Europeans, and were Christianized. Yet in the final analysis this availed them little. Although white rhetoric relied on the concept of "the heathen savage" to justify the taking of lands, it mattered not at all that these people bore little resemblance to the stereotype. Their land was demanded by whites, for whites, and they were forced to move.[2]

After the Civil War, the inventions of barbed wire, the artesian well, and the repeating rifle made possible white conquest and cultivation of the Plains, which whites had not wanted before. The deliberate killing of the buffalo hastened the downfall of the powerful Plains tribes, and the bitter Indian Wars finished the process. Government policy was capricious, as alternating humane and punitive measures were proposed and initiated. The brutal treatment of early reservation Native Americans, tragically symbolized by the Wounded Knee Massacre,[3] aroused moral indignation in some quarters and genocidal determination in others. In dialectic fashion, these two responses were synthesized in the concept of assimilation. It made the moralists happy, because it was "doing good" for Native Americans to give them clothing, food, education, and religion; it satisfied the genocidal faction, because the desired end-product was the disappearance of the Native American, who would be absorbed into the dominant society as his language, customs, religion, and family structure were demolished. It was a compromise policy, designed to result in the cultural, although not physical, destruction of an entire ethnic group.

The policy of assimilation was behind the boarding-school system of the day, which forbade the speaking of any language other than English, the outlawing of Native American religious celebrations, and the Dawes Act of 1887. This act, also known as the Allotment Act, divided Native American lands into individual parcels. The manifest reason for this was to promote assimilation and to turn the Native American into a brown replica of the white farmer. However, it is interesting to note that the act also furthered exploitation of the Native Americans' resources. First, it was found that there was a good deal of land "left over" after tribally held lands had been distributed to Native American individuals. The government opened these lands to white homesteaders instead of returning them to the tribe. In addition, the farming model, which reflected white values of individuality and the private ownership of property, was not an appealing way of life to many Native Americans. . . .

Most Native Americans are poor . . . and Native Americans tend to have large families.* The birth rate is considerably higher than that of the country as a whole, and the traditional extended family still prevails in many places. Therefore, when

---

* According to the 1980 U.S. Census, the median household income for American Indians living in urban areas was $13,275, and for those in rural areas it was $11,040, with 38 percent of urban households and 46 percent of rural households earning incomes of less than $10,000 a year. This means that 31 percent of urban-dwelling Indians and 47 percent of those in rural areas were living below the poverty line.

we are talking about such low incomes, we may be talking about a group of ten or twelve people who must survive on these sub-poverty level earnings.[4]

Not only is income low, but when we examine the sources of Native American income we find that a large part of it comes from government assistance, veterans' aid, land leases, and government employment. It is difficult for Native Americans to obtain ordinary nongovernment employment. This is partly because most reservations are well out of commuting range of the better employment markets. It is also due to lack of education at a time when arbitrary standards are set for hiring, such as the requirement of a high-school diploma for work on an assembly line. Lack of training in the more marketable skills in a changing economy is also a handicap as machines take over many of the tasks for which antiquated technical schools have trained Native American youth. We should also note that discrimination in hiring practices plays an important role in limiting the availability of good employment for Native Americans.

. . . . [E]ven a well-trained and educated Native American has problems gaining employment close to home. The result is an unemployment rate which is nearly twice the white average, and which on individual reservations has been known to run as high as 70 percent. In the city, Native Americans, like blacks, tend to be "last hired, first fired."

Making a living on the reservation, without working for the government or the Bureau of Indian Affairs (BIA), is also difficult. The land given Native Americans at the time the reservations were set out was land whites believed to be useless. Therefore Native Americans live on some of the most nonarable, nongrazable land in the country. Water may be hard to come by, as white farmers and ranchers divert it for their own purposes. This makes irrigation virtually impossible. In addition, the Native American farmer faces all the difficulties confronted by any small farmer in an era of food-industry, agricultural capitalism. To compete with the large agricultural corporations is difficult if not impossible. . . .

Education presents a dismal picture, too, with dropout rates fifty percent higher than the rest of the population. Fewer than eighteen percent of students in federally run Native American schools go on to college. Results of tests indicate that while Native American children perform almost as well as white children on achievement tests that are nonverbal, their verbal work is affected by their lack of English language skills and knowledge of white culture. . . .[6]

The Coleman report found that the deficiencies of Native American children in school work were most strongly related to language problems, "cultural deprivation," and negative self-concept.[7] Those factors frequently cited as reasons for poor performance—facilities, curriculum, and quality of teachers—were not strongly correlated with the performance of Native American youngsters. This finding is particularly significant if we consider it in the light of a theory of institutional racism. All three of the major variables are related to each other and attributable to institutional racism.

The "language problem," as it is called, reflects the cultural white supremacy and ethnocentric Anglo bias of the educational system: the language problem would not be a problem at all if children were taught in their own language. Language is obviously a major problem for children who, at home, speak something other than standard middle-class English. Native American children who have, until first grade, spoken a tribal language or even "reservation English," find themselves in a classroom where the most basic skills are being conveyed in a language they do not comprehend. Some children literally have no idea what the teacher is saying. To compound the problem, the children are tested on these skills and their performance judged in terms of a national "norm." Small wonder that by such measures they appear to be behind majority-group children.

Incidentally, such tests are very good examples of institutional racism in action. A "correct" answer for test items is based on Anglo culture and the norms that flow from it. Especially on verbal tests, there may be no *intrinsic* correctness to a response but only a correctness as the majority culture defines it. In other words, the performance of white middle-class children establishes the norm for these tests, and the performance of other children is deemed "good" or "bad" depending on the degree to which it conforms to that norm. Thus we can see the arbitrary establishment of an ethnocentric cultural system within the educational institution.

Children who speak a language other than English are not alone in suffering from these arrangements. Children who speak an English that is not middle-class suffer as well. The black ghetto child, the reservation Native American, and the working-class white (who says "he don't" or "they was") all may do poorly on verbal tests. The unfortunate aspect of this situation, of course, is that those in the field of education (and many others) do not view correct English simply as conformity to middle-class verbal norms, but tend to equate it with intelligence. Thus children who speak some variant of the language emerge from the testing situation and from interaction with their teachers labeled *stupid*, not just speakers of another kind of English. This link between the speaking of standard English and concepts of intelligence affects both teacher expectations for students and students' feelings about themselves. . . .

NOTES

1. This tendency was evident in a display I saw in 1972 in a prominent museum in the Southwest. On one wall, the evolution of man was displayed. The progression was monkey, higher primate, Neanderthal, "Indian," and *homo sapiens*, white!

2. There are still Native Americans east of the Mississippi because many had assimilated into white society and were not defined as "Indian" at the time of the act, and also because the Seminoles refused to be removed and entered into a long-enduring armed conflict with the United States government which cost the government a fortune. The Seminoles never did move west of the Mississippi.

3. A group of Sioux returning from a religious event were disarmed and shot down by government troops in 1878. Many of the victims were women and children. The bodies were left unburied and frozen on the ground for several days and then subjected to mass burial in trenches. Photographs of this event bear uncanny resemblance to those of similar events at

Dachau and Auschwitz. For a complete description of the massacre, see *Bury My Heart at Wounded Knee*, by Dee Brown.

4. Of course the extended family can be an asset, and some have argued that it is indeed the merit of combined income which has perpetuated that family structure among Native Americans.

5. When whites later found they had missed a trick and that something of value *did* exist on Native American land, they took it back. The classic example of this trend is the case of the Black Hills, which were deemed worthless and included in the Sioux reservation until gold was discovered in them, whereupon the United States changed the treaty to remove the Hills from Sioux ownership.

6. Bruce A. Chadwick, "The Inedible Feast," in Bahr, Chadwick, and Day, *Native Americans Today*, pp. 131–45.

7. James S. Coleman et al., *Equality of Educational Opportunity* (Washington, D.C.: Government Printing Office, 1966).

Nilda

Nicholosa Mohr

"Nilda!" She heard someone calling her name and stopped to see who it was. It was Chucho, Benji's brother. "Hi, Nilda. What are you doing here?"

"Oh, hi, Chucho. I was walking my friend home."

"Wait, wait a minute. You going back home now?" he asked.

"Yes."

"O.K. Manuel is coming right down. We went to our aunt's house; you know Estelle, my mother's sister. We'll walk you back, Nilda."

"Sure," she said. "Will he be long? My mother is expecting me back right away."

"No, he'll be right back. As a matter of fact, we were outside in the street when Manuel remembered he forgot something and went back up." Chucho smiled. "Look, there he is. See?" and he pointed to a young boy who hurried towards them. He was younger than Chucho but almost the same height.

"Hi, Nilda. How are you?"

"Fine."

"Manuel, we'll take Nilda home; it will only be a minute out of our way."

"Sure, good," Manuel said.

The three young people walked silently for a while. It was windy and cold out; they all walked quickly, trying to stay warm.

"Nilda," Chucho said, "we hardly see you any more. You don't come to services very often now, do you?" He added, "You are missed."

Oh, man, thought Nilda, annoyed. They are gonna start that business again. "Well, I been busy, you know. Now that Mami is working every day, I have to help out a lot," she said.

"This weekend, Nilda, try to come," Chucho said. "It is something special. We will have our meeting right on the corner of 116th Street and Lexington Avenue. You know, right by the subway station? The musicians will play and we will set up a platform and amplifiers. We would like you to come and be with us, Nilda."

"I'll try," she said timidly. She hated those street meetings and she knew Benji hated them. She remembered the last time she had been out in the street with them and how embarrassed she had been; she had wanted to cry. Everyone pointed and looked at you, she thought. The kids who recognized her had made fun of her, shouting remarks and making faces. She recalled how she had tried to leave but couldn't, because her group had been right in the middle where everyone could see them.

"Have you been reading the Bible we gave you and the word of Jesus?" Chucho asked.

"Yes," she said. I wish he'd stop preaching all the time, Nilda said to herself. Chucho was the most religious and the oldest of Benji's brothers.

Nilda heard a siren and saw a police car speeding down the avenue. It passed them, stopped abruptly, and backed up. A police officer yelled out of the car window. "Hey, you! Wait a minute!" He stepped out of the car and ran across the avenue towards Nilda and the two boys. As he approached them, the patrol car made a U-turn and stopped in front of them. "Where you going?" the policeman asked. "What the hell are you going hanging around the streets at night?"

Nilda, for a moment, could not believe that he was talking to them. Shocked and frightened, she looked at the large policeman as he spoke to Chucho. "Where do you live?" the policeman asked, and looked angrily at Chucho and Manuel, a nightstick grasped in his hand. As Chucho answered, the other policeman got out of the car and walked towards them. "That's quite a few blocks from here. What the hell are you doing way up here, God damn it!" the first cop said.

"We went to visit our aunt who lives two blocks up," Manuel answered.

"Shut your ass. I'm talking to him," he said, angrily pointing to Chucho.

"Yes, that is right, officer," Chucho said. "We just came to visit my aunt, that's all."

"How old are you?"

"Sixteen."

"And you?" the cop asked Manuel.

"Fourteen."

"Who is this girl?"

"She's a friend and we are walking her home," Chucho said.

The two policemen stared at the boys for a while. Then the first policeman asked, "Where's the rest of you guys?"

Chucho looked, bewildered, at Manuel, who shook his head and shrugged his shoulders.

"Come on, cut the shit. We know all about the rumble between the Lightnings and the Barons." Nilda felt her insides begin to sink.

"We do not know, sir, who they are. We do not belong to any gangs," Chucho said.

Nilda did not know when or how it happened, but the first policeman held Chucho by the collar and up against the side of the building. "Look!" he shouted into Chucho's face. "Don't give me any shit, spick. I'm tired of this trouble. Now, either you tell me where you punks are, and quit lying, or I'm gonna smash your face."

"Officer, we don't know!" interrupted Manuel. He rushed to his brother, shouting, "We are of the Pentecostal faith. We do not believe. . . ."

The policeman released his grip and let go of Chucho. He picked up his nightstick and swung hard at Manuel. Nilda heard a thud and saw blood coming down the side of Manuel's face as he reeled over.

"Stop! Stop!" Chucho shouted. "He's only a kid. Please, please." The policeman kept swinging his nightstick at Manuel.

"Hey, leave me alone. Stop, hey!" Manuel cried out, trying to duck the blows of the nightstick.

The second policeman leaped towards the first policeman and grabbed the nightstick. "Ned! Take it easy, for God's sake, Ned!" he shouted. "Hold it! Christ! Come on, hold it now."

"Manuel! Manuel!" Chucho yelled and grabbed his brother, who was crying and wiping his face. His eyes, nose, mouth, and hair were full of blood. Manuel coughed and cried, clinging to Chucho.

The policeman had stopped using his nightstick and both men stood by, motionless, watching the two boys. Nilda had heard loud screams; only now, as she cried quietly, feeling the hoarseness in her throat, did she realize that it was she who had been screaming.

People started to appear; windows opened and some cars stopped to see what was going on. They gathered by the two boys and the policemen, asking questions. "What's happening? Look at that boy! He is bleeding." "Qué pasa aquí?" "Must be a fight. Officer? What happened?" "Look at those young kids in trouble."

"All right. Keep moving. Get outta here. Break it up," the policemen shouted at the onlookers. "O.K. now, we said beat it."

The policemen went up to the two boys. Manuel jumped back and whimpered. He clung to Chucho, who held him and wiped the wounds with a white handkerchief. "My brother is hurt," he said. "We need a doctor. Look," and he stepped back as if to show them Manuel. Manuel continued to cry, burying his face in Chucho's chest. Both policemen looked at each other but said nothing. Chucho continued to speak. "We are members of the Pentecostal Church on Lexington Avenue and 102nd Street, La Roca de San Sebastián. We do not believe in violence. Please," he pleaded, "take us to the hospital; my brother is hurt."

Nilda watched Manuel, who cried in pain, "Ay, man, . . . qué dolor . . . it hurts, Chucho . . . it hurts too much . . . help me." Some of the blood was drying and Manuel's face began to swell and puff up. The wind blew his soft dark hair, which was covered with red blotches.

"All right, we'll drive you down to the emergency room at Flower Fifth, but next time stay off the streets or it will be worse. Now, we won't press charges, but we don't want any crap from you. O.K.?" the first policeman said.

"Please, sir!" Chucho said. "Just take us to a hospital. We don't want no trouble."

The second policeman look at Nilda. "You get back home; a young girl like you should be off the streets. Where do you live?" he asked.

Nilda stared at him. "Not far; I can walk. It's only down a few blocks, that's all."

"All right, now get the hell off the streets and right home before we take you in."

"Yes," she said, frightened, "I'll go right home."

The policemen went to the patrol car and opened the back door. "Get in," the second policeman said, and looked at the brothers. "Go on, get in back; we'll drive you down to the hospital."

Nilda watched as Chucho almost carried Manuel to the back of the patrol car. Manuel breathed heavily and couldn't stop crying. "Don't worry, Manuel, we're going to the emergency room, man, to the hospital; hold on." The two boys disappeared into the car.

"Shit, Ned!" the second policeman said. "You oughta watch that temper."

"Bunch of bastards anyway. Spick got what he deserved," the first policeman said. . . .

5

The Circuit

Francisco Jiménez

It was that time of year again. Ito, the strawberry sharecropper, did not smile. It was natural. The peak of the strawberry season was over and the last few days the workers, most of them braceros, were not picking as many boxes as they had during the months of June and July.

As the last days of August disappeared, so did the number of braceros. Sunday, only one—the best picker—came to work. I liked him. Sometimes we talked during our half-hour lunch break. That is how I found out he was from Jalisco, the same state in Mexico my family was from. That Sunday was the last time I saw him.

When the sun had tired and sunk behind the mountains, Ito signaled us that is was time to go home. "Ya esora," he yelled in his broken Spanish. Those were the words I waited for twelve hours a day, every day, seven days a week, week after week. And the thought of not hearing them again saddened me.

As we drove home Papá did not say a word. With both hands on the wheel, he stared at the dirt road. My older brother, Roberto, was also silent. He leaned his head back and closed his eyes. Once in a while he cleared from his throat the dust that blew in from outside.

Yes, it was that time of year. When I opened the front door to the shack, I stopped. Everything we owned was neatly packed in cardboard boxes. Suddenly I felt even more the weight of hours, days, weeks, and months of work. I sat down on a box. The thought of having to move to Fresno and knowing what was in store for me there brought tears to my eyes.

That night I could not sleep. I lay in bed thinking about how much I hated this move.

A little before five o'clock in the morning, Papá woke everyone up. A few minutes later, the yelling and screaming of my little brothers and sisters, for whom the move was a great adventure, broke the silence of dawn. Shortly, the barking of the dogs accompanied them.

While we packed the breakfast dishes, Papá went outside to start the "Carcan-chita." That was the name Papá gave his old '38 black Plymouth. He bought it in a used-car lot in Santa Rosa in the winter of 1949. Papá was very proud of his little jalopy. He had a right to be proud of it. He spent a lot of time looking at other cars before buying this one. When he finally chose the "Carcanchita," he checked it thoroughly before driving it out of the car lot. He examined every inch of the car. He listened to the motor, tilting his head from side to side like a parrot, trying to detect any noises that spelled car trouble. After being satisfied with the looks and sounds of the car, Papá then insisted on knowing who the original owner was. He never did find out from the car salesman, but he bought the car anyway. Papá figured the original owner must have been an important man because behind the rear seat of the car he found a blue necktie.

Papá parked the car out in front and left the motor running. "Listo," he yelled. Without saying a word, Roberto and I began to carry the boxes out to the car. Roberto carried the two big boxes and I carried the two smaller ones. Papá then threw the mattress on top of the car roof and tied it with ropes to the front and rear bumpers.

Everything was packed except Mamá's pot. It was an old large galvanized pot she had picked up at an army surplus store in Santa María the year I was born. The pot had many dents and nicks, and the more dents and nicks it acquired the more Mamá liked it. "Mi olla," she used to say proudly.

I held the front door open as Mamá carefully carried out her pot by both handles, making sure not to spill the cooked beans. When she got to the car, Papá reached out to help her with it. Roberto opened the rear car door and Papá gently placed it on the floor behind the front seat. All of us then climbed in. Papá sighed, wiped the sweat off his forehead with his sleeve, and said wearily: "Es todo."

As we drove away, I felt a lump in my throat. I turned around and looked at our little shack for the last time.

At sunset we drove into a labor camp near Fresno. Since Papá did not speak English, Mamá asked the camp foreman if he needed any more workers. "We don't need no more," said the foreman, scratching his head. "Check with Sullivan down the road. Can't miss him. He lives in a big white house with a fence around it."

When we got there, Mamá walked up to the house. She went through a white gate, past a row of rose bushes, up the stairs to the front door. She rang the doorbell. The porch light went on and a tall husky man came out. They exchanged a few words. After the man went in, Mamá clasped her hands and hurried back to the car. "We have work! Mr. Sullivan said we can stay there the whole season," she said, gasping and pointing to an old garage near the stables.

The garage was worn out by the years. It had no windows. The walls, eaten by termites, strained to support the roof full of holes. The dirt floor, populated by earth worms, looked like a gray road map.

That night, by the light of a kerosene lamp, we unpacked and cleaned our new home. Roberto swept away the loose dirt, leaving the hard ground. Papá plugged the holes in the walls with old newspapers and tin can tops. Mamá fed my little brothers and sisters. Papá and Roberto then brought in the mattress and placed it on the far corner of the garage. "Mamá, you and the little ones sleep on the mattress. Roberto, Panchito, and I will sleep outside under the trees," Papá said.

Early next morning Mr. Sullivan showed us where his crop was, and after breakfast, Papá, Roberto, and I headed for the vineyard to pick.

Around nine o'clock the temperature had risen to almost one hundred degrees. I was completely soaked in sweat and my mouth felt as if I had been chewing on a handkerchief. I walked over to the end of the row, picked up the jug of water we had brought, and began drinking. "Don't drink too much; you'll get sick," Roberto shouted. No sooner had he said that than I felt sick to my stomach. I dropped to my knees and let the jug roll off my hands. I remained motionless with my eyes glued on the hot sandy ground. All I could hear was the drone of insects. Slowly I began to recover. I poured water over my face and neck and watched the dirty water run down my arms to the ground.

I still felt a little dizzy when we took a break to eat lunch. It was past two o'clock and we sat underneath a large walnut tree that was on the side of the road. While we ate, Papá jotted down the number of boxes we had picked. Roberto drew designs on the ground with a stick. Suddenly I noticed Papá's face turn pale as he looked down the road. "Here comes the school bus," he whispered loudly in alarm. Instinctively, Roberto and I ran and hid in the vineyards. We did not want to get in trouble for not going to school. The neatly dressed boys about my age got off. They carried books under their arms. After they crossed the street, the bus drove away. Roberto and I came out from hiding and joined Papá. "Tienen que tener cuidado," he warned us.

After lunch we went back to work. The sun kept beating down. The buzzing insects, the wet sweat, and the hot dry dust made the afternoon seem to last forever. Finally the mountains around the valley reached out and swallowed the sun.

Within an hour it was too dark to continue picking. The vines blanketed the grapes, making it difficult to see the bunches. "Vámonos," said Papá, signaling to us that it was time to quit work. Papá then took out a pencil and began to figure out how much we had earned our first day. He wrote down numbers, crossed some out, wrote down some more. "Quince," he murmured.

When we arrived home, we took a cold shower underneath a water-hose. We then sat down to eat dinner around some wooden crates that served as a table. Mamá had cooked a special meal for us. We had rice and tortillas with "carne con chile," my favorite dish.

The next morning I could hardly move. My body ached all over. I felt little control over my arms and legs. This feeling went on every morning for days until my muscles finally got used to the work.

It was Monday, the first week of November. The grape season was over and I could now go to school. I woke up early that morning and lay in bed, looking at the stars and savoring the thought of not going to work and of starting sixth grade for the first time that year. Since I could not sleep, I decided to get up and join Papá and Roberto at breakfast. I sat at the table across from Roberto, but I kept my head down. I did not want to look up and face him. I knew he was sad. He was not going to school today. He was not going tomorrow, or next week, or next month. He would not go until the cotton season was over, and that was sometime in February. I rubbed my hands together and watched the dry, acid stained skin fall to the floor in little rolls.

When Papá and Roberto left for work, I felt relief. I walked to the top of a small grade next to the shack and watched the "Carcanchita" disappear in the distance in a cloud of dust.

Two hours later, around eight o'clock, I stood by the side of the road waiting for school bus number twenty. When it arrived I climbed in. Everyone was busy either talking or yelling. I sat in an empty seat in the back.

When the bus stopped in front of the school, I felt very nervous. I looked out the bus window and saw boys and girls carrying books under their arms. I put my hands in my pant pockets and walked to the principal's office. When I entered I heard a woman's voice say: "May I help you?" I was startled. I had not heard English for months. For a few seconds I remained speechless. I looked at the lady who waited for an answer. My first instinct was to answer her in Spanish, but I held back. Finally, after struggling for English words, I managed to tell her that I wanted to enroll in the sixth grade. After answering many questions, I was led to the classroom.

Mr. Lema, the sixth grade teacher, greeted me and assigned me a desk. He then introduced me to the class. I was so nervous and scared at that moment when everyone's eyes were on me that I wished I were with Papá and Roberto picking cotton. After taking roll, Mr. Lema gave the class the assignment for the first hour. "The first thing we have to do this morning is finish reading the story we began yesterday," he said enthusiastically. He walked up to me, handed me an English book, and asked me to read. "We are on page 125," he said politely. When I heard this, I felt my blood rush to my head; I felt dizzy. "Would you like to read?" he asked hesitantly. I opened the book to page 125. My mouth was dry. My eyes began to water. I could not begin. "You can read later," Mr. Lema said understandingly.

For the rest of the reading period I kept getting angrier and angrier with myself. I should have read, I thought to myself.

During recess I went into the restroom and opened my English book to page 125. I began to read in a low voice, pretending I was in class. There were many words I did not know. I closed the book and headed back to the classroom.

Mr. Lema was sitting at his desk correcting papers. When I entered he looked up at me and smiled. I felt better. I walked up to him and asked if he could help me with the new words. "Gladly," he said.

The rest of the month I spent my lunch hours working on English with Mr. Lema, my best friend at school.

One Friday during lunch hour Mr. Lema asked me to take a walk with him to the music room. "Do you like music?" he asked me as we entered the building.

"Yes, I like corridos," I answered. He then picked up a trumpet, blew on it and handed it to me. The sound gave me goose bumps. I knew that sound. I had heard it in many corridos. "How would you like to learn how to play it?" he asked. He must have read my face because before I could answer, he added: "I'll teach you how to play it during our lunch hours."

That day I could hardly wait to tell Papá and Mamá the great news. As I got off the bus, my little brothers and sisters ran up to meet me. They were yelling and screaming. I thought they were happy to see me, but when I opened the door to our shack, I saw that everything we owned was neatly packed in cardboard boxes.

The Asian Woman in America

Gloria L. Kumagai

Both females and males, regardless of their racial ethnic group, are seriously limited in their information about Asian women. Far too often the system educates individuals about race and sex as two distinct and separate categories. Consequently, Asian women, as well as other women of color, are viewed either as members of their ethnic group or their sexual group, and rarely as members of both groups simultaneously. This paper presents an overview of the historical context and the present-day status of Asian women in America as well as implications for education and change.

Asian women have been in the United States for over 120 years. Their roots were started in the 1850's when a large influx of Chinese came into this country. These immigrants entered the United States with hopes of earning enough money so that they could return to China and buy land. They had no intention to reside permanently in this country. Natural catastrophies of flood and famine and the political disasters of unrest and rebellion in China were factors causing the Chinese to seek their fortunes overseas. Within this mass movement, there were few Chinese women. In fact, by 1890, there were only 3,868 Chinese females compared to 103,620 Chinese males (Jung, 1974).

One of the inevitable conditions resulting from the disproportionate sex ratio between the Chinese male and Chinese female was prostitution. According to Jung, several hundred Chinese prostitutes arrived by ship from Hong Kong as early as 1852:

> The majority of these women were not originally prostitutes but had been sold to men in Hong Kong who later forced them into prostitution. (Jung, 1974)

This condition existed through the years. In the late 1880's and early 1900's, the Chinese women in the United States were severely oppressed as they were mere slaves and sexual commodities.

The Chinese Exclusion Act of 1882 prohibited the entry of Chinese women who were not the wives of classes of Chinese exempt from the Act. Those classes were merchants, students, and teachers. Since the bulk of Chinese immigrants were laborers, their wives, if they were married, were not allowed to immigrate. This situation further added to the imbalanced sex ratio. In addition, states passed miscegenation laws which prevented Chinese males from intermarrying with white females. The result was that Chinese immigrant men lived out lonely, desolate lives in this country while attempting to amass their fortunes. The development of a Chinese bachelor society was a product of the imbalanced sex ratio.

Chinese women were permitted to enter this country in 1943 when the Chinese Exclusion Act of 1882 was repealed. Amendments to the Immigration Act of 1924 and the War Brides Act of 1947 promoted family unity and helped to equalize the sex ratio in the Chinese American population. However, this population is still experiencing the consequences of the Exclusion Act as reflected in the highly imbalanced sex ratio in certain age categories.

The life of Chinese immigrant women in this country has been described by Jen:

> Once settled in America, the Chinese immigrant mother is faced with the economic struggle of survival in a strange, hostile country. She is too often the "cheap labor" for white America's ruling class . . . sewing a $50.00 dress for 50¢, washing dishes at a "cheap" Chinese restaurant, making beds for tourists in a luxury hotel, or keeping house for those who just "love their industrious, amusing Chinese domestics." (Jen, 1971)

The lives of Chinese immigrant women have been patterned on the Confucian ethic—to serve their fathers in youth, husbands in marriage, and their sons in old age. The basic elements of Chinese society were filial piety and the strong family unit. Consequently, Chinese women have sacrificed for their families without complaint because all of their hopes are expressed through their children. Their individuality becomes defined in terms of their role within the family and the family's position within society:

> She demands from her daughters and daughters-in-law subservience to their husbands' careers and wishes. "It is the woman and her mother who is chastised when her home, cooking, or children are unpleasant," she tells us. And when either sons or daughters are involved in politics, she implores us not to challenge the authorities. When we protest against the racist war or go on strike for Asian studies programs, she cries and tells us that we must be faithful to the welfare of our family, that all else is beyond our concern. (Jen, 1971)

The cultural values of passivity and submission are passed on to Chinese American females who are born in this country.

The immigration of Japanese women was similar to that of Chinese women in that very few came during the late 1800's. However, unlike the Chinese pattern, Japanese women began coming in a continuous stream from 1900 to 1920. The reason for this difference was that many young Japanese male immigrants began to bring over wives. Census figures show that in 1900, there were 985 females out of a total Japanese population of 24,326; and by 1920, there were 22,193 women out of a total Japanese population of 111,010 (Gee, 1974).

The "picture bride" practice was the major way for single Japanese male immigrants to acquire wives. This practice was an extension of the traditional arranged marriage system in Japan:

> Picture bride marriages grew out of the *omiaikekkon* or arranged marriage. An agreed upon go-between or go-betweens carried out the negotiations between Japanese families throughout the selection process, and the initial customary meeting or *omiai* between prospective brides and bridegrooms often was preceded by an exchange of photographs, especially in cases in which the families were separated by long distance. Apart from the fact that the partners to a union neither met during the course of negotiations nor were both present at the wedding ceremony, the picture bride marriage satisfied all the recognized social conventions regarding marriage in Japan. (Gee, 1974)

Picture-bride marriages were perceived by the surrounding dominant white society as "an immoral social custom antithetical to American Christian ideals" (Gee, 1974). Whites rationalized that because Japanese immigrants participated in such a degrading practice, they would never be able to assimilate or "melt" into the mainstream of the United States. Claims such as these led to the Japanese government discontinuing the issuance of passports to picture brides in 1920. This act, "along with the subsequent 1924 Immigration Act left 42.5 percent of the adult Japanese males still single in America with no hopes of getting married" (Gee, 1974).

The overall importance of the immigration of Japanese women was that they made the Japanese American family unit possible. This unit produced children who were born in the United States and were U.S. citizens by birth. This second generation represented "the transition from a society of single male sojourners to permanent immigrants" (Gee, 1974).

Japanese pioneer women in the United States are known as Issei, referring to first generation present in this country. These Issei women did not lead an easy life. They immediately began to work alongside their husbands because of constant deprivation and the need for money. Two women recounted:

> At the beginning I worked with my husband picking potatoes or onions and putting them in sacks. Working with rough-and-tumble men, I became weary to the bones; waking up in the mornings I could not bend over the wash basin.
> Sunlight came out about 4:00 A.M. during the summer in the Yokima Valley. I arose at 4:30. After cooking breakfast, I went out to the fields. There was no electric stove or gas like now. It took over one hour to cook, burning kindling wood. (Gee, 1974)

The responsibilities of childbearing and housekeeping were additional burdens for Issei women. Childbirth was probably the greatest hardship due to the lack of professional health care. For example, doctors were not readily available in rural areas where immigrants lived, were too expensive, or would not treat Japanese women. Thus, the alternatives were to deliver by oneself or use the services of a midwife.

> Post-natal recuperation was a luxury, in most households. Since wives were economic units crucial to the family incomes, they often worked until the day of childbirth and were working within three days afterwards. (Fujitomi and Wong, 1973)

Child raising usually was the sole responsibility of women as a result of the distinct sexual division of labor within the home. One Issei woman recalled:

> My husband is a Meiji man. He did not think of helping in the house or with the children. No matter how busy I may have been, he never changed the baby's diapers. Though it may not be right to say this ourselves, we Issei pioneer women from Japan worked solely for our husbands. At mealtime, whenever there was not enough food, we served a lot to our husbands and took very little for ourselves. (Gee, 1974)

Japanese pioneer women were extraordinary women. They had the physical stamina and moral courage to persist and survive from the time they left Japan through their adaptation to life in America. They had the strength to survive despite the formidable conditions in which they lived and faced each day.

Second generation Japanese women in America are called Nisei. Both Issei and Nisei women went through upheaval from their homes and communities and relocation to concentration camps in this country during World War II. Cultural values of submission and passivity have persisted in forming the lives of Nisei women:

> Duty and obligation continue to guide the Nisei woman's behavior and lifestyle. As a young girl, she was raised to become a respectful wife and good mother to her sons. Getting a college education was not important, so only a minority of the Nisei women have college degrees. Today, the Nisei women, typically, hold occupations as factory workers, waitresses, secretaries, nurses, and teachers. The major concern of the Nisei women is their families. Like the Issei family, the Nisei family is vertically structured. The husband is the decision maker, the head of the household. . . . Mothers continue to live vicariously through their children, encouraging all of them, regardless of sex, to pursue, at least, a college degree. In order to keep their children through school, the Nisei women will sacrifice their own luxuries to provide the children with the opportunities denied themselves. (Fujitomi and Wong, 1973)

The behaviors and lifestyles of Nisei women have influenced Japanese American women of the third and fourth generations.

Besides Asian women of Chinese and Japanese ancestry, there are other women of Asian ancestry in this country, i.e., Korean, Filipino, Vietnamese, South Sea Islands, and Hawaiian. Early immigration patterns of these groups are similar to those of the Chinese and Japanese: men came first and in greater numbers than women.

Today Asians comprise the second largest ethnic group immigrating to the United States. Therefore, a proportion of Asian women in this country are foreign born. For these women, the basic struggle for survival is often complicated by their inadequate language skills in English, and they are limited to Asian ghetto areas where their native languages are spoken.

Many aspects of the history of Asian American women in this country are still ongoing. For example, Asian immigrants as well as citizens are still victims of the "cheap labor" syndrome. The importance of knowing about history is that much of it defines the present situation of Asian American women. . . .

Asian American women are victims of both sexual and racial stereotyping—a position of double jeopardy. The most common stereotypes are:

1. The docile, submissive Asian female who makes the perfect wife.
2. The exotic sexpot who will cater to the whims of any man. Epithets are Suzy Wong, dragon lady, and geisha girl.

These stereotypes have often been viewed as positive by both females and males. However, the use of them is negative in that such stereotypes do not permit people to perceive and deal with Asian American women as real human beings with ideas, aspirations, talents, and feelings. Thus, they are denied respect and dignity.

Women of Asian ancestry have been stereotyped since they immigrated to this country. Chinese immigrant women were viewed as degraded animal-like creatures. Negative perceptions of these women were formed during the anti-Chinese period of 1870 to 1900 in America. At later times, these views were directed toward women of other Asian groups when they entered this country.

After World War II, U.S. soldiers brought back the impressions of Japanese women as perfect wives—domestic and excellent homemakers. This image has been generalized onto Japanese American women as well as other Asian American women. The belief that Asian American women are the same as Asian women in Asia is not only illogical, it is clearly . . . discriminatory. Asian American women are distinct from Asian women in Asia but are not perceived to be distinct by people in this country.

An interesting aspect of the stereotypes about Asian American females is that they are either positive or negative, depending largely upon how favorably their particular ethnic group is being viewed by others. Thus, during the anti-Chinese period in this country, stereotypes of Chinese women were highly negative as they were for Japanese American females during World War II; after World War II, the stereotypes became "positive" for Japanese American women as they did for Chinese American women after Richard Nixon's visit to China in the early 1970's. These negative and positive stereotypes are paradoxical and were most recently encountered during the Vietnam War and the influx of refugees to this country.

The media has reinforced to a great extent the prevailing attitudes and stereotypes of Asian Americans during a given period. At the present, there are two major roles for Asian American women in the movies and television shows. They either fall under the Suzy Wong category or the passive, docile, and accommodating woman. Since there is a lack of Asian American females in a variety of other roles and job positions in the media industry, there are few positive role models for Asian American females, young or old. This aspect is especially detrimental to the self-concept of these individuals. . . .

NOTES

A *Study of Selected Socioeconomic Characteristics of Ethnic Minorities Based on the 1970 Census, Vol. II: Asian Americans.* Washington, D.C.: Department of HEW, July, 1974.

Chen, May Ying. "Teaching a Course on Asian American Women," in Emma Gee et al. (ed.), *Counterpoint: Perspectives on Asian America.* Los Angeles: UCLA, 1976, pp. 234–39.

Fujitomi, Irene, and Diane Wong. "The New Asian-American Women," in Stanley Sue and Nathaniel N. Wagner (eds.), *Asian-Americans: Psychological Perspectives.* Palo Alto: Science and Behavior Books, Inc., 1973, pp. 252–63.

Gee, Emma. "Issei: The First Women." *Civil Rights Digest,* 6:3, Spring, 1974, pp. 48–53.

Jen, Lai. "Oppression and Survival." *Asian Women*. Berkeley: University of California, 1971, pp. 24–26.

Jung, Betty. "Chinese Immigrants." *Civil Rights Digest*, 6:3, Spring, 1974, pp. 46–47.

Loo, Leslie. "You Decide! The Dilemma of One Asian American Woman." *Trends*, 5:4, March/April, 1973, pp. 26–27.

Yoshioka, Robert B. "Asian American Women: Stereotyping Asian Women." *Civil Rights Digest*, 6:3, Spring, 1974, p. 45.

7

A Farewell to Manzanar

Jeanne Wakatsuki Houston and James D. Houston

At seven I was too young to be insulted. The camp worked on me in a much different way. I wasn't aware of this at the time, of course. No one was, except maybe Mama, and there was little she could have done to change what happened.

It began in the mess hall. Before Manzanar, mealtime had always been the center of our family scene. In camp, and afterward, I would often recall with deep yearning the old round wooden table in our dining room in Ocean Park, the biggest piece of furniture we owned, large enough to seat twelve or thirteen of us at once. A tall row of elegant, lathe-turned spindles separated this table from the kitchen, allowing talk to pass from one room to the other. Dinners were always noisy, and they were always abundant with great pots of boiled rice, platters of home-grown vegetables, fish Papa caught.

He would sit at the head of this table, with Mama next to him serving and the rest of us arranged around the edges according to age, down to where Kiyo and I sat, so far away from our parents, it seemed at the time, we had our own enclosed nook inside this world. The grownups would be talking down at their end, while we two played our secret games, making eyes at each other when Papa gave the order to begin to eat, racing with chopsticks to scrape the last grain from our rice bowls, eyeing Papa to see if he had noticed who won.

Now, in the mess halls, after a few weeks had passed, we stopped eating as a family. Mama tried to hold us together for a while, but it was hopeless. Granny was too feeble to walk across the block three times a day, especially during heavy weather, so May brought food to her in the barracks. My older brothers and sisters, meanwhile, began eating with their friends, or eating somewhere blocks away, in the hope of finding better food. The word would get around that the cook over in Block 22, say, really knew his stuff, and they would eat a few meals over there, to test the rumor. Camp authorities frowned on mess hall hopping and tried to stop it, but the good cooks liked it. They liked to see long lines outside their kitchens and would work overtime to attract a crowd.

Younger boys, like Ray, would make a game of seeing how many mess halls they could hit in one meal period—be the first in line at Block 16, gobble down your food, run to 17 by the middle of the dinner hour, gulp another helping, and hurry to 18 to make the end of that chow line and stuff in the third meal of the evening. They didn't *need* to do that. No matter how bad the food might be, you could always eat till you were full.

Kiyo and I were too young to run around, but often we would eat in gangs with other kids, while the grownups sat at another table. I confess I enjoyed this part of it at the time. We all did. A couple of years after the camps opened, sociologists studying the life noticed what had happened to the families. They made some recommendations, and edicts went out that families *must* start eating together again. Most people resented this; they griped and grumbled. They were in the habit of eating with their friends. And until the mess hall system itself could be changed, not much could really be done. It was too late.

My own family, after three years of mess hall living, collapsed as an integrated unit. Whatever dignity or feeling of filial strength we may have known before December 1941 was lost, and we did not recover it until many years after the war, not until after Papa died and we began to come together, trying to fill the vacuum his passing left in all our lives.

The closing of the camps, in the fall of 1945, only aggravated what had begun inside. Papa had no money then and could not get work. Half of our family had already moved to the east coast, where jobs had opened up for them. The rest of us were relocated into a former defense workers' housing project in Long Beach. In that small apartment there never was enough room for all of us to sit down for a meal. We ate in shifts, and I yearned all the more for our huge round table in Ocean Park.

Soon after we were released I wrote a paper for a seventh-grade journalism class, describing how we used to hunt grunion before the war. The whole family would go down to Ocean Park Beach after dark, when the grunion were running, and build a big fire on the sand. I would watch Papa and my older brothers splash through the moonlit surf to scoop out the fish, then we'd rush back to the house where Mama would fry them up and set the sizzling pan on the table, with soy sauce and horseradish, for a midnight meal. I ended the paper with this sentence: "The reason I want to remember this is because I know we'll never be able to do it again."

You might say it would have happened sooner or later anyway, this sliding apart of such a large family, in postwar California. People get married; their interests shift. But there is no escaping the fact that our internment accelerated the process, made it happen so suddenly it was almost tangible.

Not only did we stop eating at home, there was no longer a home to eat in. The cubicles we had were too small for anything you might call "living." Mama couldn't cook meals there. It was impossible to find any privacy there. We slept there and spent most of our waking hours elsewhere.

Mama had gone to work again soon after we arrived. The call went out for people with any kind of skill to offer their services. Thousands were responding, with great surges of community spirit, sometimes with outright patriotism, wanting "to do their part." Woody signed on as a carpenter. One of my brothers-in-law was a roofing foreman. Another ran a reservoir crew. Mama had worked as a dietician in Washington after she was married. In camp this was high-priority training. In addition to the daily multitude, those amateur cooks were faced with allergy cases, diabetics, nursing mothers, infants who required special feedings. For Mama it was also a way to make a little money. Nineteen dollars a month. This was top wage for an internee. Unskilled labor started at eight. All volunteer of course. You didn't have to get out of bed in the morning if you didn't want to. Mama wanted the work. She had a monthly fee to pay the warehouse in Los Angeles where she had stored what remained of our furniture and silver just before we evacuated. She worried about this constantly.

She worried about Papa too. Letters from him trickled in, once or twice a month, with half the words blacked out, calling her "Sweetheart" for the first time in fifteen years. She was always distracted, staring at things I could never see. I would try to get her attention, grab her around the legs. At night, in bed, she would hug me close. But during the day she never seemed to notice me.

Adrift, I began to look elsewhere for attention and thus took the first steps out of my child's realm toward a world of grownups other than my parents. Though I was only seven, my images of certain people from this period are very precise, because I had begun to *see* adults for the first time. On Terminal Island I first *saw* Orientals, those demon-children who had terrorized me. At Manzanar, past the fear of slanted eyes and high cheekbones, I watched with fresh amazement the variety of faces and bodies and costumes all around me. This may have resulted, in part, from the life Manzanar had forced upon us all. Once the weather warmed up, it was an out-of-doors life, where you only went "home" at night, when you finally had to: 10,000 people on an endless promenade inside the square mile of barbed wire that was the wall around our city.

One of our neighbors was a tall, broad woman, taller than anyone in camp, as far as I recall. She walked erectly and wore an Aunt Jemima scarf around her head. She was married to a Japanese man, and they had adopted a little Japanese girl I sometimes played with. But this woman, I realized much later, was half-black, with light mulatto skin, passing as a Japanese in order to remain with her husband. She wore scarfs everywhere to cover her give-away hair.

In the barracks facing ours there lived an elegant woman who astounded me each time I saw her. She and her husband both came from Japan, and her long aristocratic face was always a ghastly white. In traditional fashion she powdered it with rice flour every morning. By old-country standards this made her more beautiful. For a long time I thought she was diseased.

Two more white faces stand out in my memory, a pair of nurses I saw from time to time in the clinic. They wore white shoes, white hose, and white dresses. Above their bleached faces their foreheads had been shaved halfway over their scalp's curve to make a sharp widow's peak where starched black hair began to arch upward, reminding me of a cobra's hood. Their lips were gone. Their brows were plucked. They were always together, a pair of reptilian kabuki creatures at loose in the camp hospital.

You might say they were the negatives for two other women I soon began to see almost every day and, in fact, saw more of for a while than I did my mother. Their robes were black, their heads were hooded in white. Sister Mary Suzanne was about forty then, a frail, gentle woman from Japan who could speak no English. Sister Mary Bernadette was a feisty, robust little Canadian Japanese who spoke both languages fluently.

They were Maryknoll nuns, members of that missionary order whose special task is to go into a country, with knowledge of its language, and convert its people to the Catholic faith. Before the war they had run an orphanage in Los Angeles for children of Japanese ancestry. Evacuated to Manzanar and given the job of caring for some fifty orphans interned there, they set up what came to be known as "Children's Village," and they had one barracks turned into a chapel. They were joined by Father Steinback, one of the few Caucasians to live among us inside the compound and eat in our mess halls. He was greatly admired for this, and many internees converted to Catholicism before the camp was closed.

I was almost one of them. Papa stepped in just before my baptism day. If he had been there during those early months I probably would never have started spending time with the Maryknolls. He was always suspicious of organized religions. I think he had already tried to scare me away from Catholics. That was one of his prime methods of instruction: fear. On my way home from school each day in Ocean Park I would break into a run as I passed the local Catholic church. The nuns I glimpsed were robed and ghostly figures I wanted no part of.

Culturally we were like those Jews who observe certain traditions but never visit a synagogue. We kept a little Buddhist shrine in the house, and we celebrated a few Japanese holidays that were religiously connected—the way Christmas is. But we never said prayers. I had never been inside a Buddhist church. And as for Christianity, I had not heard the word God until we reached Terminal Island. I first heard about Jesus when the one friend I made there—another Japanese girl—took me to a Baptist Sunday School on the island, where a Caucasian teacher bewildered me with pictures of lambs and donkeys and golden-domed pavilions.

For some reason these did not appeal to me nearly as much as the stories of the saints and martyrs I heard a few months later when I began to study catechism with the Maryknolls. Soon I was over there every afternoon and most of Sunday. With no regular school to attend and no home to spend time in, it's no mystery that I should have been drawn to these two kind and generous women. They had organized a recreation program. They passed out candy. But what kept me coming back, once I started, were the tales of the unfortunate women like Saint Agatha, whose breasts were cut off when she refused to renounce her faith.

I had to walk nearly a mile to reach their chapel, and walk a mile back. That summer it was miserably hot, over one hundred degrees most days. Yet I made the trip gladly. A big homely girl about twenty years old who wore boys' shoes and an Eisenhower jacket taught catechism to the younger kids. She loved to sit us down and fix us with the eye of a mother superior and tell us about Saint Agatha, or Saint Juliana, who was boiled alive, or Saint Marcella, who was whipped to death by the Goths.

I was fascinated with the miseries of women who had suffered and borne such afflictions. On my way home, I would hike past row upon row of black barracks, watching mountains waver through that desert heat, with the sun trying to dry up my very blood, and imagine in some childish way that I was among them, that I too was up there on the screen of history, in a white lace catechism dress, sweating and grimy, yet selflessly carrying my load.

I fulfilled this little fantasy one blistering afternoon when the heat finally got me. Sunstroke. While crossing one of the wide sandy firebreaks that separated some of the blocks, I passed out.

This put me in bed for a week. After I recovered, several months went by before I resumed my catechism. For one thing, Papa discouraged me. It was just before this happened that he had returned from Fort Lincoln. He was back among us, making decisions, giving commands. For a while it seemed we would almost be a family again. But it didn't turn out that way. He was not the same man. Something terrible had happened to him in North Dakota.

He arrived at Manzanar on a Greyhound bus. We all went down to the main gate to meet him, everyone but Woody's wife, Chizu, who was in the camp hospital. The previous day she'd given birth to Papa's first grandson. She named him George, in honor of Papa's return. Two of my sisters were pregnant at the time, and they were there at the gate in hot-weather smocks, along with Woody, who had left the hospital long enough to welcome Papa back, and Granny and Mama and the rest of the family, a dozen of us standing in the glare, excited, yet very reverent as the bus pulled in.

The door whished open, and the first thing we saw was a cane—I will never forget it—poking from the shaded interior into sunlight, a straight, polished maple limb spotted with dark lidded eyes where small knotholes had been stained and polished.

Then Papa stepped out, wearing a fedora hat and a wilted white shirt. This was September 1942. He had been gone nine months. He had aged ten years. He looked over sixty, gaunt, wilted as his shirt, underweight, leaning on that cane and favoring his right leg. He stood there surveying his clan, and nobody moved, not even Mama, waiting to see what he would do or say, waiting for some cue from him as to how we should deal with this.

I was the only one who approached him. I had not thought of him much at all after he was taken away. He was simply gone. Now I was so happy to see him that I ran up and threw my arms around his waist and buried my face in his belt. I thought

I should be laughing and welcoming him home. But I started to cry. By this time everyone was crying. No one else had moved yet to touch him. It was as if the youngest, the least experienced, had been appointed to display what the others, held back by awe or fear, or some old-country notion of respect for the patriarch, could not. I hugged him tighter, wanting to be happy that my father had come back. Yet I hurt so inside I could only welcome him with convulsive tears.

A Cultural Aversion

Caroline Wang

"When you write that $500 check," says Sue Lee, "the politicians are going to expect to do something for you—if it's from anybody else besides an Asian."

In San Francisco, where Asian-Americans make up a highly visible one-quarter of the population, none of the elected supervisors are Asian-American, and only two Asian-Americans hold mayoral appointments in administrative positions, according to Lee, a special assistant in the Office of Housing and Development.

This quality of being seen but not heard—or listened to—plagues Americans of Asian descent, the so-called "Model Minority," who want to participate in the political arena.

Except for "a proclivity to eat in Chinese restaurants," as one observer puts it, city administrators rate poorly when it comes to assessing the Asian-American community. Faced with this ignorance, or indifference, Asian-Americans have begun to examine their relationship to the political system.

For many, the root of the problem lies not so much in how to politically organize Asian-Americans as in how to deal with the cultural mindsets that shape their participation in the public arena. Sociologist Lucie Cheng, director of UCLA's Asian-American Studies Center, believes that Chinese, for example, avoid seeking individual success and admire those who shun visibility. "I don't think many Americans would say 'David Stockman is my role model,' although he has a lot of power, clearly. They want to be the Reagans—people in the limelight."

Many Chinese leaders, she says, tend to work in the background, and the admired person is the one "who has the real influence."

Like many Asian-Americans of his generation, Allen Seid remembers his parents warning him about arousing attention and stirring controversy. "I recall my parents telling me, 'Hey, you don't make noises on streetcars or the bus. You might get into trouble. It's tough to defend yourself against whites.' "

"The other side,"he goes on, "is the burden—you don't want to disgrace your race."

Seid is 49. A psychiatrist, he is also a principal founder of the most influential pan-Asian political organization in the state, Asian Pacific Advocates for California (APAAC). His own growing immersion in politics over the last decade underscores the kinds of social pressures pushing more and more Asian-Americans to overcome the "model minority" mindset.

Increasing Violence

In San Francisco's Chinatown, for example, elderly women can be seen scavenging dumpsters for edible scraps, and community workers say that 95 percent of all housing violates the building code. For low-income residents and refugees, help with food, shelter, legal and social services are simple matters of survival.

Seid notes a disturbing increase in the level of violence aimed at Asian-Americans, such as depicted in Louis Malle's recent film *Alamo Bay*, which he compares to the anti-Asian atmosphere of the 1860s. "The incidences are so similar, it's scary."

Other Asian-American professionals emphasize the need for greater fairness, singling out how American stereotypes of Asians often block their advance. Diane Wong, a San Francisco editor, tells of a friend, who has been stuck at mid-point on the executive ladder for seven years. She feels those "who make decisions about what we are capable of doing—such as being authoritative or aggressive—are limiting the opportunities for Asian-Americans."

Spurred in part by such pressures, the younger generation of Asian-Americans has enrolled in law school in growing numbers, many aspiring to political office. Yet their families still pressure them to avoid certain fields. "Our parents think it is safer for us to go into accounting or engineering—not as much discrimination because you're dealing with numbers," says Wong. "If you want to be a writer, that's going into the wrong field."

She notes teachers and counselors, too, often steer Asian-Americans "out of areas that require verbal skills and written skills"—which subtly inhibits the development of leaders, as "communication is crucial to leadership."

Individual efforts to shed these trappings are sometimes guileless and spontaneous. Independent filmmaker Arthur Dong recalls that he ran for cheerleader at a junior high school where cheerleaders were all white girls.

"I broke the sex barriers and the race barriers," he says, adding that while his intention was simply "to have fun," the result was to make him stronger in a positive way. "I don't go along with the shape," he says. "It's made me say, 'I'm not like that, I'm like this.' "

Institutional efforts have been slow to develop. Two California groups have enjoyed some success—Seid's APAAC and Asian-Americans for Community Involvement (AACI) of Santa Clara County which he also helped found. Both reflect a great diversity by including destitute and wealthy Southeast Asian refugees, first-to-fifth generation Americans of Asian descent and members ranging in age from under 20 to over 60.

Both groups worked to block the Simpson-Mazzoli immigration bill and are currently fighting attempts to resurrect it. APAAC also plays a leading role in raising a cry against anti-Asian violence.

Ironically, just as APAAC has begun to establish itself, the Democratic Party leadership has eliminated its Asian Pacific Caucus. Soon afterward, the Republicans announced they expect to recognize such a caucus in time for the 1988 election.

Republicans are attracted to the variety in the Asian community, notes Henry Der, executive director of Chinese for Affirmative Action. "They see it as an opportunity to take advantage of the strong entrepreneurship of the Southeast Asian community and their anti-Communist sentiment.

But some Asian-American leaders question whether the Republicans will deal with discrimination any better than the Democrats. Meanwhile, groups like APAAC and AACI are working to mobilize their own power.

They want to make their own destiny "instead of allowing someone else to determine what role we'll play in society," says Seid, who remains a key figure in both groups. "We've got a lot to learn as a people—how to use political power."

Being Black Is Dangerous to Your Health

Denise Foley

At 16, Deirdre appears to have all the advantages of her white classmates—a good family, a good education, promising job prospects when she graduates from college. In fact, Deirdre has all the advantages but one, the most important one.

Because she is black, she is 1.3 times as likely to die of heart disease and cancer and three times as likely to die of conditions associated with pregnancy and child-birth as her white classmates.

At 55, Earl has never missed a day's work in his 35-year career as a loading-dock foreman. These days, he dreams of retiring with his wife to a little farm in North

Carolina, where they'll live the simple life on his small pension and Social Security. But Earl may not live long enough to realize his dream.

Because he is black, he is almost twice as likely to die of stroke, 2.2 times as likely to die of diabetes mellitus, 3.2 times as likely to die of kidney disease and almost 6 times as likely to be murdered as his white co-workers. In fact, on the average, black men like Earl don't survive long enough to collect Social Security.

Today, after more than a century of social progress, a young black girl can grow up to be Miss America, a young black boy to be an astronaut, and the son of a struggling black sharecropper can become mayor of the fifth largest city in the nation. But when it comes to health, it's a different story. Disease appears to have its own kind of bigotry.

"Former National Urban League President Vernon Jordan put it very well," says Ed Pitt, co-author of the League's *Black Health Status Report*. "He said, 'Being black is dangerous to your health.' "

Indeed, statistically, being black seems to be a risk factor in almost every killer disease.

Black death rates are higher for all but two of the 15 leading causes of death in the United States. (Those two are suicide and chronic obstructive pulmonary diseases.) The most chilling are infant and maternal mortality rates. A black child is almost twice as likely to die before its first birthday than a white child—and is three times as likely to be left motherless. Though infant mortality rates have been steadily declining for both races, the gap between the two shows no sign of diminishing.

Heredity? That's the easy answer, but not the real one.

Blacks are not being felled in such large numbers by genetics, but by lifestyle risk factors such as poor diet and stress, alterable behaviors that can affect anyone. There is, of course, a complicating factor. For black people, these high-risk behaviors are, in large part, a legacy of economic deprivation and social oppression.

A Look at Hypertension

Hypertension is a good example. Among blacks, high blood pressure is a virtual epidemic. One out of every four blacks is hypertensive compared to one out of 10 people in the white population. The course the disease takes is particularly vicious. Hypertensive blacks have higher blood pressure than hypertensive whites, which in turn may contribute to the greater incidences of hypertension-related diseases such as coronary heart disease, stroke, and kidney disease, says Gerald Thomson, M.D., a leading expert on black hypertension. "Depending on age, the death rates from those diseases are several times higher for blacks. For young blacks—those under 50— they're four to five times higher," says Dr. Thomson, who is director of medicine at New York's Harlem Hospital and professor of medicine at Columbia University.

There is some speculation that a greater percentage of blacks have an inability to excrete excess sodium, but the hardest evidence points to lifestyle. Some studies indicate that blacks have tended to eat more salt than whites. But, even more important, they seem to eat less potassium. Potassium has been shown to regulate blood pressure in several significant ways, including helping the body excrete excess sodium.

In fact, when a Veterans Administration study measured sodium and potassium excretion in a racially mixed group of untreated mild and moderate hypertensives, both blacks and whites were excreting about the same amount of sodium. But the blacks excreted about two-thirds as much potassium as their white counterparts.

Researcher William Cushman, M.D., attributes the marked difference to potassium intake.

"Blacks are simply getting less potassium in their diet," says Dr. Cushman, chief of the hypertension clinic at the Veterans Administration Medical Center in Jackson, Mississippi. "Urinary excretion of electrolytes is almost always a reflection of dietary intake. Other studies done in Evans County, Georgia, and in the Bogalusa Heart Study reported similar findings. And though we don't know for sure why, we can conjecture: It's more expensive to eat a high-potassium diet. Fresh fruit, vegetables and lean meats are costly. It could possibly be something in cooking practices. It has been proved that when vegetables are cooked for a long time, as they are in Southern-style cooking, potassium leaches out. But what it may all come down to is economics."

The Poverty Risk Factor

In several studies, poverty has been pinpointed as a risk factor in hypertension for both blacks *and* whites. And poverty may have another kind of fall-out—by limiting access to health care.

Hypertensive blacks in Edgecombe County, a poor, rural community in North Carolina, reported less use of medical care than their white counterparts, with more difficulties getting into the health-care system and less satisfaction with the treatment they received. It is probably no coincidence that black hypertensives in the ongoing Edgecombe high-blood-pressure study were also "worse off," according to researchers, particularly younger black men, many of whom were unaware their blood pressures were high and, in fact, have the highest death rates from hypertension-related diseases.

There appears to be a strange mythology at work when it comes to black health, particularly when the focus is on heart disease. Blacks are widely thought to have some inherent protections against coronary heart disease, particularly myocardial infarctions (heart attacks) and angina pectoris. There is some evidence from a number of leading studies that blacks have a higher level of blood fibrinolytic activity—an ability to resist clotting—and a higher ratio of high-density lipoproteins to low-density lipoproteins, a factor that is believed to protect against the collection of cholesterol plaque in the arteries. But the bottom line is that heart disease is the leading cause of death among blacks and their mortality rates are actually higher than most white populations in the world.

Richard F. Gillum, M.D., of the University of Minnesota, is a researcher in the area of blacks and coronary heart disease. In an article in the *American Heart Journal*, he postulated that the "myth" of black immunity to heart disease is the result of a tragedy of errors: statistical mistakes, lack of accurate data, underdiagnoses and inadequate accessibility of blacks to modern diagnostic techniques and medical services. Not only do blacks have higher rates of death from heart disease, says Dr. Gillum, there are certain important differences in their disease experience. Though blacks and whites suffer from heart attacks and angina with about the same frequency, evidence shows that the conditions are more often fatal in blacks. Though many researchers are still pursuing the genetic angle, Dr. Gillum suggests that the statistics may reflect lack of adequate diagnosis and treatment rather than anything physiological.

That is not to say there aren't some correctable lifestyle factors involved in the development of disease in blacks. Studies show that more black men than white men smoke, a risk factor in both cardiovascular diseases and cancer. More black women than white women are obese, a cardiovascular risk factor that may also account for the extraordinarily high rate of type II diabetes—often called adult-onset diabetes—in middle-aged and older black women.

In fact, says James R. Gavin III, M.D., Ph.D., assistant professor of medicine at Washington University School of Medicine, in St. Louis, Missouri, 60 to 90 percent of all type II diabetics develop the disease because of obesity.

"That is very important," he says. "Here is the one factor over which we may exert a great deal of control. If these people lose weight, the improvement in glucose tolerance will very often greatly exceed the amount of weight loss. The loss of just a few pounds will result in a great improvement in carbohydrate tolerance. At normal weight, glucose tolerance actually may be normal."

There is some suspicion that the predisposition to obesity has a genetic connection, though the precise link is murky. The environmental factors are clearer: For many blacks, a good, healthful weight-loss diet simply isn't affordable.

"When we look at the eating habits of our urban patients, we see diets rich in simple carbohydrates and saturated fats," says Dr. Gavin. "Lean meats, vegetables and complex carbohydrates are generally precluded because of economics. . . ."

It is well known that nutritional deficiencies over time lead not only to specific ailments such as scurvy and beriberi, but also leave the body more vulnerable to infection and disease. Poor prenatal nutrition is widely recognized as a primary factor in the distressingly high infant-mortality rates among blacks.

Low birth weight and prematurity are leading causes of death among infants. According to the latest figures, 12.5 percent of all black infants weighed less than the standard weight of five pounds, eight ounces at birth and 17 percent were premature, a fact that in itself accounts for at least some of the low-birth-weight babies born to black mothers. Another figure too is significant—the month prenatal care begins. Although most black mothers begin care early—as do most white mothers— 9 percent received either delayed or no care prior to the birth of their babies.

"And you've got to look at the population whose babies are dying," says Byllye Avery, executive director of the fledgling National Black Women's Health Project, headquartered in Atlanta. "They're of lower economic status and many of them are teenagers. Now, teenagers can have healthy babies. But if a teenager denies her pregnancy and doesn't get the proper food, she gets a little sickly baby. And that starts the chain."

Teenage mothers tend to be the children of teenage mothers. "If you look at a lot of teenage black mothers, they have mamas who are grandmas in their 30's—and great-grandmas in their 40's," says Ms. Avery. "So you aren't starting out with a healthy group of people. Instead, you've got a group of people predisposed toward high-risk pregnancy."

For that reason, groups like the National Urban League focus much of their attention on prenatal care and nutrition for the young, usually unwed mother, and fight tooth and nail to preserve federal nutrition programs that have been rapidly disappearing.

The Cancer Epidemic

Less attention has been paid to cancer, which has been insidiously gaining ground among blacks even as death rates for some cancers drop among whites. Just this year, Lucius C. Earles III, M.D., president of the black National Medical Association, called cancer an epidemic in the black community.

Cancer is perhaps the best example of how social and economic conditions dictate the individual experience blacks have with disease. While medical advances in diagnostic techniques have increased the amount of early detection—often the difference between life and death with cancer—blacks are not being diagnosed in the early, curable stages.

In fact, a national survey by the American Cancer Society showed that urban blacks tend to be less knowledgeable about cancer's warning signs, less likely to see a doctor and more likely to underestimate both the prevalence of cancer and chance for a cure.

Even after cancer is detected, the black experience is different. Survival rates are far lower than for whites, according to a study by the National Cancer Institute, which suggested that the wide variation in survival figures was due not to any genetic cause but because blacks, for economic or social reasons, were less likely to get the most up-to-date treatment or follow-up care.

Dietary deficiencies of vitamins A and C, two vitamins believed to protect against cancer, may also play a role in the gloomier cancer prognosis for blacks. In the case of esophageal cancer, which kills blacks at a rate four times higher than whites, smoking and drinking may be implicated, although the link is uncertain.

The Stress of Being Black

Stress may also play a role in the higher death rates from cancer and other diseases among blacks, although the connection, again, is not clear. Studies have shown that stress acts on the body directly by suppressing the disease-fighting capabilities of the immune system. Indirectly, it may increase life-threatening behaviors such as drinking and drug abuse which, in turn, can lead to nutritional deficiencies and diseases like cirrhosis of the liver. Stress may also be a factor in high blood pressure.

"I don't think it's a coincidence that most of the diseases that affect blacks more severely are the so-called stress diseases," says Byllye Avery.

Women seem particularly hard hit by stress. In a national survey, black women reported not only the lowest level of positive well-being, but more than half reported moderate to severe levels of distress, and a third showed a level of distress comparable to that reported by many mental patients.

Clearly, improving the black health picture is far from simple. Lifestyle changes—losing weight, reducing salt, eating three well-balanced meals a day, quitting smoking—require more than vigorous individual effort when poor health habits are dictated by economic or social conditions.

For most of us, good health is a priceless commodity. For many blacks, it's just expensive.

"The basic solution isn't personal," says Alvin F. Poussaint, M.D., professor of psychiatry at Harvard Medical School. "It's a full-employment economy, government support services such as health care, health education, prenatal nutrition programs, that insure good health from infancy on. It's not in the national interest to have families and children in such dire straits. It's too much of a risk for us not to insure that healthy children are born. To allow the birth of a defective infant that society has to take care of for 60 years—when it can be avoided—makes no sense. It's bad economics, bad medicine, and bad preventive medicine."

10

Barbie Doll

Marge Piercy

This girlchild was born as usual
and presented dolls that did pee-pee
and miniature GE stoves and irons
and wee lipsticks the color of cherry candy.
Then in the magic of puberty, a classmate said:
You have a great big nose and fat legs.

She was healthy, tested intelligent,
possessed strong arms and back,
abundant sexual drive and manual dexterity.
She went to and fro apologizing.
Everyone saw a fat nose on thick legs.

She was advised to play coy,
exhorted to come on hearty,
exercise, diet, smile and wheedle.
Her good nature wore out
like a fan belt.
So she cut off her nose and her legs
and offered them up.

In the casket displayed on satin she lay
with the undertaker's cosmetics painted on,
a turned-up putty nose,
dressed in a pink and white nightie.
Doesn't she look pretty? everyone said.
Consummation at last.
To every woman a happy ending.

11

is not so gd to be born a girl

Ntozake Shange

Is not so gd to be born a girl/ some times. that's why societies usedta throw us away/ or sell us/ or play with our vaginas/ cuz that's all girls were gd for/ at least women cd carry things & cook/ but to be born a girl is not good sometimes/ some places/ such abominable things cd happen to us. i wish it waz gd to be born a girl everywhere/ then i wd know for sure that no one wd be infibulated/ that's a word no one wants us to know/ "infibulation" is sewing our vaginas up with cat gut or weeds or nylon thread to insure our virginity/ virginity insurance=infibulation/ that can also make it impossible for us to live thru labor/ make it impossible for the baby to live thru labor/ infibulation lets us get infections that we cant mention cuz disease in the ovaries is a sign that we're dirty anyway/ so wash yrself cuz once infibulated we have to be cut open to have you know what/ the joy of the phallus/ that we may know nothing abt/ ever/ especially if something else not good that happens to little girls happens/ if we've been excised/ had our labia removed with glass or scissors/ if we've lost our clitoris because our pleasure is profane & the presence of our naturally evolved clitoris wd disrupt the very unnatural dynamic of polygamy/ so with no clitoris, no labia, & infibulation/ we're sewn-up, cut-up, pared down & sore if not dead/ & oozing puss, if not terrified that so much of our body waz wrong & did not belong on earth/ such thoughts lead to a silence/ that hangs behind veils & straight jackets/ it really is not so good to be born a girl when we have to be infibulated, excised, clitorectomized & still be afraid to walk the streets or stay home at night.

i'm so saddened that being born a girl makes it dangerous to attend midnight mass unescorted. some places if we're born girls & some one else who's very sick & weak & cruel/ attacks us & breaks our hymen/ we have to be killed/ sent away from our families/ forbidden to touch our children. these strange people who wound little girls are known as attackers, molesters, & rapists. they are known all over the world & are proliferating at a rapid rate. to be born a girl who will always have to worry not only abt the molesters, the attackers & the rapists/ but also abt their peculiarities/ does he stab too/ or shoot/ does he carry an ax/ does he spit on you/ does he know if he doesn't drop sperm we cant prove we've been violated/ those subtlties make being a girl too complex/ for some of us & we go crazy/ or never go anyplace.

some of us have never had an open window or a walk alone/ but sometimes our homes are not safe for us either/ rapists & attackers & molesters are not strangers to everyone/ they are related to somebody/ & some of them like raping & molesting their family members better than a girl-child they don't know yet/ this is called incest & girl children are discouraged from revealing attacks from uncle or daddy/cuz what wd mommy do/ after all daddy may have seen to it that abortions were outlawed in his state/ so that mommy might have too many children/ to care abt some "fun" daddy might have been having with the 2 year old/ she's a girl after all/we have to get used to it/ but infibulation, excision, clitorectomies, rape, & incest/are irrevocable life-deniers/ life-stranglers & disrespectful of natural elements/i wish these things wdnt happen anywhere anymore/ then i cd say it waz gd to be born a girl everywhere/ even though gender is not destiny/right now being born a girl is to be born threatened/ i dont respond well to threats/ i want being born a girl to be a cause for celebration/ cause for protection & nourishment of our birth-right/ to live freely with passion, knowing no fear/ that our species waz somehow incorrect.

& we are now plagued with rapists & clitorectomies. we pay for being born girls/ but we owe no one anything/ not our labia, not our clitoris, not our lives. we are born girls & live to be women who live our own lives/ to live our lives/
to have/
our lives/
to live.

12

Poem for the Young White Man Who Asked Me How I, an Intelligent, Well-Read Person Could Believe in the War Between Races

Lorna Dee Cervantes

In my land there are no distinctions.
The barbed wire politics of oppression
have been torn down long ago. The only reminder
of past battles, lost or won, is a slight
rutting in the fertile fields.

In my land
people write poems about love,
full of nothing but contented childlike syllables.
Everyone reads Russian short stories and weeps.
There are no boundaries.
There is no hunger, no
complicated famine or greed.

I am not a revolutionary.
I don't even like political poems.
Do you think I can believe in a war between races?
I can deny it. I can forget about it
when I'm safe,
living on my own continent of harmony
and home, but I am not
there.

I believe in revolution
because everywhere the crosses are burning,
sharp-shooting goose-steppers round every corner,
there are snipers in the schools . . .
(I know you don't believe this.
You think this is nothing
but faddish exaggeration. But they
are not shooting at you.)

I'm marked by the color of my skin.
The bullets are discrete and designed to kill slowly.
They are aiming at my children.
These are facts.
Let me show you my wounds: my stumbling mind, my
"excuse me" tongue, and this
nagging preoccupation
with the feeling of not being good enough.

These bullets bury deeper than logic.
Racism is not intellectual.
I can not reason these scars away.

Outside my door
there is a real enemy
who hates me.

I am a poet
who yearns to dance on rooftops,
to whisper delicate lines about joy
and the blessings of human understanding.
I try. I go to my land, my tower of words and
bolt the door, but the typewriter doesn't fade out
the sounds of blasting and muffled outrage.
My own days bring me slaps on the face.
Every day I am deluged with reminders
that this is not
my land

and this is my land.

I do not believe in the war between races

but in this country
there is war.

13

Is the Binge-Purge Cycle Catching?

Susan Squire

The college campus is surely the most fertile land of all for sowing the seeds of all types of chaotic eating behavior. Not only does college represent the challenge of separation—for many it means leaving home for the first time with all that that implies, from doing laundry to establishing your own curfew to selecting your own meals—but it also means an increase in social and academic pressures and a new anxiety about the future. In fact, the emotional stress of the experience causes an estimated 20 percent of college women to stop menstruating or have highly irregular menstrual periods.

The residential college environment itself, a community of peers with no parents around, provides endless opportunities for pass-along behaviors to soften classical collegiate depression. Drugs. Alcohol. Smoking. Dieting. Bingeing and vomiting. As the *Dartmouth Alumni Magazine* reported, "Inside a stall in a women's bathroom on campus, a woman wrote: 'I starve myself, then I gorge myself on garbage and make myself throw up afterward. I am getting out of control and am really disgusted with myself. Does anyone else have this problem?' In response, several others scrawled 'YES, YES, YES!' "

In an academically competitive college environment, the daily pressure and accompanying risk of developing a stress-related eating behavior mounts. A bingeing-and-dieting premed student at the Massachusetts Institute of Technology, where maybe 23 percent of the students are female, explained: "You can't come here and not know what you want to do. I know I can do the work required, but there are always those nagging doubts: Am I asking too much? Is this out of my range? At a place like this, with so many more men than women, the pressure to look good in order to get your share of men may not be as intense, but the academic pressure causes lots of women I know to turn to food for alleviation. I'm certainly one of them."

David M. Garner and Paul E. Garfinkel, researchers at Toronto General Hospital, have surveyed thousands of women about eating behavior. Dr. Garner calculates that a significant percentage—about 12 percent—of college-age women have *serious* difficulties with their eating behavior. These women, Dr. Garner explains, worry about food almost constantly, and all use drastic weight-control techniques, including laxatives and diuretics, as well as vomiting.

Michael G. Thompson, Ph.D., and Donald M. Schwartz, Ph.D., surveyed "problem-free" and "anorexic-like" groups of normal-weight college women, and then compared the two groups with a third: women with anorexia nervosa. "The most dramatic finding," Thompson and Schwartz reported, "was the prevalence of anorexic-like behaviors among normally functioning college women. These women were not impaired in their work, though they often felt like they were struggling. The frequently intense feelings of inadequacy they reported appeared to arise from violation of high standards." As far as dieting goes, it was so widespread that the researchers found it impossible to measure. Almost all the anorexic-like women and many of the problem-free women simply said that they were *always* dieting. "The overall impression," the researchers wrote, "is of women—anorexic and anorexic-like and problem-free—experiencing their hunger as exaggerated and obscene, secretly wishing to gratify their impulse to eat, and constantly fighting this impulse."

In a study at Ohio State University at Columbus, Judith Cusin, M.S.W., and Dr. Dale Svendsen looked at three groups of female subjects: 944 sorority women, 38 upper-level dance majors, and 244 regular coeds. They found that 9 percent of the regulars, 16 percent of the sorority members, and 23 percent of the dance majors showed serious eating problems that indicated the symptoms of anorexia nervosa.

When they broke down the responses, the researchers found that 44.8 percent of the regular coeds, 53.5 percent of the sorority women, and 64.8 percent of the dancers answered "often," "very often," or "always" to "being preoccupied with a desire to be thinner."

It figures that sorority women, who have chosen a more socially oriented campus life and therefore tend to be even more appearance-conscious than other coeds, would score higher than the latter.

Holly, a member of a University of California at Berkeley sorority for three years, says that people often joke, "Oh, she's throwing up," when a member starts to lose weight. "I've walked into the bathroom at the sorority house and immediately had to leave because it smelled so bad from vomit." Though everyone in Holly's sorority worries about gaining weight, methods other than self-induced vomiting are frequently used to prevent the terror of fat. "A lot of us count calories, most everyone goes on fad diets, and people say things like, 'I wish I could have anorexia for just a week or two.'

"Drinking is big on campus," Holly adds, "and lots of girls save all their calories for drinking by taking diet pills so they don't eat. One girl passed out at a party because she'd taken so many diet pills and was drinking so much."

Renee, now a senior at the University of Arizona, says that she and other sorority members are open about their bulimic behavior, especially if they're bored. "We go out together and spend thirty dollars on food, knowing all the time that we'll throw it up. If we're somewhere with only one bathroom we take turns throwing up, but if there are stalls we'll do it at the same time."

Like most bulimic vomiters, between binges Renee tries to diet. On diet days, she avoids social eating whenever possible. Unlike others who engage in the behavior, Renee is not ashamed of it and is, in fact, completely open about it—with her boyfriends and family as well as with her sorority sisters. Once, her brother wanted her to join him and several other friends for dinner at a French restaurant. "I told him I was dieting and I couldn't go, but he insisted. I said okay, after I explained to him that I'd have to throw up the food. At the restaurant after the meal, I got up and announced to the table that I was going off to vomit, and everyone applauded."

Renee doesn't binge and vomit every day; the longest she's gone without throwing up has been three weeks. But once she starts, often in response to being upset with her boyfriend and not being able to show her feelings, she usually repeats it three or four times, until she's so exhausted that she goes to sleep. Despite her efforts to control her weight, Renee now weighs 130 and she hates it. "I'm bothered more by being heavy than by bingeing and vomiting. My weight is my life, and when I'm fat, I'm completely miserable."

What does Renee plan to do about her problems? "Maybe once I graduate and get out of the sorority life, the bingeing and vomiting will go away. But I doubt it. The only real reason I want to stop is I'm afraid all the vomiting might affect my unborn children. Otherwise, I just want to be thin, whatever it takes."

Another high-risk area of college life where bingeing and vomiting is peer-approved is competitive athletics. Karen Lee-Benner, R.N., M.S.N., clinical coordinator of UCLA's Eating Disorders Clinic, treated two world-class gymnasts for bulimia. She says that at least one of those patients told her that the entire gymnastics team would binge and vomit together following a meet—a purely social thing.

One star gymnast on a major university's female team developed anorexia nervosa in conjunction with bingeing and vomiting up to 10 times a day and had to be hospitalized. She'd been in training since the age of 10. For all those years, keeping slim wasn't just desirable; her future as an athlete literally depended upon it. The day-in, day-out pressure to maintain control starting at such a young age, combined with a certain personality and family background, ultimately took a permanent toll.

Even without the intensified peer pressure that comes with sorority life or the performance pressure of competitive college athletics, there's always the famous "Freshman 10" to struggle with. It's the 10 pounds that so many women put on during their first year in college when they are separated from the family refrigerator and easy access to their mother's marketing lists, and confront instead starch- and sugar-laden dorm food. Freshman men tend to lose weight that first year, which can be an annoyance to their female peers. "In a coed situation," says one Radcliffe sophomore, "you want to eat what the men eat, but you gain and they lose."

Jan had never had a weight or eating problem before entering college, but she slowly began to put on weight her first year at a large Midwestern university, where she lived on campus in a dorm. Jan went on a diet—lots of exercise and skipping meals—and dropped 15 pounds. Then the weight crept back on, the comments started from her mother, her sisters, and her boyfriend, and Jan began to binge regularly every time she was criticized about her weight. At a family picnic the summer before her junior year, "my cousin, who was anorexic, gave me the idea to vomit. She had learned it from her roommate, who'd heard it from her sister."

Once she'd learned about vomiting, Jan was eager to return to school where she could binge and vomit without her mother nosing around. She knew it was wrong, but thought it was a great way to be able to eat what she wanted. Ultimately, Jan's bingeing and vomiting severely disrupted her life.

Again, it was the combination of a stressful environment with a certain vulnerable personality and probably a particular family history *along with* constant indulgence in a potentially addictive behavior that created such danger for Jan. Relatively few college women would be suffering from all those factors at once; a far greater majority binge and diet, or binge and vomit only on special occasions.

Overall, the very nature of the college lifestyle may create, especially for the female student, an upsetting tension between work orientation and dating concerns, says Dr. Raymond C. Hawkins, psychological consultant at the Austin (Texas) Stress Clinic. Interpersonal problems—such as rejection in love or academic difficulties—may precipitate overeating, with the expectation that "eating will make me feel better and who else cares about me anyway, so I might as well eat."

Dr. Hawkins's on-campus research shows a roller-coaster effect between interpersonal relationships, lack of self-esteem, and confusion over professional goals. Bingeing has a knockout effect on such conflicts. The feelings that follow the binge—guilt and self-deprecation, plus the fear of weight gain—distract the binger from the original problem. At this point, says Dr. Hawkins, the binger makes the logical error of redefining her problem as being the uncontrolled eating itself, or her overweight appearance.

Because Dr. Hawkins believes that working to clarify professional goals is a firmer ground on which to build self-esteem than romantic relationships, which tend to be much less controllable, he emphasizes career planning in treatment of college women with food-control problems. Feeling directed plays a crucial role in getting a college woman past chaotic eating behavior, Dr. Hawkins stresses. When she gets involved with a new idea or project, she relates to her body more positively, he says. The trick is to make that state of mind a permanent one by focusing closely on that idea or project—and channeling it to a viable direction for the future.

14

When the Boss Wants Sex

Yla Eason

Florine Mitchell watched the lights blink through each number as the elevator sped to the top floor. She and her boss were on their way to get her desk supplies. "Have you ever made love to a white man?" her boss asked casually. Florine wrinkled her brow and stared at him in disbelief. "Would you slap my face if I made a pass at you?" he inquired in the same tone. Florine shook her head quickly in astonishment and searched the elevator walls for something on which to focus. Suddenly the doors opened and she broke her silence with a sigh. Florine looked at her watch. She had been on this new job one hour.

Florine was exposed to something just then dawning on the American consciousness and rising in the courts. In 1976, no one was sure what to call it. Today that something is clearly defined as sexual harassment. Unfortunately for Florine Mitchell (not her real name), that precise definition did not come soon enough.

Later, as she stepped into the storage room, her boss told his new assistant manager how attractive she was and leaned forward to kiss her. Blocking his move, Florine announced, "I don't go for that, and I wish you wouldn't try it again. As long as I've worked, I've never gotten involved with anybody on the job, especially my *boss*." He apologized.

At lunch he talked about the sad sexual relationship he shared with his wife. "We sleep in separate bedrooms," he confessed. Florine was edgy, and she told him that she felt awkward listening to him discuss his personal life. Again, he apologized.

"I like you," her boss declared three days later. "Don't like me." Florine snapped, trying not to bruise his ego. "I have a boyfriend I'm in love with, and I have no intentions of cutting out on him." This time her boss didn't apologize. Instead he said, "Think about it." Florine was thoroughly confused. It puzzled her that a man in his position was coming on to her this way.

When she discovered in her desk a lewd cartoon, which her superior laughingly admitted placing there, she threatened to tell *his* superior. "Go ahead," he mockingly advised. "He's my best friend."

"You're gonna make love to me," he insisted a few days later. He then explained the details of an out-of-town trip he was arranging to the branch office. After the meeting, he continued, she would spend the night with him at a hotel. This offer frightened her, and she thought quickly about the mortgage note she had to make next month, her two sons, her separation from her husband and her family several hundred miles away. If she'd had this job longer, she could collect unemployment. Florine decided she couldn't quit now. She would reason with him. She would go on the trip "strictly for the job" and come back that night. He repeated his request. "No way in hell," she stressed. "Think about it," he said.

Had sexual harassment been a more publicized issue, Florine would have known what her options were. She also would have known that hers was not an isolated case. Statistics say 50 to 80 percent of all women in the work place have been subject to verbal or physical harassment. Of the four and a half million Black women who work, only a few escape the hazard. . . .

Less than two months later, Florine Mitchell was fired. Shortly afterward she filed a suit alleging sexual harassment, saying she was fired because she refused to sleep with him. He denied all her charges and claimed he never propositioned her. She lost her case and is now raising money to appeal the decision. Florine believes the court ruled in her boss' favor because neither the judge nor the jury understood what sexual harassment was, nor could they believe a Black woman would be so naively vulnerable.

No one bothered to point out to the court then, or most recently, that Black women have been in the forefront of the movement against sexual harassment. Black women have filed the cases that have resulted in (1) a legal definition of sexual harassment, (2) the identification of sexual advances on the job as sex discrimination, (3) the prohibition against sexual harassment under Title VII of the Civil Rights Act of 1964, and (4) the determination that employers can be liable for sexual harassment.

Munford v. *J. T. Barnes* was the first harassment case granted a jury trial. *Williams* v. *Saxbe* established that dismissal because of refusing sexual advances was sex discrimination. *Barnes* v. *the EPA* (Environmental Protection Agency) defined sexual harassment and declared it illegal under Title VII. *Miller* v. *Bank of America* confirmed that an employer is liable for the sexual harassment acts of its supervisors, and *Alexander* v. *Yale University* argued that the university is responsible for acknowledging and acting on the sexual harassment complaints of students against faculty.

These cases, all brought by Black women, helped shape the new employer guidelines on sexual harassment issued by the Equal Employment Opportunity Commission (EEOC) in September 1980. EEOC, the agency charged with enforcing the antidiscrimination laws, Title VII of the Civil Rights Act of 1964, defines sexual harassment as an unwanted and unwelcome sexual advance, request for sexual favors, or any other verbal or physical conduct of a sexual nature that occurs on the job. Although sexual harassment usually takes place between a superior and a subordinate, the EEOC's new rules cover harassment of employees by other employees and by customers. And though all court cases to date involve the harassment of a female by a male, men are equally protected from harassment in the policy.

The EEOC specifically states that sexual harassment is an illegal act when one of three conditions is met. *One,* when submission is made a condition of employment; *two*, when it unreasonably interferes with one's work performance; or *three*, when it creates an intimidating, hostile or offensive working environment.

If 50 to 80 percent of working women have been sexually harassed, 50 percent of those harassed fail to report it, according to Working Women's Institute, a sexual harassment counseling service in New York. Susan Meyer, the institute's executive director, adds, "Very often we ignore our feelings about it. There is a lot of ambivalence among women because society blames us for men coming on to us." Susan Meyer, who is white, credits Black women with taking the lead in this movement before many white women considered it serious.

One speculation as to why we have so aggressively pursued this issue is that as the last hired and first fired, we have the least to lose. History shows that the most oppressed people tend to be in the forefront of civil uprisings. Moreover, we are sensitized to discriminatory acts on the job and thus more aware of and less conditioned to abiding by them.

Paulette Barnes, herself a victim of sexual harassment (*Barnes* v. *Train*), offers another theory. "White women tend to go along with a problem on the job because they have been brought up by white men to feel like 'you have to do what you have to do to get where you're going.' " She adds, however, that Black women are the ones "stigmatized as being involved in sex (on the job)." Unfortunately, too, because some women are willing to exchange sexual encounters for promotions and raises on the job, other women are expected to do the same.

"Women who say yes have set a norm," declares Paulette Barnes, who assumed the position of administrative assistant to a man who, ironically, was an equal-opportunity director. Two months after she started there, he told her, "I remember the first day I saw you. You had on a little yellow dress, and I said, golly, that's my type of woman. I could help you further your career." Then he crudely described what type of sexual pleasure he imagined her having with him. Paulette "cussed him out in a nice way" and continued her work. A week later he timidly approached her to see whether they were still friends. Reassured, he invited her to the annual backyard barbecue for employees at his home. Paulette attended with her two children, the man she was dating and his son. The next day at work, her boss was furious. "Why you brought that man to my house, I don't know," he said in a rage. "If you want to throw your men in my face, you're gonna have to get another job." "I'm not going nowhere," a defiant Paulette responded. Two months later she had to go—he abolished her job.

In 1972, when she brought her case to the court, there was no name for sexual harassment and she was told to bring a charge of racial discrimination instead (a white man was later hired at a higher salary for her position).

The woman who preceded Paulette as administrative assistant testified on Paulette's behalf that the director had expected sexual compliance from his subordinates. The woman, who was white, had slept with her supervisor because she knew it was necessary to get the job and to keep moving up in her position. However, she had also documented everything. She showed Christmas and Valentine's cards, receipts for gifts and the dates of their sexual meetings. Paulette lost and took her case to appeals court, where the judge ruled that her boss' request for sexual favors was sex discrimination and therefore against the law. She received a cash settlement.

But Paulette Barnes has been relatively more fortunate than others. Diane Williams, the first person to win a sexual harassment case, has yet to collect the money awarded in her 1972 case. The U.S. Justice Department, which she sued, is refusing to pay her legal fees, and Diane says they "are in the thousands."

Diane Williams was 24, single and a Justice Department public information specialist in Washington, D.C. Though married, her superior sent her a card saying, "Seldom a day goes by without a thought of you." Moreover, he repeatedly asked her to go to the movies, join him for drinks and accompany him to dinner. Each time she said no. Soon after she was fired. She took her boss to court, where he claimed they were having an affair and charged that when it ended she sued out of jealous anger. Before winning her case, she had two administrative hearings within the department and was in three different courts with her case. She says it was an arduous process. "It took a lot out of my personal life."

For most women who fight a sexual harassment case, it is an emotionally draining battle that causes depression and periods of self-doubt and loss of self-esteem. They report not feeling good about themselves, mainly because their private life is an open book during the trial process. Often their love relationships suffer, their subsequent work performance is less confident, they are shunned by other workers and employers as troublemakers. In addition, the experience is often handled by the courts as if it were a rape case, which causes more women to be reluctant about disclosing its existence. "My lawyer asked me if I could handle the court's bringing up the fact that I had two children but didn't marry their father," recounts Paulette Barnes. "I told her, 'I faced it then, and I can deal with it again.'"

Then there are those few women who are flattered by their boss' attention until it jeopardizes their job or gets out of hand and they have difficulty explaining why they endured the treatment before. Also, there are those who do not want to cause trouble and thus say nothing and start looking for a new place to work. But it is the humiliation of realizing they have been victimized that gnaws at most women's self-concept after these experiences—explaining it to themselves is the hardest part.

And justification is not easy, because studies show age, dress, position, looks, education, romance and love have nothing to do with whom a man will choose to harass. Any woman can have sex appeal—and beauty, as the cliche goes, is in the eye of the beholder. One woman seeking counseling after an incident threw her hands up totally perplexed. "Look at me," she explained, "I'm 50 years old!"

Dr. Cynthia D. Barnes, a respected New York–based psychiatrist, says one reason we women are so unraveled by the experience is that we never thought it could happen. "You never think a man is going to do this. Even when there have been many things that actually led up to it, women are shocked, embarrassed, distraught." This reaction occurs, she adds, because of the way women are raised to think about men. "Women are also taught that men are there to take care of them. It's hard to think that a man who is there to protect you is also assaulting you."

Florine Mitchell bears out that analysis. She says that at first "I wondered why he acted that way, and I thought he was silly, but harmless. It took me a while to figure out he was hitting on me." When it dawned on her what she had endured as his employee, "I became withdrawn and ashamed of myself. I blamed myself and tried to figure out what I did wrong." She broke up with her boyfriend because she had trouble relating to men afterward. During a discussion with a man, he attempted a harmless joke, and she cut him off, cracked on him and tried to belittle him. She accepted a job at lower pay with no raise for three years because she had a female boss and she refused to look for better employment because she was afraid she would have to work for a man. She was unable to keep a relationship going with a man, spent a lot of time alone at home crying, sought counseling and reports that it took her four years to start feeling good about herself and to realize that all men aren't deceptive. But she adds today, "It [sexual harassment] is the greatest pain anyone can experience at any one time." She says that when she realized she was not at fault for what happened to her, she could accept herself again.

Suffering continues for the victims, Cynthia Barnes says, because "for many women, it's hard to blame the man. They learn from their parents that relationships with men represent a dual-edged sword—men may exploit you as well as guard you. So when it happens, women don't want to believe it. They think maybe this is a caring statement rather than sexual harassment." Susan Meyer adds that there is no rationale for the treatment. "Sexual harassment is a power play. In many ways it's a game where men play out their economic power over women." Women testify to this, saying that what surprised them most when it happened was its spontaneity and the man's lack of guilt. One woman, an executive with a New York hair-care company, reports how she was standing in her office when the president of the division walked in, dropped down on his knees and ran his hand up and down her leg. The experience so shocked her that she just stood and stared at him. When she asked him why, he simply replied, "I looked and I had to touch. I couldn't help it." She was outraged, first because he felt that free to invade her privacy and second because he was white.

Many women say sexual harassment becomes more insidious when the player is a white male. "Historically, it just recreates that whole plantation, master-slave scene, and it must bring back what our great, great grandmothers went through. It perhaps evokes more rage than if it was a Black man," comments Cynthia Barnes. However, sexual harassment does not seem to break down neatly into the white-oppressor, Black-victim syndrome. Both Diane Williams and Paulette Barnes had Black male supervisors. Diane says of her experience, "It was horrible. I was furious having to hear him deliberately say all the nasty things about me he could, especially since he's a Black man. We don't need to tear each other apart; we have too much coming from the other communities for that."

Cynthia Barnes adds, "With Black men, it probably brings about more disgust. Since the sixties we've gotten a sense of brotherhood and sisterhood, and to have one of your own perpetuating this brings about a feeling of being betrayed. One woman who was harassed on her job by a white male and later harassed by a Black male for whom she temporarily worked said, "When he put his hand up my thigh, I kept saying to myself, 'Oh, no, not you too.' " She had known the man several years and considered herself his friend but never had one sexual thought about him. "What surprised me was that he thought I would respond favorably."

"When accused of sexual harassment, men often respond that they were only trying to initiate a close personal relationship with a woman they liked very much," states Catherine A. MacKinnon in her book *Sexual Harassment of Working Women* (Yale University Press). Some men clearly resent the fact that they cannot proposition a woman at work. Author Gay Talese was quoted as saying, "Whether he's effective or not, a man is always going to chase; it's simply part of his emotional and physical makeup." The person's professional position, however, adds to the anxiety of the woman on the receiving end, and often her desire not to be bothered is ignored. "Men are brought up to see women as someone to take care of their needs," states Cynthia Barnes. "Men have never been taught to shift from the social view of a woman to the professional. A woman is a woman; thus comes the need for sexual dominance."

Paulette Barnes says her boss was never reprimanded. None of the other women report any action against their supervisors either, which suggests that society tolerates this behavior. All of the men either denied anything had happened or said what did occur was taken out of context. Paulette, asked what type of male would harass, replied, "It's usually somebody that nobody else wants. If you work for a good-looking man who has himself together, chances are he already has lady friends and doesn't need to pressure anybody to be with him." The harasser, adds Paulette, uses his position to act like a ladies' man in situations where he knows the rejection rate will be low.

In spite of the man's motivation, a woman has to be careful about how she handles his actions. Another woman, Jane Parker (not her real name), who worked at the U.S. post office for seven years, asked her new supervisor why she was having trouble getting emergency leave. "You know why," he shot back. She told him no, she didn't. "You could avoid all this if you would just act right," he said, winking his eye. Asked to explain what he meant, he made his request to have sex with her, in vulgar descriptive detail. "Either that," he concluded, "or I'll make you sorry you ever worked here. In fact, I'll see to it that you get fired." He then arrogantly pointed his finger in her face and thumped her breast. A livid Jane Parker slapped his hand and yelled at him in a loud voice, insisting that he never touch her again. Two days later she was fired for "physically assaulting a superior." When she attempted to get unemployment, her request was denied because witnesses saw her strike him. Her case is still in litigation.

Although the post office adamantly maintains that it is not responsible, the new EEOC guidelines state that an "organization is responsible for its acts and those of its agents and supervisory employees with respect to sexual harassment regardless of whether the employer knew or should have known of their occurrences." Interestingly enough, the case that first raised the issue of employer liability was brought by a Black woman, Margaret Miller, against the Bank of America in San Francisco, Calif.

A few weeks after her superior assumed his new position as the manager of Margaret Miller's department, he appeared at her doorstep uninvited. "I've never felt this way about a Black chick before," he confessed and told the keypunch operator that he could "get her off the machines," if she cooperated with his desires. She refused his romantic overtures, although he continued to pester her regarding when she would invite him to dinner. A couple of months later, she was fired for "insubordination." Margaret Miller charged in court that the bank had a policy of "permitting males in supervisory positions to put Black female employees in subsidiary roles demeaning their dignity—a role that Black females had to play to remain employed." She lost her first case because the bank had a policy against her supervisor's behavior and it charged that since she did not report the incidents, it was not liable. She took her case to appeals court, where the judge ruled in her favor, saying that the employer was liable for "the torts [wrongful acts] of its employees acting in the course of their employment." Margaret Miller received an out-of-court cash settlement.

Fighting a court case is a costly and exhausting process and requires a good lawyer, a lot of time—digging up details and recalling events—and stamina. First, legal fees can average $100 an hour. It doesn't take long to run up a big bill if the lawyer spends 20 hours on your case. Second, one must present evidence that proves one's claim: witnesses to events, memos, letters, details of conversations, people who have had similar experiences, personnel files, statistics on hiring procedures and practices, employment records. Third, a person needs patience, determination, a sense of purpose and strength to endure the questioning and what some call the "debilitating lies" that arise during the process. Also, courts are often hostile and unsympathetic toward Black women, especially if the case is against a white male with some authority or social position.

Barbara Sims (not her real name), who brought the first student-initiated case of sexual harassment to court, claims she lost her case because the judge, a white female, refused to allow much of her supporting evidence in court.

When Barbara was a college sophomore, she alleges, a professor asked her, "How bad do you want an A in this course?" She shunned his bait, saying, "I would like an A, but it's not an insane desire of mine." "I would really hate to give you a C," he repeated until it sounded threatening. He then asked, "Will you make love to me?" Barbara quickly answered no. He commented on her body and she asked to leave. She was almost at her dorm before she realized her refusal meant she would get a C on her paper. "I was shocked, then I got angry," she says. For this to happen in an academic environment, she says, creates "an assumption of my inferiority as a Black person as well as my lack of seriousness as a woman." He denied her charges.

In court the judge did not permit students who had experienced harassment under the professor to testify, because they had graduated. Although Barbara told her dean immediately after the incident, and the dean said there was nothing that could be done, that conversation was not allowed to be presented as testimony. Also, she had given a written statement regarding the incident to a Black professor, but neither his testimony nor that statement was allowed. "It was all incredibly racist," asserts Barbara. Her lawyer, a white woman, says she was "shocked by the callousness" of the court. She adds that the case was lost because "the judge didn't want to believe us." They were "procedurally restricted," she says, from mentioning any other cases that related to Barbara's charge.

After Barbara's case, the college instituted a policy whereby women who had been harassed could initiate a formal complaint; none existed at the time Barbara complained. Today companies and organizations, warned by EEOC that they have an obligation to create a working environment free of harassment, are issuing rules of behavior to employees. American Telephone and Telegraph, with more than 85,000 Black women employees in its Bell system nationwide, recently issued a statement saying, "An employee who has been found guilty of sexually harassing another employee can get fired for it."

As more women are made aware of the rules against sexual harassment and how it operates, fewer incidences will be allowed to continue. However, the price associated with confronting the issue remains high. Of particular concern to most women is how their spouses respond. Neither Florine Mitchell nor Paulette Barnes told their male companions about the incident when it occurred. They cited fear of his "causing a scene" and their not wanting to hurt him by telling him about another man's abusive behavior. Both women said they were "protecting" their man against possibly reacting physically against their boss. "Women don't tell because they are embarrassed it happened, and they know they are bringing themselves up for scrutiny as to whether or not they were provocative and encouraged it," psychiatrist Cynthia Barnes explains. In order to combat the problem more effectively, she believes, "women have to stop being so trusting. Women like to be nice, but we must be aware that there's a potential attraction, and to most men there's not much difference between a working woman and a woman who exists for his sexual gratification."

Susan Meyer (of Working Women's Institute) adds, "As women, we need to be clear about our role as workers. We need to take ourselves seriously and be aware of our rights on the job. When we are harassed, we can't say, 'I'm imagining it.' Chances are you aren't the only one he has harassed." Florine Mitchell agrees that a woman who has been harassed should talk about it with other women at work. "People knew it was happening on my job, but it was kept very hush-hush. I thought I could ignore the man. My way to handle it was to leave him alone—show him no encouragement and he would get tired. I thought as long as I'm doing a good job, he can't fire me."

Although Florine Mitchell is still fighting her battle, she has assumed a new position as a manager for another concern. Her former boss continues to deny having harassed her, and she occasionally must talk with him in her new position. Barbara Sims is now a law student at the University of California in Berkeley and says she might appeal her decision; Diane Williams is finishing her last year of law school as well. Paulette Barnes is an instructor of air traffic controllers in Oklahoma

City, Okla. The sexual harassment events profoundly changed their lives, but none regrets her decision to fight. Paulette says she spoke up because "I was a mother who was working, and I had kids to support. Suppose I didn't take a stand there and ten or 15 years from now my daughter comes along and it's still happening." Diane Williams concurs. "So many of us have to work; therefore the situation has to be corrected. I have too much confidence in myself as a person and as a professional to subject myself to that treatment."

15

He Defies You Still:
The Memoirs of a Sissy

Tommi Avicolli

> *You're just a faggot*
> *No history faces you this morning*
> *A faggot's dreams are scarlet*
> *Bad blood bled from words that scarred*[1]

Scene One

A homeroom in a Catholic high school in South Philadelphia. The boy sits quietly in the first aisle, third desk, reading a book. He does not look up, not even for a moment. He is hoping no one will remember he is sitting there. He wishes he were invisible. The teacher is not yet in the classroom so the other boys are talking and laughing loudly.

Suddenly, a voice from beside him:

"Hey, you're a faggot, ain't you?"

The boy does not answer. He goes on reading his book, or rather pretending he is reading his book. It is impossible to actually read the book now.

"Hey, I'm talking to you!"

The boy still does not look up. He is so scared his heart is thumping madly; it feels like it is leaping out of his chest and into his throat. But he can't look up.

"Faggot, I'm talking to you!"

To look up is to meet the eyes of the tormentor.

Suddenly, a sharpened pencil point is thrust into the boy's arm. He jolts, shaking off the pencil, aware that there is blood seeping from the wound.

"What did you do that for?" he asks timidly.

"Cause I hate faggots," the other boy says, laughing. Some other boys begin to laugh, too. A symphony of laughter. The boy feels as if he's going to cry. But he must not cry. Must not cry. So he holds back the tears and tries to read the book again. He must read the book. Read the book.

When the teacher arrives a few minutes later, the class quiets down. The boy does not tell the teacher what has happened. He spits on the wound to clean it, dabbing it with a tissue until the bleeding stops. For weeks he fears some dreadful infection from the lead in the pencil point.

Scene Two

The boy is walking home from school. A group of boys (two, maybe three, he is not certain) grab him from behind, drag him into an alley and beat him up. When he gets home, he races up to his room, refusing dinner ("I don't feel well," he tells his mother through the locked door) and spends the night alone in the dark wishing he would die. . . .

These are not fictitious accounts—I *was* that boy. Having been branded a sissy by neighborhood children because I preferred jump rope to baseball and dolls to playing soldiers, I was often taunted with "hey sissy" or "hey faggot" or "yoo hoo honey" (in a mocking voice) when I left the house.

To avoid harassment, I spent many summers alone in my room. I went out on rainy days when the street was empty.

I came to like being alone. I didn't need anyone, I told myself over and over again. I was an island. Contact with others meant pain. Alone, I was protected. I began writing poems, then short stories. There was no reason to go outside anymore. I had a world of my own.

> *In the schoolyard today*
> *they'll single you out*
> *Their laughter will leave your ears ringing*
> *like the church bells*
> *which once awed you.* . . .[2]

School was one of the more painful experiences of my youth. The neighborhood bullies could be avoided. The taunts of the children living in those endless repetitive row houses could be evaded by staying in my room. But school was something I had to face day after day for some two hundred mornings a year.

I had few friends in school. I was a pariah. Some kids would talk to me, but few wanted to be known as my close friend. Afraid of labels. If I was a sissy, then he had to be a sissy, too. I was condemned to loneliness.

Fortunately, a new boy moved into our neighborhood and befriended me; he wasn't afraid of the labels. He protected me when the other guys threatened to beat me up. He walked me home from school; he broke through the terrible loneliness. We were in third or fourth grade at the time.

We spent a summer or two together. Then his parents sent him to camp and I was once again confined to my room.

Scene Three

High school lunchroom. The boy sits at a table near the back of the room. Without warning, his lunch bag is grabbed and tossed to another table. Someone opens it and confiscates a package of Tastykakes; another boy takes the sandwich. The empty bag is tossed back to the boy who stares at it, dumbfounded. He should be used to this; it has happened before.

Someone screams, "faggot," laughing. There is always laughter. It does not annoy him anymore.

There is no teacher nearby. There is never a teacher around. And what would he say if there were? Could he report the crime? He would be jumped after school if he did. Besides, it would be his word against theirs. Teachers never noticed anything. They never heard the taunts. Never heard the word, "faggot." They were the great deaf mutes, pillars of indifference; a sissy's pain was not relevant to history and geography and god made me to love honor and obey him, amen.

Scene Four

High school Religion class. Someone has a copy of *Playboy*. Father N. is not in the room yet; he's late, as usual. Someone taps the boy roughly on the shoulder. He turns. A finger points to the centerfold model, pink fleshy body, thin and sleek. Almost painted. Not real. The other asks, mocking voice, "Hey, does she turn you on? Look at those tits!"

The boy smiles, nodding meekly; turns away.

The other jabs him harder on the shoulder, "Hey, whatsamatter, don't you like girls?"

Laughter. Thousands of mouths; unbearable din of laughter. In the Arena: thumbs down. Don't spare the queer.

"Wanna suck my dick? Huh? That turn you on, faggot!"

The laughter seems to go on forever. . . .

Behind you, the sound of their laughter
echoes a million times
in a soundless place
They watch how you walk/sit/stand/breathe. . . .[3]

What did being a sissy really mean? It was a way of walking (from the hips rather than the shoulders); it was a way of talking (often with a lisp or in a high-pitched voice); it was a way of relating to others (gently, not wanting to fight, or hurt anyone's feelings). It was being intelligent ("an egghead" they called it sometimes); getting good grades. It means not being interested in sports, not playing football in the street after school; not discussing teams and scores and playoffs. And it involved not showing fervent interest in girls, not talking about scoring with tits or *Playboy* centerfolds. Not concealing naked women in your history book; or porno books in your locker.

On the other hand, anyone could be a "faggot." It was a catch-all. If you did something that didn't conform to what was the acceptable behavior of the group, then you risked being called a faggot. If you didn't get along with the "in" crowd, you were a faggot. It was the most commonly used put-down. It kept guys in line. They became angry when somebody called them a faggot. More fights started over someone calling someone else a faggot than anything else. The word had power. It toppled the male ego, shattered his delicate facade, violated the image he projected. He was tough. Without feeling. Faggot cut through all this. It made him vulnerable. Feminine. And feminine was the worst thing he could possibly be. Girls were fine for fucking, but no boy in his right mind wanted to be like them. A boy was the opposite of girl. He was not feminine. He was not feeling. He was not weak.

Just look at the gym teacher who growled like a dog; or the priest with the black belt who threw kids against the wall in rage when they didn't know their Latin. They were men, they got respect.

But not the physics teacher who preached pacifism during lectures on the nature of atoms. Everybody knew what he was—and why he believed in the anti-war movement.

My parents only knew that the neighborhood kids called me names. They begged me to act more like the other boys. My brothers were ashamed of me. They never said it, but I knew. Just as I knew that my parents were embarrassed by my behavior.

At times, they tried to get me to act differently. Once my father lectured me on how to walk right. I'm still not clear on what that means. Not from the hips, I guess; don't "swish" like faggots do.

A nun in elementary school told my mother at Open House that there was "something wrong with me." I had draped my sweater over my shoulders like a girl, she said. I was a smart kid, but I should know better than to wear my sweater like a girl!

My mother stood there, mute. I wanted her to say something, to chastise this nun; to defend me. But how could she? This was a nun talking—representative of Jesus, protector of all that was good and decent.

An uncle once told me I should start "acting like a boy" instead of like a girl. Everybody seemed ashamed of me. And I guess I was ashamed of myself, too. It was hard not to be.

Scene Five

Priest: Do you like girls, Mark?
Mark: Uh-huh.
Priest: I mean *really* like them?
Mark: Yeah—they're okay.
Priest: There's a role they play in your salvation. Do you understand it, Mark?
Mark: Yeah.
Priest: You've got to like girls. Even if you should decide to enter the seminary, it's
    important to keep in mind God's plan for a man and a woman. . . .[4]

Catholicism of course condemned homosexuality. Effeminacy was tolerated as
long as the effeminate person did not admit to being gay. Thus, priests could be
effeminate because they weren't gay.

As a sissy, I could count on no support from the church. A male's sole purpose
in life was to father children—souls for the church to save. The only hope a
homosexual had of attaining salvation was by remaining totally celibate. Don't even
think of touching another boy. Don't even think of touching another boy. To think
of a sin was a sin. And to sin was to put a mark upon the soul. Sin—if it was a
serious offense against god—led to hell. There was no way around it. If you sinned,
you were doomed.

Realizing I was gay was not an easy task. Although I knew I was attracted to boys
by the time I was about eleven, I didn't connect this attraction to homosexuality. I
was not queer. Not I. I was merely appreciating a boy's good looks, his fine features,
his proportions. It didn't seem to matter that I didn't appreciate a girl's looks in the
same way. There was no twitching in my thighs when I gazed upon a beautiful girl.
But I wasn't queer.

I resisted that label—queer—for the longest time. Even when everything
pointed to it, I refused to see it. I was certainly not queer. Not I.

We sat through endless English classes, and History courses about the wars
between men who were not allowed to love each other. No gay history was ever
taught. No history faces you this morning. You're just a faggot. Homosexuals had
never contributed to the human race. God destroyed the queers in Sodom and
Gomorrah.

We learned about Michelangelo, Oscar Wilde, Gertrude Stein—but never that
they were queer. They were not queer. Walt Whitman, the "father of American
poetry," was not queer. No one was queer. I was alone, totally unique. One of a
kind. Were there others like me somewhere? Another planet, perhaps?

In school, they never talked of the queers. They did not exist. The only hint we
got of this other species was in religion class. And even then it was clouded in
mystery—never spelled out. It was a sin. Like masturbation. Like looking at *Playboy*
and getting a hard-on. A sin.

Once a progressive priest in senior year religion class actually mentioned
homosexuals—he said the word—but was into Erich Fromm, into homosexuals as

pathetic and sick. Fixated at some early stage; penis, anal, whatever. Only hetero-sexuals passed on to the nirvana of sexual development.

No other images from the halls of the Catholic high school except those the other boys knew: swishy faggot sucking cock in an alley somewhere, grabbing asses in the bathroom. Never mentioning how much straight boys craved blowjobs, it was part of the secret.

It was all a secret. You were not supposed to talk about the queers. Whisper maybe. Laugh about them, yes. But don't be open, honest; don't try to understand. Don't cite their accomplishments. No history faces you this morning. You're just a faggot   faggot   no history   just a faggot

Epilogue

The boy marching down the Parkway. Hundreds of queers. Signs proclaiming gay pride. Speakers. Tables with literature from gay groups. A miracle, he is thinking. Tears are coming loose now. Someone hugs him.

> *You could not control*
> *the sissy in me*
> *nor could you exorcise him*
> *nor electrocute him*
> *You declared him illegal illegitimate*
> *insane and immature*
> *But he defies you still.*[5]

NOTES

1. From the poem "Faggot" by Tommi Avicolli, published in *GPU News*, Sept. 1979.
2. Ibid.
3. Ibid.
4. From the play *Judgment of the Roaches* by Tommi Avicolli, produced in Philadelphia at the Gay Community Center, the Painted Bride Arts Center and the University of Pennsylvania; aired over WXPN-FM, in four parts; and presented at the Lesbian/Gay Conference in Norfolk, VA, July, 1980.
5. From the poem "Sissy Poem," published in *Magic Doesn't Live Here Anymore* (Philadelphia: Spruce Street Press, 1976).

Real Men Don't Cry... and Other "Uncool" Myths

Phil W. Petrie

Things were not going well. Do they ever for young couples struggling to understand each other, raise a family, pay the mortgage and at least keep the Joneses in sight? I had wanted to comfort my pregnant wife, soothe her with words that would temper the harshness of our reality. The baby was due in two months and my employer had just informed me that I didn't have hospitalization coverage for childbirth. I was frustrated and wanted to scream, lay my head in my wife's lap and cry. I needed to be soothed as well as she. She wanted to talk about our predicament, needed to talk it out. So did I, but I couldn't. I felt that I had failed her. Guilt stood at my side. But how could she know any of that, since all I did was to turn on the stereo system—my electronic security blanket—and listen to Miles Davis. I was cool. Her words shot through the space of "All Blues." "You're a cold SOB," she hissed.

She's being emotional again, I thought, Just like a woman. I, on the other hand, was controlling the situation because I was cool—which in reality was only a few degrees away from being cold. Wasn't that what she really wanted from me as head of the household—control? Wasn't Freud correct when he proclaimed that our anatomy was our destiny (that is, our genitals determine our behavior)? In spite of her protestations that we had to talk, there was nothing in my upbringing that negated for me the power of coolness. I knew by the example of my elders that men controlled themselves and women did not.

In Mt. Olive, the Baptist church of my youth, it was expected that the "sisters" would "carry on" at church services. And they did. Moved by something that the preacher had said or by the mystery of a song, they would leap from their seats, run, scream, hurtle down the aisles. Transformed. Private feeling was suddenly public spectacle. Ushers came. White-gloved hands brushed away the tears. The men of the church, the elders, sat glued to their seats. I watched, instructed by this example of male control. I watched in silence but wished that I could know the electric transformation that moved those souls to dance.

"The larger culture creates expectations for males," says Dr. Walter Tardy, a psychiatrist in New York City. "In spite of the Women's Liberation Movement, men still live in a very macho culture and role play. Women tend to display their feelings more."

One of the roles men play is that of the rational being devoid of strong emotions. Profound feelings, it is thought, will interfere with the male task, whether that means making it at the nine-to-five or making it at war. Objective decisions must be made without distracting emotions, which women are thought to be prone to—even by some other women. For many persons, "being a man" is synonymous with being emotionless—cool.

One need not be told this. Like air, it seems to be a pervasive part of the male atmosphere. If one missed it at church (as I did not), one might pick it up at the barbershop or the playground—places where the elements of the culture are passed on without the benefit of critical examination.

Didn't Wimpy Sheppard tell me at Tom Simon's Barbershop that only babies, women and sissies cried? A man, he said, ain't supposed to cry. That's why my father, at the death of his mother, slipped out to the backyard away from his family to sit among the chickens and wail. How could I explain to my wife—to myself—that I couldn't rest my head in her lap and weep? I had to protect my masculinity. Asking me to cry, to drop my cool, was asking me to redefine my life.

Says Margo Williams, a widow residing in San Diego, California, with her two children, "If you can't let down to your mate, friend or what have you, then you have to ask yourself what the relationship is all about—is it worth being involved with? For me, it's not about my man being strong and hard. I want him to be a human being—warm, sensitive and willing to share his life with me."

What if he balks? Williams is asked. "If the relationship is a serious one, I would urge him to let us try to work through the problems," she says. "I would want to establish a relationship wherein we could express to each other our needs and wants—even express our dislikes. We have to establish an honest relationship."

Dr. Tardy cautions that "there are degrees of honesty. Do you tell the truth all of the time, or is a white lie something appropriate? One can only be just so honest. The truth may set you free, but some truths should be withheld because they can hurt more than they help. But even if you don't tell it all, you must tell *something*. Communications is the key."

Therein lies the danger of being cool and playing roles. In doing this, one reveals a persona rather than a person, plays a part rather than being part of the relationship. Communication, by its root definition, means "sharing, making something common between people." It is this fear of sharing—giving up something—that drives some men into being noncommunicative except in the area of sex.

Robert Staples, a sociologist, states in his book *Black Masculinity* (Black Scholar Press) that when Black men "have been unable to achieve status in the workplace, they have exercised the privilege of their manliness and attempted to achieve it [power] in the bedroom. Feeling a constant need to affirm their masculinity, tenderness and compassion are eschewed as signs of weakness, which leaves them vulnerable to the ever-feared possibility of female domination."

It could be argued that in today's climate of women's liberation, all men are on the defensive because of the developing assertiveness of women. No doubt some men—if not many—use sex as a controlling force. "But," says Wilbur Suesberry, a pediatrician practicing in Compton, California, "I don't believe that sex is racially restrictive. Black sexuality is a myth started and supported by whites and perpetuated by Blacks. Men find it difficult to express their inner feelings but they must find a way to do it. If you have things pent up inside of you and they do not come out in a healthy way, then they exit in an unhealthy way. Sex as an outlet for your emotions is not good. To communicate you can't sulk or take to the bed, you must talk" Talk? Yes, talk is a more precise method of communicating than sex, intuition or an "understanding."

"The birth is due in two months," she persisted. "What are we going to do?" Annoyed, not at her but at the apparent futility of the situation, I turned up the record player and went deeper into myself. Didn't she understand me well enough to know that I would do something? Hadn't I always? Couldn't she look at me and see that I was worried too? Didn't she trust me well enough to know that I would do something? All of those questions might have been eliminated with my telling her simply and directly what my feelings really were. How could she really know them unless she were a mind reader, just as I didn't know what she felt? Screaming and crying isn't quite the same thing as communicating effectively. I pulled her to me, caressed her.

Hugging and kissing are not substitutes for words, for language. Talking to each other allows us to bring order to the disruption and confusion engendered by silence. *Talk to me,* Little Willie John used to sing, *talk to me in your own sweet gentle way.*

This simple verbal act is made all the more difficult for men (and women, for that matter) if we don't know (or won't admit) what our feelings really are. We can't talk about things if we can't conceptualize them. Communication is more than mouthing words or rapping. I see it as defining an aspect of one's life by framing that aspect into words and then sharing it with someone. It is not only a problem for lovers; it also bedevils fathers and sons, mothers and daughters. It is problematic because it drives you within. The first act of communication is with your self—"the private self," Dr. Tardy calls it. This journey within involves both introspection and openness.

Yet what I face within myself—if indeed I face it—may never be completely shared with anyone. An insistance that I communicate *all* of my feelings is asking too much. We men are now being urged not only to redefine our roles and relationships with our mates and society but also to become vulnerable by revealing our private selves to another public, although it may be a public of only one. The degree to which I can do this—express *some* of my feelings—is determined by the self-awareness I have of myself and the trust I have for my spouse.

I closet my feelings out of self-protection and fear of the unknown. Women in their newfound drive for liberation have the example of men to direct them. It seems that all women are asking for is some of the prerogatives once claimed by men only. But what is to be the model for me? White men? I think not. Granted they are the movers and shakers within this society, but the madness of the world that they have created does not make them legitimate role models. Yet for many Black women the term *man* is synonymous with *white man.* I resent being asked to pattern myself after a man whose reality—full of avarice and destruction—is so antithetical to mine. I hold on to my cool.

For Black men, being cool is not just an attitude; it becomes a political stance, a metaphor for power. To give that up is, in effect, to render oneself powerless—to lose control. For Black men, who control so little, to lose this cool is to lose a weapon in their arsenal for survival. Do Black women know that?

"Maybe you could call somebody [white?] who can help," she suggested, determined to get a word out of me. And if I can't find someone white to help us with my problems, I thought, then I can fold up and cry to you. Ugh. Is this what you ask of me: to imitate white men or act like women (that is, take control or cry)? What brave new world are you asking me to enter into by dropping my cool, discarding my role as leader, drowning my strength with tears? It is a scenario that no other group of men in history has ever played. Yet you ask me, the most politically weak person within the society, to lead the way to this new world. How can you ask me that, baby? And if I go, will you cast me aside as being weak? You scream about a man who is strong enough to cry, strong enough to admit weaknesses, and at the same time you want a "take-charge" person, a man who won't let anyone run over him. Caught between such confusion, I turn to the ball game, to the television, to the silence within myself. Love is withheld. Restrained. Tentative.

"I think that our generation is too tentative," says Lee Atkins, a publishing-company sales representative living in Chicago. "Those of us born in the 1940's and before were given too many caveats. Black men or boys were told not to do this and not to do that. Avoid the police. Stay out of trouble. All of this was done to protect us in an extremely racist and hostile society. In effect, we were being told: behave or you will be destroyed." That made us cautious and we are now paying the price for all that caution. As men we find that we are too careful, too private, not open and not willing to explore. We find it difficult to open up even to those we care about the most.

"Those kids born in the 1950's and 1960's," Atkins continues, "were born into a world where the expectations for the Black male were more positive. A whole set of new possibilities was suddenly available. Sexually, things were more permissive, and in the do-your-own-thing attitude of the 1960's and 1970's Black men were actually encouraged to be more unconventional, to open up."

This has led to young Black men who are more candid about their feelings, more carefree in their attitudes. "I would be surprised," says Dr. Tardy, "if these young adults weren't more open in their dealings with each other. The drawback may be that they don't want to establish the permanent relations that were expected in the past. I can imagine that many young women will say that the young men today aren't 'serious' or are too much into themselves. That's the legacy of hanging loose."

Whether we are young or old, one thing is certain: we men cannot expect to go through a lifetime in silence, repressing our feelings, denying our emotions, without being run down by frustrations, failed opportunities and unfulfilled promises. And why would we do this? Is it because of the protrusion dangling between our legs? Is it because we hold on to a fixed role in a changing world? Or is it because of our fear of losing an imagined power? Perhaps the answer is all of the above. If so, we must rush to get rid of these contrived ghosts. In the real world our women are calling to us. How long will they keep it up before they give up? Or as writer Amiri Baraka asks, "How long till the logic of our lives runs us down?"

She stood before me pleading, belly swollen with my seed. She wasn't asking for much, just that I talk to her. She was richly human and was demanding that I be nothing less, saying that I couldn't be a man until I showed that I was human— warm, tender, compassionate, feeling, and able to express that feeling. It was difficult, but with a guide so dedicated to my good health I began the journey from within to without that day. We found the money for the hospital. But more important, I found that I could talk to her about me, could share my life in trust with her. I write this as a souvenir of remembrance—a gift for her.

17

Divorce Law and Policy:
The Rising Backlash

Marianne Takas

In 1982, I was one of the over one million American women who faced divorce. I was, unquestionably, one of the very lucky ones: I was young, healthy, white, and employed. I was also—and this is crucial—childless. It was therefore more irritating than devastating to learn that, like most postdivorce women, I could expect to live at a much lower standard of living than my former spouse. I wouldn't be compensated for putting him through postgraduate school (a program that promised to perhaps double his earnings), but I wouldn't be homeless, either.

In the months that followed, though, a thought haunted me: suppose I hadn't been white, educated, and financially advantaged? Suppose, more simply, I'd had a child? How much more dangerous the inequities would have been.

"Motherhood," says Lillian Kozak, chair of New York State NOW's Domestic Relations Law Task Force, "puts a woman behind the eight ball. Child-raising can be a wonderful thing, but in our society it has no monetary value and accumulates no economic rights. If at any time the wage-earning father decides to leave, the mother and children can be financially devastated."

The facts support Kozak's claim. There are now more than eight million women raising children under 21 whose fathers are not living in the household, the U.S. Bureau of Census reports. Fully one third of them live below the poverty level. Nearly two thirds . . . collect no child support at all. And among the "lucky few" who do get some support, the average amount received is about $115 per child per month. According to Wayne Dixon, author of *Child Support Enforcement: Unequal Protection Under the Law* (Forum Foundation), white families average about $121 per child per month and black families about $71.

Alimony, once an important means of avoiding postdivorce poverty (particularly for older women or the mothers of young children), is now all but unknown. Fewer than 5 percent of all divorced, nonremarried women are entitled to receive alimony in a given year—and fewer still actually collect.

All women, married or unmarried, employed within and/or outside the home are at risk. With the corporate world still largely insensitive to the needs of workers with family responsibilities, even professional couples face hard choices if they want to have children. Commonly, one parent—nearly always the woman—finds that she must interrupt or scale down her career in order to meet the family's needs at home. Coupled with the prevailing wage discrimination against women, the result is a serious disparity in earning power. The family becomes dependent upon the support of the male wage earner—and ripe for economic disaster if that support is withdrawn.

Until recently, the legal system's increasing role in impoverishing women and children was not fully recognized. We knew about the growing "feminization of poverty" but were largely unaware of how changes in divorce policy and practice had contributed to the crisis. We had anecdotal reports, occasional data, and a growing sense of misgiving, but little solid statistical analysis. Those of us still married or not yet married could reassure ourselves that the problem was an isolated one of a few stingy or irresponsible men. My husband (or lover or future husband), we could tell ourselves, would never do that to me. And I would never be so vulnerable.

Enter Lenore Weitzman, bearer of the bad news. Weitzman, associate professor of sociology at Stanford University in California, was the major researcher on a 10-year study of the effects of California's widely-hailed—and widely-imitated—no-fault divorce law. In her shocking and important new book, *The Divorce Revolution: The Unexpected Social and Economic Consequences for Women and Children in America* (The Free Press), Weitzman documents and explains how new divorce policies in California have resulted in severe financial losses to women and children. Her major finding: the effect of the average divorce decree is to decrease the standard of living of the woman and any minor children in her household by 73 percent, while actually *increasing* that of the man by 42 percent.

"The framers of the no-fault divorce laws," explains Weitzman, "were totally preoccupied with the negative aspects of the traditional adversarial system. In the past, to get a divorce, people were required to prove fault—that a spouse had done something improper like adultery or physical cruelty. That could bring out the worst in people in terms of anger and recriminations, and the legislators hoped that no-fault laws would reduce acrimony and restore dignity to the parties.

"What they didn't consider, however, was that requiring proof of fault had long provided the one protection for economically dependent homemakers and women raising children. If a woman hadn't given her husband grounds for divorce—hadn't committed adultery or other forbidden behavior—she had some leverage. She could agree to ask for the divorce herself on the grounds of the husband's behavior, but only if he first provided adequate support for her and the children."

As support levels declined under no-fault, property divisions also became less fair. California is a community property state, but the law has never dictated an exact formula for division if the spouses divorce. Before no-fault was instituted, reports Weitzman, property divisions tended to be along lines of family need, with a custodial mother and children retaining the family home and enough other property to avoid sudden poverty. More recently, rigid 50/50 divisions have become the norm.

The result, says Weitzman: an *illusion* of equality, with the man retaining a full half of the property, while the woman and an average two children must share the remaining half. Frequently, to accomplish the split, the family home is sold, so that the mother must find new living arrangements for herself and the children.

Ironically, Weitzman's disturbing statistics come from a state that many analysts believe is actually less unfair to women than most. For if California's community property law now results in a 50/50 split between unequal family units, women and children may fare even worse under the more common equitable division laws, which theoretically provide for a fair—but not necessarily equal—split of family assets. Thus, for example, a special study by Harriet N. Cohen and Adria S. Hillman for the New York Task Force on Women in the Courts showed that in the average property division, the man actually received substantially *more* than the woman and children combined.

Those who criticize the growing inequities under no-fault divorce laws do not, however, generally advocate a return to fault requirements. At best, explains NOW's Lillian Kozak, the old fault requirements provided only a crude bargaining tool that helped some women to escape the effects of the underlying problem: the failure of both law and society to recognize and reward the essential services offered by most women in the home.

"What we really need," says Kozak, "are laws and policies that recognize the family as a cooperative unit. If the facts show that a man within a family has been free to pursue his career fully while the woman has taken on most of the child-care responsibility—whether she's also held an outside job or not—his greater earning power is a family asset.

"That means that not only property, but also in the years after the divorce that income should continue to be shared. Otherwise, it's like dividing up a business partnership by giving half the capital and inventory to each partner—but letting one of them keep the entire income-producing business."

Despite isolated advances, however, the dominant trend seems to be in precisely the opposite direction. The practical problem of negotiating alimony, for example, has been eclipsed by arguments that the concept itself is outdated. It's best for everyone if the parties get a fresh start, runs the modern theory. Isn't that what women's liberation is all about?

That upbeat view totally overlooks the role of alimony in sharing family earning power and compensating for past and present services within the family. Yet it has no doubt contributed to the declining levels and poor enforcement of alimony awards. In real-dollar terms, child-support awards have declined in recent years, a casualty, perhaps, of the growing resistance to *any* postdivorce income transfers.

The growing trend toward these harsh interpretations of "equality" in divorce is not limited to finances. Indeed, perhaps the most disturbing example of ignoring family realities occurs in the custody area. Parents should have equal custodial *rights* to a child, some policymakers argue—even if the mother has always taken the major *responsibility* for the child's care and continues to do so.

Could all these changes reflect an excess of innocence, a naïve belief that women and men are indeed equal both in financial status and family responsibilities? Perhaps, but around the divorce drama these days there seems to be an ominous and growing hostility toward "uppity" women: women who have careers. Women who want out of marriages. Women who think they don't need men any more, and need a lesson they won't forget.

"Women file for divorce in most cases because they are 'pissed off,'" writes Ken Pangborn, president of Men International, Inc., in the February, 1985, issue of "Legal Beagle: A Family Law Reform Newsletter." "Greed is a powerful motive. . . . The feminist agenda, when examined closely, is *not* a cry for a fair share of the pie. . . . It is an angry demand for the pie and the kitchen it was cooked in, along with everything else."

The solution, according to Pangborn? Since women cannot be trusted, men should strike back—by aggressively seeking sole custody of their children.

It would be comforting to believe that such extremes are limited to a few extremists—and indeed there *are* numerous calm, fair-minded male voices in the storm. Yet a glance at the steady stream of divorce advocacy books for men, written by male lawyers and published by prestigious houses, is indeed deeply disturbing.

The Lion's Share: A Combat Manual for the Divorcing Male, by J. Alan Ornstein, for example, is dedicated in part to divorcing women, the "Bitches of Buchenwald" [with their] female chauvinistic greed." Leonard Kerpelman, author of *Divorce: A Guide for Men,* advises men to use "primitive democratic means" to reach their goals, explaining, "If [judges] see one person hollering and the other submitting, they'll rule for the one hollering." That same angry, competitive mentality pervades two books by Maurice Franks: *How To Avoid Paying Alimony* and the more recent *Winning Custody*.

Perhaps the most chilling of all is *How To Win Custody*, by Louis Kiefer. Kiefer, a lawyer who won sole custody of his own children, offers helpful advice on using accusations of lesbianism as a bargaining technique, and on how to kidnap a child from the custodial mother.

[It is 1984, and] I am talking with an old college friend. It's a local call, for by happy coincidence we again live in the same town. The call, however, like many of our recent conversations, is not a happy one.

"I'm sorry, Marianne," she says, her voice straining to hide pain and panic. "I can't make it today. I know it's your birthday, and I feel just terrible."

I'm disappointed, too, but mostly I'm concerned. Gradually at first, then in a rush of tears, she explains. Her husband (who refuses to meet me) doesn't approve of me because I'm a lawyer and divorced and live in a co-op house in Cambridge. She never dares to visit me unless he's out of town, but this time she thought she'd slip off quietly between loads at the Laundromat. He guessed her plan somehow, smashed two glasses against the wall, and raced off in the car with their three-year-old daughter.

Days later, when the crisis is past, she calls me from work. "I want to leave him," she says, "but I'm afraid. He says he'll get custody of Jennifer, and I'll never see her any more. You know about these things, Marianne. Can he do that?"

My heart breaks for her, because I know the risk is serious. I cannot honestly tell her, no, your child is safe if only you will leave this dangerous man.

"In recent years, when women began to get 'uppity'—began seeking economic independence and reproductive rights," says psychiatrist Phyllis Chesler, author of *Mothers on Trial: The Battle for Children and Custody* (McGraw-Hill, 1986), "the deepest patriarchal response was to go for the kids. Because when you go for the children, that keeps women in marriages that are bad, keeps them at home afraid to pursue careers. They're afraid to 'break the rules' that have traditionally defined good mothers. In fact, however, they're at risk even if they *don't* break the rules.

Chesler's book, based upon hundreds of interviews with mothers, fathers, children, and professionals working with divorcing families, focuses in part upon an in-depth study of 60 mothers challenged for custody of their children between 1960 and 1981. The mothers studied had been married an average of nine years, had an average of two children, and had completed an average of three years of college. All the mothers had been primary caretakers of the children prior to the custody fight. Among the children's fathers, 87 percent had not been directly involved in child care before seeking custody, and 67 percent had not paid child support upon separations. Permanent custody was nonetheless awarded to 70 percent of the fathers.

In a legal climate in which male custody victories appear not to require actual prior involvement in child-raising, the potential for abuse is rife. While some men may in fact be involved in child-raising during marriage, the law does not require or even encourage them to do so. Worse yet, children can be used as pawns for bargaining or expressing anger. Thus, in Weitzman's study [only 13 percent of the fathers] actually sought physical custody of the children—but fully one third used custody threats to gain leverage in financial bargaining.

According to Nancy Polikoff, staff attorney of the Women's Legal Defense Fund, the recent advance in male custody rights at first seemed reasonable even to feminist advocates. "In the early 1970s," explains Polikoff, "we saw a trend away from assuming that the mother was always the caretaker of the children and should therefore be their custodian. That seemed fine. We assumed that courts would then make a gender-neutral inquiry into who had actually been caring for the children, and whoever it was, the mother or the father, would be more likely to get custody.

"Well, it hasn't turned out that way. Instead of replacing an assumption that the mother was caring for the children with a gender-neutral inquiry, we've instead seen the work of the child-raiser gradually devalued or ignored. Today the use of other factors to determine custody is flourishing. Courts look at financial status, the nicer home, even the new spouse the man is statistically more likely to have. Then, too, money generally buys the ability to litigate more effectively. In the end, the relationship between mother and child, the work that she's done raising the children, and the importance of continuity of care to the children is all but forgotten."

Why would judges and legislators, presumably concerned about child welfare, so easily disregard an involved mother's role in child-raising, favoring instead a financially dominant father? Why, for that matter, would millions of ordinary men turn their backs on their own children, allowing them to live in relative poverty? And why does our society overlook or even condone the inequities, almost as if we believed that women who leave (or fail to satisfy) men deserve to suffer?

In recent months, while speaking publicly about the child-support crisis, I have been besieged by the voices of angry men.

"I'm one of those Deadbeat Dads you keep talking about," says one man belligerently. (In fact, I never use that term.) "And I'll tell you why. She turns the kids against me. She uses this snide tone when I call on the phone, 'Oh, it's your dad again.' I figure I can't compete, so I just don't call *or* support."

"These women, they leave a guy and run off with another," argues another man, "and they think we'll pay for their kids?"

A middle-aged judge speaks to me scoldingly, like a father admonishing his errant child. "I've always taken care of my wife, but you ladies wanted to be liberated. Well, I guess you'll just have to live with the consequences."

It is easy to see viciousness in these comments, the hostile backlash of men losing control. And yet, I have to say honestly that I hear real pain in their voices, see real anguish in their eyes. Even their anger is understandable—it is just grossly misdirected.

Everyone—men and women—feels hurt and anger when a relationship ends.

But men have the social permission to act out their anger, and social encouragement to substitute expressions of control for true expressions of emotion. Undoubtedly, many men do feel cheated out of fatherhood and, more than that, out of the ability to be intimate. Yet that painful sense of isolation begins long before a divorce, and even long before the marriage. "What's all this talk about absent fathers?" asks a friend of mine, worrying about his own ability to father effectively. "I never knew my dad, and he lived with us my whole life."

The traditional social contract offered to men in our society is not much better than that traditionally offered to women. Be controlled and effective and a good breadwinner, men are told, and in return we'll let you rule the family. It's not emotionally sustaining even when it "works," because power and control are substituted for—and prevent—real intimacy and sharing.

Typically, as in Chesler's study, the men who fight the hardest and most cruelly tend to be those who lacked a positive emotional connection to the family *during* the marriage. Their rage is not so much because they fear losing important intimate relationships, but because they suspect they never truly had them, and may lack the capacity to develop them.

But if the anger is understandable, the destructive response cannot be justified. To understand the reasons is like understanding the reasons a batterer batters or a molester molests. At the bottom line, the violent behavior must stop.

There are available remedies—proposed policies that would promote equity and fairness while recognizing individual family differences. In custody disputes, WLDF's Polikoff and other commentators point to case law in West Virginia, Minnesota, Pennsylvania, and Oregon that offers a gender-neutral standard based on continuity of care to the children. If, in West Virginia or Minnesota, a mother has been the child's primary caregiver prior to divorce and is not unfit, there is a presumption in favor of retaining her as the custodian. If a fit father has fulfilled that role, he receives the presumption in his favor. In Pennsylvania and Oregon, while presumption is not the standard, positive consideration is given to the role of the primary caregiver.

(If child-raising responsibilities have truly been shared, of course, the parents may agree on joint custody. Studies show that parents who have shared child-raising during the marriage are the most likely to choose joint custody, and the most likely to make it work. Court-imposed joint custody, however, is the least likely to be successful, often creating conflict and inequity.)

Once custody is determined based on continuity of care and the best interests of the children, advocates note, financial arrangements should ensure that each new family unit achieves a standard of living equal to the other. This means first that property is divided to reflect the needs of all family members, so that, for example, a three-person family of mother and two children would receive a three-person share—not an amount equal or less than the father alone.

Similarly, alimony and child-support levels should be set to allow the children and their caretaker to enjoy the same standard of living as the noncustodial parent.

One excellent method of doing this is known as income equalization. Simply stated, standardized government cost-of-living charts are used to determine comparable incomes for a family of one, two, or more at any given standard of living. Total family income is then divided so that each family unit is at the same level. Yet despite the ready availability of the charts (and law review articles explaining their use), no state presently uses the income-equalization method.

Finally, since a court order is only a piece of paper until enforced, aggressive enforcement of support orders is needed. Recent federal legislation, the Child Support Enforcement Amendments of 1984 (see "Gazette," June, 1985), requires states to improve their mechanisms for child-support collection. Yet organized political pressure is needed on the state level—first, to ensure that the laws really are implemented; second, to see that these much-needed reforms are extended to alimony collection as well; finally, to urge the adoption of reasonable guidelines offering adequate support levels.

As the need for reform becomes ever more clear, women's activism on divorce equity is increasing. Just as we struggle for the freedom to choose or not choose men as partners, to marry or not to marry, and to have or not have children, we must also struggle to make those choices meaningful and safe. By insisting that our partings with men be free of oppression and coercion, we open the door to equality between women and men *within* relationships.

18

At a Welfare Hotel, Mothers Find Support in Weekly Talks

Sara Rimer

"I'm getting ready to walk away and leave them all here—the baby, too," the mother of four said in an agitated voice. "I can't take it. I tell you, I'm getting ready to crack some heads."

"You know what you do when you feel that way?" another mother said. "You talk to God."

"You get a babysitter," said another mother. "Then you go and find someone to talk to."

This was not just any group of women discussing the pressures of motherhood.

These women knew the mother of four was deadly serious because all of them had felt just as desperate at some point.

This was another weekly meeting of a group of mothers who are struggling to raise their children at the Martinique Hotel, a welfare hotel at Broadway and 32d Street that is crowded with 400 homeless families.

The meeting of the group, formed two years ago by the Hudson Guild, a 90-year-old Manhattan settlement house, is known as Coffee Hour. It has become an oasis of talk and understanding in a place where the first lesson a mother learns is to trust no one and where each week brings crises and continued stress—everything from sudden loss of food stamps to the inability to find an apartment within the welfare rent allotment. The women have become the closest thing to a community inside the Martinique.

"I met all my friends at Coffee Hour," said Azalee Green, the mother of five. "Coffee Hour is like a family."

Like many of the other women, Gloria Magriz said she had spent most of her first two months at the Martinique in her room with her three children, going out only to do errands.

"I was scared," Miss Magriz, 22 years old, said. "You have no friends when you come here. You can't trust people."

Coffee Hour, open to all women at the Martinique, helped bring her out of her room. "I listened to the other women," she said. "Their problems sounded bigger than mine. They had kids taken away from them. Or their husbands beat them, or they didn't have enough food so their kids went hungry."

Sometimes as many as 20 women come to Coffee Hour, sometimes only six or seven. Some bring their babies. Lately, they have been meeting huddled in their winter coats in the hotel's cold ballroom, warming themselves with coffee and cookies provided by the Hudson Guild. They keep talking despite constant interruptions—children running through the room, announcements that the ballroom is needed for the free lunch program.

"Such Survivors"

The group discussions are led by Evelyn Vega, a Hudson Guild social worker who offers counseling and referral services to families at the hotel. Each week, the women discuss a different topic from a list they have submitted. Suggestions include:

"How to help each other."

"How to understand my son's problems at school and home."

"How to get an apartment for my kids."

"How to love our family."

"These women are such survivors," Miss Vega said. "They love their children so much."

The women talk in sad, angry voices of the other mothers whom they watch giving up, escaping in drugs or simply leaving their children to fend for themselves. Last summer one mother died of a drug overdose. The women raised money to buy suits for her sons, 12 and 14 years old, to wear to her funeral.

Last month, an 18-year-old mother of three left her children, whose ages range from 3 months to 3 years. Another member of the group, Pat Stanley, is taking care of them in hopes their mother will return. Miss Stanley has three rooms for her own 11 children.

"I sympathize with her," Miss Stanley said. "I know what it is to be depressed. One time I got so depressed I didn't leave my apartment for 10 days."

Stigma of Hotel Life

At one meeting, a 19-year-old pregnant mother of two broke down. She said she felt too overwhelmed to accomplish the smallest task, like cleaning the rugs in her room. After the meeting, the other women cleaned her rugs.

One subject that comes up repeatedly is the stigma that comes with living in a welfare hotel. It is particularly hard on children, who are taunted for being "hotel kids." At a recent meeting, Miss Stanley said her 11-year-old son, who prides himself on being tough, had come home from school close to tears.

"His teacher made a remark about him being at the Martinique," she said. "She said, 'I heard about the robbing and mugging that goes on there.' "

Some of the Coffee Hour mothers have become role models for the others. One of them is Miss Green—"the mother of the Martinique," as some call her—whose efforts to transform her hotel room into a home are discussed in admiring tones.

A Makeshift Kitchen

The rooms at the Martinique don't come with cooking facilities, only small refrigerators. Dishes are washed in bathroom sinks. But Miss Green managed to convert her closet into a makeshift kitchen, with a hotplate and two nightstands pushed together for a counter.

"She's got her room so nice," said another Coffee Hour mother, Shirley Dingle. "She says, 'Why not fix it up? Who knows how long we're going to be here?' "

Inspired by her friend, Miss Dingle, 35, decorated the walls of her room with framed color photographs of her four children. With a string and a yellow curtain, she improvised a room divider for privacy.

Like the other families at the hotel, the mothers in the group have come to the Martinique through a variety of circumstances—burned out of their apartments, evicted, or forced to leave buildings that have been abandoned. Still others had to leave the overcrowded apartments of relatives with whom they were living.

"Give Each Other Strength"

When new families arrive, the women from Coffee Hour offer comfort and advice. "This is a neighborhood," Miss Green tells them. "There are good streets and bad streets, weak families and good families."

At a recent meeting, there was one newcomer, a woman with eight children, who said she had been evicted the week before from her apartment in Brooklyn. The other women explained Coffee Hour to her.

"It's a place where us ladies can get together and talk about our problems," Miss Dingle said.

"We give each other strength," Miss Stanley said.

"I'll be riding in the elevator and people say, 'You gotta be careful in here,' " the new woman told them. "I don't trust anyone. I won't loan anything to anyone—not even a cigarette."

The other women said they had felt that way, too. "But you got to remember the times when there are five days before your check comes," one said, "and you're digging through your ashtrays, looking for a cigarette. You can't make it alone in here."

19

Listening

Sey Chassler

One morning, about 20 years ago, my wife and I were arguing about whether or not I ever listened to her. It was one of those arguments that grow into passion and pain and, often, for me at least, into a kind of hysteria. This one became one of those that do not go away with the years. Suddenly, she threw something at me, and said: "From now on you do the shopping, plan the meals, take care of the house, everything. I'm through!"

I was standing in the kitchen looking at the shelves of food, at the oven, at the sink, at the refrigerator, at the cleaning utensils. At my wife.

My reaction was orgasmic. Somewhere inside of me there was screaming, hurting, a volcanic gush of tears flooded my head and broke down over me. I shook and sobbed. I was terrified. No matter what, I knew I could not handle the burden. I could not do my job and be responsible for the entire household. How could I get through a day dealing with personnel, budgets, manuscripts, art departments, circulation statistics, phone calls, people, agents, management, writers, and *at the same time* plan dinner for tonight and tomorrow night and breakfast and a dinner party Thursday night and shopping for it all and making sure the house is in good shape and the woman who cleans for us is there and on time and the laundry done and the children taken to the doctor, and the children taken care of? How could *any* one person do all that and stay sane? No one could do that properly. No one. Natalie simply watched me for a while. Finally she said: "Okay. Don't worry. I'll keep on doing it." She put on her coat and went to her office.

Despite her simple statement that she would go on doing it, I stood awhile telling myself that *no one* could do all of that. No one. There was a *click* in my head—and it dawned on me that *she* was doing it.

How invisible my wife's life was to me. How invisible to men women are.

Shortly afterward, in 1963 or 1964, not long after *The Feminine Mystique* was published, Betty Friedan and I were invited to speak to the nation's largest organization of home economists. As executive editor of *Redbook* magazine, I was asked to talk about the magazine's view of women. Betty was talking about the thesis of her book—that all American women were trapped in their homebound positions and that women's magazines, among others, put out propaganda to keep them trapped.

I had read *The Feminine Mystique*, of course, and felt I was fully prepared to answer it and, thereby, to defend not only *Redbook* from Friedan's attack but to defend American women, as well.

In mid-speech I proclaimed that, despite what Friedan had written, women, in this day and in this country, were free to be whatever they wished to be, that they were not children to be told what they might and might not do, that they could work at whatever profession they chose or whatever job, that they were free to be wives if they wished, and truck drivers if they wished, and mothers if they wished or homemakers if they wished. The list was growing longer and the speech was getting more and more impassioned in its proclamation of freedoms. I paused and waited for the applause. I had, after all, just proclaimed freedom throughout the land! I looked out at the audience. The hall was silent.

My pause became a dark empty cavern, and I could feel myself groping for a way out, wondering what had gone awry. I felt naked, stripped bare before 800 women. I could not understand what I had said that was wrong. Looking for comfort, I thought of my wife, and—*click!* I suddenly realized that my wife was a woman who was free to choose a career and *had*—but who also had delayed that career until her children—*her* children!—were in school. She was not as free as I thought, nor was any married woman.

While my enthusiasm had diminished, I went on with my speech. But whatever it was that had clicked in my head first in the kitchen and then in Kansas City, stayed there. And for a long time afterward, there were things going on in my head that I couldn't quite get hold of.

Whatever they were, I found myself listening for clicks in my head while thinking about, talking to, or dealing with women. And since I worked with more than 60 women every day and came home to my wife every night, I had a good deal of listening to do.

At home one night after dinner, I sat down to read the paper, as usual, while my wife went into the kitchen to do the dishes. I could see her in the kitchen. She looked happy, or at least not unhappy, there in the pretty kitchen she had designed—and she was probably appreciating the change of pace after a hard day as chief of service in a mental hospital dealing with a staff of three or four dozen employees and a hundred or more patients, some of whom threatened her from time to time. Yes, she was using the time well, since she had no hobbies to break the tension. I was feeling comfortably and happily married, when—*click!*—the view changed, and I saw a hardworking woman doing something she'd rather not be doing just now.

When my wife finished and sat down near me, I kissed her with a special tenderness, I thought. She didn't. As a matter of fact, she turned the other cheek. Something was going on in both our heads.

The next night *I* decided to do the dishes and she read the paper. At the sink, I began to think about male arrogance. Why did I have the choice of doing or not doing the dishes, while my wife did not? By the same token, why had she had to wait until our children were in school to exercise her "free" choice of working at her career? Our jobs were equally pressured and difficult (hers more harrowing than mine) and yet, if I chose to sit and read after dinner, I could. She could not, unless I decided she could by *offering* to do the dishes. My definition of freedom was based on a white male conception: the notion that because I am free, because I can make choices, anyone can make choices. I was defining "anyone" in my terms, in masculine terms. I am anyone, unqualified. She is anyone, gender female. So you can take your tender kisses and shove them.

I felt I had caught the edge of an insight about the condition of women and while I wanted to, I found I couldn't discuss it with men; it made them uneasy and defensive. They'd fight off the conversation. They'd say things like "But that's the way it is supposed to be, Sey. Forget it!" After a while, I began to feel like one of those people who carry signs in the street announcing the end of the world. Pretty soon I got defensive, too—and my questions produced terrific dinner-table fights with other male guests. The women almost always remained silent, seeming to enjoy watching the men wrestle. The men were convinced that I was a nut. And several, including my father, accused me of "coming out for women," because in my job as editor of a women's magazine that would be "smart" and "profitable."

I certainly couldn't talk to any woman directly, because I was embarrassed. I didn't believe women would tell me the truth—and, more important, I was not going to let them know I was worried or thinking about the matter or afraid to find the answer.

If you are one of those men who feel trapped by women, who think they are fine for sex but interfere with living, all of the above may not be very clear to you. Maybe the following will set some clicks off for you.

The other day I was reading *The Intimate Male*, by Linda Levine, ACSW, and Lonnie Barbach, Ph.D. It is one of those books in which men reveal all their sexual secrets, fantasies, and so on. It is supposed to help us understand each other, I guess. All I ever get out of such books is the discovery that other guys and I share the same fantasies. Well, in this one, I read about a guy who likes his wife to walk around the house without any underwear under her skirt. Innocent enough, you guess? But what he *really* likes is to "lay on the floor while my wife does the dishes, and look up her dress"!

I told this story to a couple of men I know, and they thought it beat all hell how he got his wife to walk around without her pants on. They loved it. Hey, what a crazy guy!

But wait. Let's try it from the wife's point of view: here is this nice woman who has spent her day working somewhere, either out on a job of some kind or taking care of this romantic fellow's house. She is about as beat as he is by the end of the day and maybe she'll be ready for sex later, but not right now. Right now her hands are full of dirty dishes and wet garbage, so what can she be thinking of? *He* doesn't have to do anything but work his eyeballs.

Everyone to her or his own kink, of course. But it isn't kink that is going on here. What is going on here is a neat exercise in power. The man on the floor is proving to his wife and to himself that he is the boss. He can take his pleasure while she works. Of course, she can tell him to knock it off and keep her pants on, but that is going to make him very unhappy. Unhappy enough maybe to go out for a few beers until she comes to her senses. "This freaking wife of mine," he'll say to the guys in the bar, "every time I want it, she's doing the dishes or too tired or something."

So the chances are she doesn't tell him to knock it off, because the implied threat of walking out for a while gains the husband the privilege of turning his wife into a dancing girl while she's doing the dishes. In other words, here is a neat form of blackmail—"Do as I say, or you'll get my mad side and everyone will know I married a cold little bitch." This is known as dominance—and you should have heard a click in your head.

The episode on the kitchen floor is, admittedly, a bit unusual. That sort of thing doesn't go on with most people. Here's one that is more familiar. As reported in *The Wall Street Journal* in a story on sex discrimination in law firms, King & Spalding of Atlanta had a company picnic last summer. Initially proposed for the festivities was a "wet T-shirt" contest, but, in the end, the firm merely decided to hold a bathing-suit competition. It was open only to the company's women summer associates. A third-year law student from Harvard University won. While awarding her the prize, a partner of the firm said, "She has the body we'd like to see more of." King & Spalding is no small company. Among its clients are Coca-Cola Company, Cox Broadcasting Corporation, and General Motors.

The question here is: why would a Harvard law student parade around in a bathing suit for a bunch of rowdy male lawyers? It's easy to say she was looking for a job with a good firm. Since the bathing-suit competition incident, King & Spalding has promised it will not practice sex discrimination, and the student who won the contest has agreed to join the firm. But the question remains: why would she enter such a contest?

I refer you to the woman in the kitchen, above. Why did she take her pants off?

Dominance. Male dominance. Someone calls the shots, someone else does as she is told.

What would you say to your boss if he announced that he was thinking of having a wet jockstrap contest at the company picnic? Or if your best girl asked you to take your pants off, while you crawled under the car to have a look at the manifold? What would you say? If your wife asked you to stay home with the baby or to meet the plumber or to do the shopping or to clean the toilet bowl some day, what would you say?

Click?

My wife and I have been married 41 years. We think of ourselves as being happily married—and we are. But the dominance is there. It means that in my relationship with my wife, I am almost totally the boss. When we have a discussion (that's marital-ese for argument), more often than not it is I who declare when the end of it arrives. If we make a plan together and she does most of the work on the plan, it is given to me for *approval*. If I do most of the work on the plan, I submit it to her for her *information*. If she agrees to the plan, she'll say "Good, should we do it?" If I agree to the plan, I'll say, "Good, let's go." That doesn't mean that I make all the decisions, control all the funds, make all the choices, talk louder than she does. I don't have to. It simply means that I do not have to ask my wife for permission to do anything. Whether she does or says anything about it or not, everything my wife does is to a large extent qualified by what I think or will think. In effect, she must ask my permission. What's more, as husband, I seem—no matter how I try to avoid it— to assign all the jobs in our family. In effect, I win all the arguments–even the ones we don't have. That's emotional dominance—and it means that everything that occurs between us, everything we do together, is monitored by me.

Once during a lecture tour I was talking to undergraduates at the University of Indiana about the Women's Movement and how important it is. One of the women, a senior, asked a question and then she said: "I don't want to get married when I graduate. I want to be someone." *Click.*

That statement haunts me. I never had to say anything like that. I had always thought I would get married *and* be somebody. What's more, I took it for granted that my wife would be responsible for the family in addition to her job. I would love and care for my children, but I wouldn't have to deal with their phone calls at the office. They'd call my wife at the office. That's what mommies are for, aren't they? No one had to tell the children that. No one had to tell me that. No one had to tell my wife that. We all *knew* it. And everyone knew that men not only had freedom of choice but freedom to grant permission to women to make choices.

I had freedom, yes, but as my children were growing up, as I looked at my family, I began to struggle with a barely conscious knowledge that the happy group of people with whom I lived—my two sons, my daughter, my wife—were feeling uneasy when I was around. They shifted stiffly, muffled their voices, stifled their laughter when I arrived in their midst. They could feel the dominant grown male arrive. I didn't want that. It was simply there—where I was.

As the years went by and my consciousness grew, I began to recall for examination not only those uneasy days, but really angry ones. What was I angry about? I was angry that I was not always my wife's center of attention. I had been brought up thinking I would be. That made our early days very rough, indeed. I was angry when our first son was born. Those were the days when women had babies and men simply were proud, frightened, and prepared to pay the bills.

The birth of my first child was traumatic, as it was with each of the others. Beyond admiring the growing child in my wife's body, I played virtually no part in any of their births. As each child was about to be born, I got to drive my wife to the hospital. I was kept in the waiting room for expectant fathers. I could read and smoke and bite my nails. No one came to tell me anything. The movies had told me childbirth is painful, dangerous, life-threatening for a woman. I stood in the corner of the waiting room—all three times—fearful, out of touch with whatever dark things were happening in an operating room somewhere above me, sick with wanting to be near my wife.

In the evening before my second son was born, it was extremely hot, and the nurses sent me home to await his arrival. Nervous and feeling abandoned, I took a shower with an electric fan whirring in the bathroom. As I reached for the towel, I stuck my fingers into the metal blades of the fan. I screamed for my wife and cursed that she was not there. I raced around looking for bandages, found a handkerchief, wrapped it around my fingers, shoved a months-old condom on them to stem the flow of blood, dressed, ran to a doctor down the street, was stitched up, and finally rushed off to the hospital—to wait. And he was born. But I didn't get to see him right away.

It was always the same: when my first son was born, they didn't let me see him for a while. A nurse simply came and told me to be proud. "It's a boy!" she said. I had to ask if my wife was all right. I had to ask when I would see our baby. After a half hour or so, they took me up to a nursery window and pointed to a bundle in a tiny basket. They took me to see my wife and let me kiss her. They sent me away. They did the same with our second son. They did the same with my daughter. Only, they didn't say, "Be proud," they said, "You have a beautiful little girl this time!" I was proud. But they did not let me use my love, touch my world.

I was angry. I felt left out, put off, unable to feel entirely that I, too, had had a baby, had given (*given*) birth to a child—just as my wife had. I think sometimes that the anger of those days has carried into all of our lives. I, in some kind of crazy partnership with my past, my traditions, put it there—in the lives of my wife, and of our children.

Now, as I look back at the time of the births, when I was kept out, given no choice over urgent and vital matters affecting my life, I understand how it feels to be a woman and have no choices—how it feels not to be heard. I have finally discovered what it is to be like the undergraduate who wanted to be someone. She, too, I realize now was in a waiting room waiting to be proud—and knowing her pride would be controlled by others.

Last year, after a board meeting of one of the nation's best-known women's organizations, I was sitting with a group of women who are legislators, corporate executives, lawyers, broadcasters—big shots. One of them said: "We've been at it for about twenty years now, and we've made real progress—why then does the pain still linger?" Another answered simply: "Because the men still keep the lid on."

Click.

The Women's Movement has made some remarkable changes in our lives, but it hasn't changed the position of the male much at all. Men still make the moves. They are the ones who, in their own good time, move in. And in their own good time, move out. Someone makes the rules, someone else does as she is told.

About eight years ago, my wife suggested—finally—that I must be hard of hearing because I never seemed to hear what she said, even though I answered all questions and conducted real conversations with her. She made me promise to see an ear doctor. I did. He found nothing wrong. When I told him that this whole idea was my wife's, he sent me home. "Most of my male patients," he said, "are here on the advice of their wives." I laughed. But . . . *click!*

We don't have to listen. As men we simply are in charge. It comes with the territory. Popeye sings "I am what I am." God said the same thing to Moses in the wilderness. Male images. They're built into us. Images of dominance.

I got to be the editor of *Redbook* because I was the second in line. There was at least one woman on the staff who could have done the job as well or better than I, but the president of the company had, in his time, passed over many women—and this time there was no exception. While I knew about editing and writing and pictures, I didn't know beans about fiction or recipes and fashion and cosmetics and all of those things; still, having the responsibility and the authority, I had to act as if I did. I was forced, therefore, to listen very carefully to the women who worked with me and whose help I needed. And, listening, I learned to talk with them and talking with them I began to hear them.

Most of the editors in the company were women, most of the sales and business people were men. The men could never figure out how to talk to the women. They seemed to think that I had learned some secrets about women, and they'd stop me in the halls and say things like "How can I tell Anne such and such about this advertising account?" And I'd say, "Just tell her." And they'd say, "But can you say that to a woman? Will she understand?"

Click.

In the beginning, I found myself using my position as a male. I *talked* to the men; I gave orders to the women.

By the same token, the men and women dealt with me differently. In an argument, a man would feel comfortable telling me I was wrong and, if necessary, call me a damn fool. Two hours later we'd be working together without grudge. But most women would give silent assent and do as they were told. They obeyed. The stronger ones *would* call me stupid or whatever they needed to, but they (and I) would hurt for days. They had breached the rules. Some would come up to apologize, and we both would wind up with tears in our eyes. Dominance. When we learned to work with each other as equals, we learned to be angry as equals—and to respect each other, to love each other as equals.

And yet, while I began to feel some measure of equality with the women, I could not, for a very long time, figure out how to achieve the kind of camaraderie, the palship, the mutual attachment to team, the soldierly equality of action, that men feel for each other. I could never feel comfortable putting my arm around a woman as we walked down a corridor talking business or conspiring against some agent or corporate plan—as I would with a man. Out of sheer good feeling and admiration for a job well done and a fight well fought, there were days when I wanted to throw my arms around women I worked with—as I would with a man—but I never really felt fully free to.

While it was hard to achieve camaraderie, as we worked hand-in-hand, eye-to-eye, shoulder-to-shoulder, mind-to-mind warm, erotic, sexy—yet not sexy—feelings would begin to flow. While they were mutual, they were not feelings to be turned into acts of sex. They were feelings that came out of—and went into—the intensity of the work at hand.

What were they like, these erotic feelings? They were like the feelings of a locker room after a game played hard and won. They felt like sweat. They felt like heroism. They felt like bodies helping bodies. They felt like those urges that make it all right to smack a guy on the ass in congratulation and gratitude, to throw your arms around him and hug him for making the winning point. And they felt like the secret admiration of his body—because he was a hero—as he stood in the shower. How marvelous to feel that way about a woman—and not want to go to bed with her! Just to admire and love her for being with you—and for helping you to play the game. I recommend the feeling. And I think, perhaps, in prehistory when female and male hunted and gathered side-by-side in the frightening wilderness—sharing their fears, their losses, their gains and their triumphs equally—it must have been this way. In the time before the gods. In the time before I-am-what-I-am.

I was telling a woman friend about all of this. She asked: "Do you deal with your women colleagues and friends differently from the way you deal with your wife?"

Click.

I was sitting with a man friend, when, in relation to nothing in particular, he said: "Guys get to be heroes. Girls get to be cheerleaders. Guys get to be dashing womanizers, great studs. Women get to be sluts."

Click.

A lot of us men think of these things and we hurt when we do. And a lot of us—most of us—simply don't think of these things. Or we think of them as something that will go away—the complaints from women will go away, as they always seem to.

Still, as men, we recognize Freud's question: "Good God, what do women *want?*"

To be heard.

My 89-year-old mother, married 65 years to my 89-year-old father, says to him, "Someday you'll let me talk when I want to."

On the grimy wall of the 23rd Street station of the New York subway a woman's hand has written: "Women Lib gonna get your girl!"

In H.G. Wells's book, *The Passionate Friends*, Mary writes to Stephen: "Womankind isn't human, it's reduced human."

Margaret Mead, in a conversation, remarks that in American households, the man decides whether the toilet paper leads from the top of the roll or the bottom of the roll.

Will men ever appreciate fully what women are saying?

I don't think I will ever, fully. No matter what clicks in my head.

The world belongs to men. It is completely dominated by us—and by our images.

What men see when they look out and about are creatures very like themselves—in charge of everything. What women see when they look out and about is that the creatures in charge of everything are *unlike* themselves.

If you are a man, think of a world, your world, in which for everything you own or do or think you are accountable to women. Women are presidents, bankers, governors, door holders, traffic cops, airline pilots, bosses, supervisors, landlords. Shakespeare. The whole structure is completely dominated by women. Your doctor, your lawyer, your priest, minister, rabbi are women. The figure on the cross is a woman. God is a woman. Every authoritative voice and every authoritative image is the image and voice of women: Buddha, Mohammed, Moses, Matthew, Luke, Paul, the guy who does the voice-over on the commercial and Ben Franklin—all are women. So are Goliath and David. So are the Supreme Court, the tax collector, the head of the CIA, the mechanic who fixes your transmission, the editor of your daily newspaper, the doctor who handed you to your mother. Jack the Giant Killer. Walter Mondale. St. Patrick. Ronald Reagan is a woman. Walter Cronkite is a woman. George Steinbrenner is a woman. Think of such a world. The Pope is a woman. JR is a woman. Casper Weinberger. Think of yourself in such a world. Think of your father in it. Think of *him* as a woman. Think about it.

Don't just brush it off, for Mary's sake—think about it.

Suggestions for Further Reading

R. M. Brown: *RubyFruit Jungle*, Bantam, New York, 1977.

J. David (ed): *The American Indian: The First Victim*, William Morrow & Co., New York, 1972.

J. Gwaltney: *Drylongso: A Self-Portrait of Black America*, Vintage Books, New York, 1981.

A. Haley: *The Autobiography of Malcolm X*, Grove Press, New York, 1964.

M. H. Kingston: *The Woman Warrior*, Vintage Books, New York, 1977.

A. Moody: *Coming of Age in Mississippi*, Dell Publishing Co., New York, 1968.

C. Moraga & G. Anzaldua (eds.): *This Bridge Called My Back: Writings by Radical Women of Color*, Kitchen Table: Women of Color Press, New York, 1981.

G. Naylor: *The Women of Brewster Place*, Penguin Books, New York, 1983.

E. Rivera: *Family Installments: Memories of Growing Up Hispanic*, Penguin Books, 1983.

L. B. Rubin: *Intimate Strangers: Men and Women Together*, Harper and Row, New York, 1983.

L. B. Rubin: *Worlds of Pain: Life in the Working Class Family*, Basic Books, New York, 1976.

A. K. Shulman: *Memories of an Ex-Prom Queen*, Knopf, New York, 1972.

L. M. Silko: *Ceremony*, New American Library, New York, 1977.

B. Smith (ed): *Home Girls: A Black Feminist Anthology*, Kitchen Table: Women of Color Press, New York, 1983.

S. Turkle: *Working*, Avon Books, New York, 1972.

Chinese Historical Society of Southern California: *Linking Our Lives: Chinese American Women of Los Angeles*, Chinese Historical Society of Southern California, Los Angeles, California, 1984.

How It Happened: The Legal Status of Women and People of Color in the United States

It is clear that being born a woman, a person of color, or both, in addition to being poor, makes it far more likely that an individual will have less education, inferior health care, a lower standard of living, and a diminished set of aspirations compared with those who are born white, wealthy, and male. How does this happen? Is the lack of equality of opportunity and condition documented in the first three parts of this book accidental and aberrant? Or is it the inevitable result of a system designed to perpetuate the privileges of wealthy, white males? To answer these questions, we must turn to history.

But whose history shall we study? History can be written from many perspectives. The lives of "great men" will vary greatly depending upon whether their biographers are their mothers, their peers, their wives, their lovers, their children, or their servants. And there is no basis for singling out one point of view as more correct or appropriate than any other, for each tells us part of the history of the person. Furthermore, we might ask why history should be the history of "great men" exclusively. What about the lives of valets, dancers, carpenters, teachers, and mothers? Aren't their experiences essential to reconstructing the past? Can history omit the lives of the majority of people in a society and still claim to give us an accurate account of the past?

We can even question who decides what counts as history. In the past, the war diaries of generals were kept as prized historical documents, whereas diaries written by women giving an account of their daily lives were ignored or discounted. What makes one invaluable and the other irrelevant? Many historians have chosen to call one particular point of view *history* and have used it to evaluate the relevance and worth of all else—this point of view being that of white men of property. It is this point of view that has permeated our American history texts and classes. The greatest secret kept by many traditional history texts was that women and people of color and working people created the wealth and culture of this country.

History, we are told, involves collecting and studying facts. But what counts as a "fact," and who decides which facts are important? Whose interests are served or furthered by these decisions? For many years, one of the first "facts" that grade-school children learned was that Christopher Columbus discovered America. And yet this "history" is neither clear nor incontrovertible. It is a piece of the past examined from the point of view of white Europeans; it is to their interest to persuade others to believe it, since this "fact" undermines the claims of others. American Indians might well ask how Columbus could have discovered America in 1492 if they had already been living here for thousands of years. Teaching children that bit of fiction about Columbus served to render Native Americans invisible and thus tacitly excused or denied the genocide carried out by European settlers.

During the contemporary period, many new approaches to history have arisen to remedy the omissions and distortions of the past. Women's history, Black history, gay history, ethnic history, labor history, and others all propose to transform traditional history so that it more accurately reflects the reality of people's lives past and present.

Part IV does not attempt to provide a comprehensive history of the American Republic since its beginning. Rather, it is designed to trace the legal status of people of color and white and Black women since the first Europeans came to this land. This is done by reproducing legal documents that highlight developments in legal status. In a few cases, these legal documents are supplemented with materials that help paint a clearer picture of the issues involved or their implications.

Much is left out by adopting this framework for our study. Most significantly, the actual political and social movements that brought about the changes in the legal realm are omitted. For this reason, students are urged to supplement their study of the legal documents with the rich accounts of social history from the "Suggested Readings" listed at the end of Part IV.

However, the legal documents themselves are fascinating. They make it possible for us to reduce hundreds of years of history to a manageable size. We can thus form a picture of the rights and status of many so-called minority groups in this country, a picture that contrasts sharply with the one usually offered in high-school social-studies classes. Most importantly, the documents can help us answer the question raised by material in the first three parts of this text: how did it happen that all women and all people of color came to have such limited access to power and opportunity?

The readings here show that, from the country's inception, the laws and institutions of the United States were designed to create and maintain the privileges of wealthy white males. The discrimination documented in the early parts of this book is no accident. It has a long and deliberate history. Understanding this history is essential if we are to create a more just and democratic society.

On July 4, 1776, the thirteen colonies set forth a declaration of independence from Great Britain. In that famous document, the founders of the Republic explained their reasons for separating from the homeland and expressed their hopes for the new republic. In lines that are rightly famous and often quoted, the signatories proclaimed that "all Men are created equal, that they are endowed by their Creator with certain unalienable Rights, that among these are Life, Liberty and the Pursuit of Happiness." They went on to assert that "to secure these Rights, Governments are instituted among Men, deriving their just Powers from the Consent of the Governed." When these words were written, however, a large portion of the population of the United States had no legal rights whatsoever. American Indians, women, indentured servants, poor white men who did not own property, and, of course, slaves could not vote, nor were they free to exercise their liberty or pursue their happiness in the same way that white men with property could. When the authors of the Declaration of Independence proclaimed that all men were created equal and endowed with unalienable rights, they meant "men" quite literally and white men specifically. Negro slaves, as it turned out, were worth "three fifths of all other Persons," a figure stipulated in Article I, Section 2, of the United States Constitution. This section of the Constitution, which is often referred to as the "three-fifths compromise," undertook to establish how slaves would be counted for the purposes of determining taxes as well as for calculating representation of the states in Congress.

Faced with the need for an enormous work force to cultivate the land, the European settlers first tried to enslave the American Indian population. Later, the settlers brought over large numbers of "indentured workers" from Europe. These workers were poor white men, women, and children, some serving prison sentences at home, who were expected to work in the colonies for a certain period of time and then receive their freedom. When neither of these populations proved suitable, the settlers began importing African Negroes to serve their purposes.

Records show that the first African Negroes were brought to this country as early as 1526. Initially, the Negroes appear to have had the same status as indentured servants, but the laws reflect a fairly rapid distinction between the two groups. Maryland law made this distinction as early as 1640; Massachusetts legally recognized slavery in 1641; Virginia passed a law making Negroes slaves for life in 1661; and so it went until the number of slaves grew to roughly 600,000 at the time of the signing of the Declaration of Independence.[1] Numerous legal documents, such as An Act for the Better Ordering and Governing of Negroes and Slaves passed in South Carolina in 1712 and excerpted in Selection 1, prescribed the existence of the slaves, as did the acts modeled on An Act Prohibiting the Teaching of Slaves to Read, a North Carolina statute reprinted here in Selection 3.

When the early European settlers came to this country, there were approximately 2.5 million Native Americans living on the land that was to become the

United States. These Indian peoples were divided among numerous separate and autonomous tribes, each with its own highly developed culture and history. The white man quickly lumped these diverse peoples into a single and inferior category, "Indians," and set about destroying their culture and seizing their lands. The Indian Removal Act of 1830 (Selection 4) was fairly typical of the kinds of laws that were passed to carry out the appropriation of Indian lands. Believing the Indians to be inherently inferior to whites, the United States government had no hesitation about legislating the removal of the Indians from valuable ancestral lands to ever more remote and barren reservations. The dissolution of the Indian tribal system was further advanced by the General Allotment Act (Dawes Act) of 1887, which divided tribal landholdings among individual Indians and thereby successfully undermined the tribal system and the culture of which it was a part. In addition, this act opened up lands within the reservation area for purchase by the United States government, which then made those lands available to white settlers for homesteading (see Selection 16). Many supporters of the allotment policy, who were considered "friends" of the Indians, argued that the benefits of individual ownership would have a "civilizing effect" on them.[2] Instead, it ensured a life of unrelenting poverty for most because it was usually impossible for a family to derive subsistence from the use of a single plot of land and without the support of the tribal community.

While John Adams was involved in writing the Declaration of Independence, his wife, Abigail Adams, took him to task for failing to accord women the same rights and privileges as men. "I cannot say that you are very generous to the ladies; for whilst you are proclaiming peace and good will to men, emancipating all nations, you insist upon retaining an absolute power over wives."[3] Although law and custom consistently treated women as if they were physically and mentally inferior to men, the reality of women's lives was very different. Black female slaves were forced to perform the same inhuman fieldwork as Black male slaves and were expected to do so even in the final weeks of pregnancy. They were routinely beaten and abused without regard for the supposed biological fragility of the female sex. White women settlers gave birth to large numbers of children, ten and twelve being quite common and as many as twenty births not being unusual. And they did so in addition to working side by side with men to perform all those duties necessary to survival in a new and unfamiliar environment. When her husband died, a woman often assumed his responsibilities as well. It was not until well into the 1800s, primarily as a result of changes brought about by the Industrial Revolution, that significant class differences began to affect the lives and work of white women.

As women, both Black and white, became increasingly active in the antislavery movement during the 1800s, many noticed certain similarities between the legal status of women and the legal status of slaves. Participants at the first women's rights convention held at Seneca Falls, New York, in 1848 listed women's grievances and specified their demands. At this time, married women were regarded as property of their husbands and had no direct legal control over their own wages, their property, or even their children. The Declaration of Sentiments issued at Seneca Falls was modeled on the Declaration of Independence in the hope that men would extend the declaration's rights to women. It is reprinted in this part along with selections from a variety of sources from that period that reflect the most typical male responses to women's demands for the vote and other rights. Similar emotional attacks are still used today to ridicule and then dismiss contemporary feminist demands.

The abysmal legal status of women and people of color in the United States during the nineteenth century is graphically documented in a series of court decisions reproduced in this part. In *People v. Hall*, 1854, the California Supreme Court decided that a California statute barring Indians and Negroes from testifying in court cases involving whites also applied to Chinese Americans. The judges asserted that the Chinese are "a race of people whom nature has marked as inferior, and who are incapable of progress or intellectual development beyond a certain point." The extent of anti-Chinese feeling in parts of the United States can be further inferred from portions of the California Constitution adopted in 1876 and included in this part.

In a more famous case, *Dred Scott v. Sanford*, 1857, the United States Supreme Court was asked to decide whether Dred Scott, a Negro, was a citizen of the United States with the rights that that implied. Scott, a slave who had been taken from Missouri, a slave state, into the free state of Illinois for a period of time, argued that because he was free and had been born in the United States, he was therefore a citizen. The Court ruled that this was not the case and, using reasoning that strongly parallels *People v. Hall*, offered a survey of United States law and custom to show that Negroes were never considered a part of the people of the United States. In *Bradwell v. Illinois*, 1873, the Supreme Court ruled that women could not practice law and used the opportunity to carefully distinguish the rights and prerogatives of women from those of men. The Court maintained that "civil law, as well as nature herself, has always recognized a wide difference in the respective spheres and destinies of man and woman" and went on to argue that women belong in the "domestic sphere."

During the period in which these and other court cases were brought, the United States moved toward and ultimately fought a bloody civil war. Allegedly fought "to free the slaves," much more was at stake. The Civil War reflected a struggle to the death between the Southern aristocracy, whose wealth was based on land and whose power rested on a kind of feudal economic-political order, and the Northern capitalists, who came into being by virtue of the Industrial Revolution and who wished to restructure the nation's economic-political institutions to better serve the needs of the new industrial order. Chief among these needs was a large and mobile work force for the factories in the North. Hundreds of thousands of soldiers died in the bloody conflict, while other men purchased army deferments and used the war years to amass tremendous personal wealth. On the Confederate side, men who owned fifty or more slaves were exempted from serving in the army, while wealthy Northern men were able to purchase deferments from the Union for the sum of $300. Among those who purchased deferments and went on to become millionaires as a result of war profiteering were John D. Rockefeller, Andrew Carnegie, J. Pierpont Morgan, Philip Armour, James Mellon, and Jay Gould.[4]

In September 1862, President Abraham Lincoln signed the Emancipation Proclamation (Selection 9) as part of his efforts to bring the Civil War to an end by
forcing the Southern states to concede. It did not free all slaves; it freed only those in
states or parts of states in rebellion against the federal government. Only in September 1865, after the conclusion of the war, were all slaves freed by the Thirteenth
Amendment (Selection 10). However, Southern whites did not yield their privileges
easily. Immediately after the war, the Southern states began to pass laws known as
"The Black Codes," which attempted to reestablish the relations of slavery. Some of
these codes are described in this part in a selection written by W. E. B. Du Bois.

In the face of such efforts to deny the rights of citizenship to Black men,
Congress passed the Fourteenth Amendment (Selection 10) in July 1868. This
amendment, which continues to play a major role in contemporary legal battles
over discrimination, includes a number of important provisions. It explicitly extended citizenship to all those born or naturalized in the United States and guarantees all citizens "due process" and "equal protection" of the law. In addition, it
cancelled all debts incurred by the Confederacy in its unsuccessful rebellion while
recognizing the validity of the debts incurred by the federal government. This meant
that wealthy Southerners who had extended large sums of money or credit to the
Confederacy would lose it, while wealthy Northern industrialists would be paid.

Southern resistance to extending the rights and privileges of citizenship to Black
men persisted, and the Southern states used all their powers, including unbridled
terror and violence, to subvert the intent of the Thirteenth and Fourteenth Amendments. The Fifteenth Amendment (Selection 10), which explicitly granted the vote
to Black men, was passed in 1870 but it was received by the Southern states with as
little enthusiasm as had greeted the Thirteenth and Fourteenth Amendments.

As the abolitionist movement grew and the Civil War became inevitable, many
women's rights activists, also active in the struggle to free the slaves, argued that the
push for women's rights should temporarily defer to the issue of slavery. In fact, after
February 1861, no women's rights conventions were held until the end of the war.
Although Black and white women had long worked together in both movements, the
question of which struggle took precedence created serious splits among women's
rights activists, including such strong Black allies as Frederick Douglass and Sojourner Truth. Some argued that the evils of slavery were so great that they took
precedence over the legal discrimination experienced by middle-class white women.
They resented attempts by Elizabeth Cady Stanton and others to equate the condition
of white women with that of Negro slaves and argued, moreover, that the women's
rights movement had never been concerned with the extraordinary suffering of Black
women or the special needs of working women. The explicitly racist appeals made by
some white women activists as they sought white men's support for women's suffrage
did nothing to bridge this schism. While Black men received the vote in 1868, at least
on paper, women would have to continue their fight until the passage of the Nineteenth Amendment (Selection 18) in 1920. As a result, many women and Blacks saw
each other as adversaries or obstacles in their struggle for legal equality, deflecting

their attention from the privileged white men who provoked the conflict and whose power was reinforced by it.

One special cause for bitterness was the Fourteenth Amendment's reference to *male* inhabitants and the right to vote. This was the first time that voting rights had explicitly been rendered gender-specific. The Fourteenth Amendment was tested in 1874 by *Minor v. Happersett* (Selection 13), in which the court was asked to rule directly on the question of whether women had the vote by virtue of their being citizens of the United States. The Court ruled unanimously that women did *not* have the vote, arguing that women, like criminals and mental defectives, could legitimately be denied the vote by the states.[5] In a somewhat similar case, *Elk v. Wilkens*, 1884 (Selection 15), John Elk, an American Indian who had left his tribe and lived among whites, argued that he was a citizen by virtue of the Fourteenth Amendment and should not be denied the right to vote by the state of Nebraska. The Supreme Court ruled that neither the Fourteenth nor Fifteenth Amendments applied to Elk. Native Americans became citizens of the United States three years later, under one of the provisions of the Dawes Act of 1887.

Unsuccessful in their attempts to reinstate some form of forced servitude by passage of "The Black Codes," Southern states began to legalize the separation of the races in all aspects of public and private life. In *Plessy v. Ferguson*, 1896, (Selection 17), the Supreme Court was asked to rule on whether segregation by race in public facilities violated the Thirteenth and Fourteenth Amendments. In a ruling that was to cruelly affect several generations of Black Americans, the Supreme Court ruled that restricting Negroes to the use of "separate but equal" public accommodations did not deny them equal protection of the law. This decision remained in effect for almost sixty years until *Brown v. Board of Education of Topeka*, 1954 (Selection 20). In the historic *Brown* decision, the Court ruled, in effect, that "separate" could not possibly be "equal." Nonetheless, abolishing segregation on paper was one thing; actually bringing about the integration of public facilities was another. The integration of public schools, housing, and employment in both the North and the South has been a long and often bloody struggle that continues to this day.

The racist attitudes toward Chinese Americans, reflected in the nineteenth-century California statutes and constitution as we have already seen, extended toward Japanese Americans as well. This racism erupted during the twentieth century after the bombing of Pearl Harbor by Japan on December 7, 1941. Anti-Japanese feelings ran so high that President Franklin Roosevelt issued an executive order allowing the military to designate "military areas" from which it could then exclude any persons it chose. On March 2, 1942, the entire West Coast was designated as such an area, and within a few months, everyone of Japanese ancestry (defined as those having as little as one-eighth Japanese blood) was evacuated. More than 110,000 people of Japanese descent, most of them American citizens, were forced to leave their homes and jobs and to spend the war years in so-called relocation camps behind barbed wire.[6] Although the United States was also at war with Germany, no such barbaric treatment was afforded German Americans. The military evacuation of Japanese Americans was challenged in *Korematsu* v. *United States*, 1944. In its decision, excerpted in Selection 19, the Supreme Court upheld the forced evacuation.

The twentieth century has seen the growth of large and diverse movements for race and gender justice. These movements precipitated the creation of a number of commissions and government agencies, which were to research and enforce equal treatment for people of color and women; the passage of a number of statutes to this end; and a series of Supreme Court decisions in the area. For women, one of the most significant Court decisions of the recent past was *Roe* v. *Wade*, 1973 (Selection 21), which, for the first time, gave women the right to terminate pregnancy by abortion. Rather than affirming a woman's right to control her body, however, the *Roe* decision is based upon the right to privacy. The impact of *Roe* was significantly blunted by *Harris* v. *McRae*, 1980, in which the Court ruled that the right to privacy did not require public funding of medically necessary abortions for women who could not afford them. In practice, this meant that white middle-class women who chose abortion could exercise their right but that many poor white women and women of color could not. The single biggest defeat for the Women's Movement of this period was the failure to pass the much misunderstood Equal Rights Amendment, which is reproduced in Selection 24.

The most serious issues facing proponents of civil rights today involve the ways to create a society of equals in light of our country's history of institutionalized racism and sexism, as well as the long-term effects of slavery and discrimination. The final selections in this part discuss key affirmative-action cases of the contemporary period in the context of the ongoing debate over goals, quotas, and so-called reverse discrimination.

NOTES

1. W. Z. Foster: *The Negro People in American History*, International Publishers, New York, 1954, p. 37.

2. United States Commission on Civil Rights: *Indian Tribes: A Continuing Quest for Survival*, a report of the United States Commission on Civil Rights, June 1981, p. 34.

3. Letter to John Adams, May 7, 1776.

4. H. Wasserman: *Harvey Wasserman's History of the United States*, Harper & Row, New York, 1975, p. 3.

5. E. Flexner: *Century of Struggle*, Harvard University Press, Cambridge, Massachusetts, 1976, p. 172.

6. R. E. Cushman & R. F. Cushman: *Cases in Constitutional Law*, Appleton-Century-Crofts, New York, 1958, p. 127.

An Act for the Better Ordering and Governing of Negroes and Slaves, South Carolina, 1712

Colonial America had a role for the Negro. But the presence of a servile population, presumably of inferior stock, made it necessary to adopt measures of control. As might be expected, the southern colonies had the most highly developed codes governing Negroes. In 1712 South Carolina passed "An Act for the better ordering and governing of Negroes and Slaves." This comprehensive measure served as a model for slave codes in the South during the colonial and national periods. Eight of its thirty-five sections are reproduced below.

Whereas, the plantations and estates of this province cannot be well and sufficiently managed and brought into use, without the labor and service of negroes and other slaves; and forasmuch as the said negroes and other slaves brought unto the people of this Province for that purpose, are of barbarous, wild, savage natures, and such as renders them wholly unqualified to be governed by the laws, customs, and practices of this Province; but that it is absolutely necessary, that such other constitutions, laws and orders, should in this Province be made and enacted, for the good regulating and ordering of them, as may restrain the disorders, rapines and inhumanity, to which they are naturally prone and inclined, and may also tend to the safety and security of the people of this Province and their estates; to which purpose,

I. *Be it therefore enacted*, by his Excellency, William, Lord Craven, Palatine, and the rest of the true and absolute Lords and Proprietors of this Province, by and with the advice and consent of the rest of the members of the General Assembly, now met at Charlestown, for the South-west part of this Province, and by the authority of the same, That all negroes, mulatoes, mustizoes or Indians, which at any time heretofore have been sold, or now are held or taken to be, or hereafter shall be bought and sold for slaves, are hereby declared slaves; and they, and their children, are hereby made and declared slaves, to all intents and purposes; excepting all such negroes, mulatoes, mustizoes or Indians, which heretofore have been, or hereafter shall be, for some particular merit, made and declared free, either by the Governor and council of this Province, pursuant to any Act or law of this Province, or by their respective owners or masters; and also, excepting all such negroes, mulatoes, mustizoes or Indians, as can prove they ought not to be sold for slaves. And in case any negro, mulatoe, mustizoe or Indian, doth lay claim to his or her freedom, upon all or any of the said accounts, the same shall be finally heard and determined by the Governor and council of this Province.

II. And for the better ordering and governing of negroes and all other slaves in this Province, *Be it enacted* by the authority aforesaid, That no master, mistress, overseer, or other person whatsoever, that hath the care and charge of any negro or slave, shall give their negroes and other slaves leave, on Sundays, hollidays, or any other time, to go out of their plantations, except such negro or other slave as usually wait upon them at home or abroad, or wearing a livery; and every other negro or slave that shall be taken hereafter out of his master's plantation, without a ticket, or leave in writing, from his master or mistress, or some other person by his or her appointment, or some white person in the company of such slave, to give an account of his business, shall be whipped; and every person who shall not (when in his power) apprehend every negro or other slave which he shall see out of his master's plantation, without leave as aforesaid, and after apprehended, shall neglect to punish him by moderate whipping, shall forfeit twenty shillings, the one half to the poor, to be paid to the church wardens of the Parish where such forfeiture shall become due, and the other half to him that will inform for the same, within one week after such neglect; and that no slave may make further or other use of any one ticket than was intended by him that granted the same, every ticket shall particularly mention the name of every slave employed in the particular business, and to what place they are sent, and what time they return; and if any person shall presume to give any negro or slave a ticket in the name of his master or mistress, without his or her consent, such person so doing shall forfeit the sum of twenty shillings; one half to the poor, to be disposed of as aforesaid, the other half to the person injured, that will complain against the person offending, within one week after the offence committed. And for the better security of all such persons that shall endeavor to take any runaway, or shall examine any slave for his ticket, passing to and from his master's plantation, it is hereby declared lawful for any white person to beat, maim or assult, and if such negro or slave cannot otherwise be taken, to kill him, who small refuse to shew his ticket, or, by running away or resistance, shall endeavor to avoid being apprehended or taken.

III. *And be it further enacted* by the authority aforesaid, That every master, mistress or overseer of a family in this Province, shall cause all his negro houses to be searched diligently and effectually, once every fourteen days, for fugitive and runaway slaves, guns, swords, clubs, and any other mischievous weapons, and finding any, to take them away, and cause them to be secured; as also, for clothes, goods, and any other things and commodities that are not given them by their master, mistress, commander or overseer, and honestly come by; and in whose custody they find any thing of that kind, and suspect or know to be stolen goods, the same they shall seize and take into their custody, and a full and ample description of the particulars thereof, in writing, within ten days after the discovery thereof, either to the provost marshall, or to the clerk of the parish for the time being, who is hereby required to receive the same, and to enter upon it the day of its receipt, and the particulars to file and keep to himself; and the clerk shall set upon the posts of the church door, and the provost marshall upon the usual public places, or places of notice, a short brief, that such lost goods are found; whereby, any person that hath lost his goods may the better come to the knowledge where they are; and the owner going to the marshall or clerk, and proving, by marks or otherwise, that the goods lost belong to him, and paying twelve pence for the entry and declaration of the same, if the marshall or clerk be convinced that any part of the goods certified by him to be found, appertains to the party inquiring, he is to direct the said party inquiring to the place and party where the goods be, who is hereby required to make restitution of what is in being to the true owner; and every master, mistress or overseer, as also the provost marshall or clerk, neglecting his duty in any the particulars aforesaid, for every neglect shall forfeit twenty shillings.

IV. And for the more effectual detecting and punishing such persons that trade with any slave for stolen goods, *Be it further enacted* by the authority aforesaid, That where any person shall be suspected to trade as aforesaid, any justice of the peace shall have power to take from him suspected, sufficient recognizance, not to trade with any slave contrary to the laws of this Province; and if it shall afterwards appear to any of the justices of the peace, that such person hath, or hath had, or shipped off, any goods, suspected to be unlawfully come by, it shall be lawful for such justice of the peace to oblige the person to appear at the next general sessions, who shall there be obliged to make reasonable proof, of whom he brought, or how he came by, the said goods, and unless he do it, his recognizance shall be forfeited. . . .

VII. And *whereas*, great numbers of slaves which do not dwell in Charlestown, on Sundays and holidays resort thither, to drink, quarrel, fight, curse and swear, and profane the Sabbath, and using and carrying of clubs and other mischievous weapons, resorting in great companies together, which may give them an opportunity of executing any wicked designs and purposes, to the damage and prejudice of the inhabitants of this Province; for the prevention whereof, *Be it enacted* by the authority aforesaid, That all and every the constables of Charlestown, separately on every Sunday, and the holidays at Christmas, Easter and Whitsonside, together with so many men as each constable shall think necessary to accompany him, which he is hereby empowered for that end to press, under the penalty of twenty shillings to the person that shall disobey him, shall, together with such persons, go through all or any the streets, and also, round about Charlestown, and as much further on the neck as they shall be informed or have reason to suspect any meeting or concourse of any such negroes or slaves to be at that time, and to enter into any house, at Charlestown, or elsewhere, to search for such slaves, and as many of them as they can apprehend, shall cause to be publicly whipped in Charlestown, and then to be delivered to the marshall, who for every slave so whipped and delivered to him by the constable, shall pay the constable five shillings, which five shillings shall be repaid the said marshall by the owner or head of that family to which the said negro or slave doth belong, together with such other charges as shall become due to him for keeping runaway slaves; and the marshall shall in all respects keep and dispose of such slave as if the same was delivered to him as a runaway, under the same penalties and forfeiture as hereafter in that case is provided; and every constable of Charlestown which shall neglect or refuse to make search as aforesaid, for every such neglect shall forefit the sum of twenty shillings. . . .

IX. *And be it further enacted* by the authority aforesaid, That upon complaint made to any justice of the peace, of any heinous or grievous crime, committed by any slave or slaves, as murder, burglary, robbery, burning of houses, or any lesser crimes, as killing or stealing any meat or other cattle, maiming one the other, stealing of fowls, provisions, or such like trespasses or injuries, the said justice shall issue out his warrant for apprehending the offender or offenders, and for all persons to come before him that can give evidence; and if upon examination, it probably appeareth, that the apprehended person is guilty, he shall commit him or them to prison, or immediately proceed to tryal of the said slave or slaves, according to the form hereafter specified, or take security for his or their forthcoming, as the case shall require, and also to certify to the justice next to him, the said cause, and to require him, by virtue of this Act, to associate himself to him, which said justice is hereby required to do, and they so associated, are to issue their summons to three sufficient freeholders, acquainting them with the matter, and appointing them a day, hour and place, when and where the same shall be heard and determined, at which day, hour and place, the said justices and freeholders shall cause the offenders and evidences to come before them, and if they, on hearing the matter, the said freeholders being by the said justices first sworn to judge uprightly and according to evidence, and diligently weighing and examining all evidences, proofs and testimonies (and in case of murder only, if on violent presumption and circumstances), they shall find such negro or other slave or slaves guilty thereof, they shall give sentence of death, if the crime by law deserve the same, and forthwith by their warrant cause immediate execution to be done, by the common or any other executioner, in such manner as they shall think fit, the kind of death to be inflicted to be left to their judgment and discretion; and if the crime committed shall not deserve death, they shall then condemn and adjudge the criminal or criminals to any other punishment, but not extending to limb or disabling him, without a particular law directing such punishment, and shall forthwith order execution to be done accordingly.

X. And in regard great mischiefs daily happen by petty larcenies committed by negroes and slaves of this Province, *Be it further enacted* by the authority aforesaid, That if any negro or other slave shall hereafter steal or destroy any goods, chattels, or provisions whatsoever, of any other person than his master or mistress, being under the value of twelve pence, every negro or other slave so offending, and being brought before some justice of the peace of this Province, upon complaint of the party injured, and shall be adjudged guilty by confession, proof, or probable circumstances, such negro or slave so offending, excepting children, whose punishment is left wholly to the discretion of the said justice, shall be adjudged by such justice to be publicly and severely whipped, not exceeding forty lashes; and if such negro or other slave punished as aforesaid, be afterwards, by two justices of the peace, found guilty of the like crimes, he or they, for such his or their second offence, shall either have one of his ears cut off, or be branded in the forehead with a hot iron, that the mark thereof may remain; and if after such punishment, such negro or slave for his third offence, shall have his nose slit; and if such negro or other slave, after the third time as aforesaid, be accused of petty larceny, or of any of the offences before mentioned, such negro or other slave shall be tried in such manner as those accused of murder, burglary, *etc.* are before by this Act provided for to be tried, and in case they shall be found guilty a fourth time, of any the offences before mentioned, then such negro or other slave shall be adjudged to suffer death, or other punishment, as the said justices shall think fitting; and any judgment given for the first offence, shall be a sufficient conviction for the first offence; and any after judgment after the first judgment, shall be a sufficient conviction to bring the offender within the penalty of the second offence, and so for inflicting the rest of the punishments; and in case the said justices and freeholders, and any or either of them, shall neglect or refuse to perform the duties by this Act required of them, they shall severally, for such their defaults, forfeit the sum of twenty-five pounds. . . .

XII. *And it is further enacted* by the authority aforesaid, That if any negroes or other slaves shall make mutiny or insurrection, or rise in rebellion against the authority and government of this Province, or shall make preparation of arms, powder, bullets or offensive weapons, in order to carry on such mutiny or insurrection, or shall hold any counsel or conspiracy for raising such mutiny, insurrection or rebellion, the offenders shall be tried by two justices of the peace and three freeholders, associated together as before expressed in case of murder, burglary. *etc.*, who are hereby empowered and required to try the said slaves so offending, and inflict death, or any other punishment, upon the offenders, and forthwith by their warrant cause execution to be done, by the common or any other executioner, in such manner as they shall think fitting; and if any person shall make away or conceal any negro or negroes, or other slave or slaves, suspected to be guilty of the beforementioned crimes, and not upon demand bring forth the suspected offender or offenders, such person shall forfeit for every negro or slave so concealed or made away, the sum of fifty pounds; *Provided, nevertheless*, that when and as often as any of the beforementioned crimes shall be committed by more than one negro, that shall deserve death, that then and in all such cases, if the Governor and council of this Province shall think fitting, and accordingly shall order, that only one or more of the said criminals should suffer death as exemplary, and the rest to be returned to the owners, that then, the owners of the negroes so offending, shall bear proportionably the loss of the said negro or negroes so put to death, as shall be allotted them by the said justices and freeholders; and if any person shall refuse his part so allotted him, that then, and in all such cases, the said justices and freeholders are hereby required to issue out their warrant of distress upon the goods and chattels of the person so refusing, and shall cause the same to be sold by public outcry, to satisfy the said money so allotted him to pay, and to return the overplus, if any be, to the owner; *Provided, nevertheless,* that the part allotted for any person to pay for his part or proportion of the negro or negroes so put to death, shall not exceed one sixth part of his negro or negroes so excused and pardoned; and in case that shall not be sufficient to satisfy for the negro or negroes that shall be put to death, that the remaining sum shall be paid out of the public treasury of this Province. *

2

The "Three-fifths Compromise":
The U.S. Constitution, Article I, Section 2

One of the major debates in the Constitutional Convention hinged on the use of slaves in computing taxes and fixing representation. Southern delegates held that slaves should be computed in determining representation in the House, but that they should not be counted in determining a state's share of the direct tax burden. The northern delegates' point of view was exactly the opposite. A compromise was reached whereby three fifths of the slaves were to be counted in apportionment of representation and in direct taxes among the states. Thus the South was victorious in obtaining representation for her slaves, even though delegate Luther Martin might rail that the Constitution was an insult to the Deity "who views with equal eye the poor African slave and his American master." The "three-fifths compromise" appears in Article I, Section 2.

Representatives and direct Taxes shall be apportioned among the several States which may be included within this Union, according to their respective Numbers, which shall be determined by adding to the whole Number of free Persons, including those bound to Service for a Term of Years, and excluding Indians not taxed, three fifths of all other Persons.

*Thomas Cooper and David J. McCord, eds., *Statutes at Large of South Carolina* (10 vols., Columbia, 1836–1841), VII, 352–357.

3

An Act Prohibiting the Teaching of Slaves to Read*

To keep the slaves in hand it was deemed necessary to keep them innocent of the printed page. Otherwise they might read abolitionist newspapers that were smuggled in, become dissatisfied, forge passes, or simply know too much. Hence most states passed laws prohibiting anyone from teaching slaves to read or write. The North Carolina statute was typical.

An Act to Prevent All Persons from Teaching Slaves to Read or Write, the Use of Figures Excepted

Whereas the teaching of slaves to read and write, has a tendency to excite dissatisfaction in their minds, and to produce insurrection and rebellion, to the manifest injury of the citizens of this State:

Therefore,

Be it enacted by the General Assembly of the State of North Carolina, and it is hereby enacted by the authority of the same, That any free person, who shall hereafter teach, or attempt to teach, any slave within the State to read or write, the use of figures excepted, or shall give or sell to such slave or slaves any books or pamphlets, shall be liable to indictment in any court of record in this State having jurisdiction thereof, and upon conviction, shall, at the discretion of the court, if a white man or woman, be fined not less than one hundred dollars, nor more than two hundred dollars, or imprisoned; and if a free person of color, shall be fined, imprisoned, or whipped, at the discretion of the court, not exceeding thirty-nine lashes, nor less than twenty lashes.

II. *Be it further enacted,* That if any slave shall hereafter teach, or attempt to teach, any other slave to read or write, the use of figures excepted, he or she may be carried before any justice of the peace, and on conviction thereof, shall be sentenced to receive thirty-nine lashes on his or her bare back.

III. *Be it further enacted,* That the judges of the Superior Courts and the justices of the County Courts shall give this act in charge to the grand juries of their respective counties.

*Acts Passed by the General Assembly of the State of North Carolina at the Session of 1830–1831 (Raleigh, 1831), 11.

4

The Indian Removal Act, May 28, 1830

The Indian Removal Act of May 28, 1830, authorized the president to negotiate an exchange of lands in the west for those held by Indian tribes in any state or territory. To this end, Congress appropriated $500,000. "Thousands of Indian people, almost the entire population that had existed in the southeastern United States were moved west. . . . Although removal was theoretically based upon consent of those removed, it is clear that the eastern tribes were coerced."*

5

Declaration of Sentiments and Resolutions, Seneca Falls Convention, 1848

The Declaration of Sentiments, adopted in July 1848 at Seneca Falls, New York, at the first woman's-rights convention, is the most famous document in the history of feminism. Like its model, the Declaration of Independence, it contains a bill of particulars. Some people at the meeting thought the inclusion of disfranchisement in the list of grievances would discredit the entire movement, and when the resolutions accompanying the Declaration were put to a vote, the one calling for the suffrage was the only one that did not pass unanimously. But it did pass and thus inaugurated the woman-suffrage movement in the United States.

*Indian Tribes: A Continuing Quest for Survival (A Report of the United States Civil Rights Commission, June 1981).

Declaration of Sentiments

When, in the course of human events, it becomes necessary for one portion of the family of man to assume among the people of the earth a position different from that which they have hitherto occupied, but one to which the laws of nature and of nature's God entitle them, a decent respect to the opinions of mankind requires that they should declare the causes that impel them to such a course.

We hold these truths to be self-evident: that all men and women are created equal; that they are endowed by their Creator with certain inalienable rights; that among these are life, liberty, and the pursuit of happiness; that to secure these rights governments are instituted, deriving their just powers from the consent of the governed. Whenever any form of government becomes destructive of these ends, it is the right of those who suffer from it to refuse allegiance to it, and to insist upon the institution of a new government, laying its foundation on such principles, and organizing its powers in such form, as to them shall seem most likely to effect their safety and happiness. Prudence, indeed, will dictate that governments long established should not be changed for light and transient causes; and accordingly all experience hath shown that mankind are more disposed to suffer, while evils are sufferable, than to right themselves by abolishing the forms to which they were accustomed. But when a long train of abuses and usurpations, pursuing invariably the same object, evinces a design to reduce them under absolute depotism, it is their duty to throw off such government, and to provide new guards for their future security. Such has been the patient sufferance of the women under this government, and such is now the necessity which constrains them to demand the equal station to which they are entitled.

The history of mankind is a history of repeated injuries and usurpations on the part of man toward woman, having in direct object the establishment of an absolute tyranny over her. To prove this, let facts be submitted to a candid world.

He has never permitted her to exercise her inalienable right to the elective franchise.

He has compelled her to submit to laws, in the formation of which she had no voice.

He has withheld from her rights which are given to the most ignorant and degraded men—both natives and foreigners.

Having deprived her of this first right of a citizen, the elective franchise, thereby leaving her without representation in the halls of legislation, he has oppressed her on all sides.

He has made her, if married, in the eye of the law, civilly dead.

He has taken from her all right in property, even to the wages she earns.

He has made her, morally, an irresponsible being, as she can commit many crimes with impunity, provided they be done in the presence of her husband. In the covenant of marriage, she is compelled to promise obedience to her husband, he becoming, to all intents and purposes, her master—the law giving him power to deprive her of her liberty, and to administer chastisement.

He has so framed the laws of divorce, as to what shall be the proper causes, and in case of separation, to whom the guardianship of the children shall be given, as to be wholly regardless of the happiness of women—the law, in all cases, going upon the false supposition of the supremacy of man, and giving all power into his hands.

After depriving her of all rights as a married woman, if single, and the owner of property, he has taxed her to support a government which recognizes her only when her property can be made profitable to it.

He has monopolized nearly all the profitable employments, and from those she is permitted to follow, she receives but a scanty remuneration. He closes against her all the avenues to wealth and distinction which he considers most honorable to himself. As a teacher of theology, medicine, or law, she is not known.

He has denied her the facilities for obtaining a thorough education, all colleges being closed against her.

He allows her in Church, as well as State, but a subordinate position, claiming Apostolic authority for her exclusion from the ministry, and, with some exceptions, from any public participation in the affairs of the Church.

He has created a false public sentiment by giving to the world a different code of morals for men and women, by which moral delinquencies which exclude women from society, are not only tolerated, but deemed of little account in man.

He has usurped the prerogative of Jehovah himself, claiming it as his right to assign for her a sphere of action, when that belongs to her conscience and to her God.

He has endeavored, in every way that he could, to destroy her confidence in her own powers, to lessen her self-respect, and to make her willing to lead a dependent and abject life.

Now, in view of this entire disfranchisement of one-half the people of this country, their social and religious degradation—in view of the unjust laws above mentioned, and because women do feel themselves aggrieved, oppressed, and fraudulently deprived of their most sacred rights, we insist that they have immediate admission to all the rights and privileges which belong to them as citizens of the United States.

In entering upon the great work before us, we anticipate no small amount of misconception, misrepresentation, and ridicule; but we shall use every instrumentality within our power to effect our object. We shall employ agents, circulate tracts, petition the State and National legislatures, and endeavor to enlist the pulpit and the press in our behalf. We hope this Convention will be followed by a series of Conventions embracing every part of the country.

Resolutions

WHEREAS, The great precept of nature is conceded to be, that "man shall pursue his own true and substantial happiness." Blackstone in his Commentaries remarks, that this law of Nature being coeval with mankind, and dictated by God himself, is of course superior in obligation to any other. It is binding over all the globe, in all countries and at all times; no human laws are of any validity if contrary to this, and such of them as are valid, derive all their force, and all their validity, and all their authority, mediately and immediately, from this original; therefore,

Resolved, That such laws as conflict, in any way, with the true and substantial happiness of woman, are contrary to the great precept of nature and of no validity, for this is "superior in obligation to any other."

Resolved, That all laws which prevent woman from occupying such a station in society as her conscience shall dictate, or which place her in a position inferior to that of man, are contrary to the great precept of nature, and therefore of no force or authority.

Resolved, That woman is man's equal—was intended to be so by the Creator, and the highest good of the race demands that she should be recognized as such.

Resolved, That the women of this country ought to be enlightened in regard to the laws under which they live, that they may no longer publish their degradation by declaring themselves satisfied with their present position, nor their ignorance, by asserting that they have all the rights they want.

Resolved, That inasmuch as man, while claiming for himself intellectual superiority, does accord to woman moral superiority, it is pre-eminently his duty to encourage her to speak and teach, as she has an opportunity, in all religious assemblies.

Resolved, That the same amount of virtue, delicacy, and refinement of behavior that is required of woman in the social state, should also be required of man, and the same transgressions should be visited with equal severity on both man and woman.

Resolved, That the objection of indelicacy and impropriety, which is so often brought against woman when she addresses a public audience, comes with a very ill-grace from those who encourage, by their attendance, her appearance on the stage, in the concert, or in feats of the circus.

Resolved, That woman has too long rested satisfied in the circumscribed limits which corrupt customs and a perverted application of the Scriptures have marked out for her, and that it is time she should move in the enlarged sphere which her great Creator has assigned her.

Resolved, That it is the duty of the women of this country to secure to themselves their sacred right to the elective franchise.

Resolved, That the equality of human rights results necessarily from the fact of the identity of the race in capabilities and responsibilities.

Resolved, therefore, That, being invested by the Creator with the same capabilities, and the same consciousness of responsibility for their exercise, it is demonstrably the right and duty of woman, equally with man, to promote every righteous cause by every righteous means; and especially in regard to the great subjects of morals and religion, it is self-evidently her right to participate with her brother in teaching them, both in private and in public, by writing and by speaking, by any instrumentalities proper to be used, and in any assemblies proper to be held; and this being a self-evident truth growing out of the divinely implanted principles of human nature, any custom or authority adverse to it, whether modern or wearing the hoary sanction of antiquity, is to be regarded as a self-evident falsehood, and at war with mankind.

[All the above resolutions had been drafted by Elizabeth Cady Stanton. At the last session of the convention Lucretia Mott offered the following, which, along with all the other resolutions except the ninth, was adopted unanimously.—*Ed.*]

Resolved, That the speedy success of our cause depends upon the zealous and untiring efforts of both men and women, for the overthrow of the monopoly of the pulpit, and for the securing to woman an equal participation with men in the various trades, professions, and commerce.

⑥

The Antisuffragists: *Selected Papers, 1852–1887*

Editorial, New York *Herald* (1852)*

The farce at Syracuse has been played out. . . .

Who are these women? What do they want? What are the motives that impel them to this course of action? The *dramatis personae* of the farce enacted at Syracuse present a curious conglomeration of both sexes. Some of them are old maids, whose personal charms were never very attractive, and who have been sadly slighted by the masculine gender in general; some of them women who have been badly mated, whose own temper, or their husbands', has made life anything but agreeable to them, and they are therefore down upon the whole of the opposite sex; some, having so much of the virago in their disposition, that nature appears to have made a mistake in their gender—mannish women, like hens that crow; some of boundless vanity and egotism, who believe that they are superior in intellectual ability to "all the world and the rest of mankind," and delight to see their speeches and addresses in print; and man shall be consigned to his proper sphere—nursing the babies,

*"The Woman's Rights Convention—The Last Act of the Drama," editorial, New York *Herald*, September 12, 1852.

washing the dishes, mending stockings, and sweeping the house. This is "the good time coming." Besides the classes we have enumerated, there is a class of wild enthusiasts and visionaries—very sincere, but very mad—having the same vein as the fanatical Abolitionists, and the majority, if not all of them, being, in point of fact, deeply imbued with the anti-slavery sentiment. Of the male sex who attend these Conventions for the purpose of taking part in them, the majority are hen-pecked husbands, and all of them ought to wear petticoats. . . .

How did woman first become subject to man as she now is all over the world? By her nature, her sex, just as the negro is and always will be, to the end of time, inferior to the white race, and, therefore, doomed to subjection; but happier than she would be in any other condition, just because it is the law of her nature. The women themselves would not have this law reversed. . . .

What do the leaders of the Woman's Rights Convention want? They want to vote, and to hustle with the rowdies at the polls. They want to be members of Congress, and in the heat of debate to subject themselves to coarse jests and indecent language. . . . They want to fill all other posts which men are ambitious to occupy—to be lawyers, doctors, captains of vessels, and generals in the field. How funny it would sound in the newspapers, that Lucy Stone, pleading a cause, took suddenly ill in the pains of parturition, and perhaps gave birth to a fine bouncing boy in court! Or that Rev. Antoinette Brown was arrested in the middle of her sermon in the pulpit from the same cause, and presented a "pledge" to her husband and the congregation; or, that Dr. Harriot K. Hunt, while attending a gentleman patient for a fit of the gout or *fistula in ano*, found it necessary to send for a doctor, there and then, and to be delivered of a man or woman child—perhaps twins. A similar event might happen on the floor of Congress, in a storm at sea, or in the raging tempest of battle, and then what is to become of the woman legislator?

New York State Legislative Report (1856)*

Mr. Foote, from the Judiciary Committee, made a report on Women's rights that set the whole House in roars of laughter:

"The Committee is composed of married and single gentlemen. The bachelors on the Committee, with becoming diffidence, having left the subject pretty much to the married gentlemen, they have considered it with the aid of the light they have before them and the experience married life has given them. Thus aided, they are enabled to state that the ladies always have the best place and choicest titbit at the table. They have the best seat in the cars, carriages, and sleighs; the warmest place in the winter, and the coolest place in the summer. They have their choice on which side of the bed they will lie, front or back. A lady's dress costs three times as

*This Report on Woman's Rights, made to the New York State Legislature and concerning a petition for political equality for women, was printed in an Albany paper in March 1856.

much as that of a gentleman; and, at the present time, with the prevailing fashion, one lady occupies three times as much space in the world as a gentleman.

"It has thus appeared to the married gentlemen of your Committee, being a majority (the bachelors being silent for the reason mentioned, and also probably for the further reason that they are still suitors for the favors of the gentler sex), that, if there is any inequality or oppression in the case, the gentlemen are the sufferers. They, however, have presented no petitions for redress; having, doubtless, made up their minds to yield to an inevitable destiny. . . ."

Orestes A. Brownson, The Woman Question (1869 and 1873)*

The conclusive objection to the political enfranchisement of women is, that it would weaken and finally break up and destroy the Christian family. The social unit is the family, not the individual; and the greatest danger to American society is, that we are rapidly becoming a nation of isolated individuals, without family ties or affections. The family has already been much weakened, and is fast disappearing. We have broken away from the old homestead, have lost the restraining and purifying associations that gathered around it, and live away from home in hotels and boarding-houses. We are daily losing the faith, the virtues, the habits, and the manners without which the family cannot be sustained; and when the family goes, the nation goes too, or ceases to be worth preserving. . . .

Extend now to women suffrage and eligibility; give them the political right to vote and to be voted for; render it feasible for them to enter the arena of political strife, to become canvassers in elections and candidates for office, and what remains of family union will soon be dissolved. The wife may espouse one political party, and the husband another, and it may well happen that the husband and wife may be rival candidates for the same office, and one or the other doomed to the mortification of defeat. Will the husband like to see his wife enter the lists against him, and triumph over him? Will the wife, fired with political ambition for place or power, be pleased to see her own husband enter the lists against her, and succeed at her expense? Will political rivalry and the passions it never fails to engender increase the mutual affection of husband and wife for each other, and promote domestic union and peace, or will it not carry into the bosom of the family all the strife, discord, anger, and division of the political canvass? . . .

Woman was created to be a wife and a mother; that is her destiny. To that destiny all her instincts point, and for it nature has specially qualified her. Her

*The following document consists of two articles by Orestes A. Brownson: "The Woman Question. Article I [from the *Catholic World*, May 1869]," in Henry F. Brownson, ed., *The Works of Orestes A. Brownson*, XVIII (Detroit, 1885), 388–89; and "The Woman Question. Article II [a review of Horace Bushnell, *Women's Suffrage: The Reform against Nature* (New York, 1869), from *Brownson's Quarterly Review* for October 1873]," in Henry F. Brownson, *op. cit.*, p. 403.

proper sphere is home, and her proper function is the care of the household, to manage a family, to take care of children, and attend to their early training. For this she is endowed with patience, endurance, passive courage, quick sensibilities, a sympathetic nature, and great executive and administrative ability. She was born to be a queen in her own household, and to make home cheerful, bright, and happy.

We do not believe women, unless we acknowledge individual exceptions, are fit to have their own head. The most degraded of the savage tribes are those in which women rule, and descent is reckoned from the mother instead of the father. Revelation asserts, and universal experience proves that the man is the head of the woman, and that the woman is for the man, not the man for the woman; and his greatest error, as well as the primal curse of society is that he abdicates his headship, and allows himself to be governed, we might almost say, deprived of his reason, by woman. It was through the seductions of the woman, herself seduced by the serpent, that man fell, and brought sin and all our woe into the world. She has all the qualities that fit her to be a help-meet of man, to be the mother of his children, to be their nurse, their early instructress, their guardian, their life-long friend; to be his companion, his comforter, his consoler in sorrow, his friend in trouble, his ministering angel in sickness; but as an independent existence, free to follow her own fancies and vague longings, her own ambition and natural love of power, without masculine direction or control, she is out of her element, and a social anomaly, sometimes a hideous monster, which men seldom are, excepting through a woman's influence. This is no excuse for men, but it proves that women need a head, and the restraint of father, husband, or the priest of God.

Remarks of Senator George G. Vest in Congress (1887)*

Mr. VEST. . . . If this Government, which is based on the intelligence of the people, shall ever be destroyed it will be by injudicious, immature, or corrupt suffrage. If the ship of state launched by our fathers shall ever be destroyed, it will be by striking the rock of universal, unprepared suffrage. . . .

The Senator who last spoke on this question refers to the successful experiment in regard to woman suffrage in the Territories of Wyoming and Washington. Mr. President, it is not upon the plains of the sparsely settled Territories of the West that woman suffrage can be tested. Suffrage in the rural districts and sparsely settled regions of this country must from the very nature of things remain pure when corrupt everywhere else. The danger of corrupt suffrage is in the cities, and those masses of population to which civilization tends everywhere in all history. Whilst the country has been pure and patriotic, cities have been the first cancers to appear upon the body-politic in all ages of the world.

*The following remarks of Senator George G. Vest (Democrat, Missouri) may be found in the *Congressional Record*, 49th Congress, 2d Session, January 25, 1887, p. 986.

Wyoming Territory! Washington Territory! Where are their large cities? Where are the localities in those Territories where the strain upon popular government must come? The Senator from New Hampshire [Henry W. Blair—*Ed.*], who is so conspicuous in this movement, appalled the country some months since by his ghastly array of illiteracy in the Southern States. . . . That Senator proposes now to double, and more than double, that illiteracy. He proposes now to give the negro women of the South this right of suffrage, utterly unprepared as they are for it.

In a convention some two years and a half ago in the city of Louisville an intelligent negro from the South said the negro men could not vote the Democratic ticket because the women would not live with them if they did. The negro men go out in the hotels and upon the railroad cars. They go to the cities and by attrition they wear away the prejudice of race; but the women remain at home, and their emotional natures aggregate and compound the race-prejudice, and when suffrage is given them what must be the result? . . .

I pity the man who can consider any question affecting the influence of woman with the cold, dry logic of business. What man can, without aversion, turn from the blessed memory of that dear old grandmother, or the gentle words and caressing hand of that dear blessed mother gone to the unknown world, to face in its stead the idea of a female justice of the peace or township constable? For my part I want when I go to my home—when I turn from the arena where man contends with man for what we call the prizes of this paltry world—I want to go back, not to be received in the masculine embrace of some female ward politician, but to the earnest, loving look and touch of a true woman. I want to go back to the jurisdiction of the wife, the mother; and instead of a lecture upon finance or the tariff, or upon the construction of the Constitution, I want those blessed, loving details of domestic life and domestic love.

. . . I speak now respecting women as a sex. I believe that they are better than men, but I do not believe they are adapted to the political work of this world. I do not believe that the Great Intelligence ever intended them to invade the sphere of work given to men, tearing down and destroying all the best influences for which God has intended them.

The great evil in this country to-day is in emotional suffrage. The great danger to-day is in excitable suffrage. If the voters of this country could think always coolly, and if they could deliberate, if they could go by judgment and not by passion, our institutions would survive forever, eternal as the foundations of the continent itself; but massed together, subject to the excitements of mobs and of these terrible political contests that come upon us from year to year under the autonomy of our Government, what would be the result if suffrage were given to the women of the United States?

Women are essentially emotional. It is no disparagement to them they are so. It is no more insulting to say that women are emotional than to say that they are delicately constructed physically and unfitted to become soldiers or workmen under the sterner, harder pursuits of life.

What we want in this country is to avoid emotional suffrage, and what we need is to put more logic into public affairs and less feeling. There are spheres in which feeling should be paramount. There are kingdoms in which the heart should reign supreme. That kingdom belongs to woman. The realm of sentiment, the realm of love, the realm of the gentler and the holier and kindlier attributes that make the name of wife, mother, and sister next to that of God himself.

I would not, and I say it deliberately, degrade woman by giving her the right of suffrage. I mean the word in its full signification, because I believe that woman as she is to-day, the queen of the home and of hearts, is above the political collisions of this world, and should always be kept above them. . . .

It is said that the suffrage is to be given to enlarge the sphere of woman's influence. Mr. President, it would destroy her influence. It would take her down from that pedestal where she is to-day, influencing as a mother the minds of her offspring, influencing by her gentle and kindly caress the action of her husband toward the good and pure.

7

People v. Hall, 1854

Bias against Chinese and other colored "races" was endemic in Nineteenth Century California, but perhaps no single document so well demonstrates that bias as this majority opinion handed down by the Chief Justice of the California Supreme Court. Since Chinese miners lived in small, segregated groups, the practical effect of this decision was to declare "open season" on Chinese, since crimes against them were likely to be witnessed only by other Chinese.

The People, Respondent, v. George W. Hall, Appellant

The appellant, a free white citizen of this State, was convicted of murder upon the testimony of Chinese witnesses.

The point involved in this case, is the admissibility of such evidence.

The 394th section of the Act Concerning Civil Cases, provides that no Indian or Negro shall be allowed to testify as a witness in any action or proceeding in which a White person is a party.

The 14th section of the Act of April 16th, 1850, regulating Criminal Proceedings, provides that "No Black, or Mulatto person, or Indian, shall be allowed to give evidence in favor of, or against a white man."

The true point at which we are anxious to arrive, is the legal signification of the words, "Black, Mulatto, Indian and White person," and whether the Legislature adopted them as generic terms, or intended to limit their application to specific types of the human species.

Before considering this question, it is proper to remark the difference between the two sections of our Statute, already quoted, the latter being more broad and comprehensive in its exclusion, by use of the word "Black," instead of Negro.

Conceding, however, for the present, that the word "Black," as used in the 14th section, and "Negro," in 394th, are convertible terms, and that the former was intended to include the latter, let us proceed to inquire who are excluded from testifying as witnesses under the term "Indian."

When Columbus first landed upon the shores of this continent, in his attempt to discover a western passage to the Indies, he imagined that he had accomplished the object of his expedition, and that the Island of San Salvador was one of those Islands of the Chinese sea, lying near the extremity of India, which had been described by navigators.

Acting upon this hypothesis, and also perhaps from the similarity of features and physical conformation, he gave to the Islanders the name of Indians, which appellation was universally adopted, and extended to the aboriginals of the New World, as well as of Asia.

From that time, down to a very recent period, the American Indians and the Mongolian, or Asiatic, were regarded as the same type of human species. . . .

. . . That this was the common opinion in the early history of American legislation, cannot be disputed, and, therefore, all legislation upon the subject must have borne relation to that opinion. . . .

. . . In using the words, "No Black, or Mulatto person, or Indian shall be allowed to give evidence for or against a White person," the Legislature, if any intention can be ascribed to it, adopted the most comprehensive terms to embrace every known class or shade of color, as the apparent design was to protect the White person from the influence of all testimony other than that of persons of the same caste. The use of these terms must, by every sound rule of construction, exclude every one who is not of white blood. . . .

. . . We have carefully considered all the consequences resulting from a different rule of construction, and are satisfied that even in a doubtful case we would be impelled to this decision on grounds of public policy.

The same rule which would admit them to testify, would admit them to all the equal rights of citizenship, and we might soon see them at the polls, in the jury box, upon the bench, and in our legislative halls.

This is not a speculation which exists in the excited and overheated imagination of the patriot and statesman, but it is an actual and present danger.

The anomalous spectacle of a distinct people, living in our community, recognizing no laws of this State except through necessity, bringing with them their prejudices and national feuds, in which they indulge in open violation of law; whose mendacity is proverbial; a race of people whom nature has marked as inferior, and who are incapable of progress or intellectual development beyond a certain point, as their history has shown; differing in language, opinions, color, and physical conformation; between whom and ourselves nature has placed an impassable difference, is now presented, and for them is claimed, not only the right to swear away the life of a citizen, but the further privilege of participating with us in administering the affairs of our Government. . . .

. . . For these reasons, we are of opinion that the testimony was inadmissible. . . .

Dred Scott v. Sanford, 1857

The question is simply this: Can a negro, whose ancestors were imported into this country, and sold as slaves, become a member of the political community formed and brought into existence by the Constitution of the United States, and as such become entitled to all the rights, and privileges, and immunities, guarantied by that instrument to the citizen? One of which rights is the privilege of suing in a court of the United States in the cases specified in the Constitution.

It will be observed, that the plea applies to that class of persons only whose ancestors were negroes of the African race, and imported into this country, and sold and held as slaves. The only matter in issue before the court, therefore, is whether the descendants of such slaves, when they shall be emancipated, or who are born of parents who had become free before their birth, are citizens of a State, in the sense in which the word citizen is used in the Constitution of the United States. And this being the only matter in dispute on the pleadings, the court must be understood as speaking in his opinion of that class only, that is, of those persons who are the descendants of Africans who were imported into this country, and sold as slaves.

It becomes necessary, therefore, to determine who were citizens of the several States when the Constitution was adopted. And in order to do this, we must recur to the Governments and institutions of the thirteen colonies, when they separated from Great Britain and formed new sovereignties, and took their places in the family of independent nations. We must inquire who, at that time, were recognised as the people or citizens of a State, whose rights and liberties had been outraged by the English Government; and who declared their independence, and assumed the powers of Government to defend their rights by force of arms.

In the opinion of the court, the legislation and histories of the times, and the language used in the Declaration of Independence, show, that neither the class of persons who had been imported as slaves, nor their descendants, whether they had become free or not, were then acknowledged as a part of the people, nor intended to be included in the general words used in that memorable instrument.

It is difficult at this day to realize the state of public opinion in relation to that unfortunate race, which prevailed in the civilized and enlightened portions of the world at the time of the Declaration of Independence, and when the Constitution of the United States was framed and adopted. But the public history of every European nation displays it in a manner too plain to be mistaken.

They had for more than a century before been regarded as beings of an inferior order, and altogether unfit to associate with the white race, either in social or political relations; and so far inferior, that they had no rights which the white man was bound to respect; and that the negro might justly and lawfully be reduced to slavery for his benefit. He was bought and sold, and treated as an ordinary article of merchandise and traffic, whenever a profit could be made by it. This opinion was at that time fixed and universal in the civilized portion of the white race. It was regarded as an axiom in morals as well as in politics, which no one thought of disputing, or supposed to be open to dispute; and men in every grade and position in society daily and habitually acted upon it in their private pursuits, as well as in matters of public concern, without doubting for a moment the correctness of this opinion.

And in no nation was this opinion more firmly fixed or more uniformly acted upon than by the English Government and English people. They not only seized them on the coast of Africa, and sold them or held them in slavery for their own use; but they took them as ordinary articles of merchandise to every country where they could make a profit on them, and were far more extensively engaged in this commerce than any other nation in the world.

The opinion thus entertained and acted upon in England was naturally impressed upon the colonies they founded on this side of the Atlantic. And, accordingly, a negro of the African race was regarded by them as an article of property, and held, and bought and sold as such, in every one of the thirteen colonies which united in the Declaration of Independence, and afterwards formed the Constitution of the United States. The slaves were more or less numerous in the different colonies, as slave labor was found more or less profitable. But no one seems to have doubted the correctness of the prevailing opinion of the time.

The legislation of the different colonies furnishes positive and indisputable proof of this fact.

The language of the Declaration of Independence is equally conclusive:

It begins by declaring that, "when in the course of human events it becomes necessary for one people to dissolve the political bands which have connected them with another, and to assume among the powers of the earth the separate and equal station to which the laws of nature and nature's God entitle them, a decent respect for the opinions of mankind requires that they should declare the causes which impel them to the separation."

It then proceeds to say: "We hold these truths to be self-evident: that all men are created equal; that they are endowed by their Creator with certain unalienable rights; that among them is life, liberty, and the pursuit of happiness; that to secure these rights, Governments are instituted, deriving their just powers from the consent of the governed."

The general words above quoted would seem to embrace the whole human family, and if they were used in a similar instrument at this day would be so understood. But it is too clear for dispute, that the enslaved African race were not intended to be included, and formed no part of the people who framed and adopted this declaration; for if the language, as understood in that day, would embrace them, the conduct of the distinguished men who framed the Declaration of Independence would have been utterly and flagrantly inconsistent with the principles they asserted; and instead of the sympathy of mankind, to which they so confidently appealed, they would have deserved and received universal rebuke and reprobation.

Yet the men who framed this declaration were great men—high in literary acquirements—high in their sense of honor, and incapable of asserting principles inconsistent with those on which they were acting. They perfectly understood the meaning of the language they used, and how it would be understood by others; and they knew that it would not in any part of the civilized world be supposed to embrace the negro race, which, by common consent, had been excluded from civilized Governments and the family of nations, and doomed to slavery. They spoke and acted according to the then established doctrines and principles, and in the ordinary language of the day, and no one misunderstood them. The unhappy black race were separated from the white by indelible marks, and laws long before established, and were never thought of or spoken of except as property, and when the claims of the owner or the profit of the trader were supposed to need protection.

This state of public opinion had undergone no change when the Constitution was adopted, as is equally evident from its provisions and language.

The brief preamble sets forth by whom it was formed, for what purposes, and for whose benefit and protection. It declares that it is formed by the *people* of the United States; that is to say, by those who were members of the different political communities in the several States; and its great object is declared to be to secure the blessings of liberty to themselves and their posterity. It speaks in general terms of the *people* of the United States, and of *citizens* of the several States, when it is providing for the exercise of the powers granted or the privileges secured to the citizen. It does not define what description of persons are intended to be included under these terms, or who shall be regarded as a citizen and one of the people. It uses them as terms so well understood, that no further description or definition was necessary.

But there are two clauses in the Constitution which point directly and specifically to the negro race as a separate class of persons, and show clearly that they were not regarded as a portion of the people or citizens of the Government then formed.

One of these clauses reserves to each of the thirteen States the right to import slaves until the year 1808, if it thinks proper. And the importation which it thus sanctions was unquestionably of persons of the race of which we are speaking, as the traffic in slaves in the United States had always been confined to them. And by the other provision the States pledge themselves to each other to maintain the right of property of the master, by delivering up to him any slave who may have escaped from his service, and be found within their respective territories. By the first above-mentioned clause, therefore, the right to purchase and hold this property is directly sanctioned and authorized for twenty years by the people who framed the Constitution. And by the second, they pledge themselves to maintain and uphold the right of the master in the manner specified, as long as the Government they then formed should endure. And these two provisions show, conclusively, that neither the description of persons therein referred to, nor their descendants, were embraced in any of the other provisions of the Constitution; for certainly these two clauses were not intended to confer on them or their posterity the blessings of liberty, or any of the personal rights so carefully provided for the citizen.

Upon the whole, therefore, it is the judgment of this court, that it appears by the record before us that the plaintiff in error is not a citizen of Missouri, in the sense in which that word is used in the Constitution; and that the Circuit Court of the United States, for that reason, had no jurisdiction in the case, and could give no judgment in it. Its judgment for the defendant must, consequently, be reversed, and a mandate issued, directing the suit to be dismissed for want of jurisdiction. *

9

The Emancipation Proclamation

Abraham Lincoln

Emancipation Proclamation by the President of the United States of America: A Proclamation

January 1, 1863

Whereas, on the twenty-second day of September, in the year of our Lord one thousand eight hundred and sixty two, a proclamation was issued by the President of the United States, containing, among other things, the following, to wit:

"That on the first day of January, in the year of our Lord one thousand eight

*Benjamin C. Howard, *Report of the Decision of the Supreme Court of the United States in the Case of Dred Scott* . . . (Washington, 1857), 9, 13–14, 15–17, 60.

hundred and sixty-three, all persons held as slaves within any State or designated part of a State, the people whereof shall then be in rebellion against the United States, shall be then, thenceforward, and forever free; and the Executive Government of the United States, including the military and naval authority thereof, will recognize and maintain the freedom of such persons, and will do no act or acts to repress such persons, or any of them, in any efforts they may make for their actual freedom.

"That the Executive will, on the first day of January aforesaid, by proclamation, designate the States and parts of States, if any, in which the people thereof, respectively, shall then be in rebellion against the United States; and the fact that any State, or the people thereof, shall on that day be, in good faith, represented in the Congress of the United States by members chosen thereto at elections wherein a majority of the qualified voters of such State shall have participated, shall, in the absence of strong countervailing testimony, be deemed conclusive evidence that such State, and the people thereof, are not then in rebellion against the United States."

Now, therefore I, Abraham Lincoln, President of the United States, by virtue of the power in me vested as Commander-in-Chief, of the Army and Navy of the United States in time of actual armed rebellion against authority and government of the United States, and as a fit and necessary war measure for suppressing said rebellion, do, on this first day of January, in the year of our Lord one thousand eight hundred and sixty-three, and in accordance with my purpose so to do publicly proclaimed for the full period of one hundred days, from the day first above mentioned, order and designate as the States and parts of States wherein the people thereof respectively, are this day in rebellion against the United States, the following, to wit:

Arkansas, Texas, Louisiana, (except the Parishes of St. Bernard, Plaquemines, Jefferson, St. Johns, St. Charles, St. James[,] Ascension, Assumption, Terrebonne, Lafourche, St. Mary, St. Martin, and Orleans, including the City of New-Orleans) Mississippi, Alabama, Florida, Georgia, South-Carolina, North-Carolina, and Virginia (except the forty-eight counties designated as West Virginia, and also the counties of Berkley, Accomac, Northampton, Elizabeth-City, York, Princess Ann, and Norfolk, including the cities of Norfolk & Portsmouth [)]; and which excepted parts are, for the present, left precisely as if this proclamation were not issued.

And by virtue of the power, and for the purpose aforesaid, I do order and declare that all persons held as slaves within said designated States, and parts of States, are, and henceforward shall be free; and that the Executive government of the United States, including the military and naval authorities thereof, will recognize and maintain the freedom of said persons.

And I hereby enjoin upon the people so declared to be free to abstain from all violence, unless in necessary self-defence; and I recommend to them that, in all cases when allowed, they labor faithfully for reasonable wages.

And I further declare and make known, that such persons of suitable condition, will be received into the armed service of the United States to garrison forts, positions, stations, and other places, and to man vessels of all sorts in said service.

And upon this act, sincerely believed to be an act of justice, warranted by the Constitution, upon military necessity, I invoke the considerate judgment of mankind, and the gracious favor of Almighty God.

In witness whereof, I have hereunto set my hand and caused the seal of the United States to be affixed.

Done at the City of Washington, this first day of January, in the year of our Lord one thousand eight hundred and sixty-three, and of the Independence of the United States of America the eighty-seventh.

By the President:
Abraham Lincoln

William H. Steward,
Secretary of State*

10

United States Constitution:
Thirteenth (1865), Fourteenth (1868), and Fifteenth (1870) Amendments

Amendment XIII (Ratified December 6, 1865). *Section 1.* Neither slavery nor involuntary servitude, except as a punishment for crime whereof the party shall have been duly convicted, shall exist within the United States, or any place subject to their jurisdiction.

Section 2. Congress shall have power to enforce this article by appropriate legislation.

Amendment XIV (Ratified July 9, 1868). *Section 1.* All persons born or naturalized in the United States, and subject to the jurisdiction thereof, are citizens of the United States and of the state wherein they reside. No State shall make or enforce any law which shall abridge the privileges or immunities of citizens of the United

*Basler, *op. cit.*, VI, 28–30.

States; nor shall any State deprive any person of life, liberty, or property, without due process of law; nor deny to any person within its jurisdiction the equal protection of the laws.

Section 2. Representatives shall be apportioned among the several states according to their respective numbers, counting the whole number of persons in each state, excluding Indians not taxed. But when the right to vote at any election for the choice of Electors for President and Vice-President of the United States, Representatives in Congress, the executive and judicial officers of a State, or the members of the Legislature thereof, is denied to any of the male inhabitants of such State, being twenty-one years of age, and, citizens of the United States, or in any way abridged, except for participation in rebellion, or other crime, the basis of representation therein shall be reduced in the proportion which the number of such male citizens shall bear to the whole number of male citizens twenty-one years of age in such State.

Section 3. No person shall be a Senator or Representative in Congress, or elector of President and Vice-President, or hold any office, civil or military, under the United States, or under any State, who, having previously taken an oath, as a member of Congress, or as an officer of the United States, or as an executive or judicial officer of any State, to support the Constitution of the United States, shall have engaged in insurrection or rebellion against the same, or given aid or comfort to the enemies thereof. But Congress may by a vote of two-thirds of each House, remove such disability.

Section 4. The validity of the public debt of the United States, authorized by law, including debts incurred for payment of pensions and bounties for services in suppressing insurrection or rebellion, shall not be questioned. But neither the United States nor any State shall assume or pay any debt or obligation incurred in aid of insurrection or rebellion against the United States, or any claim for the loss or emancipation of any slave; but all such debts, obligations, and claims, shall be held illegal and void.

Section 5. The Congress shall have power to enforce, by appropriate legislation, the provisions of this article.

Amendment XV (Ratified February 3, 1970). *Section 1.* The right of citizens of the United States to vote shall not be denied or abridged by the United States or by any State on account of race, color, or previous condition of servitude.

Section 2. The Congress shall have power to enforce this article by appropriate legislation.

11

The Black Codes

W. E. B. Du Bois

The whole proof of what the South proposed to do to the emancipated Negro, unless restrained by the nation, was shown in the Black Codes passed after Johnson's accession, but representing the logical result of attitudes of mind existing when Lincoln still lived. Some of these were passed and enforced. Some were passed and afterward repealed or modified when the reaction of the North was realized. In other cases, as for instance, in Louisiana, it is not clear just which laws were retained and which were repealed. In Alabama, the Governor induced the legislature not to enact some parts of the proposed code which they overwhelmingly favored.

The original codes favored by the Southern legislatures were an astonishing affront to emancipation and dealt with vagrancy, apprenticeship, labor contracts, migration, civil and legal rights. In all cases, there was plain and indisputable attempt on the part of the Southern states to make Negroes slaves in everything but name. They were given certain civil rights: the right to hold property, to sue and be sued. The family relations for the first time were legally recognized. Negroes were no longer real estate.

Yet, in the face of this, the Black Codes were deliberately designed to take advantage of every misfortune of the Negro. Negroes were liable to a slave trade under the guise of vagrancy and apprenticeship laws; to make the best labor contracts, Negroes must leave the old plantations and seek better terms; but if caught wandering in search of work, and thus unemployed and without a home, this was vagrancy, and the victim could be whipped and sold into slavery. In the turmoil of war, children were separated from parents, or parents unable to support them properly. These children could be sold into slavery, and "the former owner of said minors shall have the preference." Negroes could come into court as witnesses only in cases in which Negroes were involved. And even then, they must make their appeal to a jury and judge who would believe the word of any white man in preference to that of any Negro on pain of losing office and caste.

The Negro's access to the land was hindered and limited; his right to work was curtailed; his right of self-defense was taken away, when his right to bear arms was stopped; and his employment was virtually reduced to contract labor with penal servitude as a punishment for leaving his job. And in all cases, the judges of the Negro's guilt or innocence, rights and obligations were men who believed firmly, for the most part, that he had "no rights which a white man was bound to respect."

Making every allowance for the excitement and turmoil of war, and the mentality of a defeated people, the Black Codes were infamous pieces of legislation.

Let us examine these codes in detail.[1] They covered, naturally, a wide range of subjects. First, there was the question of allowing Negroes to come into the state. In South Carolina the constitution of 1865 permitted the Legislature to regulate immigration, and the consequent law declared "that no person of color shall migrate into and reside in this State, unless, within twenty days after his arrival within the same, he shall enter into a bond, with two freeholders as sureties . . . in a penalty of one thousand dollars, conditioned for his good behavior, and for his support."

Especially in the matter of work was the Negro narrowly restricted. In South Carolina, he must be especially licensed if he was to follow on his own account any employment, except that of farmer or servant. Those licensed must not only prove their fitness, but pay an annual tax ranging from $10–$100. Under no circumstances could they manufacture or sell liquor. Licenses for work were to be granted by a judge and were revokable on complaint. The penalty was a fine double the amount of the license, one-half of which went to the informer.

Mississippi provided that "every freedman, free Negro, and mulatto shall on the second Monday of January, one thousand eight hundred and sixty-six, and annually thereafter, have a lawful home or employment, and shall have written evidence thereof . . . from the Mayor . . . or from a member of the board of police . . . which licenses may be revoked for cause at any time by the authority granting the same."

Detailed regulation of labor was provided for in nearly all these states.

Louisiana passed an elaborate law in 1865, to "regulate labor contracts for agricultural pursuits." Later, it was denied that this legislation was actually enacted but the law was published at the time and the constitutional convention of 1868 certainly regarded this statute as law, for they formally repealed it. The law required all agricultural laborers to make labor contracts for the next year within the first ten days of January, the contracts to be in writing, to be with heads of families, to embrace the labor of all the members, and to be "binding on all minors thereof." Each laborer, after choosing his employer, "shall not be allowed to leave his place of employment, until the fulfillment of his contract, unless by consent of his employer, or on account of harsh treatment, or breach of contract on the part of the employer; and if they do so leave, without cause or permission, they shall forfeit all wages earned to the time of abandonment. . . .

"In case of sickness of the laborer, wages for the time lost shall be deducted, and where the sickness is feigned for purposes of idleness, . . . and also should refusal to work be continued beyond three days, the offender shall be reported to a justice of the peace, and shall be forced to labor on roads, levees, and other public works, without pay, until the offender consents to return to his labor. . . .

"When in health, the laborer shall work ten hours during the day in summer, and nine hours duing the day in winter, unless otherwise stipulated in the labor contract; he shall obey all proper orders of his employer or his agent; take proper care of his work mules, horses, oxen, stock; also of all agricultural implements; and employers shall have the right to make a reasonable deduction from the laborer's wages for injuries done to animals or agricultural implements committed to his care, or for bad or negligent work. Bad work shall not be allowed. Failing to obey reasonable orders, neglect of duty and leaving home without permission, will be deemed disobedience. . . . For any disobedience a fine of one dollar shall be imposed on the offender. For all lost time from work hours, unless in case of sickness, the laborer shall be fined twenty-five cents per hour. For all absence from home without leave, the laborer will be fined at the rate of two dollars per day. Laborers will not be required to labor on the Sabbath except to take the necessary care of stock and other property on plantations and do the necessary cooking and household duties, unless by special contract. For all thefts of the laborers from the employer of agricultural products, hogs, sheep, poultry or any other property of the employer, or willful destruction of property or injury, the laborer shall pay the employer double the amount of the value of the property stolen, destroyed or injured, one half to be paid to the employer, and the other half to be placed in the general fund provided for in this section. No live stock shall be allowed to laborers without the permission of the employer. Laborers shall not receive visitors during work hours. All difficulties arising between the employers and laborers, under this section, shall be settled, and all fines be imposed, by the former; if not satisfactory to the laborers, an appeal may be had to the nearest justice of the peace and two freeholders, citizens, one of said citizens to be selected by the employer and the other by the laborer; and all fines imposed and collected under this section shall be deducted from the wages due, and shall be placed in a common fund, to be divided among the other laborers employed on the plantation at the time when their full wages fall due, except as provided for above."

Similar detailed regulations of work were in the South Carolina law. Elaborate provision was made for contracting colored "servants" to white "masters." Their masters were given the right to whip "moderately" servants under eighteen. Others were to be whipped on authority of judicial officers. These officers were given authority to return runaway servants to their masters. The servants, on the other hand, were given certain rights. Their wages and period of service must be specified in writing, and they were protected against "unreasonable" tasks, Sunday and night work, unauthorized attacks on their persons, and inadequate food.

Contracting Negroes were to be known as "servants" and contractors as "masters." Wages were to be fixed by the judge, unless stipulated. Negroes of ten years of age or more without a parent living in the district might make a valid contract for a year or less. Failure to make written contracts was a misdemeanor, punishable by a fine of $5 to $50; farm labor to be from sunrise to sunset, with intervals for meals; servants to rise at dawn, to be careful of master's property and answerable for property lost or injured. Lost time was to be deducted from wages. Food and clothes might be deducted. Servants were to be quiet and orderly and to go to bed at reasonable hours. No night work or outdoor work in bad weather was to be asked, except in cases of necessity, visitors not allowed without the master's consent.

Servants leaving employment without good reason must forfeit wages. Masters might discharge servants for disobedience, drunkenness, disease, absence, etc. Enticing away the services of a servant was punishable by a fine of $20 to $100. A master could command a servant to aid him in defense of his own person, family or property. House servants at all hours of the day and night, and at all days of the weeks, "must answer promptly all calls and execute all lawful orders. . . ."

Mississippi provided "that every civil officer shall, and every person may, arrest and carry back to his or her legal employer any freedman, free Negro, or mulatto who shall have quit the service of his or her employer before the expiration of his or her term of service without good cause; and said officer and person shall be entitled to receive for arresting and carrying back every deserting employee aforesaid the sum of five dollars, and ten cents per mile from the place of arrest to the place of delivery, and the same shall be paid by the employer and held as a set-off for so much against the wages of said deserting employee."

It was provided in some states, like South Carolina, that any white man, whether an officer or not, could arrest a Negro. "Upon view of a misdemeanor committed by a person of color, any person present may arrest the offender and take him before a magistrate, to be dealt with as the case may require. In case of a misdemeanor committed by a white person toward a person of color, any person may complain to a magistrate, who shall cause the offender to be arrested, and according to the nature of the case, to be brought before himself, or be taken for trial in the district court."

On the other hand, in Mississippi, it was dangerous for a Negro to try to bring a white person to court on any charge. "In every case where any white person has been arrested and brought to trial, by virtue of the provisions of the tenth section of the above recited act, in any court in this State, upon sufficient proof being made to the court or jury, upon the trial before said court, that any freedman, free Negro or mulatto has falsely and maliciously caused the arrest and trial of said white person or persons, the court shall render up a judgment against said freedman, free Negro or mulatto for all costs of the case, and impose a fine not to exceed fifty dollars, and imprisonment in the county jail not to exceed twenty days; and for a failure of said freedman, free Negro or mulatto to pay, or cause to be paid, all costs, fines and jail fees, the sheriff of the county is hereby authorized and required, after giving ten days' public notice, to proceed to hire out at public outcry, at the court-house of the county, said freedman, free Negro or mulatto, for the shortest time to raise the amount necessary to discharge said freedman, free Negro or mulatto from all costs, fines, and jail fees aforesaid."

Mississippi declared that: "Any freedman, free Negro, or mulatto, committing riots, routs, affrays, trespasses, malicious mischief and cruel treatment to animals, seditious speeches, insulting gestures, language or acts, or assaults on any person, disturbance of the peace, exercising the functions of a minister of the gospel without a license from some regularly organized church, vending spirituous or intoxicating liquors, or committing any other misdemeanor, the punishment of which is not specifically provided for by law, shall, upon conviction thereof, in the county court, be fined not less than ten dollars, and not more than one hundred dollars, and may be imprisoned, at the discretion of the court, not exceeding thirty days. . . ."

The most important and oppressive laws were those with regard to vagrancy and apprenticeship. Sometimes they especially applied to Negroes; in other cases, they were drawn in general terms but evidently designed to fit the Negro's condition and to be enforced particularly with regard to Negroes.

The Virginia Vagrant Act enacted that "any justice of the peace, upon the complaint of any one of certain officers therein named, may issue his warrant for the apprehension of any person alleged to be a vagrant and cause such person to be apprehended and brought before him; and that if upon due examination said justice of the peace shall find that such person is a vagrant within the definition of vagrancy contained in said statute, he shall issue his warrant, directing such person to be employed for a term not exceeding three months, and by any constable of the county wherein the proceedings are had, be hired out for the best wages which can be procured, his wages to be applied to the support of himself and his family. The said statute further provides, that in case any vagrant so hired shall, during his term of service, run away from his employer without sufficient cause, he shall be apprehended on the warrant of a justice of the peace and returned to the custody of his employer, who shall then have, free from any other hire, the services of such vagrant for one month in addition to the original term of hiring, and that the employer shall then have power, if authorized by a justice of the peace, to work such vagrant with ball and chain. The said statute specified the persons who shall be considered vagrants and liable to the penalties imposed by it. Among those declared to be vagrants are all persons who, not having the wherewith to support their families, live idly and without employment, and refuse to work for the usual and common wages given to other laborers in the like work in the place where they are."

In Florida, January 12, 1866: "It is provided that when any person of color shall enter into a contract as aforesaid, to serve as a laborer for a year, or any other specified term, on any farm or plantation in this State, if he shall refuse or neglect to perform the stipulations of his contract by willful disobedience of orders, wanton impudence or disrespect to his employer, or his authorized agent, failure or refusal to perform the work assigned to him, idleness, or abandonment of the premises or the employment of the party with whom the contract was made, he or she shall be liable, upon the complaint of his employer or his agent, made under oath before any justice of the peace of the county, to be arrested and tried before the criminal court of the county, and upon conviction shall be subject to all the pains and penalties prescribed for the punishment of vagrancy."

In Georgia, it was ruled that "All persons wandering or strolling about in idleness, who are able to work, and who have no property to support them; all persons leading an idle, immoral, or profligate life, who have no property to support them and are able to work and do not work; all persons able to work having no visible and known means of a fair, honest, and respectable livelihood; all persons having a fixed abode, who have no visible property to support them, and who live by stealing or by trading in, bartering for, or buying stolen property; and all professional gamblers living in idleness, shall be deemed and considered vagrants, and shall be indicated as such, and it shall be lawful for any person to arrest said vagrants and have them bound over for trial to the next term of the country court, and upon conviction, they shall be fined and imprisoned or sentenced to work on the public works, for not longer than a year, or shall, in the discretion of the court, be bound over for trial to the next term of the country court, and upon conviction, they shall be fined and imprisoned or sentenced to work on the public works, for not longer than a year, or shall, in the discretion of the court, be bound out to some person for a time not longer than one year, upon such valuable consideration as the court may prescribe."

Mississippi provided "That all freedmen, free Negroes, and mulattoes in this state over the age of eighteen years, found on the second Monday in January, 1866, or thereafter, with no lawful employment or business, or found unlawfully assembling themselves together, either in the day or night time, and all white persons so assembling with freedmen, free Negroes or mulattoes, or usually associating with freedmen, free Negroes or mulattoes on terms of equality, or living in adultery or fornication with a freedwoman, free Negro or mulatto, shall be deemed vagrants, and on conviction thereof shall be fined in the sum of not exceeding, in the case of a freedman, free Negro or mulatto, fifty dollars, and a white man two hundred dollars and imprisoned, at the discretion of the court, the free Negro not exceeding ten days, and the white men not exceeding six months."

Sec. 5 provides that "all fines and forfeitures collected under the provisions of this act shall be paid into the county treasury for general county purposes, and in case any freedman, free Negro or mulatto, shall fail for five days after the imposition of any fine or forfeiture upon him or her, for violation of any of the provisions of this act to pay the same, that it shall be, and is hereby made, the duty of the Sheriff of the proper county to hire out said freedman, free Negro or mulatto, to any person who will, for the shortest period of service, pay said fine or forfeiture and all costs; *Provided*, a preference shall be given to the employer, if there be one, in which case the employer shall be entitled to deduct and retain the amount so paid from the wages of such freedman, free Negro or mulatto, then due or to become due; and in case such freedman, free Negro or mulatto cannot be hired out, he or she may be dealt with as a pauper. . . ."

In Alabama, the "former owner" was to have preference in the apprenticing of a child. This was true in Kentucky and Mississippi.

Mississippi "provides that it shall be the duty of all sheriffs, justices of the peace, and other civil officers of the several counties in this state to report to the probate courts of their respective counties semi-annually, at the January and July terms of said courts, all freedmen, free Negroes and mulattoes, under the age of eighteen, within their respective counties, beats, or districts, who are orphans, or whose parent or parents have not the means, or who refuse to provide for and support said minors, and thereupon it shall be the duty of said probate court to order the clerk of said court to apprentice said minors to some competent and suitable person, on such terms as the court may direct, having a particular care to the interest of said minors;

Provided, that the former owner of said minors shall have the preference when, in the opinion of the court, he or she shall be a suitable person for that purpose. . . ."

"Capital punishment was provided for colored persons guilty of willful homicide, assault upon a white woman, impersonating her husband for carnal purposes, raising an insurrection, stealing a horse, a mule, or baled cotton, and housebreaking. For crimes not demanding death Negroes might be confined at hard labor, whipped, or transported; 'but punishments more degrading than imprisonment shall not be imposed upon a white person for a crime not infamous.' "[2]

In most states Negroes were allowed to testify in courts but the testimony was usually confined to cases where colored persons were involved, although in some states, by consent of the parties, they could testify in cases where only white people were involved. . . .

Mississippi simply reenacted her slave code and made it operative so far as punishments were concerned. "That all the penal and criminal laws now in force in this State, defining offenses, and prescribing the mode of punishment for crimes and misdemeanors committed by slaves, free Negroes or mulattoes, be and the same are hereby reenacted, and declared to be in full force and effect, against freedmen, free Negroes, and mulattoes, except so far as the mode and manner of trial and punishment have been changed or altered by law."

North Carolina, on the other hand, abolished her slave code, making difference of punishment only in the case of Negroes convicted of rape. Georgia placed the fines and costs of a servant upon the master. "Where such cases shall go against the servant, the judgment for costs upon written notice to the master shall operate as a garnishment against him, and he shall retain a sufficient amount for the payment thereof, out of any wages due to said servant, or to become due during the period of service, and may be cited at any time by the collecting officer to make answer thereto."

The celebrated ordinance of Opelousas, Louisiana, shows the local ordinances regulating Negroes. "No Negro or freedman shall be allowed to come within the limits of the town of Opelousas without special permission from his employer, specifying the object of his visit and the time necessary for the accomplishment of the same.

"Every Negro freedman who shall be found on the streets of Opelousas after ten o'clock at night without a written pass or permit from his employer, shall be imprisoned and compelled to work five days on the public streets, or pay a fine of five dollars.

"No Negro or freedman shall be permitted to rent or keep a house within the limits of the town under any circumstances, and anyone thus offending shall be ejected, and compelled to find an employer or leave the town within twenty-four hours.

"No Negro or freedman shall reside within the limits of the town of Opelousas who is not in the regular service of some white person or former owner, who shall be held responsible for the conduct of said freedman.

"No Negro or freedman shall be permitted to preach, exhort, or otherwise declaim to congregations of colored people without a special permission from the

Mayor or President of the Board of Police, under the penalty of a fine of ten dollars or twenty days' work on the public streets.

"No freedman who is not in the military service shall be allowed to carry firearms, or any kind of weapons within the limits of the town of Opelousas without the special permission of his employer, in writing, and approved by the Mayor or President of the Board.

"Any freedman not residing in Opelousas, who shall be found within its corporate limits after the hour of 3 o'clock, on Sunday, without a special permission from his employer or the Mayor, shall be arrested and imprisoned and made to work two days on the public streets, or pay two dollars in lieu of said work."[3]

Of Louisiana, Thomas Conway testified February 22, 1866: "Some of the leading officers of the state down there—men who do much to form and control the opinions of the masses—instead of doing as they promised, and quietly submitting to the authority of the government, engaged in issuing slave codes and in promulgating them to their subordinates, ordering them to carry them into execution, and this to the knowledge of state officials of a higher character, the governor and others. And the men who issued them were not punished except as the military authorities punished them. The governor inflicted no punishment on them while I was there, and I don't know that, up to this day, he has ever punished one of them. These codes were simply the old black code of the state, with the word 'slave' expunged, and 'Negro' substituted. The most odious features of slavery were preserved in them. . . ."[4]

NOTES

1. Quotations from McPherson, *History of United States During Reconstruction*, pp. 29–44.
2. Simkins and Woody, *South Carolina During Reconstruction*, pp. 49, 50.
3. Warmoth, *War, Politics and Reconstruction*, p. 274.
4. *Report on the Joint Committee on Reconstruction*, 1866, Part IV, pp. 78–79.

12

Bradwell v. *Illinois*, 1873

Mid-nineteenth century feminists, many of them diligent workers in the cause of abolition, looked to Congress after the Civil War for an express guarantee of equal rights for men and women. Viewed in historical perspective, their expectations appear unrealistic. A problem of far greater immediacy faced the nation. Moreover, the common law heritage, ranking the married woman in relationship to her husband as "something better than his dog, a little dearer than his horse,"[1] was just beginning to erode. Nonetheless, the text of the fourteenth amendment appalled the proponents of a sex equality guarantee. Their concern centered on the abortive second section of the amendment, which placed in the Constitution for the first time the word "male." Threefold use of the word "male," always in conjunction with the term "citizens," caused concern that the grand phrases of the first section of the fourteenth amendment would have, at best, qualified application to women.[2]

For more than a century after the adoption of the fourteenth amendment, the judiciary, with rare exceptions, demonstrated utmost deference to sex lines drawn by the legislature. . . .

The Court's initial examination of a woman's claim to full participation in society through entry into a profession traditionally reserved to men came in 1873 in Bradwell v. Illinois.[3] Myra Bradwell's application for a license to practice law had been denied by the Illinois Supreme Court solely because she was a female. The Supreme Court affirmed this judgment with only one dissent, recorded but not explained, by Chief Justice Chase. Justice Miller's opinion for the majority was placed on two grounds: (1) since petitioner was a citizen of Illinois, the privileges and immunities clause of article IV, section 2 of the Federal Constitution[4] was inapplicable to her claim; and (2) since admission to the bar of a state is not one of the privileges and immunities of United States citizenship, the fourteenth amendment did not secure the asserted right. Justice Bradley, speaking for himself and Justices Swayne and Field, chose to place his concurrence in the judgment on broader grounds. He wrote[5]:

> [T]he civil law, as well as nature herself, has always recognized a wide difference in the respective spheres and destinies of man and woman. Man is, or should be, woman's protector and defender. The natural and proper timidity and delicacy which belongs to the female sex evidently unfits it for many of the occupations of civil life. The constitution of the family organization, which is founded in the divine ordinance, as well as in the nature of things, indicates the domestic sphere as that which properly belongs to the domain and functions of womanhood. The harmony, not to say identity, of interests and views which belong, or should belong, to the family institution is repugnant to the idea of a woman adopting a distinct and independent career from that of her husband. So firmly fixed was this sentiment in the founders of the common law that it became a maxim of that system of jurisprudence that a woman had no legal existence separate from her husband, who was regarded as her head and representative in the social state and, notwithstanding some recent modifications of this civil status, many of the special rules of law flowing from and dependent upon this cardinal principle still exist in full force in most States. One of these is, that a married woman is incapable, without her husband's consent, of making contracts which shall be binding on her or him. This very incapacity was one circumstance which the Supreme Court of Illinois deemed important in rendering a married

woman incompetent fully to perform the duties and trusts that belong to the office of an attorney and counsellor.

It is true that many women are unmarried and not affected by any of the duties, complications, and incapacities arising out of the married state, but these are exceptions to the general rule. The paramount destiny and mission of woman are to fulfil the noble and benign offices of wife and mother. This is the law of the Creator. And the rules of civil society must be adapted to the general constitution of things, and cannot be based upon exceptional cases.

The humane movements of modern society, which have for their object the multiplication of avenues for woman's advancement, and of occupations adapted to her condition and sex, have my heartiest concurrence. But I am not prepared to say that it is one of her fundamental rights and privileges to be admitted into every office and position, including those which require highly special qualifications and demanding special responsibilities. In the nature of things it is not every citizen of every age, sex, and condition that is qualified for every calling and position. It is the prerogative of the legislator to prescribe regulations founded on nature, reason, and experience for the due admission of qualified persons to professions and callings demanding special skill and confidence. This fairly belongs to the police power of the State; and, in my opinion, in view of the peculiar characteristics, destiny, and mission of woman, it is within the province of the legislature to ordain what offices, positions, and callings shall be filled and discharged by men, and shall receive the benefit of those energies and responsibilities, and that decision and firmness which are presumed to predominate in the sterner sex.

Although the method of communication between the Creator and the judge is never disclosed, "divine ordinance" has been a dominant theme in decisions justifying laws establishing sex-based classifications.[6] Well past the middle of the twentieth century laws delineating "a sharp line between the sexes"[7] were sanctioned by the judiciary on the basis of lofty inspiration as well as restrained constitutional interpretation. . . .

NOTES

1. Alfred Lord Tennyson, Locksley Hall (1842); see Johnston, Sex and Property: The Common Law Tradition, The Law School Curriculum, and Developments Toward Equality, 47 N.Y.U.L.Rev. 1033, 1044–1070 (1972); pp. 163–183 infra.

2. E. Flexner, Century of Struggle 142–55 (1959).

3. 83 U.S. (16 Wall.) 130, 21 L.Ed. 442 (1873).

4. Article IV, section 2 reads: "The Citizens of each State shall be entitled to all Privileges and Immunities of Citizens in the several States."

5. 83 U.S. (16 Wall.) at 141–42.

6. E.g., State v. Heitman, 105 Kan. 139, 146–47, 181 P. 630. 633–34 (1919); State v. Bearcub, 1 Or.App. 579, 580, 465 P.2d 252, 253 (1970).

7. Goesaert v. Cleary, 335 U.S. 464, 466, 69 S.Ct. 198, 199, 93 L.Ed. 163, 165 (1948). *Goesaert* was disapproved in Craig v. Boren, 429 U.S. 190, 210 n. 23, 97 S.Ct. 451, 463, 50 L.Ed.2d 397, 414 (1976).

13

Minor v. Happersett, 1875

"In this case the court held that although women were citizens, the right to vote was not a privilege or immunity of national citizenship before adoption of the 14th Amendment, nor did the amendment add suffrage to the privileges and immunities of national citizenship. Therefore, the national government could not require states to permit women to vote."*

14

California Constitution, 1876

In 1876, at the height of the anti-Chinese movement, California adopted a new constitution. Its anti-Chinese provisions, largely unenforceable, represent an accurate measure of public feeling.

Article XIX

Section 1. The Legislature shall prescribe all necessary regulations for the protection of the State, and the counties, cities, and towns thereof, from the burdens and evils arising from the presence of aliens, who are or may become vagrants, paupers, mendicants, criminals, or invalids afflicted with contagious or infectious diseases, and from aliens otherwise dangerous or detrimental to the well-being or peace of the State, and to impose conditions upon which such persons may reside in the State,

*From *Congressional Quarterly's Guide to the U.S. Supreme Court,* 1979, p. 631.

and to provide means and mode of their removal from the State upon failure or refusal to comply with such conditions; provided, that nothing contained in this section shall be construed to impair or limit the power of the Legislature to pass such police laws or other regulations as it may deem necessary.

Section 2. No corporation now existing or hereafter formed under the laws of this State, shall, after the adoption of this Constitution, employ, directly or indirectly, in any capacity, any Chinese or Mongolian. The Legislature shall pass such laws as may be necessary to enforce this provision.

Section 3. No Chinese shall be employed on any State, county, municipal, or other public work, except in punishment for crime.

Section 4. The presence of foreigners ineligible to become citizens of the United States is declared to be dangerous to the well-being of the State, and the Legislature shall discourage their immigration by all the means within its power. Asiatic coolieism is a form of human slavery, and is forever prohibited in this State; and all contracts for coolie labor shall be void. All companies or corporations, whether formed in this country or any foreign country, for the importation of such labor, shall be subject to such penalties as the Legislature may prescribe. The Legislature shall delegate all necessary power to the incorporated cities and towns of this State for the removal of Chinese without the limits of such cities and towns, or for their location within prescribed portions of those limits; and it shall also provide the necessary legislation to prohibit the introduction into this State of Chinese after the adoption of this Constitution. This section shall be enforced by appropriate legislation.

15

Elk v. *Wilkins,* November 3, 1884

John Elk, an Indian who had voluntarily separated himself from his tribe and taken up residence among the whites, was denied the right to vote in Omaha, Nebraska, on the ground that he was not a citizen. The Supreme Court considered the question of whether Elk had been made a citizen by the Fourteenth Amendment and decided against him.

. . . . The plaintiff, in support of his action, relies on the first clause of the first section of the Fourteenth Article of Amendment of the Constitution of the United

States, by which "all persons born or naturalized in the United States, and subject to the jurisdiction thereof, are citizens of the United States and of the State wherein they reside;" and on the Fifteenth Article of Amendment, which provides that "the right of citizens of the United States to vote shall not be denied or abridged by the United States or by any State on account of race, color, or previous condition of servitude." . . .

The petition, while it does not show of what Indian tribe the plaintiff was a member, yet, by the allegations that he "is an Indian, and was born within the United States," and that "he had severed his tribal relation to the Indian tribes," clearly implies that he was born a member of one of the Indian tribes within the limits of the United States, which still exists and is recognized as a tribe by the government of the United States. Though the plaintiff alleges that he "had fully and completely surrendered himself to the jurisdiction of the United States," he does not allege that the United States accepted his surrender, or that he has ever been naturalized, or taxed, or in any way recognized or treated as a citizen, by the State or by the United States. Nor is it contended by his counsel that there is any statute or treaty that makes him a citizen.

The question then is, whether an Indian, born a member of one of the Indian tribes within the United States, is, merely by reason of his birth within the United States, and of his afterwards voluntarily separating himself from his tribe and taking up his residence among white citizens, a citizen of the United States, within the meaning of the first section of the Fourteenth Amendment of the Constitution. . . .

Indians born within the territorial limits of the United States, members of, and owing immediate allegiance to, one of the Indian tribes (an alien, though dependent, power), although in a geographical sense born in the United States, are no more "born in the United States and subject to the jurisdiction thereof," within the meaning of the first section of the Fourteenth Amendment, than the children of subjects of any foreign government born within the domain of that government, or the children born within the United States, of ambassadors or other public ministers of foreign nations.

This view is confirmed by the second section of the Fourteenth Amendment, which provides that "representatives shall be apportioned among the several States according to their respective numbers, counting the whole number of persons in each State, excluding Indians not taxed." Slavery having been abolished, and the persons formerly held as slaves made citizens, this clause fixing the apportionment of representatives has abrogated so much of the corresponding clause of the original Constitution as counted only three-fifths of such persons. But Indians not taxed are still excluded from the count, for the reason that they are not citizens. Their absolute exclusion from the basis of representation, in which all other persons are now included, is wholly inconsistent with their being considered citizens. . . .

The plaintiff, not being a citizen of the United States under the Fourteenth Amendment of the Constitution, has been deprived of no right secured by the Fifteenth Amendment, and cannot maintain this action.*

---

*112 *United States Reports: Cases Adjudged in the Supreme Court*, Banks & Brothers, New York.

16

The General Allotment Act (Dawes Act), February 8, 1887

This Act authorized the president of the United States to divide lands held by Indian tribes among individual Indians and declared Indians who received these allotments to be citizens of the United States. According to the act, each family head received 160 acres of land and each single person, 80 acres. Title to the land was held in trust for at least twenty-five years, though civilized Indians could end the trust period and become citizens. More importantly, surplus lands within the reservation boundaries were made available for purchase by the United States government and then opened to homesteading. This act, and numerous other similar acts of Congress that followed it, had the effect of breaking up tribal relations.[1]

NOTE

1. *Indian Tribes: A Continuing Quest for Survival* (A Report of the United States Commission on Civil Rights, June 1981).

17

Plessy v. *Ferguson*, 1896

After the collapse of Reconstruction governments, southern whites began gradually to legalize the informal practices of segregation which obtained in the South. One such law was passed by the Louisiana legislature in 1890 and provided that "all railway companies carrying passengers . . . in this State shall provide separate but equal accommodations for the white and colored races."

Plessy *vs.* Ferguson *tested the constitutionality of this recent trend in southern legislation. Plessy was a mulatto who, on June 7, 1892, bought a first-class ticket on the East Louisiana Railway for a trip from New Orleans to Covington, La., and sought to be seated in the "white" coach. Upon conviction of a violation of the 1890 statute, he appealed to the Supreme Court of Louisiana, which upheld his conviction, and finally to the U.S. Supreme Court, which pronounced the Louisiana law constitutional, on May 18, 1896. The defense of Plessy and attack on the Louisiana statute was in the hands of four men, the most famous of whom was Albion W. Tourgée. M. J. Cunningham, Attorney General of Louisiana, was assisted by two other lawyers in defending the statute. The majority opinion of the Court was delivered by Justice Henry B. Brown. John Marshall Harlan dissented and Justice David J. Brewer did not participate, making it a 7–1 decision.*

In his dissent to this decision Harlan asserted that "Our Constitution is color-blind, and neither knows nor tolerates classes among citizens. In respect of civil rights, all citizens are equal before the law." He offered the prophecy that "the judgment rendered this day will, in time, prove to be quite as pernicious as the decision made by this tribunal in the Dred Scott *case."*

The constitutionality of this act is attacked upon the ground that it conflicts both with the Thirteenth Amendment of the Constitution, abolishing slavery, and the Fourteenth Amendment, which prohibits certain restrictive legislation on the part of the States.

1. That it does not conflict with the Thirteenth Amendment, which abolished slavery and involuntary servitude, except as a punishment for crime, is too clear for argument. Slavery implies involuntary servitude—a state of bondage: the ownership of mankind as a chattel, or at least the control of the labor and services of one man for the benefit of another, and the absence of a legal right to the disposal of his own person, property and services. . . .

A statute which implies merely a legal distinction between the white and colored races—a distinction which is founded in the color of the two races, and which must always exist so long as white men are distinguished from the other race by color—has no tendency to destroy the legal equality of the two races, or reestablish a state of involuntary servitude. Indeed, we do not understand that the Thirteenth Amendment is strenuously relied upon by the plaintiff in error in this connection.

2. By the Fourteenth Amendment, all persons born or naturalized in the United States, and subject to the jurisdiction thereof, are made citizens of the United States and of the State wherein they reside; and the States are forbidden from making or enforcing any law which shall abridge the privileges or immunities of citizens of the United States, or shall deprive any person of life, liberty or property without due process of law, or deny to any person within their jurisdiction the equal protection of the laws. . . .

The object of the amendment was undoubtedly to enforce the absolute equality of the two races before the law, but in the nature of things it could not have been intended to abolish distinctions based upon color, or to enforce social, as distinguished from political equality, or a commingling of the two races upon terms unsatisfactory to either. Laws permitting, and even requiring, their separation in places where they are liable to be brought into contact do not necessarily imply the inferiority of either race to the other, and have been generally, if not universally, recognized as within the competency of the state legislatures in the exercise of their police power. The most common instance of this is connected with the establishment of separate schools for white and colored children, which has been held to be a valid exercise of the legislative power even by courts of States where the political rights of the colored race have been longest and most earnestly enforced. . . .

While we think the enforced separation of the races, as applied to the internal commerce of the State, neither abridges the privileges or immunities of the colored man, deprives him of his property without due process of law, nor denies him the equal protection of the laws, within the meaning of the Fourteenth Amendment, we are not prepared to say that the conductor, in assigning passengers to the coaches according to their race, does not act at his peril, or that the provision of the second section of the act, that denies to the passenger compensation in damages for a refusal to receive him into the coach in which he properly belongs, is a valid exercise of the legislative power. Indeed, we understand it to be conceded by the State's attorney, that such part of the act as exempts from liability the railway company and its officers is unconstitutional. The power to assign to a particular coach obviously implies the power to determine to which race the passenger belongs, as well as the power to determine who, under the laws of the particular State, is to be deemed a white, and who a colored person. . . .

It is claimed by the plaintiff in error that, in any mixed community, the reputation of belonging to the dominant race, in this instance the white race, is *property*, in the same sense that a right of action, or of inheritance, is property. Conceding this to be so, for the purposes of this case, we are unable to see how this statute deprives him of, or in any way affects his right to, such property. If he be a white man and assigned to a colored coach, he may have his action for damages against the company for being deprived of his so called property. Upon the other hand, if he be a colored man and be so assigned, he has been deprived of no property, since he is not lawfully entitled to the reputation of being a white man.

In this connection, it is also suggested by the learned counsel for the plaintiff in error that the same argument that will justify the state legislature in requiring railways to provide separate accommodations for the two races will also authorize them to require separate cars to be provided for the people whose hair is of a certain color, or who are aliens, or who belong to certain nationalities, or to enact laws requiring colored people to walk upon one side of the street, and white people upon the other, or requiring white men's houses to be painted white, and colored men's black, or their vehicles or business signs to be of different colors, upon the theory that one side of the street is as good as the other, or that a house or vehicle of one color is as good as one of another color. The reply to all this is that every exercise of the police power must be reasonable, and extend only to such laws as are enacted in good faith for the promotion for the public good, and not for the annoyance or oppression of a particular class. . . .

We consider the underlying fallacy of the plaintiff's argument to consist in the assumption that the enforced separation of the two races stamps the colored race with a badge of inferiority. If this be so, it is not by reason of anything found in the act, but solely because the colored race chooses to put that construction upon it. The argument necessarily assumes that if, as has been more than once the case, and is not unlikely to be so again, the colored race should become the dominant power in the state legislature, and should enact a law in precisely similar terms, it would thereby relegate the white race to an inferior position. We imagine that the white race, at least, would not acquiesce in this assumption. The argument also assumes that social prejudices may be overcome by legislation, and that equal rights cannot be secured to the negro except by an enforced commingling of the two races. We cannot accept this proposition. If the two races are to meet upon terms of social equality, it must be the result of natural affinities, a mutual appreciation of each other's merits and a voluntary consent of individuals.*

18

United States Constitution:
Nineteenth Amendment (1920)

Amendment XIX (ratified August 18, 1920). *Section 1.* The right of citizens of the United States to vote shall not be denied or abridged by the United States or by any State on account of sex.

Section 2. Congress shall have power to enforce this Article by appropriate legislation.

Plessy vs. Ferguson, 163 U.S. 537 *United States Reports: Cases Adjudged in the Supreme Court* (New York, Banks & Brothers, 1896).

Korematsu v. United States, 1944

The present case involved perhaps the most alarming use of executive military author-
ity in our nation's history. Following the bombing of Pearl Harbor in December,
1941, the anti-Japanese sentiment on the West Coast brought the residents of the
area to a state of near hysteria; and in February, 1942, President Roosevelt issued
an executive order authorizing the creation of military areas from which any or all
persons might be excluded as the military authorities might decide. On March 2, the
entire West Coast to a depth of about forty miles was designated by the command-
ing general as Military Area No. 1, and he thereupon proclaimed a curfew in that
area for all persons of Japanese ancestry. Later he ordered the compulsory evacuation
from the area of all persons of Japanese ancestry, and by the middle of the summer
most of these people had been moved inland to "war relocation centers," the Ameri-
can equivalent of concentration camps. Congress subsequently made it a crime to
violate these military orders. Of the 112,000 persons of Japanese ancestry involved,
about 70,000 were native-born American citizens, none of whom had been specifi-
cally accused of disloyalty. Three cases were brought to the Supreme Court as chal-
lenging the right of the government to override in this manner the customary civil
rights of these citizens. In Hirabayashi v. United States, 320 U. S. 81 (1943), the
Court upheld the curfew regulations as a valid military measure to prevent espio-
nage and sabotage. "Whatever views we may entertain regarding the loyalty to this
country of the citizens of Japanese ancestry, we cannot reject as unfounded the
judgment of the military authorities and of Congress that there were disloyal mem-
bers of that population, whose number and strength could not be precisely and
quickly ascertained. We cannot say that the war-making branches of the Govern-
ment did not have ground for believing that in a critical hour such persons could not
readily be isolated and separately dealt with, and constituted a menace to the na-
tional defense and safety. . . ." While emphasizing that distinctions based on ances-
try were "by their very nature odious to a free people" the Court nonetheless felt
"that in time of war residents having ethnic affiliations with an invading enemy
may be a greater source of danger than those of a different ancestry."

While the Court, in the present case, held valid the discriminatory mass
evacuation of all persons of Japanese descent, it also held in Ex parte Endo, 323
U. S. 283 (1944), that an American citizen of Japanese ancestry whose loyalty to
this country had been established could not constitutionally be held in a War Re-
location Center but must be unconditionally released. The government had allowed

persons to leave the Relocation Centers under conditions and restrictions which aimed to guarantee that there should not be "a dangerously disorderly migration of unwanted people to unprepared communities." Permission to leave was granted only if the applicant had the assurance of a job and a place to live, and wanted to go to a place "approved" by the War Relocation Authority. The Court held that the sole purpose of the evacuation and detention program was to protect the war effort against sabotage and espionage. "A person who is concededly loyal presents no problem of espionage or sabotage. . . . He who is loyal is by definition not a spy or a saboteur." It therefore follows that the authority to detain a citizen of Japanese ancestry ends when his loyalty is established. To hold otherwise would be to justify his detention not on grounds of military necessity but purely on grounds of race.

Although no case reached the Court squarely challenging the right of the government to incarcerate citizens of Japanese ancestry pending a determination of their loyalty, the tenor of the opinions leaves little doubt that such action would have been sustained. The present case involved only the right of the military to evacuate such persons from the West Coast. Mr. Justice Murphy, one of three dissenters, attacked the qualifications of the military to make sociological judgments about the effects of ancestry, and pointed out that the time consumed in evacuating these persons (eleven months) was ample for making an orderly inquiry into their individual loyalty.

Mr. Justice Black delivered the opinion of the Court, saying in part:

The petitioner, an American citizen of Japanese descent, was convicted in a federal district court for remaining in San Leandro, California, a "Military Area," contrary to Civilian Exclusion Order No. 34 of the Commanding General of the Western Command, U. S. Army, which directed that after May 9, 1942, all persons of Japanese ancestry should be excluded from that area. No question was raised as to petitioner's loyalty to the United States. The Circuit Court of Appeals affirmed, and the importance of the constitutional question involved caused us to grant certiorari.

It should be noted, to begin with, that all legal restrictions which curtail the civil rights of a single racial group are immediately suspect. That is not to say that all such restrictions are unconstitutional. It is to say that courts must subject them to the most rigid scrutiny. Pressing public necessity may sometimes justify the existence of such restrictions; racial antagonism never can.

In the instant case prosecution of the petitioner was begun by information charging violation of an Act of Congress, of March 21, 1942, 56 Stat. 173, which provides that " . . . whoever shall enter, remain in, leave, or commit any act in any military area or military zone prescribed, under the authority of an Executive order of the President, by the Secretary of War, or by any military commander designated by the Secretary of War, contrary to the restrictions applicable to any such area or zone or contrary to the order of the Secretary of War or any such military commander, shall, if it appears that he knew or should have known of the existence and extent of the restrictions or order and that his act was in violation thereof, be guilty of a misdemeanor and upon conviction shall be liable to a fine of not to exceed $5,000 or to imprisonment for not more than one year, or both, for each offense."

Exclusion Order No. 34, which the petitioner knowingly and admittedly violated was one of a number of military orders and proclamations, all of which were substantially based upon Executive Order No. 9066, 7 Fed. Reg. 1407. That order, issued after we were at war with Japan, declared that "the successful prosecution of the war requires every possible protection against espionage and against sabotage to national-defense material, national-defense premises, and national-defense utilities. . . ."

One of the series of orders and proclamations, a curfew order, which like the exclusion order here was promulgated pursuant to Executive Order 9066, subjected all persons of Japanese ancestry in prescribed West Coast military areas to remain in their residences from 8 p.m. to 6 a.m. As is the case with the exclusion order here, that prior curfew order was designed as a "protection against espionage and against sabotage." In Kiyoshi Hirabayashi v. United States, 320 U. S. 81, we sustained a conviction obtained for violation of the curfew order. The Hirabayashi conviction and this one thus rest on the same 1942 Congressional Act and the same basic executive and military orders, all of which orders were aimed at the twin dangers of espionage and sabotage.

The 1942 Act was attacked in the Hirabayashi case as an unconstitutional delegation of power; it was contended that the curfew order and other orders on which it rested were beyond the war powers of the Congress, the military authorities and of the President, as Commander in Chief of the Army; and finally that to apply the curfew order against none but citizens of Japanese ancestry amounted to a constitutionally prohibited discrimination solely on account of race. To these questions, we gave the serious consideration which their importance justified. We upheld the curfew order as an exercise of the power of the government to take steps necessary to prevent espionage and sabotage in an area threatened by Japanese attack.

In the light of the principles we announced in the Hirabayashi case, we are unable to conclude that it was beyond the war power of Congress and the Executive to exclude those of Japanese ancestry from the West Coast war area at the time they did. True, exclusion from the area in which one's home is located is a far greater deprivation than constant confinement to the home from 8 p.m. to 6 a.m. Nothing short of apprehension by the proper military authorities of the gravest imminent danger to the public safety can constitutionally justify either. But exclusion from a threatened area, no less than curfew, has a definite and close relationship to the prevention of espionage and sabotage. The military authorities, charged with the primary responsibility of defending our shores, concluded that curfew provided inadequate protection and ordered exclusion. They did so, as pointed out in our Hirabayashi opinion, in accordance with Congressional authority to the military to say who should, and who should not, remain in the threatened areas.

In this case the petitioner challenges the assumptions upon which we rested our conclusions in the Hirabayashi case. He also urges that by May 1942, when Order

No. 34 was promulgated, all danger of Japanese invasion of the West Coast had disappeared. After careful consideration of these contentions we are compelled to reject them.

Here, as in the Hirabayashi case, ". . .we cannot reject as unfounded the judgment of the military authorities and of Congress that there were disloyal members of that population, whose number and strength could not be precisely and quickly ascertained. We cannot say that the warmaking branches of the Government did not have ground for believing that in a critical hour such persons could not readily be isolated and separately dealt with, and constituted a menace to the national defense and safety, which demanded that prompt and adequate measures be taken to guard against it."

Like curfew, exclusion of those of Japanese origin was deemed necessary because of the presence of an unascertained number of disloyal members of the group, most of whom we have no doubt were loyal to this country. It was because we could not reject the finding of the military authorities that it was impossible to bring about an immediate segregation of the disloyal from the loyal that we sustained the validity of the curfew order as applying to the whole group. In the instant case, temporary exclusion of the entire group was rested by the military on the same ground. The judgment that exclusion of the whole group was for the same reason a military imperative answers the contention that the exclusion was in the nature of group punishment based on antagonism to those of Japanese origin. That there were members of the group who retained loyalties to Japan has been confirmed by investigations made subsequent to the exclusion. Approximately five thousand American citizens of Japanese ancestry refused to swear unqualified allegiance to the United States and to renounce allegiance to the Japanese Emperor, and several thousand evacuees requested repatriation to Japan.

We uphold the exclusion order as of the time it was made and when the petitioner violated it. . . . In doing so, we are not unmindful of the hardships imposed by it upon a large group of American citizens. . . . But hardships are part of war, and war is an aggregation of hardships. All citizens alike, both in and out of uniform, feel the impact of war in greater or lesser measure. Citizenship has its responsibilities as well as its privileges, and in time of war the burden is always heavier. Compulsory exclusion of large groups of citizens from their homes, except under circumstances of direst emergency and peril, is inconsistent with our basic governmental institution. But when under conditions of modern warfare our shores are threatened by hostile forces, the power to protect must be commensurate with the threatened danger. . . .

[The Court dealt at some length with a technical complication which arose in the case. On May 30, the date on which Korematsu was charged with remaining unlawfully in the prohibited area, there were two conflicting military orders outstanding, one forbidding him to remain in the area, the other forbidding him to leave but ordering him to report to an assembly center. Thus, he alleged, he was punished for doing what it was made a crime to fail to do. The Court held the orders not to be contradictory, since the requirement to report to the assembly center was merely a step in an orderly program of compulsory evacuation from the area.]

It is said that we are dealing here with the case of imprisonment of a citizen in a concentration camp solely because of his ancestry, without evidence or inquiry concerning his loyalty and good disposition towards the United States. Our task would be simple, our duty clear, were this a case involving the imprisonment of a loyal citizen in a concentration camp because of racial prejudice. Regardless of the true nature of the assembly and relocation centers—and we deem it unjustifiable to call them concentration camps with all the ugly connotations that term implies—we are dealing specifically with nothing but an exclusion order. To cast this case into outlines of racial prejudice, without reference to the real military dangers which were presented, merely confuses the issue. Korematsu was not excluded from the Military Area because of hostility to him or his race. He was excluded because we are at war with the Japanese Empire, because the properly constituted military authorities feared an invasion of our West Coast and felt constrained to take proper security measures, because they decided that the military urgency of the situation demanded that all citizens of Japanese ancestry be segregated from the West Coast temporarily, and finally, because Congress reposing its confidence in this time of war in our military leaders—as inevitably it must—determined that they should have the power to do just this. There was evidence of disloyalty on the part of some, the military authorities considered that the need for action was great, and time was short. We cannot—by availing ourselves of the calm perspective of hindsight—now say that at that time these actions were unjustified.

Affirmed.

Mr. Justice Frankfurter wrote a concurring opinion. Justices Roberts, Murphy, and Jackson each wrote a dissenting opinion.

20

Brown v. Board of Education of Topeka, 1954

Mr. Chief Justice Warren delivered the opinion of the Court.

These cases come to us from the States of Kansas, South Carolina, Virginia, and Delaware. They are premised on different facts and different local conditions, but a common legal question justifies their consideration together in this consolidated opinion.[1]

In each of the cases, minors of the Negro race, through their legal representatives, seek the aid of the courts in obtaining admission to the public schools of their community on a nonsegregated basis. In each instance, they had been denied admission to schools attended by white children under laws requiring or permitting segregation according to race. This segregation was alleged to deprive the plaintiffs of the equal protection of the laws under the Fourteenth Amendment. In each of the cases other than the Delaware case, a three-judge federal district court denied relief to the plaintiffs on the so-called "separate but equal" doctrine announced by this Court in Plessy v. Ferguson, 163 U.S. 537. Under that doctrine, equality of treatment is accorded when the races are provided substantially equal facilities, even though these facilities be separate. In the Delaware case, the Supreme Court of Delaware adhered to that doctrine, but ordered that the plaintiffs be admitted to the white schools because of their superiority to the Negro schools.

The plaintiffs contend that segregated public schools are not "equal" and cannot be made "equal," and that hence they are deprived of the equal protection of the laws. Because of the obvious importance of the question presented, the Court took jurisdiction.[2] Argument was heard in the 1952 Term, and reargument was heard this Term on certain questions propounded by the Court. . . .[3]

In approaching this problem, we cannot turn the clock back to 1868 when the Amendment was adopted, or even to 1896 when Plessy v. Ferguson was written. We must consider public education in the light of its full development and its present place in American life throughout the Nation. Only in this way can it be determined if segregation in public schools deprives these plaintiffs of the equal protection of the laws.

Today, education is perhaps the most important function of state and local governments. Compulsory school attendance laws and the great expenditures for education both demonstrate our recognition of the importance of education to our democratic society. It is required in the performance of our most basic public responsibilities, even service in the armed forces. It is the very foundation of good citizenship. Today it is a principal instrument in awakening the child to cultural values, in preparing him for later professional training, and in helping him to adjust normally to his environment. In these days, it is doubtful that any child may reasonably be expected to succeed in life if he is denied the opportunity of an education. Such an opportunity, where the state has undertaken to provide it, is a right which must be made available to all on equal terms.

We come then to the question presented: Does segregation of children in public schools solely on the basis of race, even though the physical facilities and other "tangible" factors may be equal, deprive the children of the minority group of equal educational opportunities? We believe that it does.

In Sweatt v. Painter, in finding that a segregated law school for Negroes could not provide them equal educational opportunities, this Court relied in large part on "those qualities which are incapable of objective measurement but which make for greatness in a law school." In McLaurin v. Oklahoma State Regents, the Court, in requiring that a Negro admitted to a white graduate school be treated like all other students, again resorted to intangible considerations: ". . . his ability to study, to engage in discussions and exchange views with other students, and in general, to learn his profession." Such considerations apply with added force to children in grade and high schools. To separate them from others of similar age and qualifications solely because of their race generates a feeling of inferiority as to their status in the community that may affect their hearts and minds in a way unlikely ever to be undone. The effect of this separation on their educational opportunities was well stated by a finding in the Kansas case by a court which nevertheless felt compelled to rule against the Negro plaintiffs:

> Segregation of white and colored children in public schools has a detrimental effect upon the colored children. The impact is greater when it has the sanction of the law; for the policy of separating the races is usually interpreted as denoting the inferiority of the negro group. A sense of inferiority affects the motivation of a child to learn. Segregation with the sanction of law, therefore, has a tendency to [retard] the educational and mental development of negro children and to deprive them of some of the benefits they receive in a racial[ly] integrated school system.[4]

Whatever may have been the extent of psychological knowledge at the time of Plessy v. Ferguson, this finding is amply supported by modern authority.[5] Any language in Plessy v. Ferguson contrary to this finding is rejected.

We conclude that in the field of public education the doctrine of "separate but equal" has no place. Separate educational facilities are inherently unequal. Therefore, we hold that the plaintiffs and others similarly situated for whom the actions have been brought are, by reason of the segregation complained of, deprived of the equal protection of the laws guaranteed by the Fourteenth Amendment. This disposition makes unnecessary any discussion whether such segregation also violates the Due Process Clause of the Fourteenth Amendment.

Because these are class actions, because of the wide applicability of this decision, and because of the great variety of local conditions, the formulation of decrees in these cases presents problems of considerable complexity. On reargument, the consideration of appropriate relief was necessarily subordinated to the primary question—the constitutionality of segregation in public education. We have now announced that such segregation is a denial of the equal protection of the laws. In order that we may have the full assistance of the parties in formulating decrees, the cases will be restored to the docket, and the parties are requested to present further argument on Questions 4 and 5 previously propounded by the Court for the reargument this Term.[6] The Attorney General of the United States is again invited to participate. The Attorneys General of the states requiring or permitting segregation in public education will also be permitted to appear as amici curiae upon request to do so by September 15, 1954, and submission of the briefs by October 1, 1954.

It is so ordered.

NOTES

1. In the Kansas case, Brown v. Board of Education, the plaintiffs are Negro children of elementary school age residing in Topeka. They brought this action in the United States District Court for the District of Kansas to enjoin enforcement of a Kansas statute which permits, but does not require, cities of more than 15,000 population to maintain separate school facilities for Negro and white students. Kan. Gen. Stat. §72-1724 (1949). Pursuant to that authority, the Topeka Board of Education elected to establish segregated elementary schools. Other public schools in the community, however, are operated on a nonsegregated basis. The three-judge District Court, convened under 28 U.S.C. §§2281 and 2284, found that segregation in public education has a detrimental effect upon Negro children, but denied relief on the ground that the Negro and white schools were substantially equal with respect to buildings, transportation, curricula, and educational qualifications of teachers. 98 F. Supp. 797. The case is here on direct appeal under 28 U.S.C. §1253. [The Topeka, Kansas case would be analogous to a Northern school case inasmuch as the school segregation that existed in Topeka was not mandated by state law, and some of the system was integrated. It would be eighteen years before the Court would accept another such case for review. Keyes v. School District No. 1, Denver, 445 F.2d 990 (10th Cir. 1971), cert. granted, 404 U.S. 1036 (1972)].

In the South Carolina case, Briggs v. Elliot, the plaintiffs are Negro children of both elementary and high school age residing in Clarendon County. They brought this action in the United States District Court for the Eastern District of South Carolina to enjoin enforcement of provisions in the state constitution and statutory code which require the segregation of Negroes and whites in public schools. S.C. Const., Art. XI, §7; S.C. Code §5377 (1942). The three-judge District Court, convened under 28 U.S.C. §§2281 and 2284, denied the requested relief. The court found that the Negro schools were inferior to the white schools and ordered the defendants to begin immediately to equalize the facilities. But the court sustained the validity of the contested provisions and denied the plaintiffs admission to the white schools during the equalization program. 98 F. Supp. 529. This Court vacated the District Court's judgment and remanded the case for the purpose of obtaining the court's views on a report filed by the defendants concerning the progress made in the equalization program. 342 U.S. 350. On remand, the District Court found that substantial equality had been achieved except for buildings and that the defendants were proceeding to rectify this inequality as well. 103 F. Supp. 920. The case is again here on direct appeal under 28 U.S.C. §1253.

In the Virginia case, Davis v. County School Board, the plaintiffs are Negro children of high school age residing in Prince Edward County. They brought this action in the United States District Court for the Eastern District of Virginia to enjoin enforcement of provisions in the state constitution and statutory code which require the segregation of Negroes and whites in public schools. Va. Const., §140; Va. Code §22-221 (1950). The three-judge District Court, convened under 28 U.S.C. §§2281 and 2284, denied the requested relief. The court found the Negro school inferior in physical plant, curricula, and transportation, and ordered the defendants forthwith to provide substantially equal curricula and transportation and to "proceed with all reasonable diligence and dispatch to remove" the inequality in physical plant. But, as in the South Carolina case, the court sustained the validity of the contested provisions and denied the plaintiffs admission to the white schools during the equalization program. 103 F. Supp. 337. The case is here on direct appeal under 28 U.S.C. §1253.

In the Delaware case, Gebhart v. Belton, the plaintiffs are Negro children of both elementary and high school age residing in New Castle County. They brought this action in the Delaware Court of Chancery to enjoin enforcement of provisions in the state constitution and statutory code which require the segregation of Negroes and whites in public schools. Del. Const., Art. X, §2; Del. Rev. Code §2631 (1935). The chancellor gave judgment for the plaintiffs and ordered their immediate admission to schools previously attended only by white children, on the ground that the Negro schools were inferior with respect to teacher training, pupil-teacher ratio, extracurricular activities, physical plant, and time and distance involved in travel. 87 A.2d 862. The Chancellor also found that segregation itself results in an inferior education for Negro children (see note 4, infra), but did not rest his decision on that ground. Id., at 865. The Chancellor's decree was affirmed by the Supreme Court of Delaware, which intimated, however, that the defendants might be able to obtain a modification of the decree after equalization of the Negro and white schools had been accomplished. 91 A.2d 137, 152. The defendants, contending only that the Delaware courts had erred in ordering the immediate admission of the Negro plaintiffs to the white schools, applied to this Court for certiorari. The writ was granted, 344 U.S. 891. The plaintiffs, who were successful below, did not submit a cross-petition.

2. 344 U.S. 1, 141, 891.

3. 345 U.S. 972. The Attorney General of the United States participated both Terms as amicus curiae.

4. A similar finding was made in the Delaware case: "I conclude from the testimony that in our Delaware Society, State-imposed segregation in education itself results in the Negro children, as a class, receiving educational opportunities which are substantially inferior to those available to white children otherwise similarly situated." 87 A.2d 862, 865.

5. K. B. Clark, Effect of Prejudice and Discrimination on Personality Development (Midcentury White House Conference on Children and Youth, 1950); Witmer and Kotinsky, Personality in the Making (1952), c. VI; Deutscher and Chein, The Psychological Effects of Enforced Segregation: A Survey of Social Science Opinion, 26 J. Psychol. 259 (1948); Chein, What are the Psychological Effects of Segregation Under Conditions of Equal Facilities?, 3 Int. J. Opinion and Attitude Res. 229 (1949); Brameld, Educational Costs, in

Discrimination and National Welfare (MacIver, ed., 1949), 44–48; Frazier, The Negro in the United States (1949), 674–681. And see generally Myrdal, An American Dilemma (1944).

6. "4. Assuming it is decided that segregation in public schools violates the Fourteenth Amendment

"(a) would a decree necessarily follow providing that, within the limits set by normal geographic school districting, Negro children should forthwith be admitted to schools of their choice, or

"(b) may this Court, in the exercise of its equity powers, permit an effective gradual adjustment to be brought about from existing segregated systems to a system not based on color distinctions?

"5. On the assumption on which questions 4(a) and (b) are based, and assuming further that this Court will exercise its equity powers to the end described in question 4(b),

"(a) should this Court formulate detailed decrees in these cases;

"(b) if so, what specific issues should the decrees reach;

"(c) should this Court appoint a special master to hear evidence with a view to recommending specific terms for such decrees;

"(d) should this Court remand to the courts of first instance with directions to frame decrees in these cases, and if so what general directions should the decrees of this Court include and what procedures should the courts of first instance follow in arriving at the specific terms of more detailed decrees?"

21

Roe v. Wade, 1973

This historic decision legalized a woman's right to terminate her pregnancy by abortion. The ruling was based upon the right of privacy founded on both the Fourteenth and Ninth Amendments to the Constitution. The court ruled that this right of privacy protected the individual from interference by the state in the decision to terminate a pregnancy by abortion during the early portion of the pregnancy. At the same time, it recognized the interest of the state in regulating decisions concerning the pregnancy during the latter period as the fetus developed the capacity to survive outside the woman's body.

22

Equal Protection and Affirmative Action:
Bakke and *Weber**

Two of the more controversial equal protection cases before the court in the 1970s questioned whether affirmative action programs—designed to compensate for past discrimination against blacks and other minorities—themselves denied equal protection of the laws by favoring minority over majority group members.

Initially sidestepping the issue in 1974, the court in 1978 and 1979 sought to provide an answer to this question.

- In 1978 the court held that Title VI of the Civil Rights Act of 1964, which barred discrimination in any program receiving federal financial assistance, prohibited state universities from setting racial quotas for their entering classes. But in the same decision, the court said that the equal protection clause of the 14th Amendment did not forbid state universities to consider race as one of the factors determining acceptance or rejection of a student application.
- In 1979 the court held that Title VII of the 1964 Civil Rights Act, which barred employment discrimination, did not prohibit employers from voluntarily establishing affirmative action training programs.

The *DeFunis* Case

In the 1974 case of *DeFunis* v. *Odegaard*, a five-justice majority avoided a ruling on the reverse discrimination issue by finding the case moot, no longer presenting a live controversy. The white plaintiff, who charged that he was denied admission to a state law school in order that the school might accept a less-qualified minority student, had been admitted under court order. He was scheduled to graduate from law school in the spring of 1974, only months after the court heard arguments in his case. The majority held that the case was moot since their decision on the equal

*From *Congressional Quarterly's Guide to the United States Supreme Court.*

protection issue would have no effect on the plaintiff. The dissenting justices would have preferred to resolve the substantive question. [1]

The *Bakke* Case

When the court in 1978 finally dealt with a live case of reverse discrimination, it handed down a split decision. By a 5–4 vote, the court ruled that state universities may not set aside a fixed quota of seats in each class for minority group members, denying white applicants the opportunity to compete for those places. At the same time, a different five-justice majority held that it is constitutionally permissible for admissions officers to consider race as one of the complex of factors that determine which applicant is accepted and which rejected.

Background

Allan Bakke, a 38-year-old white engineer, was twice denied admission to the medical school at the University of California at Davis. To ensure minority representation in the student body, the university had set aside 16 seats in each 100-member medical school class for minority applicants.

Challenging the program as a violation of his constitutional right to equal protection of the law, Bakke contended that he would have been admitted had it not been for this rigid preference system. In each year his application was rejected, the school did accept some minority applicants with qualifications inferior to Bakke's.

Quotas

Justice Lewis F. Powell Jr. was the only justice who agreed with both halves of the decision in *University of California Regents* v. *Bakke*. On the first decision setting aside the Davis quota system, Powell voted with Chief Justice Warren E. Burger and Justices William H. Rehnquist, Potter Stewart and John Paul Stevens. These four viewed the Bakke case as a "controversy between two specific litigants" which could be settled by applying the 1964 Civil Rights Act and which did not require consideration of constitutional issues. Title VI of the 1964 act, this majority pointed out, barred any discrimination on the ground of race, color or national origin in any program receiving federal financial assistance. When the ban was placed alongside the facts of the case, it was clear to Burger, Rehnquist, Stewart and Stevens that the university had violated the statute.

As Stevens explained:

> The University, through its special admissions policy, excluded Bakke from participation in its program of medical education because of his race. The University

also acknowledges that it was, and still is, receiving federal financial assistance. . . . The meaning of the Title VI ban on exclusion is crystal clear: Race cannot be the basis of excluding anyone from participation in a federally funded program.[2]

Powell's reasoning on this point differed from the four. Where they found no constitutional involvement, he found the scope of the Title VI ban and the equal protection clause of the 14th Amendment identical—what violated one therefore violated the other. And so he based his vote against the university's preference system on both the law and the Constitution.

The Davis special admissions program used an "explicit racial classification," Powell noted. Such classifications were not always unconstitutional, he continued, "[b]ut when a state's distribution of benefits or imposition of burdens hinges on . . . the color of a person's skin or ancestry, that individual is entitled to a demonstration that the challenged classification is necessary to promote a substantial state interest." Powell could find no substantial interest that justified establishment of the university's specific quota system. Not even the desire to remedy past discrimination was a sufficient justification, he said; such a desire was based on "an amorphous concept of injury that may be ageless in its reach into the past."[3]

Affirmative Action

But Powell's belief that not all racial classifications were unconstitutional led him to vote with the other four justices to approve the use of some race-conscious affirmative action programs. These four were Justices William J. Brennan, Jr., Thurgood Marshall, Harry A. Blackmun and Byron R. White.

Powell's vote endorsing this position was cautious; he would limit the use of these programs to situations in which past discrimination had been proved. The other four contended that the university's wish to remedy past societal discrimination was sufficient justification. For the four, Brennan wrote:

> Government may take race into account when it acts not to demean or insult any racial group, but to remedy disadvantages cast on minorities by past racial prejudice, at least when appropriate findings have been made by judicial, legislative, or administrative bodies with competence to act in this area.[4]

The four endorsed the broad remedial use of race-conscious programs, even in situations where no specific constitutional violation had been found.

The *Weber* Case

The 1979 case did not raise the constitutional issue of equal protection. It posed only the question whether the Title VII prohibition against racial discrimination in employment barred an employer from establishing an affirmative action training program that preferred blacks over whites.

By a 5–2 vote, the court held that Title VII did not bar such a program. Stewart, who had voted against racial quotas in the *Bakke* case, joined the four justices who had endorsed use of race-conscious programs in that case to form the majority in *Weber*. Chief Justice Burger and Rehnquist dissented; Powell and Stevens did not participate in the case.

Background

In 1974 Kaiser Aluminum and the United Steelworkers of America agreed upon an affirmative action plan that reserved 50 percent of all in-plant craft training slots for minorities. The agreement was a voluntary effort to increase the number of minority participants holding skilled jobs in the aluminum industry.

Brian Weber, a white, applied for a training program at the Kaiser plant where he worked in Gramercy, La. He was rejected. Weber, who had more seniority than the most junior black accepted for the program, charged that he had been a victim of "reverse discrimination." He won at both the federal district court and the court of appeals levels. The union, the company and the Justice Department then asked the Supreme Court to review the appeals court decision in three separate cases—*United Steelworkers of America* v. *Weber, Kaiser Aluminum & Chemical Corp.* v. *Weber, United States* v. *Weber*—which the court consolidated for argument and decision.[5]

Permissible Plan

Reversing the lower courts, the majority said that in passing Title VII Congress could not have intended to prohibit private employers from voluntarily instituting affirmative action plans to open opportunities for blacks in job areas traditionally closed to them:

> . . .It would be ironic indeed if a law triggered by a Nation's concern over centuries of racial injustice and intended to improve the lot of those who had "been excluded from the American dream for so long" . . . constituted the first legislative prohibition of all voluntary, private, race-conscious efforts to abolish traditional patterns of racial segregation and hierarchy.[6]

The majority carefully distinguished between the language of Title VII prohibiting racial discrimination in employment and Title VI, the section of the act reviewed in the *Bakke* case and held by a majority of the court to mean that programs receiving federal aid could not discriminate on the basis of race. In Title VI, Brennan said for the majority, "Congress was legislating to assure federal funds would not be used in an improper manner. Title VII, by contrast was enacted pursuant to the Commerce power to regulate purely private decisionmaking and was not intended to incorporate and particularize the commands of the Fifth and Fourteenth Amendments" which guarantee equal protection of the laws against federal and state infringement.[7]

In separate dissents Chief Justice Burger and Rehnquist objected to the majority's interpretation of Title VII and its legislative history. The court's judgment, Burger wrote:

> . . .is contrary to the explicit language of the statute and arrived at by means wholly incompatible with long-established principles of separation of powers. Under the guise of statutory "construction," the Court effectively rewrites Title VII to achieve what it regards as a desirable result. It "amends" the statute to do precisely what both its sponsors and its opponents agreed the statute was not *intended* to do.[8]

Rehnquist also claimed that the majority had contorted the language of Title VII. The majority opinion, he said, is "reminiscent not of jurists such as Hale, Holmes and Hughes, but of escape artists such as Houdini. . . ." The court, he continued, "eludes clear statutory language, 'uncontradicted' legislative history, and uniform precedent in concluding that employers are, after all, permitted to consider race in making employment decisions."[9]

NOTES

1. *DeFunis* v. *Odegaard*, 416 U.S. 312 (1974).
2. *University of California Regents* v. *Bakke*, 438 U.S. 265 at 412, 418 (1978).
3. Id. at 320, 307.
4. Id. at 325.
5. *United Steelworkers of America* v. *Weber*, *Kaiser Aluminum & Chemical Corp.* v. *Weber*, *United States* v. *Weber* (1979).
6. Id.
7. Id.
8. Id.
9. Id.

23

Affirmative Action in the 1980s:

Dismantling the Process of Discrimination

United States Commission on Civil Rights

During the past decade, the concept of affirmative action has emerged as the focal point of public debate over civil rights. Controversy and confusion have surrounded certain elements of affirmative action and affirmative action plans. On the surface they seem paradoxical and at odds with the goal of a "color blind" America that makes its decisions without reference to race, sex, or national origin. How can means that consciously use race, sex, and national origin be reconciled with ends that preclude any consciousness of race, sex, and national origin?

Removing the arbitrary and historic limits that discrimination has imposed on individual opportunities is a widely shared objective. There is also support for the use of affirmative action plans designed to attain these ends. Agreement often disappears, however, when those plans call for measures designated as "goals," "quotas," or other types of "preferential treatment." Many people voice concern that such affirmative measures are or may become basically indistinguishable from "quotas" used in the past to stigmatize identifiable groups and may defeat the very objective—eliminating discrimination—that affirmative action programs are designed to achieve.

This Commission has stated in other documents,[1] and restates here, its vigorous opposition to invidious quotas whose purpose is to exclude identifiable groups from opportunities. On the other hand, we maintain our unwavering support for affirmative action plans and the full range of affirmative measures necessary to make equal opportunity a reality for historically excluded groups. The Federal courts, Congress, and the executive branch as well have decried quotas born of prejudice. But they have also repeatedly ordered and permitted numerically based remedies that explicitly take race, sex, and national origin into account. . . .

In the United States, individual bias or prejudice deriving from notions of white and male supremacy and other forms of overt bigotry are the most widely recognized forms of discrimination. Over the years the American public has made progress toward rejecting such outright acts of prejudice as governmentally required segregation, the mistreatment of American Indians, racially exclusionary immigration laws, and the sometimes unintended legal subordination of women under the guise of "protective" laws. Nonetheless, practical experience in enforcing civil rights laws has shown that prejudice is perpetuated by many institutional processes and that discrimination is more complicated than individual acts of prejudice based on irrational ideas of racial and gender superiority. [2]

Despite civil rights and a noticeable improvement in public attitudes towards civil rights,[3] continued inequalities compel the conclusion that our history of racism and sexism continues to affect the present. A steady flow of data shows unmistakably that most of the historic victims of discrimination are still being victimized and that more recently arrived groups have also become victims of ongoing discriminatory attitudes and processes. Social indicators reveal persistent and widespread gaps throughout our society between the status of white males and the rest of the population.[4]

"Goals," "Quotas," and Other Types of "Preferential Treatment"

As a nation, we are committed to making our differences in skin color, gender, and ancestry sources of strength and beneficial diversity, and not grounds for oppression or mindless uniformity. Consequently, agreement on the need to identify discrimination based on race, sex, and national origin and to eliminate it through an affirmative action plan is frequently, and often easily, reached. Few fair-minded persons argue with the objective of increasing the participation of minorities and women in those areas from which they have been historically excluded. Heated controversy occurs, however, over particular methods affirmative action plans employ to achieve this common objective. The focal point of this controversy is usually not the entire affirmative action plan, nor its objective of eliminating discrimination, but those particular affirmative measures within the plan that explicitly take race, sex, and national origin into account in numerical terms. Those measures are popularly referred to as "goals," "quotas," and other types of "preferential treatment."

These terms have dominated the debate over affirmative action, often obscuring issues rather than clarifying them. The problem-remedy approach, the Commission believes, can help reorient this debate. It makes clear that the discrimination that exists within an organization forms the basis for the affirmative measures that are chosen—whether characterized as "goals," "quotas," or other types of "preferential treatment." The problem-remedy approach stresses the nature and extent of discrimination and what measures will work best to eliminate such discrimination, not what word to use to describe those measures.

The civil rights community has labored hard to define the point at which affirmative uses of race, sex, and national origin within affirmative action plans become objectionable. For many, the issue is how to distinguish a "goal," or the pursuit of a "goal," from a "quota." There is widespread acceptance of such affirmative measures as undertaking recruiting efforts, establishing special training programs, and reviewing selection procedures. On the other hand, firing whites or men to hire minorities or women, and choosing unqualified people simply to increase participation by minorities and women, are universally condemned practices. With respect to those affirmative measures that do not fall neatly on either end of this spectrum, however, distinctions are far harder to draw. These distinctions are not made easier by calling acceptable measures "goals" and objectionable ones "quotas."

For example, as part of an affirmative action plan, an employer could use any one or all of the following affirmative techniques: extensive recruiting of minorities and women; revising selection procedures so as not to exclude qualified minorities and women; assigning a "plus" over and above other factors to qualified minorities and women; specifying that among qualified applicants a certain ratio or percentage of minorities and women to white males will be selected. Similar measures could be undertaken by colleges and universities in their admissions programs.

These actions could all be taken to reach designated numerical objectives, or "goals." While the establishment of goals, and timetables to meet them, provides for accountability by setting benchmarks for success, their presence or absence does not aid in choosing which measures to use to achieve the "goals," nor make those measures any more or less affirmative in nature. The critical question is, Which affirmative measures should be used in which situations to reach the designated "goals?" The answer to this question, the Commission believes, is best found by analyzing the nature and extent of the discrimination confronting the organization.

Obviously, the last example given above of an affirmative method for reaching an objective—a percentage selection procedure—has characteristics of a "quota." But attaching this label to certain affirmative measures does not render them illegal. The preceding section of this statement explained that the lower courts have repeatedly ordered percentage and ratio selection techniques to remedy proven discrimination. In *Weber* and *Fullilove* the Supreme Court of the United States approved of measures that cannot easily evade the description of "quotas." In *Bakke* four of nine Justices approved a medical school's "set aside" program, arguing that any system that uses race, sex, or national origin as a factor in selection procedures is constitutionally no different from such a "quota" system.[5] A fifth Justice indicated such a program would be legal under circumstances not present in that case. Rigorous opposition to all "quotas," therefore, does not aid in distinguishing when to use, or not to use, these kinds of legally acceptable, and sometimes required, affirmative remedies.

A debate that hinges on whether a particular measure is a "goal" or a "quota" is unproductive both legally and as a matter of policy, in choosing which kinds of affirmative measures to use in given situations. It loses sight of the problem of discrimination by arguing over what to label remedial measures. Whichever affirmative measure may be chosen—from recruiting to openly stated percentage selection procedures, with or without specific numerical targets—depends as a matter of law and policy on the factual circumstances confronting the organization undertaking the affirmative action plan. The problem-remedy approach urges using the nature and extent of discrimination as the primary basis for deciding among possible remedies. The affirmative measure that most effectively remedies the identified discriminatory problem should be chosen.

Regardless of the particular affirmative technique that is selected, any affirmative measure will be conscious of race, sex, and national origin in order to bring minorities and women into areas from which they were formerly excluded. Experience has shown, however, that in many circumstances, without such conscious efforts related to race, sex, and national origin, opportunities for minorities and women will not be opened.

By broadening the present field of competition for opportunities, affirmative action plans function to decrease the privileges and prospects for success some white males previously, and almost automatically, enjoyed. For example, a graduate school with a virtually all-white student body that extensively recruits minorities or women is likely to fill some available positions with minorities or women, not white males. A bank with its base in the white community that invests new energies and funds in minority housing and business markets has less available capital to channel to whites. A police force that has excluded minorities or women in the past and substitutes new promotion criteria for seniority will promote some recently hired minorities or women over more senior white male police officers.

Such affirmative efforts are easier to implement when new resources are available.[6] Additional openings, increased investment funds, and more jobs add to everyone's opportunities, and no one—neither white males nor minorities and women—has any better claim to these resources than anyone else. But whether new resources become available, remain constant, or even diminish, decisions must be made. Frequently the basic choice is between present activities that, through the process of discrimination, favor white males, or affirmative action plans that consciously work to eliminate such discrimination.

The problem-remedy framework does *not* suggest that the purpose of affirmative action plans is to "prefer" certain groups over others. To criticize affirmative measures on the ground that they constitute "preferential treatment" inaccurately implies unfairness by ignoring their purpose as a means to dismantle a process that presently allocates opportunities discriminatorily.

Affirmative measures intervene in a status quo that systematically disfavors minorities and women in order to provide them with increased opportunities. While it is appropriate to debate which kinds of "preferential treatment" to use under what circumstances, the touchstone of the decision should be how the process of discrimination manifests itself and which affirmative measure promises to be the most effective in dismantling it.

What distinguishes such "preferential treatment" attributable to affirmative action plans from "quotas" used in the past[7] is the fact that the lessened opportunities for white males are incidental and not generated by prejudice or bigotry. The purpose of affirmative action plans is to eliminate notions of racial, gender, and ethnic inferiority or superiority, not perpetuate them. Moreover, affirmative action plans occur in situations in which white males as a group already hold powerful positions. Neither Federal law, Federal policy, nor this Commission endorse affirmative measures when used, as were "quotas" in the past, to stigmatize and set a ceiling on the aspirations of entire groups of people.

Support for affirmative action to dismantle the process of discrimination, however, does not mean insensitivity to the interests of white males. To the greatest extent possible, the costs of affirmative action should be borne by the decisionmakers who are responsible for discrimination, and not by white males who played no role in that process. In fashioning remedial relief for minorities and women, the courts have tried to avoid penalizing white male workers who were not responsible for the challenged discrimination. For example, rather than displacing white male employees who were hired or promoted through discriminatory personnel actions, courts in such cases have directed that the victims of the discrimination be compensated at the rate they would have earned had they been selected, until such time as they can move into the position in question without displacing the incumbent.[8] The Supreme Court has noted the availability of this "front pay" remedy as one way of "shifting to the employer the burden of the past discrimination."[9]

In addition, the law prohibits "*unnecessarily* trammeling" the interests of white males,[10] thereby protecting the existing status of white males (as distinguished from their expectations) from arbitrary affirmative action plans. Thus, there may be situations where minorities and women do not obtain the positions they might otherwise hold, because doing so would require displacing whites from their present jobs.[11] On the other hand, situations may occur in redressing discrimination that require disappointing the expectations of some individual white males.[12]

One of the most difficult areas in which to balance the national interest in eliminating discrimination against minorities and women and the interests of individual white men who may have to share with minorities and women the burden of past discrimination occurs when a downturn in business requires an employer to lay off workers. Historically, the groups hit first and hardest by recessions and depressions have been minorities and women. In the past, they were the last hired and the first fired. Today, employment provisions that call for layoffs on the basis of seniority can have the same result. In companies that used to exclude minorities and women, they will tend to have the lowest seniority and be layed off first and recalled last. To break this historical cycle and prevent recently integrated work forces from returning to their prior segregated status, this Commission has recommended, and at least one court has approved, a proportional layoff procedure.[13] Under this system, separate seniority lists for minorities, women, and white males are drawn up solely for layoff purposes, and employees are laid off from each list according to their percentages in the employer's work force.[14] There also are other methods that would preserve the opportunities created by affirmative action plans with less impact on senior white male workers, such as work sharing, inverse seniority, and various public policy changes in unemployment compensation.[15] If none of these or similar alternatives are pursued, however, the use of standard "last hired, first fired" procedures means that opportunities laboriously created in the 1970s may be destroyed during hard times in the 1980s.

In the short run, some white males will undoubtedly feel, and some may in fact be, deprived of certain opportunities as a result of affirmative action plans. Our civil rights laws, however, are a statement that such imagined or real deprivations cannot be allowed to block efforts to dismantle the process of discrimination.

Although affirmative action plans may adversely affect *individual* white males, they do not unfairly burden white males *as a class*. Their share as a class is reduced only to what it would be without discrimination against minorities and women. Emphasis on the expectations of the individual white male downplays the overall fairness of the plan, the discrimination experienced by minorities and women, and the fact that affirmative action has often produced and should continue to produce changes in our institutions that are beneficial to everyone, including white males. In eliminating the arbitrariness of some qualification standards, affirmative action can permit previously excluded white males to compete with minorities and females for jobs once closed to all of them. . . .[16]

Other Concerns

Perhaps the most serious charge against affirmative action is that affirmative remedies substitute numerical equality for traditional criteria of merit in both employment and university admissions. Neither the Nation's laws nor this Commission calls for the arbitrary lowering of valid standards. Affirmative action plans often require, however, the examination and sometimes the discarding of standards that, although traditionally believed to measure qualifications, in fact are not demonstrably related to successful performance as an employer or a student. Whether conscious or unconscious, overt or subtle, intentional or unintentional, the use of such standards may deny opportunities to minorities or women, as well as others, for reasons unrelated to real merit.

Some invalid standards used in one institution may build on discrimination that exists or has existed in other institutions. In the *Griggs* case, for example, the tests and high school diploma required as conditions of employment as a "coal handler," though invalidated because they did not measure ability to perform the job, were called into question because they operated disproportionately to exclude minorities as a result of past discrimination in education. Valid standards, however, may also exacerbate such discrimination. Because of the pervasive and cumulative effects of the process of discrimination, some minorities and women may lack the necessary skills, experience, or credentials that are valid qualifications for the positions they seek. In such situations, there are no legal obligations that would require their selection.

Instead of reinforcing such economic, social, and political disadvantages, however, civil rights law encourages organizations and institutions to develop new standards that are equally related to successful performance and do not discriminate against minorities and women, or to develop training programs that give minorities and women opportunities denied them by other sectors of our society.[17] Affirmative action, therefore, while leading to the dismantling of the process of discrimination, need not and should not endanger valid standards of merit. . . .

Arguments against affirmative action have been raised under the banner of "reverse discrimination." To be sure, there have been incidents of arbitrary action against white males because of their race or sex. But the charge of "reverse discrimination," in essence, equates efforts to dismantle the process of discrimination with that process itself. Such an equation is profoundly and fundamentally incorrect.

Affirmative measures are not an attempt to establish a system of superiority for minorities and women, as our historic and ongoing discriminatory processes too often have done for white males. Nor are affirmative measures designed to stigmatize white males, as do the abusive stereotypes of minorities and women that stem from past discrimination and are perpetuated in the present. Affirmative measures end when the discriminatory process ends, but without affirmative intervention, the discriminatory process may never end.

Properly designed and administered affirmative action plans can create a climate of equality that supports all efforts to break down the structural, organizational, and personal barriers that perpetuate injustice. They can be comprehensive plans that combat all manifestations of the complex process of discrimination. In such a climate, differences among racial and ethic groups and between men and women become simply differences, not badges that connote domination or subordination, superiority or inferiority.

NOTES

1. U.S., Commission on Civil Rights, *Toward Equal Educational Opportunity: Affirmative Admissions Programs at Law and Medical Schools* (1978); *Statement on Affirmative Action* (1977); *Statement on Affirmative Action for Equal Employment Opportunities* (1973).

2. Prior to 1964, "employment discrimination tended to be viewed as a series of isolated and distinguishable events due, for the most part, to the ill-will on the part of some identifiable individual or organization. . . . Employment discrimination, as we know today, is a far more complex and pervasive phenomenon." H. R. Rep. No. 92-238, 92d Cong., 1st Sess., *reprinted in* [1972] U.S. Code Cong. & Ad. News 2143–44.

3. Public opinion polls reveal that the expression of prejudiced attitudes towards blacks and women have continued to decline, particularly in the past decade, although such prejudice persists in a significant percentage of the public. A 1978 Gallup Poll showed declining prejudice in issues related to housing, education, and politics. Between 1965 and 1978 the number of whites who said they would move out of their neighborhoods if blacks moved in declined from 35 percent to 16 percent. Between 1973 and 1978 the number of whites who said they would object to sending their children to schools having a majority of black students

also declined from 69 percent to 49 percent of southern whites and from 63 percent to 38 percent of northern whites. Between 1969 and 1978 the number of whites who said they would vote for a qualified black Presidential candidate of their own party also increased (from 67 percent to 77 percent). *Gallup Poll*, Aug. 27–28, 1978. Between 1971 and 1978 a declining number of whites said they believed blacks to be inferior (from 22 to 15 percent) or of less native intelligence than whites (from 37 percent to 25 percent). Poll by Louis Harris and Associates for the National Conference on Christians and Jews, *Newsweek*, Feb. 26, 1979, p. 48. With regard to women, the findings are ambiguous. Attitudes toward passage of the Equal Rights Amendment, for example, have changed little. A recent Gallup Poll shows no change in the percentage of the public that supports the ERA (56 percent in both 1975 and 1980). *Gallup Poll*, July 31, 1980. Another poll, by the Roper Organization, showed a decline in support for the ERA (from 55 percent of women and 68 percent of men in 1975 to 51 percent of women and 52 percent of men in 1980). However, the same poll indicated that support for efforts to strengthen women's status had increased (from 40 percent of women and 44 percent of men in 1970 to 60 percent of women and 64 percent of men in 1980). *Virginia Slims American Women's Opinion Poll*, Roper Organization, 1980.

4. The Commission has issued a report evaluating the Nation's progress toward equality by systematically comparing the social conditions of the minority and female population to those of the majority male population. U.S. Commission on Civil Rights, *Social Indicators of Equality For Minorities and Women* (1978). According to the report, minorities and women are less likely to have completed as many years of high school or have a high school or college education than white males. If not undereducated, they tend to be educationally overqualified for the work they do and earn less than comparably educated white males. As of 1976, among those persons 25–29 years of age, 34 of every 100 white males were college educated, while only 11 out of every 100 minorities were college educated. Ibid., p. 26.

Women and minorities are more likely to be unemployed, to have less prestigious occupations than white males, and to be concentrated in different occupations. From 1970 to 1976, when unemployment rates were rising for all groups, the disparity between minority and female rates and the majority male rate generally increased; blacks, Mexican Americans, and Puerto Ricans of both sexes moved from having approximately twice the unemployment of majority males in 1970 to nearly three times the majority. Federal Contract Compliance Programs of the Department of Labor have issued sound guidance materials to employers on how to conduct a self analysis and develop affirmative action plans. Equal Employment Opportunity Commission, *Affirmative Action and Equal Employment: A Guidebook for Employers*, 1974; U.S. Department of Labor, Office of Federal Contract Compliance, *Federal Contract Compliance Manual* (1979).

5. Regents of the University of California v. Bakke, 438 U.S. 265. 378 (1978) (joint opinion of Brennan, Marshall, White, and Blackmun, JJ.)

6. For example, in United Steelworkers of America v. Weber, the employer had hired, for its craft jobs, only workers with several years experience doing such work, thereby precluding its present employees who lacked these skills, which were nearly all of them, from obtaining these higher paying positions. 443 U.S. at 198. As part of an affirmative action plan, the employer agreed to pay the cost of an on-the-job training program open to whites as well as minorities and women.

7. See, e. g., N. Belth, A *Promise to Keep*, 96–110, (1979); B. Epstein and A. Forster, "*Some of My Best Friends*," 143–58, 169–83, 220–22 (1962).

8. Patterson v. American Tobacco Co., 535 F. 2d 257, 269 (4th Cir. 1976); Bush v.

Lone Star Steel Co., 373 F. Supp. 526, 538 (N.D. Tex. 1974); United States v. U.S. Steel Corp., 371 F. Supp. 1045, 1060 n. 38 (N.D. Ala. 1973), *modified on other grounds*, 520 F. 2d 1043 (5th Cir. 1976).

9. Franks v. Bowman Transportation Co., 424 U.S. 747 n. 38 (1976). *See also* McAleer v. American Tel. & Tel. Co., 416 F. Supp. 437 (D.D.C. 1976); German v. Kipp, 427 F. Supp. 1323 (W.D. Mo. 1977), *vacated as moot*, 572 F.2d 1258 (8th Cir. 1978). *But see,* Telephone Workers Union v. N.J. Bell Telephone Co., 450 F. Supp. 284 (D.N.J. 1977). This future-oriented form of compensation is supplementary to "backpay," which compensates victims of unlawful discrimination in an effort to restore the victim to the position he or she would have been in were it not for the unlawful discrimination. When a court awards backpay, the employer pays the victim for wages wrongfully denied in the past.

10. United Steelworkers of America v. Weber, 443 U.S. 193, 208 (1979) (emphasis added).

11. "Bumping" relief (the replacing of white male workers with minority or women workers) may not be used to remedy past discrimination. *See, e.g.,* Patterson v. American Tobacco Co., 537 F.2d 257 (4th Cir. 1976) *cert. denied,* 429 U.S. 920 (1976).

12. *See* Franks v. Bowman Transportation, 424 U.S. 747, 774–77 (1976).

13. U.S. Commission on Civil Rights, *Last Hired, First Fired: Layoffs and Civil Rights* (1977); Tangren v. Wackenhut Services, Inc., 480 F. Supp. 539 (D. Nev. 1979).

14. Because "last hired, first fired" provisions generally are legal, proportional layoffs are not required by law.

15. Under worksharing agreements, employees agree to divide work and receive a reduced salary, in an effort to avoid or minimize layoffs. Inverse seniority permits the senior person, rather than the junior person, on the job to accept a temporary layoff with compensation and the right to return to his job at a later date. Changes in unemployment compensation include supplementing the wages of employees who work less than the normal 5-day work week with tax-exempt unemployment insurance benefits for the fifth day. For a discussion of these methods of minimizing or avoiding layoffs, see *Last Hired, First Fired*, pp. 49–71.

16. *See, e.g.,* and Griggs v. Duke Power Company, *supra.* (1976).

17. *See* United Steelworkers of America v. Weber, 443 U.S. 193 (1979).

The Equal Rights Amendment (Defeated)

Equality of rights under the law shall not be denied or abridged by the United States or any State on account of sex.

Suggestions for Further Reading

B. Aptheker: *Woman's Legacy Essays on Race, Sex, and Class in American History*, University of Massachusetts Press, Amherst, 1982.

R. Baxendall, L. Gordon & S. Reverby: *America's Working Women: A Documentary History—1600 to the Present*, Random House, New York, 1976.

M. F. Berry & J. W. Blassingame: *Long Memory: The Black Experience in America*, Oxford University Press, New York, 1982.

R. O. Boyer & H. Morais: *Labor's Untold Story*, United Electrical, Radio & Machine Workers of America, New York, 1972.

D. Cluster (ed): *They Should Have Served That Cup of Coffee*, South End Press, Boston, 1979.

E. Flexner: *Century of Struggle*, Harvard University Press, Cambridge, Massachusetts, 1976.

E. Gee (ed): *Counterpoint: Perspectives on Asian Americans*, Asian American Studies Center, University of California, Los Angeles, 1976.

P. Giddings: *When and Where I Enter: The Impact of Black Women on Race and Sex in America*, Bantam Books, New York, 1984.

P. Jacobs & S. Landau (eds): *To Serve the Devil*. vol. 1, *Natives and Slaves*: vol. 2, *Colonials and Sojourners: A Documentary Analysis of America's Racial History and Why It Has Been Kept Hidden*, Vintage Books, New York, 1971.

K. M. Stampp: *The Peculiar Institution: Slavery in the Ante-Bellum South*, Vintage, New York, 1956.

United States Commission on Human Rights: *Indian Tribes: A Continuing Quest for Survival*, United States Commission on Human Rights, Washington, D.C., 1981.

K. Wagenheim & O. J. Wagenheim (eds): *The Puerto Ricans: A Documentary History*, Praeger, New York, 1973.

PART V

The Prison of Race and Gender: Stereotypes, Ideology, Language, and Social Control

Mmore than two thousand years ago, Plato wrote *The Republic*, one of the most important books about politics and the social order ever written. Plato believed that people were born with different capacities and that the key to the ideal society was for each person to occupy that place in society for which he or she was naturally suited. Once those best qualified to rule were in power, the most important thing would be to guard against social change because any change would be a change for the worse.

To this end, Plato outlined a set of myths that would be taught to people at an early age to ensure that they were disinclined to tamper with the structure of the Republic. They are to be told that some people are born with iron and brass in their souls, some with silver, and others with gold, and that these metals indicate each individual's proper place in society. Those born with gold are to rule, assisted by those with silver, over those with iron and brass. Thus, the assignment of social class in Plato's Republic is to be viewed as natural and unchangeable, not arbitrary and reversible.

Plato's motives for prohibiting social change were laudable. In his Republic, the rulers, being uninterested in either personal wealth or power, would rule reluctantly out of a sense of responsibility. Guided by principles of justice and the highest considerations of morality, they would simply maintain the society so that it functioned in the best interests of all its members. For the most part, people who have exercised political power in the real world have ignored Plato's advice about what suits a person to rule, but have embraced his suggestions about how to maintain power through the exercise of social control. Tanks in the streets and armed militia are not particularly good long-term devices for keeping a population in check. Although crude force can be effective in the short run, it serves as a constant reminder to oppressed people that they are not free and gives them a focus for their anger and an impetus for rebellion.

Plato was correct that the most effective way for rulers to maintain power is to persuade those they rule that the situation is natural, inevitable, and desirable. It is here that stereotypes, ideology, and language have their role to play. Each is a way of persuading people that differences in wealth, power, and opportunity are reflections of natural differences among people, not a result of the economic and political organization of the society. Thus, each is a way of persuading people that inequality is inevitable and beyond change, not arbitrary and alterable.

In our society, stereotypes, ideology, and language have played a critical role in perpetuating racism and sexism, even at those times when the law has been used as a vehicle to fight discrimination rather than maintain it. Furthermore, race, class, and gender biases perpetuated in these subtle and largely unconscious ways manage to deflect attention from those who profit from the current organization of society. Because of this, many ordinary working people have come to believe that the greatest obstacle to their advancement comes from the demands for equity made by either women, or Black women, or white women, or people of color, or white men, or white people, rather than a small and powerful group of wealthy white men who reap the benefits of racism, sexism, and class oppression.

Stereotypes are used to ascribe incorrectly certain characteristics to whole groups of people and then explain or excuse social problems in light of these characteristics. For example, high unemployment among Black men in our society is often attributed to the "fact" that this group is "lazy" and "irresponsible" rather than to the combined effects of racism and the particular way we organize our economic life. The underrepresentation of women in positions of leadership is explained by the "fact" that they are "naturally" less aggressive than men; the large gap in wages between men and women is explained by "natural" differences in ability or by emphasizing woman's "natural" role as homemaker and man's as breadwinner and so on, rather than the needs of capitalism and male dominance.

In addition to creating and maintaining mistaken beliefs about the reason for unequal distribution of wealth, power, and opportunity, stereotypes can play an important role in reconciling individuals to discriminatory treatment. If women and people of color internalize prevailing stereotypes about their group as they are encouraged to do, they come to believe that they themselves are inadequate and unqualified, and thus they blame themselves for their failures, even when they are clearly the victims of discrimination. Stereotypes are not merely broad generalizations we impose on others; they are ways of seeing "women" or "Chicanos" or "workers" that we internalize and use to define and limit ourselves and our expectations.

Ideology, or a set of incorrect beliefs that rationalize the status quo, supports or buttresses the impact of stereotyping by further distorting our perceptions of ourselves and each other. For example, stories in the media as well as all forms of advertising create the impression that particular groups—say, women or Blacks—have made enormous strides in all areas of society, implying that they are now the recipients of special treatment that give them an advantage over white men and other groups. Never mind that statistics paint a very different picture. The force of ideology distorts our perception of the world to the extent that even women earning 59 percent of what men earn for comparable work may not recognize that they are victims of discrimination.

Moreover, negative stereotypes of women and Blacks combine with ideology so that success by members of these groups is viewed with suspicion as undeserved. Consequently, an individual can have a distorted perception of how well certain groups are doing and then blame the supposed success of these groups for his or her own frustrations and failure. For example, some people view their inability to gain admission to college as the fault of a minority group that supposedly gets preferential treatment instead of as a result of inadequate funding for public higher education.

In this way, the power of ideology helps explain why people live in one of the wealthiest societies the world has ever known, but never question why a good education continues to be a privilege enjoyed by some rather than a right for all. The same holds true with respect to housing, medical care, food, clothing, and other basic necessities. Instead of our being encouraged to ask why so much suffering and deprivation exist in the midst of such wealth, the prevailing racist and sexist ideology and stereotyping encourages us to redefine social problems as individual pathology. A good illustration of this way of seeing the world came in the mid-1980s when the mayor of New York City toured publicly financed housing facilities, which were in abominable and subhuman living condition. The mayor's comment was that some people simply prefer to live this way.

Language encourages various individuals and groups to think of themselves in ways that undermine their sense of personhood and dignity. Referring to a fifty-year-old female office worker as a "girl" is part of the package that results in paying her an inferior wage, expecting her to make coffee and run errands for her boss on her lunch hour, and failing to treat her with appropriate respect. That many women claim to be flattered by being referred to as a "girl" or being called "honey" or "sweetheart" by men they hardly know only shows how successful language and ideology have been in getting women to internalize a self-image that perpetuates their own lack of power and dignity.

The selections in Part V focus on the ways in which stereotypes, language, and ideology operate as forms of social control. They show the variety of ways in which the unconscious beliefs we hold about ourselves and others reinforce existing social roles and class positions and blunt social criticism. The first selection, "Stereotypes: Conceptual and Normative Considerations," discusses how stereotyping people distorts the accuracy of our perceptions of others and dulls our critical abilities. (The roles that stereotypes play in altering and even falsifying our perceptions are illustrated dramatically in "Bias Incident at Staten Island's Miller Field: A Tale of Two Neighborhoods," which appears in Part I.) Mark Snyder's article, "Self-Fulfilling Stereotypes," uses examples from current psychological research to show how important our expectations are in shaping our behavior and experience. Some of the most interesting studies being done in the field of education (and mentioned in Snyder's article) show that teacher's expectations are at least as important as "innate ability" in determining how well young children do in school. These expectations are often shaped unconsciously by the racist and sexist stereotypes that pervade our language.

The many ways in which our language smuggles in negative images of women and people of color are explored in the selections by Robert B. Moore and Robert Baker. Language can provide valuable clues to unconscious attitudes in a society, but some people have difficulty analyzing language because they dismiss it as trivial or because they have trouble believing that *what* we call something affects *how* we feel about it. The selections in this part ask us to take language seriously. Taken to their logical conclusion, stereotypes and ideology result in the creation of "the other," a way of seeing certain groups that strips them of their humanity and makes it possible for us to treat them in ways that would otherwise horrify us.

In the selection, "The Sacrificial Lamb," Susan Griffin explores the relationship between pornography and racism and examines the way in which widely held false perceptions of others result in acts that degrade and humiliate their victims. In "Social Effects of Some Contemporary Myths about Women," Ruth Hubbard examines some myths about women's nature and then goes on to show a direct correlation between ideology and social relations. "The Schooling of Vietnamese Immigrants" by Gail P. Kelly provides a case study in the creation and perpetuation of gender roles and race and class privilege through the use of stereotypes, language, and ideology, as we have been discussing throughout the section.

The final two selections offer more general discussions of the way in which race, class, and gender stereotypes and ideology reinforce the status quo by directing our attention away from the economic and social arrangements that perpetuate unequal treatment and encouraging us to blame the victims of these institutions for their own misery. William Ryan introduces us to the technique he calls "blaming the victim," which allows us to recognize injustice without assuming responsibility for it or acknowledging the need to make basic changes in our social and economic institutions. William Chafe examines the impact of both race and gender stereotypes and ideology by drawing an analogy between sex and race, and he argues persuasively that both racism and sexism function analogously as forms of social control. Although Chafe suggests he is comparing the experiences of white women with those of Black people, a careful reading of this essay suggests that he is really comparing the experiences of white women to those of Black men. The reader might be interested to see whether Chafe's claim about racism and sexism and social control holds up equally well when we construct similar accounts of the experiences of *Black women* as well as members of other groups discussed in this book. Chafe begins by analyzing how stereotypes, ideology, and language function to distort our expectations, perceptions, and experience and then proceeds to ask whose interests are served by this distortion.

Often, people become overwhelmed and discouraged when they realize how much our unconscious images and beliefs affect our ways of seeing each other and the world and, as a result, fail to go on to analyze the consequences of ideology. Believing that people are naturally prejudiced and can't change is one more bit of ideology that prevents us from taking control of our lives. And ideology is dangerous because it prevents us from questioning prevailing social and economic arrangements and asking whether they serve the best interest of all the people. By dividing us from each other and confusing us as to who really profits from these arrangements, ideology and stereotypes imprison us in a false world. In the next and final part of this book, a number of thinkers will offer their suggestions about how to move beyond race, class, and gender divisions.

Stereotypes: *Conceptual and Normative Considerations*

Judith Andre

A familiar battle is raging. The current skirmish involves a comic strip character, Miss Buxley, in "Beetle Bailey." Her portrayal has been called sexist: she's a dumb blonde, physically well-endowed, whose every move leaves her boss panting and unable to think. The author of the strip admits that the situation is stereotypical, but claims that "Miss Buxleys do get preferential treatment. I'm just telling the truth. . . ."[1]

Both the attack ("This is an offensive stereotype") and the defense ("I'm just telling the truth") are familiar.[2] The same battle is fought over illustrations in schoolbooks, characters in commercials, situations in sitcoms. Sometimes the battle is an inner one: realizing how blacks have been victimized by stereotypes, one may be reluctant to state some simple truth about, say, blacks and welfare.

Sometimes the question is best resolved by looking at the specific situation. The Miss Buxley character raises many interesting questions: Why is the sexual power of women over men considered funny? Why is the power of men over women— physical, economic, emotional, and political—never considered funny? What is life really like for a buxom young woman in the contemporary United States? Is it true that the Miss Buxleys of the world are treated preferentially in an office? Many stereotypes have fallen once the social scientists examined them.

In this paper, however, I will be interested in the broader question. Is there something in the nature of a stereotype that makes it objectionable, even when it (roughly) represents the truth? My discussion begins with the concept of a stereotype. How does it differ, say, from other generalizations?

Stereotypes: The Concept

The word "stereotype" first meant a metal printing plate. The Greek prefix "stereo" means "solid, hard, firm." As Rosemary Gordon points out, "The idea of unchange-ability, of monotonous regularity and formalisation was very soon abstracted from the material object itself and applied in a more metaphorical sense. . . . The use of 'stereotype' as a verb in the sense of fixing something and perpetuating it in an unchanging form can be traced back to the nineteenth century."[3] Today the term means: "a conventional, formulaic, and usually oversimplified conception, opin-ion, or belief; a person, group, event or issue considered to typify or conform to an unvarying pattern. . ."[4] As psychologists use the term, the central characteristic of a stereotype is its rigidity: it persists in spite of evidence.[5] Like most beliefs it filters the evidence, so that inconsistent information is less likely to be assimilated. But why do some beliefs have the particular inflexibility that makes them stereotypes?[6] Because stereotypes as I will define them are commonly held (rather than simply individually held) beliefs, discussion of subconscious motivation is particularly problematic. Inflexible opinions in the general public might result from conscious inflexibility on the part of relatively few opinion-makers (in other words, from deliberate indoctrina-tion). But I will assume otherwise: my discussion here will be valid to the extent that general stereotypes are a function of individual resistance to changes of mind.

An unwillingness to face something is a form of self-deception; it results from a sense of danger to oneself: a fear that the unfaced fact itself will turn out to be unpleasant, or at least that the facing of it will be. Thinking is work; an unpredict-able world is frightening. Stereotypes, like other generalizations, protect us from both effort and fear. But stereotypes differ from other generalizations in their greater immunity to revision; they are not just handy but disposable rules of thumb. Why are we so particularly unwilling to think about some things? Both logical and psychological reasons are possible. As Quine describes the web of belief, privileged beliefs are those whose denial would bring about the most change in our conceptual scheme. A principle of economy leads us, when beliefs conflict, to keep those which are more fundamental. Psychologically, some beliefs are privileged because they keep us happy (or less unhappy). Their denials are threatening. Now there are only a few kinds of situation where a belief *as such* makes us happy *overall*; ordinarily it is true beliefs which, in the long run, help us. Flame burns, and burns are painful; soup nourishes; gravity is constant. Believing these true things will make our lives better. But some beliefs make life better whether or not they are true: self-esteem is the central case. My belief that I am attractive, intelligent, and honest makes my life pleasant even if I am wrong on all counts. In fact, I may be much happier than the objectively attractive, intelligent and honest person who doesn't know her own worth. Here the content of the belief is more important than its congruence with reality (although even here that congruence also matters).

In two other areas is the content of a belief more important than its well-foundedness: where the belief itself changes the world around me, and where the world around me is invulnerable to any attempt to cope. Our beliefs about other people, for instance, shape their behavior; and our lack of awareness of impending inexorable doom is a blessing if there's nothing we could do about it anyway. (Only rarely would that be true; we might at least want to get our affairs in order. But this is nevertheless a logically possible category.)

This analysis suggests that a stereotype—which we retain in the face of contradictory evidence—must function in one of the following ways: it may be relatively fundamental to our conceptual scheme; it may protect our self-esteem; it may help bring about some desirable situation; or it may shield us from facing an unchangeable, unpleasant fact, when facing it would accomplish nothing. (I'm assuming here quite a rational subconscious; it might be safer to say that the belief *appears* to us, feels to us, important in one of the ways just mentioned, and so we resist questioning it.)

But even among rigid, logically or psychologically privileged beliefs, stereotypes form a subset. To begin with, they concern classes of people rather than the whole human race. Rigid beliefs about human beings in general are not stereotypes (except perhaps in science fiction, where "heroic Terrans" confront extraterrestrials); nor are inflexible beliefs about individuals—about celebrities or historical figures. These are myths, perhaps, but not stereotypes. This may explain why there are relatively few stereotypes about white men; white men are, in this culture, unreflectively taken to be the standard human being from whom women and other races deviate. What stereotypes there are concern not men as such, but men in relation to women: men are naturally polygamous or domestically clumsy.

In addition, stereotypes concern behavioral or psychological attributes. Fat people are believed to be jolly *and* to be bad health risks, but only the belief about their personality counts as a stereotype. A stereotype is usually a belief that members of a group will behave in certain ways—it's an expectation that something observable will happen.

A stereotype is also simple and general. The more complex and specific a statement, the less likely it is to express a stereotype. Compare, for instance, "Most great jazz musicians have been black" (a nonstereotypical claim) with "Blacks are so musical" (a stereotypical claim). This characteristic of a stereotype—generality—complements the first characteristic (rigidity); for a general statement is hard to falsify. If this particular black child is tone-deaf, he may still be good on the drums—or an inspired dancer. If he fails at all these activities, well, he's "the exception that proves the rule"—the original belief may refer to all blacks, almost all, or just a majority of them.

Simplicity is a related characteristic. The categories invoked are not only broad, they are few. Fat people are jolly, priests are dedicated, the Irish are garrulous and hard-drinking.

Finally, stereotypes ignore, or falsify, or oversimplify the causes of this behavior. Because of this, a stereotype at least suggests that the attributed behavior is inevitable; this, too, contributes to the rigidity of the belief. When a cause for the behavior is mentioned, claims gain empirical content and become falsifiable. Thus, beliefs or portrayals that include beliefs about the causes of the behavior are less likely to count as stereotypes. A nagging wife is a stereotype; a wife who nags because her only route to success is through her husband is less so. Even a false or farfetched causal claim—sociobiological speculation, for instance—at least calls attention to the question of cause, and is to that extent better than a free-floating claim such as "women are monogamous, men polygamous; they just are." But unfounded claims about genetic causes are only slightly better than what I have called "free-floating" claims (those which make no reference to cause at all). Stereotypes, in one way or the other, suggest that the behavior in question is an unalterable given. Stereotypes, then, are a subset of commonly believed generalizations about the way certain kinds of people feel and act. Stereotypes are inflexible beliefs; they involve a few broad categories only; and they imply that what they describe is inevitable.

Stereotypes as Undesirable

"Stereotype" is pejorative; there is always something objectionable in the beliefs and images to which the word refers. Once the concept of stereotype has been analyzed, the nature of that objectionableness is clearer. To begin with, a stereotype is particularly resistant to change; it keeps us from seeing the truth, should the truth be at odds with our beliefs. The truth is a good thing to know, ordinarily, since we can deal more effectively with what we see than with what we don't. The habit of seeking the truth is therefore also a good thing; it's useful, and—I will not try to defend this here—morally preferable. Ceteris paribus, then, a stereotype is a bad thing because it is unfriendly to truth.

The analysis in Part I also helps illuminate the role of stereotypes in unjust social arrangements. Remember that a stereotypical portrayal reinforces two beliefs at once: that X's are Y, and that X's are inevitably Y. If these beliefs are particularly privileged, then they must (at least seem to our subconscious) do one of the following: protect our self-esteem; underlie many other significant beliefs; help perpetuate situations pleasing to us; shield us from knowledge which is better not known. Stereotypes about minorities do all of this. They protect the self-esteem of the majority in two ways. First, some assure the majority of its superiority. ("Blacks are ignorant.") Secondly, they protect the ruling class from seeing its moral turpitude. ("Blacks are like happy children. They don't need what we need." Or, "Women haven't succeeded because they're naturally frivolous.") The realization that something could and should be changed is a moral burden. Once enlightened, I cannot think well of myself *and* remain inactive. What makes the burden worse is that stereotypes about minorities often do have a central place in our conceptual scheme. The possibility of their falsehood or mutability threatens our beliefs about many other things. When stereotypes fall, beliefs about myself—in particular, about my worth—may fall; as may beliefs about how society actually works, why it works that way, and what alternatives are available. Finally, of course, stereotypes about the disadvantaged are self-fulfilling prophecies. People act as they are expected to act, for a variety of familiar reasons.

Stereotypes concerning minorities, then, may well help perpetuate injustices. Interesting questions remain, however: are all stereotypes about minorities objectionable? For that matter, are all stereotypes as such morally objectionable? Or instead must each be examined for its possible role in perpetuating injustice?

As mentioned earlier, at least one thing counts against all stereotypes: their inflexibility. Truth is endangered, and truth is a good thing. But truth isn't the only good thing; its sacrifice is sometimes justified. And as there are arguments to be given in favor of stock figures in literature, so there are advantages to culturally shared expectations about people. These expectations make the world more predictable and hence more manageable; since they are commonly shared, they make communication easier. A stereotype may even enshrine an attribute of which the people in question are truly and proudly the possessors. Perhaps most Irish *are* religious, most nurses dedicated, most Italians warm and loving.

But "stereotype" remains a pejorative. When, then, would a portrayal of, say, a dedicated physician become objectionable? The objection might be aesthethic rather than moral; stale writing fails to do what literature should do: make us see more clearly. The aesthetic criticism, however, leads directly to the moral one. Stereotypes prevent us from seeing clearly, not only in the sense that they filter out conflicting information, but also in the sense that they keep us from understanding what they do allow us to see. This is true even of positive stereotypes about nonminorities. Suppose most physicians are in fact dedicated. What is the harm in the portrayal of one more selfless doctor? The portrayal keeps us from attending to the uniqueness of each individual. He may be heroic in some respects, conscientious in others, but occasionally imperfect. He, and we, are reluctant to admit the imperfection, and unduly shocked when we do see it; in either case we will not cope well with the problem. We are, ironically, less likely to appreciate his heroism, too—for it is simply expected. All doctors are like that.

Stereotypes, then, are bad things even when the image they convey is a positive one. Their patronizing romanticism keeps us from coping with reality, and from appreciating the individual troubles and successes of the people we meet.

What Is to Be Done?

Stereotypes are avoidable. There are many ways to portray ordinary conventional people without descending into stereotype. We need not be afraid of telling the truth. The guidelines for doing so are found in the description of a stereotype given in Part I. Stereotypes are simple, general, and causally agnostic. A portrayal of a carping mother-in-law is not stereotypical if her individuality shows. What does she complain about? What doesn't she complain about? What other characteristics does she have? Most importantly, *why* is she so unpleasant? A stereotyped portrayal would focus on just two facts: she is a mother-in-law; she carps. *That* picture reinforces the connection which most people make already and automatically. But even a portrayal that is congruent with a stereotype can challenge that stereotype by calling attention to its limited, specific applicability, and by encouraging thought about the origins of the behavior. The criminals on the TV show *Hill Street Blues* are primarily black and hispanic. But each is shown as an individual; blacks are seen in many noncriminal roles; and the social factors that promote criminality are obvious. Only for the least discerning of viewers would the show encourage the identification: "young black" = "thug."

To answer the questions which began this paper: there's a great difference between a true generalization and a stereotype. And there's nothing wrong with telling the truth; just make sure it's the whole truth. Responsible portrayals encourage us to see in one another both our individuality and our roles in a social system. Stereotypes blind us to the first, and keep us enlightened about the second. The world of the stereotype is a world of free-floating stock figures, whose behavior has no explanation (except, perhaps, in their genes). It may be a humorous world (although that's a subject for a different paper) but it is not a happy world. Nor is it a true one.

NOTES

1. Mort Walker, quoted by Sheryl Jones, "Sexism Draws Some New Battle Lines," *The Ledger-Star* (Norfolk, Virginia), December 28, 1982.

2. Another line of defense is equally familiar: "Your attempt at censorship is worse than anything I've done." However common, the defense is confused. Attempts to influence editorial discretion through reason are not censorship. If legal threats are used (say, the threat of a boycott) the question becomes more complicated. See my " 'Censorship': Some Distinctions," in *The International Journal of Applied Philosophy*, vol. 1, no. 4 (Fall 1983), pp. 25-32.

3. Rosemary Gordon, *Stereotypy of Imagery and Belief as an Ego Defense* (Cambridge: University Press, 1962), pp. 2-3.

4. *American Heritage Dictionary* (Boston: Houghton Mifflin, 1979).

5. Gordon, p. 4.

6. The dictionary speaks of community stereotypes, and does not include inflexibility as a defining characteristic. The psychologists are speaking of individually held stereotypes, and give inflexibility as their major defining characteristic. I discuss in this paper those commonly held stereotypes which are relatively inflexible; I assume that most are. Some of the objections I will make, however, apply only to those formulaic beliefs which are relatively rigid; others apply to all formulaic beliefs (about the behavior and feelings of classes of people).

2

Self-Fulfilling Stereotypes

Mark Snyder

Gordon Allport, the Harvard psychologist who wrote a classic work on the nature of prejudice, told a story about a child who had come to believe that people who lived in Minneapolis were called monopolists. From his father, moreover, he had learned that monopolists were evil folk. It wasn't until many years later, when he discovered his confusion, that his dislike of residents of Minneapolis vanished.

Allport knew, of course, that it was not so easy to wipe out prejudice and erroneous stereotypes. Real prejudice, psychologists like Allport argued, was buried deep in human character, and only a restructuring of education could begin to root it out. Yet many people whom I meet while lecturing seem to believe that stereotypes are simply beliefs or attitudes that change easily with experience. Why do some people express the view that Italians are passionate, blacks are lazy, Jews materialistic, and lesbians mannish in their demeanor? In the popular view, it is because they have not learned enough about the diversity among these groups and have not had enough contact with members of the groups for their stereotypes to be challenged by reality. With more experience, it is presumed, most people of good will are likely to revise their stereotypes.

My research over the past decade convinces me that there is little justification for such optimism—and not only for the reasons given by Allport. While it is true that deep prejudice is often based on the needs of pathological character structure, stereotypes are obviously quite common even among fairly normal individuals. When people first meet others, they cannot help noticing certain highly visible and distinctive characteristics: sex, race, physical appearance, and the like. Despite people's best intentions, their initial impressions of others are shaped by their assumptions about such characteristics.

What is critical, however, is that these assumptions are not merely beliefs or attitudes that exist in a vacuum; they are reinforced by the behavior of both prejudiced people and the targets of their prejudice. In recent years, psychologists have collected considerable laboratory evidence about the processes that strengthen stereotypes and put them beyond the reach of reason and good will.

My own studies initially focused on first encounters between strangers. It did not take long to discover, for example, that people have very different ways of treating those whom they regard as physically attractive and those whom they consider physically unattractive, and that these differences tend to bring out precisely those kinds of behavior that fit with stereotypes about attractiveness.

In an experiment that I conducted with my colleagues Elizabeth Decker Tanke and Ellen Berscheid, pairs of college-age men and women met and became acquainted in telephone conversations. Before the conversations began, each man received a Polaroid snapshot, presumably taken just moments before, of the woman he would soon meet. The photograph, which had actually been prepared before the experiment began, showed either a physically attractive woman or a physically unattractive one. By randomly choosing which picture to use for each conversation, we insured that there was no consistent relationship between the attractiveness of the woman in the picture and the attractiveness of the woman in the conversation.

By questioning the men, we learned that even before the conversations began, stereotypes about physical attractiveness came into play. Men who looked forward to talking with physically attractive women said that they expected to meet decidedly sociable, poised, humorous, and socially adept people, while men who thought that they were about to get acquainted with unattractive women fashioned images of rather unsociable, awkward, serious, and socially inept creatures. Mooveover, the men proved to have very different styles of getting acquainted with women whom they thought to be attractive and those whom they believed to be unattractive. Shown a photograph of an attractive woman, they behaved with warmth, friendliness, humor, and animation. However, when the woman in the picture was unattractive, the men were cold, uninteresting, and reserved.

These differences in the men's behavior elicited behavior in the women that was consistent with the men's stereotyped assumptions. Women who were believed (unbeknown to them) to be physically attractive behaved in a friendly, likeable, and sociable manner. In sharp contrast, women who were perceived as physically unattractive adopted a cool, aloof, and distant manner. So striking were the differences in the women's behavior that they could be discerned simply by listening to tape recordings of the woman's side of the conversations. Clearly, by acting upon their stereotyped beliefs about the women whom they would be meeting, the men had initiated a chain of events that produced *behavioral confirmation* for their beliefs.

Similarly, Susan Anderson and Sandra Bem have shown in an experiment at Stanford University that when the tables are turned—when it is women who have pictures of men they are to meet on the telephone—many women treat the men according to their presumed physical attractiveness, and by so doing encourage the men to confirm their stereotypes. Little wonder, then, that so many people remain convinced that good looks and appealing personalities go hand in hand.

Sex and Race

It is experiments such as these that point to a frequently unnoticed power of stereotypes: the power to influence social relationships in ways that create the illusion of reality. In one study, Berna Skrypnek and I arranged for pairs of previously unacquainted students to interact in a situation that permitted us to control the information that each one received about the apparent sex of the other. The two people were seated in separate rooms so that they could neither see nor hear each other. Using a system of signal lights that they operated with switches, they negotiated a division of labor, deciding which member of the pair would perform each of several tasks that differed in sex-role connotations. The tasks varied along the dimensions of masculinity and femininity: sharpen a hunting knife (masculine), polish a pair of shoes (neutral), iron a shirt (feminine).

One member of the team was led to believe that the other was, in one condition of the experiment, male; in the other, female. As we had predicted, the first member's belief about the sex of the partner influenced the outcome of the pair's negotiations. Women whose partners believed them to be men generally chose stereotypically masculine tasks; in contrast, women whose partners believed that they were women usually chose stereotypically feminine tasks. The experiment thus suggests that much sex-role behavior may be the product of other people's stereotyped and often erroneous beliefs.

In a related study at the University of Waterloo, Carl von Baeyer, Debbie Sherk, and Mark Zanna have shown how stereotypes about sex roles operate in job interviews. The researchers arranged to have men conduct simulated job interviews with women supposedly seeking positions as research assistants. The investigators informed half of the women that the men who would interview them held traditional views about the ideal woman, believing her to be very emotional, deferential to her husband, home-oriented, and passive. The rest of the women were told that their interviewer saw the ideal woman as independent, competitive, ambitious, and dominant. When the women arrived for their interviews, the researchers noticed that most of them had dressed to meet the stereotyped expectations of their prospective interviewers. Women who expected to see a traditional interviewer had chosen very feminine-looking makeup, clothes, and accessories. During the interviews (videotaped through a one-way mirror) these women behaved in traditionally feminine ways and gave traditionally feminine answers to questions such as "Do you have plans to include children and marriage with your career plans?"

Once more, then, we see the self-fulfilling nature of stereotypes. Many sex differences, it appears, may result from the images that people create in their attempts to act out accepted sex roles. The implication is that if stereotyped expectations about sex roles shift, behavior may change, too. In fact, statements by people who have undergone sex-change operations have highlighted the power of such expectations in easing adjustment to a new life. As the writer Jan Morris said in recounting the story of her transition from James to Jan: "The more I was treated as a woman, the more woman I became."

The power of stereotypes to cause people to confirm stereotyped expectations can also be seen in interracial relationships. In the first of two investigations done at Princeton University by Carl Word, Mark Zanna, and Joel Cooper, white undergraduates interviewed both white and black job applicants. The applicants were actually confederates of the experimenters, trained to behave consistently from interview to interview, no matter how the interviewers acted toward them.

To find out whether or not the white interviewers would behave differently toward white and black job applicants, the researchers secretly videotaped each interview and then studied the tapes. From these, it was apparent that there were substantial differences in the treatment accorded blacks and whites. For one thing, the interviewers' speech deteriorated when they talked to blacks, displaying more errors in grammar and pronunciation. For another, the interviewers spent less time with blacks than with whites and showed less "immediacy," as the researchers called it, in their manner. That is, they were less friendly, less outgoing, and more reserved with blacks.

In the second investigation, white confederates were trained to approximate the immediate or the nonimmediate interview styles that had been observed in the first investigation as they interviewed white job applicants. A panel of judges who evaluated the tapes agreed that applicants subjected to the nonimmediate styles performed less adequately and were more nervous than job applicants treated in the immediate style. Apparently, then, the blacks in the first study did not have a chance to display their qualifications to the best advantage. Considered together, the two investigations suggest that in interracial encounters, racial stereotypes may constrain behavior in ways to cause both blacks and whites to behave in accordance with those stereotypes.

Rewriting Biography

Having adopted stereotyped ways of thinking about another person, people tend to notice and remember the ways in which that person seems to fit the stereotype, while resisting evidence that contradicts the stereotype. In one investigation that I conducted with Seymour Uranowitz, student subjects read a biography of a fictitious woman named Betty K. We constructed the story of her life so that it would fit the stereotyped images of both lesbians and heterosexuals. Betty, we wrote, never had a steady boyfriend in high school, but did go out on dates. And although we gave her a steady boyfriend in college, we specified that he was more of a close friend than anything else. A week after we had distributed this biography, we gave our subjects some new information about Betty. We told some students that she was now living with another woman in a lesbian relationship; we told others that she was living with her husband.

To see what impact stereotypes about sexuality would have on how people remembered the facts of Betty's life, we asked each student to answer a series of questions about her life history. When we examined their answers, we found that the students had reconstructed the events of Betty's past in ways that supported their own stereotyped beliefs about her sexual orientation. Those who believed that Betty was a lesbian remembered that Betty had never had a steady boyfriend in high school, but tended to neglect the fact that she had gone out on many dates in college. Those who believed that Betty was now a heterosexual tended to remember that she had formed a steady relationship with a man in college, but tended to ignore the fact that this relationship was more of a friendship than a romance.

The students showed not only selective memories but also a striking facility for interpreting what they remembered in ways that added fresh support for their stereotypes. One student who accurately remembered that a supposedly lesbian Betty never had a steady boyfriend in high school confidently pointed to the fact as an early sign of her lack of romantic or sexual interest in men. A student who correctly remembered that a purportedly lesbian Betty often went out on dates in college was sure that these dates were signs of Betty's early attempts to mask her lesbian interests.

Clearly, the students had allowed their preconceptions about lesbians and heterosexuals to dictate the way in which they interpreted and reinterpreted the facts of Betty's life. As long as stereotypes make it easy to bring to mind evidence that supports them and difficult to bring to mind evidence that undermines them, people will cling to erroneous beliefs.

Stereotypes in the Classroom and Work Place

The power of one person's beliefs to make other people conform to them has been well demonstrated in real life. Back in the 1960s, as most people well remember, Harvard psychologist Robert Rosenthal and his colleague Lenore Jacobson entered elementary-school classrooms and identified one out of every five pupils in each room as a child who could be expected to show dramatic improvement in intellectual achievement during the school year. What the teachers did not know was that the children had been chosen on a random basis. Nevertheless, something happened in the relationships between teachers and their supposedly gifted pupils that led the children to make clear gains in test performance.

It can also do so on the job. Albert King, now a professor of management at Northern Illinois University, told a welding instructor in a vocational training center that five men in his training program had unusually high aptitude. Although these five had been chosen at random and knew nothing of their designation as high-aptitude workers, they showed substantial changes in performance. They were absent less often than were other workers, learned the basics of the welder's trade in about half the usual time, and scored a full 10 points higher than other trainees on a welding test. Their gains were noticed not only by the researcher and by the welding instructor, but also by other trainees, who singled out the five as their preferred co-workers.

Might not other expectations influence the relationships between supervisors and workers? For example, supervisors who believe that men are better suited to some jobs and women to others may treat their workers (wittingly or unwittingly) in ways that encourage them to perform their jobs in accordance with stereotypes about differences between men and women. These same stereotypes may determine who gets which job in the first place. Perhaps some personnel managers allow stereotypes to influence, subtly or not so subtly, the way in which they interview job candidates, making it likely that candidates who fit the stereotypes show up better than job-seekers who do not fit them.

Unfortunately, problems of this kind are compounded by the fact that members of stigmatized groups often subscribe to stereotypes about themselves. That is what Amerigo Farina and his colleagues at the University of Connecticut found when they measured the impact upon mental patients of believing that others knew their psychiatric history. In Farina's study, each mental patient cooperated with another person in a game requiring teamwork. Half of the patients believed that their partners knew they were patients, the other half believed that their partners thought they were nonpatients. In reality, the nonpatients never knew a thing about anyone's psychiatric history. Nevertheless, simply believing that others were aware of their history led the patients to feel less appreciated, to find the task more difficult, and to perform poorly. In addition, objective observers saw them as more tense, more anxious, and more poorly adjusted than patients who believed that their status was not known. Seemingly, the belief that others perceived them as stigmatized caused them to play the role of stigmatized patients.

Consequences for Society

Apparently, good will and education are not sufficient to subvert the power of stereotypes. If people treat others in such a way as to bring out behavior that supports stereotypes, they may never have an opportunity to discover which of their stereotypes are wrong.

I suspect that even if people were to develop doubts about the accuracy of their stereotypes, chances are they would proceed to test them by gathering precisely the evidence that would appear to confirm them.

The experiments I have described help to explain the persistence of stereotypes. But, as is so often the case, solving one puzzle only creates another. If by acting as if false stereotypes were true, people lead others, too, to act as if they were true, why do the stereotypes not come to *be* true? Why, for example, have researchers found so little evidence that attractive people are generally friendly, sociable, and outgoing and that unattractive people are generally shy and aloof?

I think that the explanation goes something like this: Very few among us have the kind of looks that virtually everyone considers either very attractive or very unattractive. Our looks make us rather attractive to some people but somewhat less attractive to other people. When we spend time with those who find us attractive, they will tend to bring out our more sociable sides, but when we are with those who find us less attractive, they will bring out our less sociable sides. Although our actual physical appearance does not change, we present ourselves quite differently to our admirers and to our detractors. For our admirers we become attractive people, and for our detractors we become unattractive. This mixed pattern of behavior will prevent the development of any consistent relationship between physical attractiveness and personality.

Now that I understand some of the powerful forces that work to perpetuate social stereotypes, I can see a new mission for my research. I hope, on the one hand, to find out how to help people see the flaws in their stereotypes. On the other hand, I would like to help the victims of false stereotypes find ways of liberating themselves from the constraints imposed on them by other members of society.

3

Racist Stereotyping in the English Language

Robert B. Moore

Language and Culture

An integral part of any culture is its language. Language not only develops in conjunction with a society's historical, economic and political evolution; it also reflects that society's attitudes and thinking. Language not only *expresses* ideas and concepts but actually *shapes* thought.[1] If one accepts that our dominant white culture is racist, then one would expect our language—an indispensable transmitter of culture—to be racist as well. Whites, as the dominant group, are not subjected to the same abusive characterization by our language that people of color receive. Aspects of racism in the English language that will be discussed in this essay include terminology, symbolism, politics, ethnocentrism, and context.

Before beginning our analysis of racism in language we would like to quote part of a TV film review which shows the connection between language and culture.[2]

> Depending on one's culture, one interacts with time in a very distinct fashion. One example which gives some cross-cultural insights into the concept of time is language. In Spanish, a watch is said to "walk." In English, the watch "runs." In German, the watch "functions." And in French, the watch "marches." In the Indian culture of the Southwest, people do not refer to time in this way. The value of the watch is displaced with the value of "what time it's getting to be." Viewing these five cultural perspectives of time, one can see some definite emphasis and values that each culture places on time. For example, a cultural perspective may provide a clue

to why the negative stereotype of the slow and lazy Mexican who lives in the "Land of Manana" exists in the Anglo value system, where time "flies," the watch "runs" and "time is money."

A Short Play on "Black" and "White" Words

Some may blackly (angrily) accuse me of trying to blacken (defame) the English language, to give it a black eye (a mark of shame) by writing such black words (hostile). They may denigrate (to cast aspersions; to darken) me by accusing me of being blackhearted (malevolent), of having a black outlook (pessimistic, dismal) on life, of being a blackguard (scoundrel)—which would certainly be a black mark (detrimental fact) against me. Some may black-brow (scowl at) me and hope that a black cat crosses in front of me because of this black deed. I may become a black sheep (one who causes shame or embarrassment because of deviation from the accepted standards), who will be blackballed (ostracized) by being placed on a blacklist (list of undesirables) in an attempt to blackmail (to force or coerce into a particular action) me to retract my words. But attempts to blackjack (to compel by threat) me will have a Chinaman's chance of success, for I am not a yellow-bellied Indian-giver of words, who will whitewash (cover up or gloss over vices or crimes) a black lie (harmful, inexcusable). I challenge the purity and innocence (white) of the English language. I don't see things in black and white (entirely bad or entirely good) terms, for I am a white man (marked by upright firmness) if there ever was one. However, it would be a black day when I would not "call a spade a spade," even though some will suggest a white man calling the English language racist is like the pot calling the kettle black. While many may be niggardly (grudging, scanty) in their support, others will be honest and decent—and to them I say, that's very white of you (honest, decent).

The preceding is of course a white lie (not intended to cause harm), meant only to illustrate some examples of racist terminology in the English language.

Obvious Bigotry

Perhaps the most obvious aspect of racism in language would be terms like "nigger," "spook," "chink," "spic," etc. While these may be facing increasing social disdain, they certainly are not dead. Large numbers of white Americans continue to utilize these terms. "Chink," "gook," and "slant-eyes" were in common usage among U.S. troops in Vietnam. An NBC nightly news broadcast, in February 1972, reported that the basketball team in Pekin, Illinois, was called the "Pekin Chinks" and noted that even though this had been protested by Chinese Americans, the term continued to be used because it was easy, and meant no harm. Spiro Agnew's widely reported "fat Jap" remark and the "little Jap" comment of lawyer John Wilson, during the Watergate hearings, are surface indicators of a deep-rooted Archie Bunkerism.

Many white people continue to refer to Black people as "colored," as for instance in a July 30, 1975 *Boston Globe* article on a racist attack by whites on a group of Black people using a public beach in Boston. One white person was quoted as follows:

> We've always welcomed good colored people in South Boston but we will not tolerate radical blacks or Communists. . . . Good colored people are welcome in South Boston, black militants are not.

Many white people may still be unaware of the disdain many African Americans have for the term "colored," but it often appears that whether used intentionally or unintentionally, "colored" people are "good" and "know their place," while "Black" people are perceived as "uppity" and "threatening" to many whites. Similarly, the term "boy" to refer to African American men is now acknowledged to be a demeaning term, though still in common use. Other terms such as "the pot calling the kettle black" and "calling a spade a spade" have negative racial connotations but are still frequently used, as for example when President Ford was quoted in February 1976 saying that even though Daniel Moynihan had left the U.N., the U.S. would continue "calling a spade a spade."

Color Symbolism

The symbolism of white as positive and black as negative is pervasive in our culture, with the black/white words used in the beginning of this essay only one of many aspects. "Good guys" wear white hats and ride white horses, "bad guys" wear black hats and ride black horses. Angels are white, and devils are black. The definition of *black* includes "without any moral light or goodness, evil, wicked, indicating disgrace, sinful," while that of *white* includes "morally pure, spotless, innocent, free from evil intent."

A children's TV cartoon program, *Captain Scarlet*, is about an organization called Spectrum, whose purpose is to save the world from an evil extraterrestrial force called the Mysterons. Everyone in Spectrum has a color name—Captain Scarlet, Captain Blue, etc. The one Spectrum agent who has been mysteriously taken over by the Mysterons and works to advance their evil aims is Captain Black. The person who heads Spectrum, the good organization out to defend the world, is Colonel White.

Three of the dictionary definitions of white are "fairness of complexion, purity, innocence." These definitions affect the standards of beauty in our culture, in which whiteness represents the norm. "Blondes have more fun" and "Wouldn't you really rather be a blonde" are sexist in their attitudes toward women generally, but are racist white standards when applied to third world women. A 1971 *Mademoiselle* advertisement pictured a curly-headed, ivory-skinned woman over the caption, "When you go blonde go all the way," and asked: "Isn't this how, in the back of your mind, you always wanted to look? All wide-eyed and silky blonde down to there, and innocent?" Whatever the advertising people meant by this particular woman's innocence, one must remember that "innocent" is one of the definitions of the word white. This standard of beauty when preached to all women is racist. The statement "Isn't this how, in the back of your mind, you always wanted to look?" either ignores third world women or assumes they long to be white.

Time magazine in its coverage of the Wimbledon tennis competition between the black Australian Evonne Goolagong and the white American Chris Evert described Ms. Goolagong as "the dusky daughter of an Australian sheepshearer," while Ms. Evert was "a fair young girl from the middle-class groves of Florida." *Dusky* is a synonym of "black" and is defined as "having dark skin; of a dark color; gloomy; dark; swarthy." Its antonyms are "fair" and "blonde." *Fair* is defined in part as "free from blemish, imperfection, or anything that impairs the appearance, quality, or character; pleasing in appearance, attractive; clean; pretty; comely." By defining Evonne Goolagong as "dusky," *Time* technically defined her as the opposite of "pleasing in appearance; attractive; clean; pretty; comely."

The studies of Kenneth B. Clark, Mary Ellen Goodman, Judith Porter and others indicate that this persuasive "rightness of whiteness" in U.S. culture affects children before the age of four, providing white youngsters with a false sense of superiority and encouraging self-hatred among third world youngsters.

Ethnocentrism or From a White Perspective

Some words and phrases that are commonly used represent particular perspectives and frames of reference, and these often distort the understanding of the reader or listener. David R. Burgest[3] has written about the effect of using the terms "slave" or "master." He argues that the psychological impact of the statement referring to "the master raped his slave" is different from the impact of the same statement substituting the words: "the white captor raped an African woman held in captivity."

> Implicit in the English usage of the "master-slave" concept is ownership of the "slave" by the "master," therefore, the "master" is merely abusing his property (slave). In reality, the captives (slave) were African individuals with human worth, right and dignity and the term "slave" denounces that human quality thereby making the mass rape of African women by white captors more acceptable in the minds of people and setting a mental frame of reference for legitimizing the atrocities perpetuated against African people.

The term slave connotes a less than human quality and turns the captive person into a thing. For example, two McGraw-Hill Far Eastern Publishers textbooks

(1970) stated, "At first it was the slaves who worked the cane and they got only food for it. Now men work cane and get money." Next time you write about slavery or read about it, try transposing all "slaves" into "African people held in captivity," "Black people forced to work for no pay" or "African people stolen from their families and societies." While it is more cumbersome, such phrasing conveys a different meaning.

Passive Tense

Another means by which language shapes our perspective has been noted by Thomas Greenfield,[4] who writes that the achievements of Black people—and Black people themselves—have been hidden in

> the linguistic ghetto of the passive voice, the subordinate clause, and the "understood" subject. The seemingly innocuous distinction (between active/passive voice) holds enormous implications for writers and speakers. When it is effectively applied, the rhetorical impact of the passive voice—the art of making the creator or instigator of action totally disappear from a reader's perception—can be devastating.

For instance, some history texts will discuss how European immigrants came to the United States seeking a better life and expanded opportunities, but will note that "slaves *were brought* to America." Not only does this omit the destruction of African societies and families, but it ignores the role of northern merchants and southern slaveholders in the profitable trade in human beings. Other books will state that "the continental railroad *was built,*" conveniently omitting information about the Chinese laborers who built much of it or the oppression they suffered.

Another example. While touring Monticello, Greenfield noted that the tour guide

> made all the black people at Monticello disappear through her use of the passive voice. While speaking of the architectural achievements of Jefferson in the active voice, she unfailingly shifted to passive when speaking of the work performed by Negro slaves and skilled servants.

Noting a type of door that after 166 years continued to operate without need for repair, Greenfield remarks that the design aspect of the door was much simpler than the actual skill and work involved in building and installing it. Yet his guide stated: "Mr. Jefferson designed these doors . . ." while "the doors *were installed* in 1809." The workers who installed those doors were African people whom Jefferson held in bondage. The guide's use of the passive tense enabled her to dismiss the reality of Jefferson's slaveholding. It also meant that she did not have to make any mention of the skills of those people held in bondage.

Politics and Terminology

"Culturally deprived," "economically disadvantaged" and "underdeveloped" are other terms which mislead and distort our awareness of reality. The application of the term "culturally deprived" and third world children in this society reflects a value judgment. It assumes that the dominant whites are cultured and all others without culture. In fact, third world children generally are bicultural, and many are bilingual, having grown up in their own culture as well as absorbing the dominant culture. In many ways, they are equipped with skills and experiences which white youth have been deprived of, since most white youth develop in a monocultural, monolingual environment. Burgest[5] suggests that the term "culturally deprived" be replaced by "culturally dispossessed," and that the term "economically disadvantaged" be replaced by "economically exploited." Both these terms present a perspective and implication that provide an entirely different frame of reference as to the reality of the third world experience in U.S. society.

Similarly, many nations of the third world are described as "underdeveloped." These less wealthy nations are generally those that suffered under colonialism and neo-colonialism. The "developed" nations are those that exploited their resources and wealth. Therefore, rather than referring to these countries as "underdeveloped," a more appropriate and meaningful designation might be "over exploited." Again, transpose this term next time you read about "underdeveloped nations" and note the different meaning that results.

Terms such as "culturally deprived," "economically disadvantaged" and "underdeveloped" place the responsibility for their own conditions on those being so described. This is known as "Blaming the Victim."[6] It places responsibility for poverty on the victims of poverty. It removes the blame from those in power who benefit from, and continue to permit, poverty.

Still another example involves the use of "non-white," "minority" or "third world." While people of color are a minority in the U.S., they are part of the vast majority of the world's population, in which white people are a distinct minority. Thus, by utilizing the term minority to describe people of color in the U.S., we can lose sight of the global majority/minority reality—a fact of some importance in the increasing and interconnected struggles of people of color inside and outside the U.S.

To describe people of color as "non-white" is to use whiteness as the standard and norm against which to measure all others. Use of the term "third world" to describe all people of color overcomes the inherent bias of "minority" and "non-white." Moreover, it connects the struggles of third world people in the U.S. with the freedom struggles around the globe.

The term third world gained increasing usage after the 1955 Bandung Conference of "non-aligned" nations, which represented a third force outside of the two world superpowers. The "first world" represents the United States, Western Europe and their sphere of influence. The "second world" represents the Soviet Union and its sphere. The "third world" represents, for the most part, nations that were, or are, controlled by the "first world" or West. For the most part, these are nations of Africa, Asia and Latin America.

"Loaded" Words and Native Americans

Many words lead to a demeaning characterization of groups of people. For instance, Columbus, it is said, "discovered" America. The word *discover* is defined as "to gain sight or knowledge of something previously unseen or unknown; to discover may be to find some existent thing that was previously unknown." Thus, a continent inhabited by millions of human beings cannot be "discovered." For history books to continue this usage represents a Eurocentric (white European) perspective on world history and ignores the existence of, and the perspective of, Native Americans. "Discovery," as used in the Euro-American context, implies the right to take what one finds, ignoring the rights of those who already inhabit or own the "discovered" thing.

Eurocentrism is also apparent in the usage of "victory" and "massacre" to describe the battles between Native Americans and whites. *Victory* is defined in the dictionary as "a success or triumph over an enemy in battle or war; the decisive defeat of an opponent." *Conquest* denotes the "taking over of control by the victor, and the obedience of the conquered." *Massacre* is defined as "the unnecessary, indiscriminate killing of a number of human beings, as in barbarous warfare or persecution, or for revenge or plunder." *Defend* is described as "to ward off attack from; guard against assault or injury; to strive to keep safe by resisting attack."

Eurocentrism turns these definitions around to serve the purpose of distorting history and justifying Euro-American conquest of the Native American homelands. Euro-Americans are not described in history books as invading Native American lands, but rather as defending *their* homes against "Indian" attacks. Since European communities were constantly encroaching on land already occupied, then a more honest interpretation would state that it was the Native Americans who were "warding off," "guarding" and "defending" their homelands.

Native American victories are invariably defined as "massacres," while the indiscriminate killing, extermination and plunder of Native American nations by Euro-Americans is defined as "victory." Distortion of history by the choice of "loaded" words used to describe historical events is a common racist practice. Rather than portraying Native Americans as human beings in highly defined and complex societies, cultures and civilizations, history books use such adjectives as "savages," "beasts," "primitive," and "backward." Native people are referred to as "squaw," "brave," or "papoose" instead of "woman," "man," or "baby."

Another term that has questionable connotations is *tribe*. The Oxford English Dictionary defines this noun as "a race of people; now applied especially to a primary aggregate of people in a primitive or barbarous condition, under a headman or chief." Morton Fried,[7] discussing "The Myth of Tribe," states that the word "did not become a general term of reference to American Indian society until the nineteenth century. Previously, the words commonly used for Indian populations were 'nation' and 'people.' " Since "tribe" has assumed a connotation of primitiveness or backwardness, it is suggested that the use of "nation" or "people" replace the term whenever possible in referring to Native American peoples.

The term *tribe* invokes even more negative implications when used in reference to American peoples. As Evelyn Jones Rich[8] has noted, the term is "almost always used to refer to third world people and it implies a stage of development which is, in short, a put-down."

"Loaded" Words and Africans

Conflicts among diverse peoples within African nations are often referred to as "tribal warfare," while conflicts among the diverse peoples within European countries are never described in such terms. If the rivalries between the Ibo and the Hausa and Yoruba in Nigeria are described as "tribal," why not the rivalries between Serbs and Slavs in Yugoslavia, or Scots and English in Great Britain, Protestants and Catholics in Ireland, or the Basques and the Southern Spaniards in Spain? Conflicts among African peoples in a particular nation have religious, cultural, economic and/or political roots. If we can analyze the roots of conflicts among European peoples in terms other than "tribal warfare," certainly we can do the same with African peoples, including correct reference to the ethnic groups or nations involved. For example, the terms "Kaffirs," "Hottentot" or "Bushmen" are names imposed by white Europeans. The correct names are always those by which a people refer to themselves. (In these instances Xhosa, Khoi-Khoin and San are correct.[9])

The generalized application of "tribal" in reference to Africans—as well as the failure to acknowledge the religious, cultural and social diversity of African peoples—is a decidedly racist dynamic. It is part of the process whereby Euro-Americans justify, or avoid confronting, their opression of third world peoples. Africa has been particularly insulted by this dynamic, as witness the pervasive "darkest Africa" image. This image, widespread in Western culture, evokes an Africa covered by jungles and inhibited by "uncivilized," "cannibalistic," "pagan," "savage" peoples. This "darkest Africa" image avoids the geographical reality. Less than 20 per cent of the African continent is wooded savanna, for example. The image also ignores the history of African cultures and civilizations. Ample evidence suggests this distortion of reality was developed as a convenient rationale for the European and American slave trade. The Western powers, rather than exploiting, were civilizing and christianizing "uncivilized" and "pagan savages" (so the rationalization went). This dynamic also served to justify Western colonialism. From Tarzan movies to racist children's books like *Doctor Dolittle* and *Charlie and the Chocolate Factory*, the image of "savage" Africa and the myth of "the white man's burden" has been perpetuated in Western culture.

A 1972 *Time* magazine editorial lamenting the demise of *Life* magazine, stated that the "lavishness" of *Life's* enterprises included "organizing safaris into darkest Africa." The same year, the *New York Times'* C.L. Sulzberger wrote that Africa has "a history as dark as the skins of many of its people." Terms such as "darkest Africa," "primitive," "tribe" ("tribal") or "jungle," in reference to Africa, perpetuate myths and are especially inexcusable in such large circulation publications.

Ethnocentrism is similarly reflected in the term "pagan" to describe traditional religions. A February 1973 *Time* magazine article on Uganda stated, "Moslems account for only 500,000 of Uganda's 10 million people. Of the remainder, 5,000,000 are Christians and the rest pagan." *Pagan* is defined as "Heathen, a follower of a polytheistic religion; one that has little or no religion and that is marked by a frank delight in and uninhibited seeking after sensual pleasures and material goods." *Heathen* is defined as "Unenlightened; an unconverted member of a people or nation that does not acknowledge the God of the Bible. A person whose culture or enlightenment is of an inferior grade, especially an irreligious person." Now, the people of Uganda, like almost all Africans, have serious religious beliefs and practices. As used by Westerners, "pagan" connotes something wild, primitive and inferior—another term to watch out for.

The variety of traditional structures that African people live in are their "houses," not "huts." A *hut* is "an often small and temporary dwelling of simple construction." And to describe Africans as "natives" (noun) is derogatory terminology—as in, "the natives are restless." The dictionary definition of *native* includes: "one of a people inhabiting a territorial area at the time of its discovery or becoming familiar to a foreigner; one belonging to a people having a less complex civilization." Therefore, use of "native," like use of "pagan" often implies a value judgment of white superiority.

Qualifying Adjectives

Words that would normally have positive connotations can have entirely different meanings when used in a racial context. For example, C. L. Sulzberger, the columnist of the *New York Times*, wrote in January 1975, about conversations he had with two people in Namibia. One was the white South African administrator of the country and the other a member of SWAPO, the Namibian liberation movement. The first is described as "Dirk Mudge, who as senior elected member of the administration is a kind of acting Prime Minister. . . ." But the second person is introduced as "Daniel Tijongarero, an intelligent Herero tribesman who is a member of SWAPO. . . ." What need was there for Sulzberger to state that Daniel Tijongarero is "intelligent"? Why not also state that Dirk Mudge was "intelligent"— or do we assume he wasn't?

A similar example from a 1968 *New York Times* article reporting on an address by Lyndon Johnson stated, "The President spoke to the well-dressed Negro officials and their wives." In what similar circumstances can one imagine a reporter finding it necessary to note that an audience of white government officials was "well-dressed"?

Still another word often used in a racist context is "qualified." In the 1960's white Americans often questioned whether Black people were "qualified" to hold public office, a question that was never raised (until too late) about white officials like Wallace, Maddox, Nixon, Agnew, Mitchell, et al. The question of qualifications has been raised even more frequently in recent years as white people question whether Black people are "qualified" to be hired for positions in industry and educational institutions. "We're looking for a qualified Black" has been heard again and again as institutions are confronted with affirmative action goals. Why stipulate that Blacks must be "qualified," when for others it is taken for granted that applicants must be "qualified."

Speaking English

Finally, the depiction in movies and children's books of third world people speaking English is often itself racist. Children's books about Puerto Ricans or Chicanos often connect poverty with a failure to speak English or to speak it well, thus blaming the victim and ignoring the racism which affects third world people regardless of their proficiency in English. Asian characters speak a stilted English ("Honorable so and so" or "Confucius say") or have a speech impediment ("roots or ruck," "very solly," "flied lice"). Native American characters speak another variation of stilted English ("Boy not hide. Indian take boy."), repeat certain Hollywood-Indian phrases ("Heap big" and "Many moons") or simply grunt out "Ugh" or "How." The repeated use of these language characterizations functions to make third world people seem less intelligent and less capable than the English-speaking white characters.

Wrap-Up

A *Saturday Review* editorial[10] on "The Environment of Language" stated that language

> . . . has as much to do with the philosophical and political conditioning of a society as geography or climate. . . . people in Western cultures do not realize the extent to which their racial attitudes have been conditioned since early childhood by the power of words to ennoble or condemn, augment or detract, glorify or demean. Negative language infects the subconscious of most Western people from the time they first learn to speak. Prejudice is not merely imparted or superimposed. It is metabolized in the bloodstream of society. What is needed is not so much a change in language as an awareness of the power of words to condition attitudes. If we can at least recognize the underpinnings of prejudice, we may be in a position to deal with the effects.

To recognize the racism in language is an important first step. Consciousness of the influence of language on our perceptions can help to negate much of that influence. But it is not enough to simply become aware of the affects of racism in conditioning attitudes. While we may not be able to change the language, we can definitely change our usage of the language. We can avoid using words that degrade people. We can make a conscious effort to use terminology that reflects a progressive perspective, as opposed to a distorting perspective. It is important for educators to provide students with opportunities to explore racism in language and to increase their awareness of it, as well as learning terminology that is positive and does not perpetuate negative human values.

NOTES

1. Simon Podair, "How Bigotry Builds Through Language," *Negro Digest*, March '67
2. Jose Armas, "Antonio and the Mayor: A Cultural Review of the Film," *The Journal of Ethnic Studies*, Fall, '75
3. David R. Burgest, "The Racist Use of the English Language," *Black Scholar*, Sept. '73
4. Thomas Greenfield, "Race and Passive Voice at Monticello," *Crisis*, April '75
5. David R. Burgest, "Racism in Everyday Speech and Social Work Jargon," *Social Work*, July '73
6. William Ryan, *Blaming the Victim*, Pantheon Books, '71
7. Morton Fried, "The Myth of Tribe," *National History*, April '75
8. Evelyn Jones Rich, "Mind Your Language," *Africa Report*, Sept./Oct. '74
9. Steve Wolf, "Catalogers in Revolt Against LC's Racist, Sexist Headings," *Bulletin of Interracial Books for Children*, Vol. 6, Nos. 3&4, '75
10. "The Environment of Language," *Saturday Review*, April 8, '67

Also see:

Roger Bastide, "Color, Racism and Christianity," *Daedalus*, Spring '67
Kenneth J. Gergen, "The Significance of Skin Color in Human Relations," *Daedalus*, Spring '67
Lloyd Yabura, "Towards a Language of Humanism," *Rhythm*, Summer '71
UNESCO, "Recommendations Concerning Terminology in Education on Race Questions," June '68

4

"Pricks" and "Chicks":
A Plea For "Persons"

Robert Baker

There is a school of philosophers who believe that one starts philosophizing not by examining whatever it is one is philosophizing about but by examining the words we use to designate the subject to be examined. I must confess my allegiance to this school. The import of my confession is that this is an essay on women's liberation.

There seems to be a curious malady that affects those philosophers who, in order to analyze anything, must examine the way we talk about it. They seem incapable of talking about anything without talking about their talk about it—and, once again, I must confess to being typical. Thus I shall argue, first, that the way in which we identify something reflects our conception of it; second, that the conception of women embedded in our language is male chauvinistic; third, that the conceptual revisions proposed by the feminist movement are confused; and finally, that at the root of the problem are both our conception of sex and the very structure of sexual identification.

Identification and Conception

I am not going to defend the position that the terms we utilize to identify something reflect our conception of it; I shall simply explain and illustrate a simplified version of this thesis. Let us assume that any term that can be (meaningfully) substituted for x in the following statements is a term used to identify something: "Where is the x?" "Who is the x?" Some of the terms that can be substituted for x in the above expressions are metaphors; I shall refer to such metaphors as metaphorical identifications. For example, southerners frequently say such things as "Where did that girl get to?" and "Who is the new boy that Lou hired to help out at the filling station?" If the persons the terms apply to are adult Afro-Americans, then "girl" and "boy" are metaphorical identifications. The fact that the metaphorical identifications in question are standard in the language relects the fact that certain characteristics of the objects properly classified as boys and girls (for example, immaturity, inability to take care of themselves, need for guidance) are generally held by those who use identifications to be properly attributable to Afro-Americans. One might say that the whole theory of southern white paternalism is implicit in the metaphorical identification "boy" (just as the rejection of paternalism is implicit in the standardized Afro-American forms of address, "man" and "woman," as in, for example, "Hey, man, how are you?").

Most of what I am going to say in this essay is significant only if the way we metaphorically identify something is not a superficial bit of conceptually irrelevant happenstance but rather a reflection of our conceptual structure. Thus if one is to accept my analysis he must understand the significance of metaphorical identifications. He must see that, even though the southerner who identifies adult Afro-American males as "boys" feels that this identification is "just the way people talk"; but for a group to talk that way it must think that way. In the next few paragraphs I shall adduce what I hope is a persuasive example of how, in one clear case, the change in the way we identified something reflected a change in the way we thought about it.

Until the 1960s, Afro-Americans were identified by such terms as "Negro" and "colored" (the respectable terms) and by the more disreputable "nigger," "spook," "kink," and so on. Recently there has been an unsuccessful attempt to replace the respectable identification with such terms as "African," and "Afro-American," and a more successful attempt to replace them with "black." The most outspoken champions of this linguistic reform were those who argued that nonviolence must be abandoned for Black Power (Stokely Carmichael, H. Rap Brown), that integration must be abandoned in favor of separation (the Black Muslims: Malcolm X, Muhammad Ali), and that Afro-Americans were an internal colony in the alien world of Babylon who must arm themselves against the possibility of extermination (the Black Panthers: Eldridge Cleaver, Huey Newton). All of these movements and their partisans wished to stress that Afro-Americans were different from other Americans and could not be merged with them because the difference between the two was as great as that between black and white. Linguistically, of course, "black" and "white" are antonyms; and it is precisely this sense of oppositeness that those who see the Afro-American as alienated, separated, and nonintegratable wish to capture with the term "black." Moreover, as any good dictionary makes clear, in some contexts "black" is synonymous with "deadly," "sinister," "wicked," "evil," and so forth. The new militants were trying to create just this picture of the black man—civil rights and Uncle Tomism are dead, the ghost of Nat Turner is to be resurrected, freedom now or pay the price, the ballot or the bullet, violence is as American as cherry pie. The new strategy was that the white man would either give the black man his due or pay the price in violence. Since conceptually a "black man" was an object to be feared ("black" can be synonymous with "deadly," and so on), while a "colored man" or a "Negro" was not, the new strategy required that the "Negro" be supplanted by the "black man." White America resisted the proposed linguistic reform quite vehemently, until hundreds of riots forced the admission that the Afro-American was indeed black.

Now to the point: I have suggested that the word "black" replaced the word

"Negro" because there was a change in our conceptual structure. One is likely to reply that while all that I have said above is well and good, one had, after all, no choice about the matter. White people are identified in terms of their skin color as whites; clearly, if we are to recognize what is in reality nothing but the truth, that in this society people are conscious of skin color, to treat blacks as equals is merely to identify them by their skin color, which is black. That is, one might argue that while there was a change in words, we have no reason to think that there was a parallel conceptual change. If the term "black" has all the associations mentioned above, that is unfortunate; but in the context the use of the term "black" to identify the people formerly identified as "Negroes" is natural, inevitable, and, in and of itself, neutral; black is, after all, the skin color of the people in question. (Notice that this defense of the natural-inevitable-and-neutral conception of identification quite nicely circumvents the possible use of such seemingly innocuous terms as "Afro-American" and "African" by suggesting that in this society it is *skin color* that is the relevant variable.)

The great flaw in this analysis is that the actual skin color of virtually all of the people whom we call "black" is not black at all. The color tones range from light yellow to a deep umber that occasionally is literally black. The skin color of most Afro-Americans is best designated by the word "brown." Yet "brown" is not a term that is standard for identifying Afro-Americans. For example, if someone asked, "Who was the brown who was the architect for Washington, D.C.?" we would not know how to construe the question. We might attempt to read "brown" as a proper name ("Do you mean Arthur Brown, the designer?"). We would have no trouble understanding the sentence "Who was the black (Negro, colored guy, and so forth) who designed Washington, D.C.?" ("Oh, you mean Benjamin Banneker.") Clearly, "brown" is not a standard form of identification for Afro-Americans. I hope that it is equally clear that "black" has become the standard way of identifying Afro-Americans not because the term was natural, inevitable, and, in the context, neutral, but because of its occasional synonymy with "sinister" and because as an antonym to "white" it best fitted the conceptual needs of those who saw race relations in terms of intensifying and insurmountable antonyms. If one accepts this point, then one must admit that there is a close connection between the way in which we identify things and the way in which we conceive them—and thus it should be also clear why I wish to talk about the way in which women are identified in English.[1] (Thus, for example, one would expect Black Muslims, who continually use the term "Black *man*"—as in "the black *man's* rights"—to be more male chauvinistic than Afro-Americans who use the term "black *people*" or "black *folk*.")

Ways of Idenitifying Women

It may at first seem trivial to note that women (and men) are identified sexually; but conceptually this is extremely significant. To appreciate the significance of this fact it is helpful to imagine a language in which proper names and personal pronouns do not reflect the sex of the person designated by them (as they do in our language). I have been told that in some oriental languages pronouns and proper names reflect social status rather than sex, but whether or not there actually exists such a language is irrelevant, for it is easy enough to imagine what one would be like. Let us then imagine a language where the proper names are sexually neutral (for example, "Xanthe"), so that one cannot tell from hearing a name whether the person so named is male or female, and where the personal pronouns in the language are "under" and "over." "Under" is the personal pronoun appropriate for all those who are younger than thirty, while "over" is appropriate to persons older than thirty. In such a language, instead of saying such things as "Where do you think *he* is living now?" one would say such things as "Where do you think *under* is living now?"

What would one say about a cultural community that employed such a language? Clearly, one would say that they thought that for purposes of intelligible communication it was more important to know a person's age grouping than the person's height, sex, race, hair color, or parentage. (There are many actual cultures, of course, in which people are identified by names that reflect their parentage; for example, Abu ben Adam means Abu son of Adam.) I think that one would also claim that this people would not have reflected these differences in the pronominal structure of their language if they did not believe that the differences between unders and overs was such that a statement would frequently have one meaning if it were about an under and a different meaning if it were about an over. For example, in feudal times if a serf said, "My lord said to do this," that assertion was radically different from "Freeman John said to do this," since (presumably) the former had the status of a command while the latter did not. Hence the conventions of Middle English required that one refer to people in such a way as to indicate their social status. Analogously, one would not distinguish between pronominal references according to the age differences in the persons referred to were there no shift in meaning involved.

If we apply the lesson illustrated by this imaginary language to our own, I think that it should be clear that since in our language proper nouns and pronouns reflect sex rather than age, race, parentage, social status, or religion, we believe one of the most important things one can know about a person is that person's sex. (And, indeed, this is the first thing one seeks to determine about a newborn babe—our first question is almost invariably "Is it a boy or a girl?") Moreover, we would not reflect this important difference pronominally did we not also believe that statements frequently mean one thing when applied to males and something else when applied to females. Perhaps the most striking aspect of the conceptual discrimination reflected in our language is that man is, as it were, essentially human, while woman is only accidentally so.

This charge may seem rather extreme, but consider the following synonyms (which are readily confirmed by any dictionary). "Humanity" is synonymous with "mankind" but not with "womankind." "Man" can be substituted for "humanity" or "mankind" in any sentence in which the terms "mankind" or "humanity" occur without changing the meaning of the sentence, but significantly, "woman" cannot.

Thus, the following expressions are all synonymous with each other: "humanity's great achievements," "mankind's great achievements," and "man's great achievements." "Woman's great achievements" is not synonymous with any of these. To highlight the degree to which women are excluded from humanity, let me point out that it is something of a truism to say that "man is a rational animal," while "woman is a rational animal" is quite debatable. Clearly, if "man" in the first assertion embraced both men and women, the second assertion would be just as much a truism as the first.[2] Humanity, it would seem, is a male prerogative. (And hence, one of the goals of woman's liberation is to alter our conceptual structure so that someday "mankind" will be regarded as an improper and vestigial ellipsis for "humankind," and "man" will have no special privileges in relation to "human being" that "women" does not have.[3])

The major question before us is, "How are women conceived of in our culture?" I have been trying to answer this question by talking about how they are identified. I first considered pronominal identification; now I wish to turn to identification through other types of noun phrases. Methods of nonpronominal identification can be discovered by determining which terms can be substituted for "woman" in such sentences as "Who is that woman over there?" without changing the meaning of the sentence. Virtually no term is interchangeable with "woman" in that sentence for all speakers on all occasions. Even "lady," which most speakers would accept as synonymous with "woman" in that sentence, will not do for a speaker who applies the term "lady" only to those women who display manners, poise, and sensitivity. In most contexts, a large number of students in one or more of my classes will accept the following types of terms as more or less interchangeable with "woman." (An asterisk indicates interchanges acceptable to both males and females; a plus sign indicates terms restricted to black students only. Terms with neither an asterisk nor a plus sign are acceptable by all males but are not normally used by females.)

A.   NEUTRAL TERMS: *lady, *gal, *girl (especially with regard to a co-worker in an office or factory), *+sister, *broad (originally in the animal category, but most people do not think of the term as now meaning pregnant cow)

B.   ANIMAL: *chick, bird, fox, vixen, filly, bitch (Many do not know the literal meaning of the term. Some men and most women construe this use as pejorative; they think of "bitch" in the context of "bitchy," that is, snappy, nasty, and so forth. But a large group of men claim that it is a standard nonpejorative term of identification—which may perhaps indicate that women have come to be thought of as shrews by a large subclass of men.)

C.   PLAYTHING: babe, doll, cuddly

D.   GENDER (association with articles of clothing typically worn by those in the female gender role): skirt, hem

E.   SEXUAL: snatch, cunt, ass, twat, piece (of ass, and so forth), lay, pussy (could be put in the animal category, but most users associated it with slang expression indicating the female pubic region), +hammer (related to anatomical analogy between a hammer and breasts). There are many other usages, for example, "bunny," "sweat hog," but these were not recognized as standard by as many as ten percent of any given class.

The students in my classes reported that the most frequently used terms of identification are in the neutral and animal classifications (although men in their forties claim to use the gender classifications quite a bit) and that the least frequently used terms of identification are sexual. Fortunately, however, I am not interested in the frequency of usage but only in whether the use is standard enough to be recognized as an identification among some group or other. (Recall that "brown" was not a standardized term of identification and hence we could not make sense out of "Who was the brown who planned Washington, D.C. ?" Similarly, one has trouble with "Who was the breasts who planned Washington, D.C. ?" but not with "Who was the babe (doll, chick, skirt, and so forth) who planned Washington, D.C. ?"

Except for two of the animal terms, "chick" and "broad"—but note that "broad" is probably neutral today—women do not typically identify themselves in sexual terms, in gender terms, as playthings, or as animals; *only males use nonneutral terms to identify women.* Hence, it would seem that there is a male conception of women and a female conception. Only males identify women as "foxes," "babes," "skirts," or "cunts" (and since all the other nonneutral identifications are male, it is reasonable to assume that the identification of a woman as a "chick" is primarily a male conception that some women have adopted).

What kind of conception do men have of women? Clearly they think that women share certain properties with certain types of animals, toys, and playthings; they conceive of them in terms of the clothes associated with the female gender role; and, last (and, if my classes are any indication, least frequently), they conceive of women in terms of those parts of their anatomy associated with sexual intercourse, that is, as the identification "lay" indicates quite clearly, as sexual partners.

The first two nonneutral male classifications, animal and plaything, are *prima facie* denigrating (and I mean this in the literal sense of making one like a "nigger"). Consider the animal classification. All of the terms listed, with the possible exception of 'bird,' refer to animals that are either domesticated for servitude (to *man*) or hunted for sport. First, let us consider the term "bird." When I asked my students what sort of birds might be indicated, they suggested chick, canary (one member, in his forties, had suggested "canary" as a term of identification), chicken, pigeon, dove, parakeet, and hummingbird (one member). With the exception of the hummingbird, which like all the birds suggested is generally thought to be diminutive and pretty, all of the birds are domesticated, usually as pets (which reminds one that "my pet" is an expression of endearment). None of the birds were predators or symbols of intelligence or nobility (as are the owl, eagle, hawk, and falcon); nor did large but beautiful birds seem appropriate (for example, pheasants, peacocks, and swans). If one construes the bird terms (and for that matter, "filly") as applicable to women because they are thought of as beautiful, or at least pretty, *then there is nothing denigrating about them.* If, on the other hand, the common properties that underlie the metaphorical identification are domesticity and servitude, then they are

indeed denigrating (as for myself, I think that both domesticity and prettiness underlie the identification). "Broad," of course, is, or at least was, clearly denigrating,
since nothing renders more service to a farmer than does a pregnant cow, and cows
are not commonly thought of as paradigms of beauty.

With one exception all of the animal terms reflect a male conception of women
either as domesticated servants or as pets, or as both. Indeed, some of the terms
reflect a conception of women first as pets and then as servants. Thus, when a
pretty, cuddly little chick grows older, she becomes a very useful servant—the egg-
laying hen.

"Vixen" and "fox," variants of the same term, are the one clear exception. None
of the other animals with whom women are metaphorically identified are generally
thought to be intelligent, aggressive, or independent—but the fox is. A chick is a
soft, cuddly, entertaining, pretty, diminutive, domesticated, and dumb animal. A
fox too is soft, cuddly, entertaining, pretty, and diminutive, but it is neither dependent nor dumb. It is aggressive, intelligent, and a minor predator—indeed, it preys
on chicks—and frequently outsmarts ("outfoxes") men.

Thus the term "fox" or "vixen" is generally taken to be a compliment by both
men and women, and compared to any of the animal or plaything terms it is indeed
a compliment. Yet considered in and of itself, the conception of a woman as a fox is
not really complimentary at all, for the major connection between *man* and fox is
that of predator and prey. The fox is an animal that men chase, and hunt, and kill
for sport. If women are conceived of as foxes, then they are conceived of as prey that
it is fun to hunt.

In considering plaything identifications, only one sentence is necessary. *All the
plaything identifications are clearly denigrating since they assimilate women to the
status of mindless or dependent objects.* "Doll" is to male paternalism what "boy" is
to white paternalism.

Up to this point in our survey of male conceptions of women, every male
identification, without exception, has been clearly antithetical to the conception of
women as human beings (recall that "man" was synonymous with "human," while
"woman" was not). Since the way we talk of things, and especially the way we
identify them, is the way in which we conceive of them, any movement dedicated to
breaking the bonds of female servitude must destroy these ways of identifying and
hence of conceiving of women. Only when both sexes find the terms "babe," "doll,"
"chick," "broad," and so forth, as objectionable as "boy" and "nigger" will women
come to be conceived of as independent *human beings.*

The two remaining unexamined male identifications are gender and sex. There
seems to be nothing objectionable about gender identifications per se. That is,
women are metaphorically identified as skirts because in this culture, skirts, like
women, are peculiarly female. Indeed, if one accepts the view that the slogan
"female and proud" should play the same role for the women's liberation movement
that the slogan "Black is beautiful" plays for the black-liberation movement, then
female clothes should be worn with the same pride as Afro clothes. (Of course, one
can agree that the skirt, like the cropped-down Afro, is a sign of bondage, and hence

both the item of clothing and the identification with it are to be rejected—that is, cropped-down Afros are to Uncle Tom what skirts are to Uncle Mom.)

The terms in the last category are obviously sexual, and frequently vulgar. For a variety of reasons I shall consider the import and nature of these identifications in the next section.

Men Ought Not to Think of Women as Sex Objects

Feminists have proposed many reforms, and most of them are clearly desirable, for example, equal opportunity for self-development, equal pay for equal work, and free day-care centers. One feminist proposal, however, is peculiarly conceptual and deeply perplexing. I call this proposal peculiarly conceptual because unlike the other reforms it is directed at getting people to think differently. The proposal is that *men should not think of women (and women should not think of themselves) as sex objects*. In the rest of the essay I shall explore this nostrum. I do so for two reasons: first, because the process of exploration should reveal the depth of the problem confronting the feminist; and second, because the feminists themselves seem to be entangled in the very concepts that obstruct their liberation.

To see why I find this proposal puzzling, one has to ask what it is to think of something as a sex object.

If a known object is an object that we know, an unidentified object is an object that we have not identified, and a desired object is an object that we desire, what then is a sex object? Clearly, a sex object is an object we have sex with. Hence, to think of a woman as a sex object is to think of her as someone to have sexual relations with, and when the feminist proposed that men refrain from thinking of women in this way, *she is proposing that men not think of women as persons with whom one has sexual relations*.

What are we to make of this proposal? Is the feminist suggesting that women should not be conceived of in this way because such a conception is "dirty"? To conceive of sex and sex organs as dirty is simply to be a prude. "Shit" is the paradigm case of a dirty word. It is a dirty word because the item it designates is taboo; it is literally unclean and untouchable (as opposed to something designated by what I call a curse word, which is not untouchable but rather something to be feared— "damn" and "hell" are curse words; "piss" is a dirty word). If one claims that "cunt" (or "fuck") is a dirty word, then one holds that what this term designates is unclean and taboo; thus one holds that the terms for sexual intercourse or sexual organs are dirty, one has accepted puritanism. If one is a puritan and a feminist, then indeed one ought to subscribe to the slogan *men should not conceive of women as sexual objects*. What is hard to understand is why anyone but a puritan (or, perhaps, a homosexual) would promulgate this slogan; yet most feminists, who are neither lesbians nor puritans, accept this slogan. Why?

A word about slogans: Philosophical slogans have been the subject of consider-able analysis. They have the peculiar property (given a certain seemingly sound background story) of being obviously true, yet obviously false. "Men should not conceive of women as sex objects" is, I suggest, like a philosophical slogan in this respect. The immediate reaction of any humanistically oriented person upon first hearing the slogan is to agree with it—yet the more one probes the meaning of the slogan, the less likely one is to give one's assent. Philosophical analysts attempt to separate out the various elements involved in such slogans—to render the true-false slogan into a series of statements, some of which are true, some of which are false, and others of which are, perhaps, only probable. This is what I am trying to do with the slogan in question. I have argued so far that one of the elements that seems to be implicit in the slogan is a rejection of women as sexual partners for men and that although this position might be proper for a homosexual or puritanical movement, it seems inappropriate to feminism. I shall proceed to show that at least two other interpretations of the slogan lead to inappropriate results; but I shall argue that there are at least two respects in which the slogan is profoundly correct—even if misleadingly stated.

One plausible, but inappropriate, interpretation of "men ought not to conceive of women as sex objects" is that men ought not to conceive of women *exclusively* as sexual partners. The problem with this interpretation is that everyone can agree with it. Women are conceived of as companions, toys, servants, and even sisters, wives and mothers—and hence not exclusively as sexual partners. Thus this slogan loses its revisionary impact, since even a male chauvinist could accept the slogan without changing his conceptual structure in any way—which is only to say that men do not usually identify or conceive of women as sexual partners (recall that the sexual method of identification is the least frequently used).

Yet another interpretation is suggested by the term "object" in "sex object," and this interpretation too has a certain amount of plausibility. Men should not treat women as animate machines designed to masturbate men or as conquests that allow men to "score" for purposes of building their egos. Both of these variations rest on the view that to be treated as an object is to be treated as less than human (that is, to be treated as a machine or a score). Such relations between men and women are indeed immoral, and there are, no doubt, men who believe in "scoring." Unfortunately, however, this interpretation—although it would render the slogan quite apt—also fails because of its restricted scope. When feminists argue that men should not treat women as sex objects, they are not *only* talking about fraternity boys and members of the Playboy Club; they are talking about all males in our society. The charge is that in our society men treat women as sex objects rather than as persons; it is this universality of scope that is lacking from the present interpretation. *Nonetheless, one of the reasons that we are prone to assent to the unrestricted charge that men treat women as sex objects is that the restricted charge is entirely correct.*

One might be tempted to argue that the charge that men treat women as sex objects is correct since such a conception underlies the most frequently used identifications, as animal and plaything; that is, these identifications indicate a sexual context in which the female is used as an object. Thus, it might be argued that the female fox is chased and slayed if she is four-legged, but chased and laid if she is two. Even if one admits the sexual context *implicit* in *some* animal and plaything identifications, one will not have the generality required; because, for the most part, the plaything and animal identifications themselves are nonsexual—most of them do not involve a sexual context. A pregnant cow, a toy doll, or a filly are hardly what one would call erotic objects. Babies do not normally excite sexual passion; and anyone whose erotic interests are directed toward chicks, canaries, parakeets, or other birds is clearly perverse. The animals and playthings to whom women are assimilated in the standard metaphorical identifications are not symbols of desire, eroticism, or passion (as, for example, a bull might be).

What is objectionable in the animal and plaything identifications is not the fact that some of these identifications reflect a sexual context but rather that—regardless of the context—these identifications reflect a conception of women as mindless servants (whether animate or inanimate is irrelevant). The point is not that men ought not to think of women in sexual terms but that they ought to think of them as human beings; and the slogan *men should not think of women as sex objects* is only appropriate when a man thinking of a woman as a sexual partner automatically conceives of her as something less than human. The point about *sex objects* is not merely that it is inappropriate for a man, when, for example, listening to a woman deliver a serious academic paper, to imagine having sexual intercourse with the woman; it is inappropriate, of course, but much in the same way that it is inappropriate to imagine playing tennis with the speaker. The difference between a tennis partner and a sex partner is that whereas there is nothing degrading about a woman's being thought of as a tennis partner, there seems to be something *degrading* about her being thought of as a man's sex partner in our society—at least outside of the circumscribed context of a love relationship. (Note that it would be inappropriate, but not necessarily degrading to the woman, for a man in the audience to imagine courting the woman, having an affair with the woman, or marrying the woman; it does degrade the woman for the man to mentally undress the woman, or imagine an act of sexual intercourse between them.) The reason why unadorned sexual partnership is degrading to the female is that in this relationship the female is conceptualized, and treated not merely as a mindless thing productive of male pleasure, but as an *object* in the Kantian sense of the term—as a person whose autonomy has been violated. Or, to put the point differently, the reason why it is degrading for a woman to be conceptualized as a sexual partner is because *rape* is our paradigm of un-adorned sexual intercourse.

Our Conception of Sexual Intercourse

Consider the terms we use to identify coitus, or more technically, the terms that function synonymously with "had sexual intercourse with" in a sentence of the form "A had sexual intercourse with B." The following is a list of some commonly used synonyms (numerous others that are not as widely used have been omitted, for example, "diddled," "laid pipe with"):

- screwed
- laid
- fucked
- had
- did it with (to)
- banged
- balled
- humped
- slept with
- made love to

Now, for a select group of these verbs, names for males are the subjects of sentences with active constructions (that is, where the subjects are said to be doing the activity); and names for females require passive constructions (that is, they are the recipients of the activity—whatever is done is done to them). Thus, we would not say "Jane did it to Dick," although we would say "Dick did it to Jane." Again, Dick bangs Jane, Jane does not bang Dick; Dick humps Jane, Jane does not hump Dick. In contrast, verbs like "did it with" do not require an active role for the male; thus, "Dick did it with Jane and Jane with Dick." Again, Jane may make love to Dick, just as Dick makes love to Jane; and Jane sleeps with Dick as easily as Dick sleeps with Jane. (My students were undecided about "laid." Most thought that it would be unusual indeed for Jane to lay Dick, unless she played the masculine role of seducer-aggressor.)

These sentences thus form the following pairs. (Those nonconjoined singular noun phrases where a female subject requires a passive construction are marked with a cross. An asterisk indicates that the sentence in question is not a sentence of English if it is taken as synonymous with the italicized sentence heading the column.[4]

- *Dick had sexual intercourse with Jane*
- Dick screwed Jane+
- Dick laid Jane+
- Dick fucked Jane+
- Dick had Jane+
- Dick did it to Jane+
- Dick banged Jane+
- Dick humped Jane+
- Dick balled Jane (?)
- Dick did it with Jane
- Dick slept with Jane
- Dick made love to Jane

- *Jane had sexual intercourse with Dick*
- Jane was banged by Dick
- Jane was humped by Dick

- *Jane was done by Dick
- Jane was screwed by Dick
- Jane was laid by Dick
- Jane was fucked by Dick
- Jane was had by Dick
- Jane balled Dick (?)
- Jane did it with Dick
- Jane slept with Dick
- Jane made love to Dick
- *Jane screwed Dick
- *Jane laid Dick
- *Jane fucked Dick
- *Jane had Dick
- *Jane did it to Dick
- *Jane banged Dick
- *Jane humped Dick

These lists make clear that within the standard view of sexual intercourse, males, or at least names for males, seem to play a different role than females, since male subjects play an active role in the language of screwing, fucking, having, doing it, and perhaps, laying, while female subjects play a passive role.

The asymmetrical nature of the relationship indicated by the sentences marked with a cross is confirmed by the fact that the form "___ed with each other" is acceptable for the sentences not marked with a cross, but not for those that require a male subject. Thus:

- *Dick and Jane had sexual intercourse with each other*
- Dick and Jane made love to each other
- Dick and Jane slept with each other
- Dick and Jane did it with each other
- Dick and Jane balled with each other (*?)
- *Dick and Jane banged with each other
- *Dick and Jane did it to each other
- *Dick and Jane had each other
- *Dick and Jane fucked each other
- *Dick and Jane humped each other
- *(?)Dick and Jane laid each other
- *Dick and Jane screwed each other

It should be clear, therefore, that our language reflects a difference between the male and female sexual roles, and hence that we conceive of the male and female roles in different ways. The question that now arises is, "What difference in our conception of the male and female sexual roles requires active constructions for males and passive for females?"

One explanation for the use of the active construction for males and the passive construction for females is that this grammatical asymmetry merely reflects the natural physiological asymmetry between men and women: the asymmetry of "to screw" and "to be screwed," "to insert into" and "to be inserted into." That is, it might be argued that the difference between masculine and feminine grammatical roles merely reflects a difference naturally required by the anatomy of males and females. This explanation is inadequate. Anatomical differences do not determine how we are to conceptualize the relation between penis and vagina during intercourse. Thus one can easily imagine a society in which the female normally played the active role during intercourse, where female subjects required active constructions with verbs indicating copulation, and where the standard metaphors were terms like "engulfing"—that is, instead of saying "he screwed her," one would say "she engulfed him." It follows that the use of passive constructions for female subjects of verbs indicating copulation does not reflect differences determined by human anatomy but rather reflects those generated by human customs.

What I am going to argue next is that the passive construction of verbs indicating coitus (that is, indicating the female position) can *also* be used to indicate that a person is being harmed. I am then going to argue that the metaphor involved would only make sense if we conceive of the female role in intercourse as that of a person being harmed (or being taken advantage of).

Passive constructions of "fucked," "screwed," and "had" indicate the female role. They also can be used to indicate being harmed. Thus, in all of the following sentences, Marion plays the female role: "Bobbie fucked Marion"; "Bobbie screwed Marion"; "Bobbie had Marion"; "Marion was fucked"; "Marion was screwed"; and "Marion was had." All of the statements are equivocal. They might literally mean that someone had sexual intercourse with Marion (who played the female role); or they might mean, metaphorically, that Marion was deceived, hurt, or taken advantage of. Thus, we say things as "I've been screwed" ("fucked," "had," "taken," and so on) when we have been treated unfairly, been sold shoddy merchandise, or conned out of valuables. Throughout this essay I have been arguing that metaphors are applied to things only if what the term *actually* applies to shares one or more properties with what the term *metaphorically* applies to. Thus, the female sexual role must have something in common with being conned or being sold shoddy merchandise. The only common property is that of being harmed, deceived, or taken advantage of. *Hence we conceive of a person who plays the female sexual role as someone who is being harmed* (that is, "screwed," "fucked," and so on).

It might be objected that this is clearly wrong, since the unsignated terms do not indicate someone's being harmed, and hence we do not conceive of having intercourse as being harmed. The point about the unsignated terms, however, is that they can take both females and males as subjects (in active constructions) and thus *do not pick out the female role*. This demonstrates that we conceive of sexual roles in such a way that only females are thought to be taken advantage of in intercourse.

The best part of solving a puzzle is when all the pieces fall into place. If the subjects of the passive construction are being harmed, presumably the subjects of the active constructions are doing harm, and, indeed, we do conceive of these subjects in precisely this way. Suppose one is angry at someone and wishes to express malevolence as forcefully as possible without actually committing an act of physical violence. If one is inclined to be vulgar one can make the sign of the erect male cock by clenching one's fist while raising one's middle finger, or by clenching one's fist and raising one's arm and shouting such things as "screw you," "up yours," or "fuck you." In other words, one of the strongest possible ways of telling someone that you wish to harm him is to tell him to assume the female sexual role relative to you. Again, to say to someone "go fuck yourself" is to order him to harm himself, while to call someone a "mother fucker" is not so much a play on his Oedipal fears as to accuse him of being so low that he would inflict the greatest imaginable harm (fucking) upon that person who is most dear to him (his mother).

Clearly, we conceive of the male sexual role as that of hurting the person in the female role—but lest the reader have any doubts, let me provide two further bits of confirming evidence: one linguistic, one nonlinguistic. One of the English terms for a person who hurts (and takes advantage of) others is the term "prick." This metaphorical identification would not make sense unless the bastard in question (that is, the person outside the bonds of legitimacy) was thought to share some characteristics attributed to things that are literally pricks. As a verb, "prick" literally means "to hurt," as in "I pricked myself with a needle"; but the usage in question is as a noun. As a noun, "prick" is a colloquial term for "penis." Thus, the question before us is what characteristic is shared by a penis and a person who harms others (or, alternatively, by a penis and by being stuck by a needle). Clearly, no physical characteristic is relevant (physical characteristics might underlie the Yiddish metaphorical attribution "schmuck," but one would have to analyze Yiddish usage to determine this); hence the shared characteristic is nonphysical; the only relevant shared nonphysical characteristic is that both a literal prick and a figurative prick are agents that harm people.

Now for the nonlinguistic evidence. Imagine two doors: in front of each door is a line of people; behind each door is a room; in each room is a bed; on each bed is a person. The line in front of one room consists of beautiful women, and on the bed in that room is a man having intercourse with each of these women in turn. One may think any number of things about this scene. One may say that the man is in heaven, or enjoying himself at a bordello; or perhaps one might only wonder at the oddness of it all. One does not think that the man is being hurt or violated or degraded—or at least the possibility does not immediately suggest itself, although one could conceive of situations where this was what was happening (especially, for example, if the man was impotent). Now, consider the other line. Imagine that the figure on the bed is a woman and that the line consists of handsome, smiling men. The woman is having intercourse with each of these men in turn. It immediately strikes one that the woman is being degraded, violated, and so forth—"that poor woman."

When one man fucks many women he is a playboy and gains status; when a woman is fucked by many men she degrades herself and loses stature.

Our conceptual inventory is now complete enough for us to return to the task of analyzing the slogan that men ought not to think of women as sex objects.

I think that it is now plausible to argue that the appeal of the slogan "men ought not to think of women as sex objects," and the thrust of much of the literature produced by contemporary feminists, turns on something much deeper than a rejection of "scoring" (that is, the utilization of sexual "conquests" to gain esteem) and yet is a call neither for homosexuality nor for puritanism.

The slogan is best understood as a call for a new conception of the male and female sexual roles. If the analysis developed above is correct, our present conception of sexuality is such that to be a man is to be a person capable of brutalizing women (witness the slogans "The marines will make a man out of you!" and "The army builds *men!*" which are widely accepted and which simply state that learning how to kill people will make a person more manly). Such a conception of manhood not only bodes ill for a society led by such men, but also is clearly inimical to the best interests of women. It is only natural for women to reject such a sexual role, and it would seem to be the duty of any moral person to support their efforts—to redefine our conceptions not only of fucking, but of the fucker (man) and the fucked (woman).

This brings me to my final point. We are a society preoccupied with sex. As I noted previously, the nature of proper nouns and pronouns in our language makes it difficult to talk about someone without indicating that person's sex. This convention would not be part of the grammar of our language if we did not believe that knowledge of a person's sex was crucial to understanding what is said about that person. Another way of putting this point is that sexual discrimination permeates our conceptual structure. Such discrimination is clearly inimical to any movement toward sexual egalitarianism and virtually defeats its purpose at the outset. (Imagine, for example, that black people were always referred to as "them" and whites as "us" and that proper names for blacks always had an "x" suffix at the end. Clearly any movement for integration as equals would require the removal of these discriminatory indicators. Thus at the height of the melting-pot era, immigrants Americanized their names: "Bellinsky" became "Bell," "Burnstein" became "Burns," and "Lubitch" became "Baker.")

I should therefore like to close this essay by proposing that contemporary feminists should advocate the utilization of neutral proper names and the elimination of gender from our language (as I have done in this essay); and they should vigorously protest any utilization of the third-person pronouns "he" and "she" as examples of sexist discrimination (perhaps "person" would be a good third-person pronoun)—for, as a parent of linguistic analysis once said, "The limits of our language are the limits of our world."

NOTES

1. The underlying techniques used in this essay were all developed primarily by Austin and Strawson to deal with the problems of metaphysics and epistemology. All I have done is to attempt to apply them to other areas; I should note, however, that I rely rather heavily on metaphorical identifications, and that first philosophy tends not to require the analysis of such

superficial aspects of language. Note also that it is an empirical matter whether or not people do use words in a certain way. In this essay I am just going to assume that the reader uses words more or less as my students do; for I gathered the data on which words we use to identify women, and so on, simply by asking students. If the reader does not use terms as my students do, then what I say may be totally inapplicable to him. The linguistic surveys on which this article is based were done on samples of student language at Wayne State University (Detroit) and Wayne County Community College (inner city centers: Detroit) during the 1970–1971 academic year. A number of surveys conducted by students at Union College in 1973 and 1974 indicate different usages. Whereas in the first survey active female constructions for verbs indicate sexual intercourse (e.g. "Jane laid Dick") were regarded as deviant, later surveys found these constructions to be acceptable. This may be explained by differences in the class structure (since Union College students are predominately white upper middle class, while WSU students are lower middle class and the WCCC students were from the black inner city), or by some more persuasive changes in conception of the woman's role.

2. It is also interesting to talk about the technical terms that philosophers use. One fairly standard bit of technical terminology is "trouser word." J. L. Austin invented this bit of jargon to indicate which term in a pair of antonyms is important. Austin called the important term a "trouser word" because "it is the use which wears the trousers." Even in the language of philosophy, to be important is to play the male role. Of course, the antifeminism implicit in the language of technical philosophy is hardly comparable to the male chauvinism embedded in commonplaces of ordinary discourse.

3. Although I thought it inappropriate to dwell on these matters in the text, it is quite clear that we do *not* associate many positions with females—as the following story brings out. I related this conundrum both to students in my regular courses and to students I teach in some experimental courses at a nearby community college. Among those students who had not previously heard the story, only native Swedes invariably resolved the problem; less than half of the students from the upper-class background would get it (eventually), while lower-class and black students virtually never figured it out. Radical students, women, even members of women's liberation groups fared no better than anyone else with their same class background. The story goes as follows: A little boy is wheeled into the emergency room of a hospital. The surgeon on emergency call looks at the boy and says, "I'm sorry I cannot operate on this child; he is my son." The surgeon was not the boy's father. In what relation did the surgeon stand to the child? Most students did not give any answer. The most frequent answer given was that the surgeon had fathered the boy illegitimately. (Others suggested that the surgeon had divorced the boy's mother and remarried and hence was not legally the boy's father.) Even though the story was related as a part of a lecture on women's liberation, at best only 20 percent of the written answers gave the correct and obvious answer—the surgeon was the boy's mother.

4. For further analysis of verbs indicating copulation see "A Note on Conjoined Noun Phrases," *Journal of Philosophical Linguistics*, vol. 1, no. 2, Great Expectations, Evanston, Ill. Reprinted with "'English Sentences Without Overt Grammatical Subject," in Zwicky, Salus, Binnick, and Vanek, eds., *Studies Out in Left Field: Defamatory Essays Presented to James D. McCawley* (Edmonton: Linguistic Research, Inc., 1971). The puritanism in our society is such that both of these articles are pseudo-anonymously published under the name of Quang Phuc Dong; Mr. Dong, however, has a fondness of citing the articles and theories of Professor James McCawley, Department of Linguistics, University of Chicago. Professor McCawley himself was kind enough to criticize an earlier draft of this essay. I should also like to thank G. E. M. Anscombe for some suggestions concerning this essay.

5

The Sacrificial Lamb

Susan Griffin

Therefore, I saw my own task especially in extracting those nuclear ideas from the extensive and unshaped substance of a general world view and remolding them into more or less dogmatic forms which in their clear delineation are adapted for holding solidly together those men who swear allegiance to them.

ADOLF HITLER, *Mein Kampf*

There are two kinds of delusion which it is possible for the civilized mind to embrace. The first delusion is a private one. The mind possessed by such a delusion is often perceived as mad. Certainly as strange. For the private delusion sets the one who believes in it apart from the rest of humanity. But exactly the opposite is true of the second delusion. This is the *mass delusion*: it consists of a *shared* set of beliefs which are untrue and which distort reality. A whole nation, for example, decides to believe that "the Jew" is evil. This type of delusion brings the man or woman who believes in it into a common circle of humanity. And because the mass delusion is a shared delusion, the mind which shares it is perceived as normal, while the same society perceives as mad the mind which sees reality.

Pornography is a mass delusion and so is racism. In certain periods of history, both of these mass delusions have been accepted as sane views of the world, by whole societies or certain sectors of society. The pornographic ideology, for instance, is perceived as a reasonable world view by parts of American and European societies today. And various forms of racism have been the official ideologies of societies, political parties, and even governments. Most notably, we remember the official racism of the Third Reich. But are we arguing that because of the prevalence of these delusional systems they are an inevitable outcome of civilization? This is indeed what the delusional mind would have us believe. And when we grow up inside a culture of denial, a culture which embodies and expresses delusion, we begin to think of this distortion as part of human nature.

We see a film in which a woman is murdered. Or a series of women are murdered, or beaten, or raped. The next day, we read in the newspaper that a woman has been shot to death by a stranger. We hear that the man next door has several times "broken down" and threatened the life of his wife, his son. An advertisement for a novel depicts a woman's throat cut open and bleeding. And in our minds all this is woven into a fabric which we imagine is inevitable.

We begin to look on the violence of men toward women as a kind of natural phenomenon. And slowly, our own behavior becomes a part of this delusion which we have called reality. If we are women, we grow up with a fear which we come to believe is as common as hunger, or thirst, or anger. This fear becomes so much a part of us that it forms a background to all our movements, and we begin to believe this fear is a part of ourselves, born at the same moment as our souls. If we are men, acts of violence toward women become part of a range of behavior which we think of as human.

And in this way, we cease to realize that culture has a profound influence on our minds and on human behavior. For in fact, it is not inevitable that the human mind choose delusion over reality. It is a choice which temporarily solves the human feeling of powerlessness before nature. Yet it is not the only choice which might solve that dilemma. For example, one can imagine that a child might, for a period of time, believe in the fantasy of mind over matter and culture over nature, and then grow beyond such a delusion, just as the child does in fact, in our society, come to understand that his infant body is separate from his mother's body, which in an earlier state of mind he did not perceive.

But in this society an event intervenes in the child's life and helps to determine what choice he or she will make. And this event is culture. Our culture offers to the mind of the child socially acceptable forms through which to hold on to delusion. These are the mass delusional forms which we know as racism and the pornographic sensibility. Through these systems of thought, the mind learns to deny the natural part of its own being. It learns to project this denied part of its own being onto another, playing out against this other its own ambivalence toward the natural self. So a woman is hated and loved, ridiculed, sought after, possessed, raped. And so, also, the black or the Jew is captured and brought into slavery, or exiled; owned or dispossessed; humiliated, excluded, attacked, and murdered.

For the pornographic mind and the racist mind are really identical, both in the symbolic content and in the psychological purposes of the delusionary systems they express. And now, if we undertake to study this mind, we shall begin to see precisely how a cultural delusion gradually shapes itself into such devastating social events as the mass murder of European Jewry, which we have come to know as the Holocaust.

Finally one comes to recognize that the contents of the racist mind are fundamentally pornographic. And with this recognition, it can be seen how the pornographic images of racism provide social forms through which private distrubances may be expressed as public conflicts. In this way, the pornographic sensibility affects history even more deeply than one would have suspected. And when one examines the dynamic shape of racist propaganda, one can see that it, too, has the same shape as the movement of the pornographic mind. Indeed, here is a classic mental pattern by which images must accelerate in their violence until they become actual events, events which devastate countless human lives.

The Chauvinist Mind

> Among our secrecies, not to despise Jews (that is, ourselves) or our darknesses, our
> blacks, or in our sexuality where it takes us . . .
>   Muriel Mukeyser, "The Despisals"

On the leaflet are two familiar figures. A monstrous black man menaces a voluptu-
ous white woman. Her dress is cut low, her skirt torn so that a thigh shows through;
the sleeves of her dress fall off her shoulders. She looks over her shoulder in fear and
runs. The man's body is huge and apelike. The expression on his face is the
personification of bestiality, greed, and lust. Under the words "Conquer and Breed,"
and above a text which warns the reader against intermarriage, these two figures act
out an age-old drama.

At the heart of the racist imagination we discover a pornographic fantasy: the
specter of miscegenation. This image of a dark man raping a fair woman embodies
all that the racist fears. The fantasy preoccupies his mind. A rational argument exists
which argues that the racist simply uses pornographic images to manipulate the
mind. But these images seem to belong to the racist. They are predictable in a way
that suggests a more intrinsic part in the genesis of this ideology.

And when we turn to pornography, we discover that just as the racist is obsessed
with a pornographic drama, the pornographer is obsessed with racism. In Juvenal,
for example, we read about the "trusty Jewess" who will "tell you dreams of any kind
you please for the minutest of coins." *Hustler* magazine displays a cartoon called
Chester the Molester (part of a series depicting child molestation as humor), in
which a man wearing a swastika on his arm hides behind a corner, holds a bat, and
dangles a dollar bill on a wire to entice a little girl away from her parents. The child
and her parents all wear yellow stars of David; each member of the family is drawn
with the stereotypical hooked nose of anti-Semitic caricature. In another cartoon, a
young black man dressed in a yellow polka-dot shirt and eating watermelon stands
outside the bars of a cage in which a monkey dressed in the same yellow shirt eats
watermelon and listens to a transistor radio. A film called *Slaves of Love* is advertised
with a portrait of two black women, naked and in chains. A white man stands over
them with a whip. Nazi memorabilia, helmets, SS uniforms, photographs of the
atrocities of concentration camps, swords, knives, are sold as pornography along
with books and films. Pornographic films bear the titles *Golden Boys of the SS, Ilse
the She-Wolf of the SS, Leiben Camp.*

Writing of the twin traditions of anti-Semitism and obscenity, Lucy Dawidowicz
tells us of a rock group called "The Dictators," who declare "we are the members of
the master race," and she lists for us a mélange of articles found in the apartment of
a Hell's Angel: devices of torture, a Nazi flag, a photograph of Hitler, Nazi propaganda, and of course, pornography. She writes "Pornography and propaganda have
reinforced each other over the decades."

Indeed, the association between pornographic thought and racist ideology is
neither casual nor coincidental. As Hannah Arendt points out, both Gobineau and

Houston Chamberlain (anti-Semitic ideologues who had a great influence on the philosophy of the Third Reich and on Hitler himself) were deeply influenced by the writing of the Marquis de Sade. Like de Sade, they "elevated cruelty to a major virtue."

We know that the sufferings women experience in a pornographic culture are different in kind and quality from the sufferings of black people in a racist society, or of Jewish people under anti-Semitism. (And we know that the hatred of homosexuality has again another effect on the lives of women and men outside of the traditional sexual roles.*) But if we look closely at the portrait which the racist draws of a man or a woman of color, or that the anti-Semite draws of the Jew, or that the pornographer draws of a woman, we begin to see that these fantasized figures resemble one another. For they are the creations of one mind. This is the chauvinist mind, a mind which projects all it fears in itself onto another: a mind which defines itself by what it hates.

The black man as stupid, as passive, as bestial; the woman as highly emotional, unthinking, a being closer to the earth. The Jews as a dark, avaricious race. The whore. The nymphomaniac. Carnal lust in a woman insatiable. The virgin. The docile slave. The effeminate Jew. The usurious Jew. The African, a "greedy eater," lecherous, addicted to uncleanness. The black woman as lust: "These sooty dames, well vers'd in Venus' school/Make love an art, and boast they kiss by rule." As easy. The Jew who practices sexual orgies, who practices cannibalism. The Jewish and the black man with enormous sexual endowment.

The famous materialism of the Jew, the black, the woman. The woman who spends her husband's paychecks on hats. The black who drives a Cadillac while his children starve. The Jewish moneylender who sells his daughter. "There is nothing more intolerable than a wealthy woman," we read in Juvenal. (And in an eighteenth-century pornographic work, the pornographer writes that his heroine had "a natty little bourgeois brain." And in a contemporary pornographic novel, the hero murders a woman because she prefers "guys who drives Cadillacs.") The appetite which swallows. The black man who takes away the white man's job or the woman who takes a man's job.

Over and over again the chauvinist draws a portrait of the other which reminds us of that part of his own mind he would deny and which he has made dark to himself. The other has appetite and instinct. The other has a body. The other has an emotional life which is uncontrolled. And in the wake of this denied self, the chauvinist constructs a false self with which he himself identifies.

Wherever we find the racist idea of another being as evil and inferior, we also discover a racial *ideal*, a portrait of the self as superior, good, and righteous. Such was certainly the case with the white Southern slave owner. The Southern white man imagined himself as the heir to all the best traditions of civilization. He thought of himself as the final repository of culture. In his own mind, he was an

---

*Homophobia is a clear mass delusional system. Yet to draw an analogy between this system and racism and pornography would require another chapter. Suffice it to mention here that the fear of homosexuals historically accompanies racism, sexism, fascism, and all forms of totalitarian or authoritarian rule.

aristocrat. Thus Southern life was filled with his pretensions, his decorum, his manners, and his ceremonies of social ascension.

Just as he conferred the black men and women he enslaved with inferior qualities, so also he blessed himself with superiorities. He was "knightly" and "magnanimous," filled with "honesty" which emanated from the "flame of his strong and steady eye." He was honorable, responsible and above all, noble.

And the anti-Semite frames himself in the same polarity. Against his portrait of the Jew, he poses himself as the ideal, the Aryan: fair, courageous, honest, physically and morally stronger.

But this is a polarity deeply familiar to us. We learn it almost at birth from our mothers and fathers. Early in our lives, the ideal of masculinity is opposed to the idea of femininity. We learn that a man is more intelligent, that he is stronger than a woman. And in pornography, the male hero possesses an intrinsic moral rightness which, like Hitler's Aryan, allows him to behave toward women in ways outside morality. For according to this ideology, he is the more valuable member of the species. As the Marquis de Sade tells us, "the flesh of women," like the "flesh of all female animals," is inferior.

It is because the chauvinist has used the idea that he is superior as a justification to enslave and exploit the other, whom he describes as inferior, that certain historians of culture have imagined the ideology of chauvinism exists only to justify exploitation. But this ideology has a raison d'être intrinsic to the mind itself. Exploring this mind, one discovers that the chauvinist values his delusion for its own sake, that above all, the chauvinist mind needs to believe in the delusion it has created. For this delusion has another purpose than social exploitation. Indeed, the delusions of the chauvinist mind are born from the same condition which gives birth to all delusion, and this condition is the mind's desire to escape truth. The chauvinist cannot face the truth that the other he despises is himself.

This is why one so often discovers in chauvinist thinking a kind of hysterical denial that the other could possibly be like the self. The chauvinist insists upon an ultimate and defining difference between himself and the other. This insistence is both the starting point and the essence of all his thinking. Thus, Hitler writes on the beginnings of his own anti-Semitism:

> One day, when passing throught the Inner City, I suddenly came across an apparition in a long caftan and wearing black sidelocks. My first thought was: is this a Jew? . . . but the longer I gazed at this strange countenance and examined it section by section, the more the first question took another shape in my brain: is this a German? . . . For the first time in my life I bought myself some anti-Semitic pamphlets for a few coins.

In this way, by inventing a figure different from itself, the chauvinist mind constructs an allegory of self. Within this allegory, the chauvinist himself represents the soul, and the knowledge of culture. Whoever is the object of his hatred represents the denied self, the natural self, the self which contains the knowledge of the body. Therefore this other must have no soul.

From the chauvinist ideology we learn, for example, that a woman's soul is smaller than a man's. The misogynist and anti-Semite Otto Weiniger tells us that a woman "can have no part in the higher, transcendental life." The church tells that in order for a woman to get into heaven she must assume the shape of a man. Her body is incapable of spirituality. She is called the "devil's gateway." She brings evil into the world.

But "blackness" also comes to stand for evil in this mind. In seventeenth-century theology, we discover the explanation that the real origin of the dark races can be found in the scriptures. According to this legend, a man named Ham, who was born on Noah's Ark, knew his wife, against God's will.* Ham disobeyed. Thus in punishment a son was born to him, named Chus, and God willed that all the "posteritie after him should be so blake and loathsome that it might remain a spectacle of disobeidiance to all the worlde."

And Adolf Hitler tells us: "The symbol of all evil assumes the shape of a Jew."

And now, if the other invented by the chauvinist mind is a body without a spirit, this dark self is also nature without a capacity for culture. Therefore the other has a kind of passivity that the chauvinist mind supposes nature to have. A woman is docile. A black man is lazy. Neither has the ingenuity and virtue necessary to create culture. For example, Alfred Rosenberg, the official anti-Semitic ideologist of the Third Reich, tells us that the Jew went into trade because he did not want to work.

For the same reason, the chauvinist mind describes the despised other as lacking the intelligence for cultural achievement. A white anthropologist argues that instead of language, the black races have "a farrago of bestial sounds resembling the chitter of apes." A gynecologist argues that a woman's ovaries are damaged by serious intellectual study. Another doctor argues that menstruation moves a woman's blood away from her brain and into her pelvis.

Here one might assume that the anti-Semitic portrait of the Jew diverges from the racist's idea of the black, or the pornographic idea of a woman, over this question of intelligence. But such is not the case. The anti-Semitic idea of Jewish intelligence, on a closer examination, comes to resemble the racist idea of black intelligence or the pornographic idea of female intelligence. In the chauvinist mind, all three are described as possessing what may be called an animal cunning. All three, for instance, are called liars. Schopenhauer calls women the masters of deceit. Hitler calls the Jew a master of lies. And the racist invents the figure of the black trickster, the con artist who can never be believed.

Thus, when the chauvinist is confronted with the fact of Jewish cultural achievement, he decides that the Jew uses culture for material ends only. We read in the writing of Alfred Rosenberg, for example, that the "Jewish art dealer of today asks

*Another scriptural interpretation has it that Ham looked on "the nakedness of his father."

only for those works which could excite sensuality." And Rosenberg goes on to declare that the Jew is incapable of thinking metaphysically.*

Thus, as the anti-Semite tells us he hates the Jewish intellectual, he speaks of the "materialism" of his thought. But the idea of the materialistic Jewish spirit is very old. It has been part of the anti-Semite's repertoire at least since the Middle Ages. In an anti-Semitic legend from pre-Renaissance England, for example, a Jewish man converts to Christianity in order to protect his material possessions. Before this conversion, he leaves an image of Saint Nicholas to guard his shop and his possessions while he is away. When he returns, his belongings have been stolen, and in anger and retribution, he beats the image of the saint until "his sydes are all bloodie." But he is not impressed by this miraculous blood. However, when the same bleeding image of the saint appears to the thief, the thief is impressed enough to return to the shopkeeper what he has stolen. And it is only then, when the shopkeeper has his goods back, that he converts to Christianity. Thus we are given a portrait of the Jew as a brutal man, without Christian compassion, whose spirituality only serves mammon.†

Similarly, and in the same historical period, woman's intelligence was described as essentially devilish. Thus the *Malleus Maleficarum* tells us that when "a woman thinks alone she thinks evil." For during the period of the witch-burnings and the Inquisition, the chauvinist mind had constructed a portrait of both female and Jewish knowledge as an intelligence of sinfulness. Both were supposed to practice a *black* magic through which they learned the secrets of the earth and manipulated the powers of nature. In the chauvinist imagination, witches were capable of causing the plague, an earthquake, a drought, a pestilence; a witch could bring about impotence or sexual ravings. And the Jew, practicing his own black magic, also caused infanticide, plague, hurricanes, earthquakes.

Significantly, the chauvinist mind of this time imagined that the Jew or the witch gained power by desecrating the religious symbols of the dominant culture. The Jew was said to steal the consecrated host in order to defile it; the witch blasphemed the cross and anointed the devil. For of course, to a mind which protects itself with a culture that denies nature, *to destroy the symbols of that culture is to invoke the powers of nature.* (And now should we be surprised to learn that both Jews and witches were burned during this period of history?)

It is essential that within its own mythology, the chauvinist mind believe that culture is more powerful than nature. Thus, over and over again, this mind invents legends in which a cultural symbol vanquishes the evil forces of nature. We have

---

*In this sense, that he would separate the material from the spiritual, the chauvinist is often an anti-intellectual. At the heart of a certain kind of intellect, we discover self-reflection. But the chauvinist deplores this. He calls it "effete." For in the act of genuine self-knowledge, we know ourselves as part of nature, and we encounter the knowledge of the body as inseparable from "culture."

†Many other such legends exist. For example, a Jew studying to be a monk is visited by the devil, who tells him that he will one day be a bishop. The Jew then steals a horse and a cloak so that he will be a more impressive candidate for this office.

the legend of a Jewish boy, for instance, thrown into the flames by his father for going to church. This boy is protected by an image of the holy virgin and passes through the flames unscathed. For as much as the chauvinist mind fears the power of nature, this mind must deny the reality of that power. It is for this same reason that the pornographer must humiliate women.

This denial reaches a fever pitch in the writings of Otto Weininger, who raves that "the absolute female has no . . . will, no sense of worth or love." He tell us, "The meaning of woman is to be meaningless." And within the allegory of the chauvinist mind this is quite literally true, for in this mind the knowledge of self which woman represents has been erased. The female is "little more than an animal," he declares, she is "nothing." Thus in one stroke he has told us that women and bestiality do not exist.

But the more the chauvinist mind denies the existence of the power of nature, the more he fears this power. The pornographer, the racist, the anti-Semite, begin to believe their own delusions. The chauvinist begins to believe he is endangered by the dark other he has invented.

And yet he cannot acknowledge his fear, because fear is another form of vulnerability. It is evidence of mortality. It is natural. It is bestial. It is part of what he wished to deny in himself from the beginning. Thus now the dark other must come also to represent another side of the chauvinist mind: the other must now symbolize the chauvinist's own fearfulness.

Therefore the chauvinist projects onto the other his own sense of inadequacy in the natural world. And therefore we understand a different meaning when we hear from the chauvinist that the black was supposed to be like a child "whom somebody had to look after . . . . a grateful—a contented, glad, loving child." Or we hear that a woman is a "kind of middle-step between the child and the man."

A monstrous black man threatens a defenseless white woman. But now we can see the meaning of this drama. Here are two aspects of the self personified. In the black man, the force of the desire, of appetite, of wanting, is played out, and in the white woman, an awareness of vulnerability, weakness, mortality, fear can be lived. Through the forms of these two imaginary figures the memories of infancy and the knowledge of the body return to haunt the mind which would erase them.

In this sense, the "purity" of the white woman is like the blank space in the chauvinist's mind, the vacuum with which he has replaced his own knowledge of himself. And the bestiality of the dark man is his own desire for that knowledge, a desire which always threatens to contaminate ignorance. Now, perhaps, we can understand the nature of Hilter's fear when he writes:

> With satanic joy in his face, the black-haired Jewish youth lurks in wait for the unsuspecting girl whom he defiles with his blood, thus stealing her from her people.

The symbol has a life of its own. A writer invents a character and suddenly the character begins to surprise that writer with her acts or his words. The chauvinist has invented the black or the Jew or the woman to contain a part of himself. And now, through these invented personae, that buried part of the self begins to speak and will not be controlled by its author. Secretly, the chauvinist longs to be overtaken by the dark self he has exiled. And he would have this dark self punish the idea of purity. Therefore he imagines that women want to be raped, because he himself does not want to remain pure.

And yet he is terrified. He does not want to *know*; he does not want to be contaminated with knowledge. He is a man split against himself. So he projects his secret desire to *know* the body onto a woman. He believes that she does not want to remain pure. He tells us, in the words of an anthropologist: "women eager for venerry prefer the embrace of Negroes to those of other men." But now he is like the hero of the pornographic novel who is enraged because his doll was unfaithful to him. He has come to believe his own fantasies. He calls the woman—whom he had venerated for purity—a "whore." He becomes terribly jealous of the prowess he has imagined the black man to have. His fantasies torture him.

His mind is filled with contradiction. He tells us the white woman is both licentious and vulnerable, eager and frightened, innocent and guilty. For in the coupling which he imagines between the defenseless white woman and the monstrous black man, the chauvinist can be both rapist and raped, seduced and seducer, punished and punisher, soiler and soiled.

He invents many ways to play out his ambivalence. He hates the other and so he forces this other away from himself. He excludes this other from places of power, and from social meeting places. And yet at the same time, through complex lines of social dependence, he ties this other to him. Fearing the actual life of the other, he makes a "doll" to stand for the other. In a bar which excludes women, he stirs his drink with sticks shaped like women's bodies. In a neighborhood which excludes black men and women, he adorns his lawn with a statue of a black "boy," and his kitchen with a plastic likeness of a "mammy." In a book written for children, the same mind which hates black people creates this fantasy of a black woman: "She is nice, good, ole, fat, big, black Mammy."

Fear and want construct a dilemma in his mind. And like the pornographer, he can never solve this dilemma. For he is at war with himself, and every allegory he constructs becomes a terrible cul-de-sac in which he must face this self again. He would separate himself from himself and yet still have himself. He would forget and yet remember. He both longs for and fears the knowledge of the body. Nature is a part of him. He cannot divide what cannot be divided. His mind is in his body. His body thinks; his mind feels. From his body, nature renders meaning. He is trapped inside what he fears.

We are familiar with the effect of this mind on our lives. It is not the mind of a single man or woman, or even of a few. Rather, this is a structure of mind which is woven into the very language of our culture and into all its institutions, habits, visions. The delusion shaped by this mind is a mass delusion and touches us all. In the wake of this delusion, millions of men and women and children have been kidnapped into slavery; men have been lynched; children murdered; women raped and murdered, held prisoner, beaten; men, women, and children systematically tortured and annihilated; people denied the most basic human rights, denied the dignity of language or meaning, denied their own names.

Whether the chauvinist mind expresses itself through racist propaganda or through pornography, its delusions are not innocent. For the mind which believes in a delusion must ultimately face reality. And because the chauvinist desperately needs to believe in his delusion, when he is faced with the real nature of the world, he must act. He must force the world to resemble his delusion. . . .

⑥

Social Effects of Some Contemporary Myths about Women

Ruth Hubbard

Social Myths and Social Control

The dominant belief system of a society is often completely intertwined and hidden in the ordinary truths and realities that the people who live in that society accept without question. This tends to obscure the fact that these beliefs are actively generated and furthered by members of the dominant group because they are consistent with that group's interests. Further, these beliefs are intended to stabilize the social conditions that are required to perpetuate the hegemony of the dominant group. This is how we must regard present day scientific ideas about women's nature. They are part of the dominant belief system, but are myths that do not offer an accurate description of women's lives or explain the differences in the social and economic status of women and men.

Oppressive ideas and explanations that derive women's roles from women's "nature" are grounded in the material conditions in which the scientists who generate them live. These scientists are predominantly university-educated, economically privileged white men, who either belong to the hegemonic group or identify with its interests. (The few women and Third World men who have recently gained access to the scientific elite generally have the same economic and educational backgrounds as the traditional, white male members and often identify with the same interests.) It is therefore not an accident that scientists' perceptions of reality, as well as their descriptions of it, often serve to perpetuate and bolster the privileges of that disproportionately small group of people who have economic and social power in society.

One way that scientific explanations have served the ends of those in power has been by "proving" that the economic, social, and political roles of members of the different classes, races, and/or other socially significant groupings within the society are consistent with their biological natures and derive naturally from them. This is the way the ideology of woman's nature functions. It provides justifications for setting limits on women's roles, activities, and aspirations that are consistent with the social needs and goals perceived by those who have power to rule the society and to generate its ruling ideas. The roles women (and men) occupy in society are thus said to originate in mother nature, rather than in the society in which we live. Internalized by women, this ideology helps to make us, too, accept our allocated roles as natural.

Although the grounding of social roles in biological differences takes a scientific form in our society, it is important to see clearly that the basis for the theories is political, not simply a matter of science gone astray. Other theories have appeared in other cultures and play similar functions there. For example, Beatrice Medicine discusses views held by the Lakota Sioux and points out the several, and sometimes contradictory ways, that notions of woman's nature are used to socialize American Indian girls to accept traditional and contemporary Native American norms, as well as Anglo ones—norms that often are oppressive, though they occasionally also acknowledge women's strengths.

Because the ideology of woman's nature plays a critical role in keeping women "in our place," in this scientific age it is important to examine scientific theories that are used to support it. Therefore I shall describe some of the ways that scientific assumptions about women's biology have led us to accept discriminatory social arrangements as appropriate and natural. Indeed, the very notion that there exists a prototypical woman who can be described in ways that reflect and have meaning for the lives of the many different women living in very different geographical, economic, political, and social needs to be challenged. For example, Marian Lowe shows that naturalistic explanations of women's status in society can be quite insidious because they can affect and literally *shape* our biology by determining the material conditions in which we live—what and how much we eat and do, how stressful our lives are, and so on. For example, women are on average weaker than men at least partly because boys are encouraged to be more active than girls from earliest childhood, and girls are admonished to act like ladies. Thus, to some extent—though we do not know how much—the biological sex differences that are not specifically involved with reproduction reflect the different ways that girls and boys and women and men live.

Women's Lives: Myth and Reality

It is important to be aware that the *ideology* of woman's nature can differ drastically from, and indeed be antithetical to, the *realities* of women's lives. In fact, the ideology often serves as a smokescreen that obscures the ways women live by making people (including women) look away from the realities or ask misleading questions about them.

What are some of the realities? One is that women, with few exceptions, work and have always worked, though the term work has over the centuries been increasingly defined to mean what men do. Women's work is often trivialized, ignored, and undervalued, both in economic and political terms. For example, it is not called work when women "only" care for their households and children. Indeed, much of the work women do does not appear in the GNP and hence has no reality and value in standard descriptions of the economy. It is a fact that women work considerably more than men if *all* the work women do is counted—on average, about 56–65 hours per week as against men's 40–48—since in addition to working for pay, most women do most or all housework, as well as most volunteer work in schools, hospitals, and other parts of the community. Women earn 57 cents for every dollar men earn, not because we do not work as much or are less effective, but because women usually are paid less than men in work places and because much of women's work is unpaid. If women stopped doing all the work for which we are not paid, this society would grind to a halt, since much of the paid work men do depends heavily on women's unacknowledged and unpaid household labor.

The ideology that labels women as the natural reproducers of the species, and men as producers of goods, has not been used to exempt women from also producing goods and services, but to shunt us out of higher paying jobs, professional work, and other kinds of paid work that require continuity and give some power over one's own and, at times, other people's lives. Most women who work for pay do so in job categories such as secretary or nurse, which involve a great deal of concealed responsibility, but are underpaid. This is one reason why affirmative action *within* job categories cannot remedy women's economic disadvantage. Women will continue to be underpaid as long as access to better paying job categories is limited by social pressures, career counseling, training and hiring practices, trade union policies, and various other subtle and not so subtle societal mechanisms (such as discouraging the interest of girls in mathematics and scientific subjects). An entire range of discriminatory practices is justified by the claim that they follow from the limits that biology places on women's capacity to work. Though exceptions are made during wars and other emergencies, these are forgotten as soon as life resumes its normal course. Then women are expected to return to their subordinate roles, not because the quality of their work during the emergencies has been inferior, but because these roles are seen as natural.

A number of women employees in the chemical and automotive industries actually have been forced to choose whether to work at relatively well-paying jobs or be able ever to have children. In one instance, five women were required to submit to sterilization *by hysterectomy* in order to avoid being transferred from work in the lead pigment department at the American Cyanamid plant in Willow Island, West Virginia to janitorial work at considerably lower wages and benefits. Even though none of these women was pregnant or planning a pregnancy in the near future (indeed, the husband of one had had a vasectomy), they were considered pregnant or "potentially pregnant" unless they could prove that they were sterile. This goes on despite the fact that exposure to lead can damage sperm as well as eggs and can affect the health of workers (male and female) as well as a "potential fetus." But it is important to notice that this vicious choice has been forced only on women who have recently entered what had previously been relatively well-paid male jobs. Women whose work routinely involves exposure to chemical or radiation hazards in traditionally female jobs such as nurses, X-ray technologists, cleaning women in surgical operating rooms, beauticians, secretaries, workers in the ceramic industry, and domestic workers are not warned about the presence of chemical or physical hazards to their health or to that of a fetus, should they be pregnant. In other words, protection of women's reproductive integrity is being used as a pretext to exclude women from better paid job categories from which they had previously been ex- cluded by discriminatory employment practices, but women (or, indeed, men) are not protected against health endangering work in general.[1]

The ideology of woman's nature that is invoked at these times would have us believe that a woman's capacity to become pregnant leaves her at all times physically disabled by comparison with men. The scientific underpinnings for these ideas were elaborated in the nineteenth century by the white, university-educated, mainly upper class men who made up the bulk of the new professions of obstetrics and gynecology, biology, psychology, sociology and anthropology. But these profession- als used their theories of women's innate frailty only to disqualify the girls and women of their own race and class who would be in competition with them for education and professional status and might also deprive them of the kinds of personal attention and services they were accustomed to receive from their mothers, wives, and sisters. They did not invoke women's weakness to mitigate the exploita- tion of poor women working long hours in homes and factories that belonged to members of the upper classes, nor against the ways Black slave women were forced to work for no wages in the plantations and homes of their white masters and mistresses. Dorothy Burnham eloquently tells us about slave women's lives.

Nineteenth century biologists and physicians claimed that women's brains were smaller than men's, and that women's ovaries and uteruses required much energy and rest in order to function properly. They "proved" that therefore young girls must be kept away from schools and colleges once they had begun to menstruate and warned that without this kind of care women's uteruses and ovaries would shrivel, and the human race would die out. Yet again, this analysis was not carried over to poor women, who were not only required to work hard, but often were said to reproduce *too* much. Indeed, the fact that they could work so hard while bearing children was taken as a sign that these women were more animal-like and less highly evolved than upper class women.

Science and Social Myths

During the last decade, many feminist scholars have reminded us of this history. They have analyzed the self-serving theories and documented the absurdity of the claims as well as their class and race biases and their glaringly political intent. But this kind of scientific mythmaking is not past history. Just as medical men and biologists in the nineteenth century fought women's political organizing for equality by claiming that our reproductive organs made us unfit for anything but child-bearing and childrearing, and Freud declared women to be intrinsically less stable and intellectually less inventive and productive than men, so beginning in the 1970s, there has been a renaissance in sex differences research that has claimed to prove scientifically that women are *innately* better than men at home care and mothering while men are *innately* better fitted than women for the competitive life of the market place.

Questionable experimental results obtained with animals (primarily that proto-typic human, the white laboratory rat) are treated as though they can be applied equally well to people. On this basis, some scientists are now claiming that the secretion of different amounts of so-called male hormones (androgens) by male and female fetuses produces life-long differences in women's and men's brains. They claim not only that these (unproved) differences in fetal hormone levels exist, but imply (without evidence) that they predispose women and men *as groups* to exhibit innate differences in our abilities to localize objects in space, in our verbal and mathematical aptitudes, in aggressiveness and competitiveness, nurturing ability, and so on.[2] Other scientists, sociobiologists, claim that some of the sex differences in social behavior that exist in our society (for example, aggressiveness, competitive-ness, and dominance among men; coyness, nurturance, and submissiveness among women) are human universals that have existed in all times and cultures. Because these traits are ever-present, they deduce that they must be adaptive (that is, promote human survival), and that they have evolved through Darwinian natural selection and are now part of our genetic inheritance.

In recent years, sociobiologists have tried to prove that women have a greater biological investment in our children than men, and that women's disproportionate contributions to child- and homecare are biologically programmed to help us insure that our "investments" mature—in other words, that our children live long enough to have children themselves. The rationale is that an organism's biological fitness, in the Darwinian sense, depends on producing the greatest possible number of offspring, who themselves survive long enough to reproduce. This is what deter-mines the frequency of occurrence of an individual's genes in successive genera-tions. Following this logic a step further, sociobiologists argue that women and men must adopt basically different strategies to maximize the spreading of genes over future generations. The calculus goes as follows: because women cannot produce as many eggs as men can sperm and, in addition, must "invest" at least the nine months of pregnancy (whereas it takes a man only the few minutes of heterosexual intercourse to send a sperm on its way to personhood), each egg and child represents a much larger fraction of the reproductive fitness a woman can achieve in her lifetime than a sperm or a child does in a man's life. From this biological asymmetry, follow female fidelity, male promiscuity, and the unequal division and valuing of labor by sex in this society. As sociobiologist, David Barash, presents it, "mother nature is sexist," so don't blame her human sons.[3]

In devising these explanations, sociobiologists ignore the fact that human societies do not operate with a few superstuds; nor do stronger or more powerful men usually have more children than weaker ones. Though men, in theory, could have many more children than women can, in most societies equal numbers of men and women engage in *producing* children, but not in caring for them. But these kinds of theories are useful to people who have a stake in maintaining present inequalities. They have a superficial ring of plausibility and thus offer naturalistic justifications for discriminatory practices.

It is important to recognize that though sociobiologists have argued that we must come to understand these intrinsic biological realities so that we may bring our social arrangements into conformity with them, scientists generally have not been reluctant to tamper with nature. Scientists are proud of the technical and chemical innovations that have transformed the natural environment. And they pride themselves on the medical innovations through which healthy women's normal biology is routinely altered by means of the pill or by surgical operations that change breast or thigh size. At present, physicians routinely intervene in the normal course of pregnancy and birth, so that in the United States one out of five births is a major surgical event—a Caesarean section. Truly, physicians and scientists are not noted for their reluctance to interfere with nature!

Though many people would like to see less interference with normal biological functions than now occurs in this overmedicated and highly technological society, the fact is that human living necessarily involves an interplay between biological and social forces. We have no way of knowing what people's "real" biology is, because the concept has no meaning. There is no such thing as human biology in the pure. In other words, what we think of as women's biology is a political construct, not a scientific one.

However, within this constraint, it is important to recognize that we have much less solid and reliable information about how our bodies function than we could have if women asked the questions that are of importance and interest to us. For example, we do not know the normal range of women's experiences of menstruation, pregnancy, childbirth, lactation, and menopause. If women want to learn about our biology, we will have to share our knowledge and experiences of how our bodies function *within the context of our lives*. We must also become alert and sensitive to the ways that many of the standard descriptions of women's biology *legitimize* women's economic and social exploitation and reinforce the status quo.

To summarize:

- People's biology develops in reciprocal and dialectical relationships with the ways in which we live. Therefore human biology cannot be analyzed or understood in social isolation.

- Reconstructions of women's "intrinsic" biological nature are scientifically meaningless and usually are politically and ideologically motivated.
- Scientists and physicians have asked scientific questions from a male-supremist perspective, with the conscious or unconscious intention of proving that a woman's place in society derives naturally from her biological being.
- It is important to dispel naturalistic explanations that provide biological justifications for the economic and social limitations with which women must struggle.
- We do not know much about how our bodies function within the context of our lives because the right questions have not yet been asked, nor in the right ways. It is therefore worthwhile for women to generate meaningful and important questions that can yield practical information about how to live more healthfully and productively.

NOTES

1. This is discussed by Jeanne M. Stellman and Mary Sue Henifin in their article, "No Fertile Women Need Apply: Employment Discrimination and Reproductive Hazards in the Workplace," in, Ruth Hubbard, Mary Sue Henifin, and Barbara Fried, eds., *Biological Woman—The Convenient Myth* (Cambridge, Mass.: Schenkman, 1982), pp. 117–145.

2. Several recent publications have been concerned with hormones and the brain. Up to date summaries to research can be found in Robert W. Goy and Bruce S. McEwen, *Sexual Differentiation of the Brain* (Cambridge, Mass.: M.I.T. Press, 1980) and in a series of review articles published in *Science* 211 (1981): 1263–1324. Articles intended for general readers have appeared in *Quest* (October, 1980), *Discover* (April, 1981), *Newsweek* (May 18, 1981), *Playboy* (January–July, 1982), and other magazines. Feminist criticisms of sex differences research, including research on hormones and the brain, can be found in Ruth Hubbard and Marian Lowe, eds., *Genes and Gender II: Pitfalls in Research on Sex and Gender* (New York: Gordian Press, 1979); Brighton Women and Science Group, eds., *Alice Through the Microscope* (London: Virago, 1980); Ruth Hubbard, Mary Sue Henifin, and Barbara Fried, eds., *Biological Woman—The Convenient Myth* (Cambridge, Mass.: Schenkman, 1982).

3. The investment calculus of sex differences in social and economic roles is presented in many recent publications on sociobiology. Examples are Edward O. Wilson, *Sociobiology: The New Synthesis* (Cambridge, Mass.: Harvard University Press, 1975), chapters 15 and 16; David Barash, *The Whispering Within* (New York: Harper & Row, 1979); Donald Symons, *The Evolution of Human Sexuality* (New York: Oxford University Press, 1979). Criticisms are included in Arthur L. Caplan, ed., *The Sociobiology Debate* (New York: Harper & Row, 1978) and in Ashley Montagu, ed., *Sociobiology Examined* (New York: Oxford University Press, 1980).

7

The Schooling of Vietnamese Immigrants*

Gail P. Kelly

In April 1975, 129,000 Vietnamese came to the United States as the long and bloody war ended. These individuals came for a variety of reasons. The most common one—and one given by Vietnamese of all classes (of rural and urban origins) and almost all occupations—was that they feared that with the fall of the Thieu government they would be unable to continue living as they had in the past.[1] Vietnamese Catholics, close to half of the immigrants, believed their churches would be closed and their priests (in rural villages, also mayors, judges, and teachers) killed.[2] (Vietnamese Catholics and the government of North Vietnam had a long history of mutual animosity.) South Vietnamese government officials and wealthy businessmen feared their social and economic positions would be undermined by the new Vietnamese government. Vietnamese who came to the United States, in short, were motivated by a desire to maintain cultural, religious, social, and economic patterns as they had known them in the cities and countryside of Vietnam. They expressed little interest in adopting new ways.

When Vietnamese first arrived in the United States, they were placed in four camps: Camp Pendleton in California, Fort Chaffee in Arkansas, Eglin Air Force Base in Florida, and Fort Indian Town Gap in Pennsylvania. The purpose of the camps was to resettle Vietnamese according to U.S. government guidelines. In the camps the U.S. government conducted health, security, and financial screening as required by immigration law and resettled Vietnamese with American sponsors. Sponsors were individuals or organizations willing to take moral and financial responsibility for individuals or family units until they became self-supporting. Government policy was to spread Vietnamese resettlement throughout the country. The sponsorship program encouraged such a diaspora, because the financial commitment that the program required Americans to make to Vietnamese was so great that few individuals or organizations could afford to undertake sponsorship. Within

*Research for this article was made possible by grants from the University of Buffalo Foundation, State University of New York at Buffalo Institutional Funds, the SUNY (State University of New York) Foundation, and the New York State Council for the Humanities.

any one community a handful of individuals or groups stepped forward to provide full financial support for the two or three years that the government required of sponsors. As a result, Vietnamese were initially relocated in parts of the United States where Americans wanted them. By the time the camps closed in late 1975, they were scattered throughout the country, isolated for the most part from other Vietnamese.

The resettlement camps were the first points of entry into the United States for Vietnamese. The camps were removed from American society: they were ringed by white lines and guarded by Military Police, and Vietnamese could not leave them; neither could Americans have free access to camps. Admission to the camps was contingent on approval by the government agencies administering them. Americans who were granted permission to enter the camps could do so only during daylight hours and were restricted to certain camp areas (recreation halls, school offices, and resettlement agency headquarters).

In the closed atmosphere of the camps Americans readied Vietnamese for entry into U.S. society. Much of this preparation consisted of formal and informal education aimed specifically at adults. The largest single activity in the camps, other than finding sponsors for Vietnamese, was education. At Fort Indian Town Gap, Pennsylvania, for example, 38 classes in the English language were conducted simultaneously for three hours, morning, noon, and night, five days a week. As of September 1975, 9,700 individuals over age 18 out of a total camp population of 16,000 attended such classes daily. Over $3.7 million was expended on education in the camps.[3]

These educational programs provided instruction in the English language. A stated aim of the classes was to prepare Vietnamese for what Americans called the refugees' "New Life" in their "New Land."[4] The nature of that preparation is the focus of this article. I will analyze formal and informal education of adults in the camps. Specifically, I will dwell on English language instruction, cultural orientation programs, and bilingual written materials for adults. . . .

Internal Colonialism: A Framework for Analyzing Camp Programs

Internal colonialism is the framework I will use in analyzing U.S. educational and resettlement policies. Internal colonialism has, in the main, been taken as the process by which one nation has subjugated another nation, taking control over its territories, polity, economy, and cultural institutions. It can be distinguished from classical colonialism in that classical colonialism entails the domination of peoples outside the boundaries of the colonizer's nation-state. Internal colonialism by this definition grows out of classical colonialism. The Indians of Latin America, for example, became internal colonies only after they were parts of overseas colonies.

Many conceptualizations of internal colonialism emphasize the fact of nation-to-nation domination, arguing that internal colonialism exists only in relations between nation-states.[5] This view distinguishes between oppression having differing roots. According to this view, the oppression born out of racial or cultural differences would not be the same as oppression whose origins lie in national differences. The above definition of internal colonialism would preclude from consideration colonized racial and ethnic minorities. That definition would exclude them simply because they did not at a point in the past hold territory within the nation-state that currently oppresses them.

To define *nation* only in terms of territoriality is to define nation on Western terms and not on the terms that many Third World peoples define nationhood. Chinese, for example, do not tie nationality to being born in China, or to its land, but rather to being literate in Chinese and versed in its culture.[6] Because of the Western-centric notion of colonialism when confined to relations between territorially defined states, a literature on internal colonialism has evolved that focuses less on the origins of the relation than on the nature of the relationships that emerge between cultural and racial groups.[7] Thus, peoples who are minorities within a nation-state who may or may not have territorial claims or have constituted a nation-state in the past can be considered colonized. By this definition, Blacks, Native Americans, and immigrant communities are internal colonies in the United States. They are internal colonies because their relationship to white, Anglo-America is analogous to that of overseas colonies to the metropole. Characteristic of that relationship is forced entry into the society and culture of the colonizer; creation of a labor force that is differentiated by caste (defined by race, culture and/or language) and controlled by and dependent on the colonizer; sharing of a single polity with the colonizer, which the colonizer dominates; and racial and cultural oppression.[8]

The relations between educational systems and internal colonialism are multifaceted. Education traditionally has been the means by which individuals are taught prevailing social norms and prepared for a place within the society. As long as the norms and behavior the school teaches are shared by all members of society, the school cannot be considered an instrument of internal colonialism, especially if relations in the society are not determined along racial/cultural lines. However, when oppression is based on racial/cultural distinctions and when the schools perpetuate them through teaching children values that are at variance with or foreign to those of their family and culture, and when it prepares students for narrow, submissive roles allocated to them by the dominant group, then the schools function to extend the internal colonial relationship. In nations where schooling is compulsory, like the United States, education becomes for the colonized the first instance of forced entry into the society and culture of the colonizer. It is the colonizer—in the United States, the white majority—who controls schools, determines educational content and the culture the schools transmit, and decides the uses of education in the society.

Schools are not only the major entry point for the colonized into the cultural and social systems set by the colonizer; schools also prepare individuals for the world of work. This the schools do not only by teaching individuals skills that are bought and sold on the labor market but also by orienting individuals to the values that employers find desirable in employees at different levels of the labor force. For some, the schools teach punctuality, respect for property not their own, obedience; for others, the schools encourage initiative and innovation and encourage students to control their means of livelihood. In internal colonies, the schools prepare individuals for the world of work according to occupations at which the schools (or more precisely those who control the schools) presume the colonized will work. Sometimes differential preparation occurs by students' achievement and presumed intelligence, as measured by tests designed by the colonizer, based on the colonizer's own cultural norms. Those who score poorly receive generalized vocational training; those who score better end up receiving technical or crafts training, while the high achievers are channeled to academic training and the managerial/professional jobs within the economy. The colonized, racially and/or culturally different from the colonizer, are trained for occupations that are both the lowest in terms of pay and prestige in the labor force. These occupations are ones that are dependent on the colonizer. In the world of work, as well as of culture, the schools deny the autonomy of the colonized. . . .

Education for the colonized perpetuates racial and cultural oppression not only through dependency teaching but also by denying, if not deprecating, the culture and race of the colonized. For example, U.S. schools have long ignored Native American cultures, except to distort them and label them as primitive.[9] The schools define how the colonized can survive within the society, for they show how income and status are tied to accepting the norms, culture, and language of the colonizer. It is not without reason, for instance, that U.S. schools, when they present Native Americans as heros to emulate, choose those who to some degree exemplify the dominant culture's values—they either made peace with the White Man or brought aspects of white culture to the colonized. In portraying Black Americans, texts written since the 1960s chose to portray Booker T. Washington and Martin Luther King, and not Malcolm X. They praise those who accept the colonizer's rules of the game and not those who exert the autonomy of the colonized.

Internal colonialism, then, can be seen as that set of relationships that fosters the dominance of groups definable by race and/or culture over a racially, culturally, and/or linguistically different group. Internal colonialism involves forced entry of the colonized into the society and culture of the colonizer, a division of labor based on race and culture in which the colonized are placed in dependency relations with the colonizer, the sharing of polity between colonizer and colonized that the colonizer dominates, and cultural oppression. Schools can become instruments of internal colonialism—they are the first point of forced entry for the colonized into the society and culture of the colonizer; they prepare the colonized for economic roles determined by the colonizer; they legitimate and normalize the polity as one that the colonizer rules for the colonized; and they become a means of cultural oppression. In short, in internal colonialism the schools teach roles and behavior appropriate to the colonized in a political, social, and economic order controlled by the colonizer. The roles the schools teach are ones that the colonizer, not the colonized, chooses, and these roles are imposed if not by the school by the economic and political order. . . .

In this article I will use the framework of internal colonialism to analyze education in the resettlement camps for Vietnamese. My analysis will show how these programs prepared Vietnamese for entry into the American lower classes while, at the same time, attempting to change their life-styles. While this is the case, I will also demonstrate that the process of internal colonialism that the programs initiated were differentiated along gender lines. Particularly striking is the degree to which the establishment of male domination within the family and the usurpation of women's roles was essentially given as compensation for the Vietnamese males' loss of class status and power in their transition from Vietnam to the United States.

Vietnamese Who Came to the United States

Vietnamese who came to the United States represented their nation's political and economic elite. As Table 1 shows, over 24 percent of heads of households were professionals, managers, and technicians; 7.2 percent were medical doctors or dentists; while another 11.7 percent were employed in clerical or sales industries (a category made up largely of lower-level government officials and businessmen). In all, about 45 percent of Vietnamese entering this country were part of the small Vietnamese ruling class, which had fought hard against social revolution. The elite nature of the Vietnamese immigrants becomes even clearer when their educational

TABLE 1   Primary Employment Skills of Heads of Households (N = 30,628)

Skill Category	Number	Percent
Medical professionals	2,210	7. 2
Professional, technical, and managerial	7,368	24. 0
Clerical and sales	3,572	11. 7
Service	2,324	7. 6
Farming, fishing, forestry	1,491	4. 9
Agricultural processing	128	0. 4
Machine trades	2,670	8. 7
Benchwork, assembly, repair	1,249	4. 1
Structural and construction	2,026	6. 6
Transportation and miscellaneous	5,165	16. 9
Did not indicate	2,425	7. 9

Note: Reports skills only, not individual's prior employment.

Source: Interagency Task Force for Indochinese Refugees, "Report to the Congress" (Washington, D.C.: Interagency Task Force for Indochinese Refugees, December 15, 1975), p. 13.

backgrounds are taken into account. About 82 percent of all Vietnamese over age 18 had secondary or better education (in Vietnam, less than 64 percent of the school-age population entered primary school). Over 20 percent of the immigrants were university-educated (2.5 percent in Vietnam received higher education).[10]

While the Vietnamese entering the United States were, taken as a whole, the elite of South Vietnam's society, there were some who had more humble origins. As Table 1 shows, about 5 percent were engaged in rural occupations. Additionally, most Vietnamese with skilled trades tended to be former soldiers, who gained their skills from the army or navy, but who were neither affluent nor powerful in Vietnam (about 4,500 Vietnamese rank-and-file soldiers and sailors came to the United States).

Men outnumbered women among the immigrants. About 45 percent were women[11] whose class origins one can only presume are similar to the men who came. The women clearly had been gainfully employed in Vietnam. Only 14 percent reported their occupations as "housewife."[12] In Vietnam urban as well as rural poor and middle-class women were in the work force, entering in increasing numbers since the war's escalation in the 1960s and the inflation that accompanied it.

In the Vietnam of the 1960s most women worked for wages out of economic necessity. Peasant women for centuries have worked the land and have been petty traders; in the forced urbanization during the war, these peasant women worked in the cities as petty traders, bar girls, laundresses, maids, and prostitutes to sustain themselves and their families. Middle-class women came into the job market in the inflation of 1960s, as men's salaries on which they had been supported no longer were adequate to sustain their families in the life-styles to which they had become accustomed.[13] Immigrants who I interviewed at Fort Indian Town Gap told me how wives of prominent civil servants, university professors, and the military opened knitting factories, began working as teletype operators, secretaries, and the like to supplement family income. In short, Vietnamese women who came to the United States had a history of working outside the home.[14]

Not only were immigrant women of all classes working women, many were the sole support of their families since the men either had been killed in the war or disabled by it and unable to work. About 21.6 percent of all immigrant households were headed by women who were their major breadwinners.[15]

Vietnamese immigrants, men and women alike, had few expectations or experiences of a life in which women were not involved in the economy and did not play a major role in both economic and family life.

English Language Instruction: Different Roles for Different Sexes

English language classes, without question, were a formal point of entry for Vietnamese into U.S. society and culture. To some extent that entry was forced, at least for men, as camp authorities pressured men into attending classes. At Fort Indian

Town Gap, camp authorities pointed out in the daily newspaper, *Dat Lanh*, that learning to speak English was the key to getting a good job and income in the United States. Those who found this incentive lacking were visited by camp administrators and urged to go to class. Vietnamese barracks leaders, appointed by Americans, were also entitled to convince recalcitrant Vietnamese that they needed to go to class.

While Americans concentrated on encouraging men to go to English classes, they made no such effort to bring women to class. In fact, women were initially discouraged from attending. When classes began, women flooded the classrooms expecting to become better equipped to enter the work force. However, camp authorities and teachers discouraged their presence. They then reduced class size by eliminating women from classes. School officials proclaimed the classes open only to heads of households since, they argued, it was they alone who would enter the work force.[16] In practice, this meant that women were excluded from class, for Americans assumed women were not heads of household. This policy, which was in effect from June to late August 1975, was justified by school personnel on several grounds. First, they argued that men, not women, would be breadwinners and, therefore, had priority in learning English. Second, they believed that permitting women in class would disrupt the Vietnamese family. Women, they said, might learn the language faster than men, and men would "lose face" because of this. This then would lead to marital conflicts and divorce. Further, they argued that there were other types of classes for women that would suit them for life in the United States: classes in birth control, child care, sewing, and cooking, as well as, after September, the Pennsylvania Commission for Women's sessions called "Women in America." Women gained free access to the language classes at Fort Indian Town Gap three months later when the camp population had diminished as refugees were resettled in the United States.

The English language classes were introductions to U.S. culture and Vietnamese potential roles, both occupational and social, within it. This was evident in the curricular materials used in class, the conduct of class, and in teacher attitudes. It was explicit in interviews I held with school personnel.

Two types of curricular materials were used in teaching English at Fort Indian Town Gap: the Survival English course developed by the Department of Health, Education and Welfare and, as a supplement, the Macmillan English Language 900 Series texts. The Survival English course, taught at three levels, had 16 lessons that covered topics (in the order presented) that included meeting strangers, finding a place to live, occupations, renting apartments, shopping, John's interest, and applying for jobs.[17] The first lesson began with greetings and sex identifications. Students were drilled on phrases such as "Hello," "Good afternoon," "My name is. . . ." "I'm a boy," "I'm a girl," and "Do you speak English?" Subsequent vocabulary taught locations of lavatories, days of the week, numbers, food, time, parts of the body, and job titles. Once vocabulary was introduced as words in isolation, lessons centered on patterned sentences and conversations. In all but 2 of the 16 lessons the conversations took place between a mythical "Mr. Brown" and "Mr.

Jones," with Mr. Brown responding to Mr. Jones's questions. For example, Mr. Jones (no doubt the Vietnamese refuge) inquired in a lesson on numbers how he might go about buying a house. In the lesson on occupations, Mr. Jones asked what kind of job might get to support his wife and two children. Mr. Jones was told that he could work as a room clerk, salesman, cashier, laborer, plumber, bricklayer, cook, cleaning person, secretary, typist, seamstress, or nurses' aide.

Women were present in the 16 units of Survival English only in two instances: in a lesson on budgeting and shopping and in one called "Conversation." One lesson contained two lines about a Miss Jones. These lines were: "Miss Jones missed the bus to the Miss Universe competition" and "She is an attractive girl."[18] The only other reference to women in the curriculum was in a set of drills on shopping that depicted women shopping for small items. In the basic classes teaching persons who knew no English, a Mrs. Brown shopped for dresses, shoes, food, aspirins, baby needs, and cosmetics, while Mr. Brown shopped for shirts, houses, cars, and furniture.[19] In the advanced classes the division of labor between the sexes was elaborated. A women named Marie compared prices of food and other commodities, thereby saving her husband *his* hard-earned money. Marie was wise and would by nothing but food without consulting her husband, Tim. In the lesson she found out where the cheapest sofa and sewing machine in town could be bought, but took her husband to the stores for him to decide whether the items should be purchased.[20]

The Macmillan English Language 900 Series, used as a supplement to the Survival English course, was not written specifically for Vietnamese refugees. It is a series of texts designed for non-English speakers, be they Italian, Arab, Chinese, German, or French. These texts, interestingly enough, are quite different from the materials devised specifically for Vietnamese. Women are not absent in the text nor so inactive. They travel, they work, go to the doctor, shop, ask questions. Despite this, the roles portrayed for women are limited to that of wife and mother. In Lesson One, Book Three (intermediate level), for example, Judy talks with John about buying a new sofa.[21] In Unit 2, Barbara and Ella talk about baking a cake for Harry, while Frank and Tom discuss hammers and nails; in Unit 4, marriage is discussed as are bridal dresses; in Unit 5, Mr. James buys a house and Mabel has coffee klatches with her new neighbors; in Unit 8, on health and sickness, Dr. Smith and his female nurse give Mrs. Adams advice on her children's health and Mr. Lewis advice on his own health and in Unit 9, mother puts children to bed and wakes them up, while father goes off to work.[22]

The curriculum materials used in teaching Vietnamese the English language, in sum, emphasized a strict division of labor between the sexes, preparing Vietnamese women not for the workplace but for narrow social roles. In many course materials, women simply did not exist. When they entered the texts, their roles were depicted solely as that of wife, mother, and shopper. In the Survival English course, designed specifically for refugees, occupations suggested for Vietnamese men often were those reserved for U.S. women. Vietnamese men were presented as qualified to become typists, seamstresses, or nurses' aides. Further, these jobs were at the very lowest ends of the occupational and salary scales in the United States. The programs were not only allocating Vietnamese men into lower-class and female occupations, they also presented immigrant men with roles traditionally reserved for U.S. women. It is Mr. Jones in the Survival English course who finds out where stores are, gets a doctor, selects a church, locates the children's school, and the like. In the Survival English materials women seemingly had no role.

The teaching materials were not the only elements in formal English instruction that attempted to rob Vietnamese women of their social and economic roles and put Vietnamese men into lower-class and female work-force jobs—teacher-student interaction in class worked similarly. An incident in an English class designed for illiterates illustrates this best. This class had more women in it than any other class I observed at Fort Indian Town Gap. (The other classes appeared to be predominantly male; advanced English classes had almost no women in them.) Because the students were illiterate, written materials could not be used. The six-week course had but three units—parts of the body and their names, foods, and jobs. All this was constructed by the teachers with the assistance of the curriculum coordinator. Vocabulary was introduced by pointing to an object or a picture of it and learning the English name for it. When pictures of objects were not available, charade was used. In one class the teacher clucked and flapped his arms like a chicken to introduce the term *chicken*. He then drilled the class on the phrase, "I want some chicken to eat."[23]

The major emphasis in the classroom was on occupations—teaching Vietnamese how to describe their work skills to prospective employers. In several classes, the teacher began with the phrase, "What kind of work do you do?" He then drew stick figures showing different kinds of work—ditch digging, selling, and the like, naming them all. After introducing phrases like "I am a ditch digger" or "I am a mechanic," he asked each of his 30 or more students, "What kind of work do you do?" The first student to respond was a young man, obviously a former soldier. He responded by imitating a gun with his fingers and replied, "I rat-a-tat-tat." The teacher corrected him with "I work with my hands." Next to recite was a middle-aged woman, who had lacquered teeth (indicating she came from a rural lower-class family). She made a motion that looked like casting nets (I found out later that she came from coastal Vung-Tau and had fished for a living). The teacher responded with "I am a housewife." The woman looked puzzled. The teacher then drew a stick figure on the blackboard representing a woman with a broom in her hand inside of a house. He repeated, "I am a housewife," pointing to the woman. She and the woman sitting with her began a lively discussion in Vietnamese and started laughing. The teacher then drilled all the women as a group repeatedly with the phrase "I am a housewife."

The United States, it has often been claimed, is a plural society with little consensus over roles, values, and behavior. In the camps, not all programs Americans developed for Vietnamese attempted to deny women roles in the economy as well as in the household or prepare the Vietnamese elite for lower-class status. Programs that did so, however, were not compulsory as was English language instruction and were not the crucial entry point into U.S. society that the schoolroom was. . . .

The Schooling of Vietnamese Immigrants and Internal Colonialism

This article has shown how educational programs for Vietnamese immigrants have contributed to the process of internal colonialism. Further, it has demonstrated that the process is different for women than it is for men. . . .

While the camp educational programs were a point of entry of Vietnamese into the society and culture of Americans, the did not serve this purpose for men and women alike. Except for "Women in America," the educational programs did not so direct Vietnamese women. Rather, they prepared Vietnamese men for integration into the U.S. work force and society—Vietnamese women were not the focus of integration efforts. "Women in America" alone tried to prepare the women for entry into the U.S. work force. However, like the other educational efforts, they impinged upon Vietnamese culture and set U.S. terms for Vietnamese adjustment to the society.

The educational programs were also instruments of internal colonialism in the way they allocated Vietnamese into the U.S. labor market. English language classes taught Vietnamese (for the most part, the professional and managerial elites of their country) to expect to become unskilled laborers, laundresses, secretaries, seamstresses, dishwashers, and the like, with marginal incomes. These were, to some extent, the jobs that Vietnamese ended up with after the camps closed. A year after the camps closed, 73 percent of the immigrants who had once been professionals, technicians, managers, and businessmen found themselves blue-collar workers; another 17 percent became clerical and sales personnel. Only 10 percent went into jobs equivalent to those they had held in Vietnam. Most worked in jobs paying minimum wages; many of these jobs were temporary. Yearly income was so low that close to 50 percent of all Vietnamese families in the United States received some form of welfare. The school programs prepared the Vietnamese for these lower-class roles.

While the educational programs fostered the lowering of Vietnamese expectations, they did so by preparing men for occupations usually reserved for women in U.S. society. However, while preparing men for women's roles, they also prepared Vietnamese men to usurp women's roles within the family. The schools taught Vietnamese men to take care of schooling, medical care, shopping, and the like. To some extent internal colonialism was providing Vietnamese men with power within the household in exchange for their loss of power within their society and nation. . . .

A final aspect of internal colonialism outlined earlier is racial and cultural oppression. In education, this has long been documented vis-à-vis Native Americans, Blacks, and Chicanos. Racial oppression has taken several forms—outright discrimination in education, either by providing separate and unequal education or by denying educational opportunity; overt cultural and racial slurs, or omission. In U.S. education oppression through omission is more often the rule than the exception today. This entails simply ignoring the internal colony. In the curriculum, often, Blacks, Native Americans, and the like simply do not exist. The actors in the world are white, male, and American. Oppression takes the form of denial. The education of Vietnamese in the camps represented cultural oppression by denial. No Vietnamese existed in the world presented to the immigrants, despite the fact that the Survival English course and "Women in America" are designed specifically for Vietnamese. In Survival English, Mr. Jones and Mr. Brown speak to one another, seek jobs, health care, apartments, and the like—the Vietnamese in these courses were not Mr. Ngo and Mr. Duc but Mr. Jones, an American.

The oppression implicit in the programs in the camps was best summed up by T.V.Q., a journalist who spent five months at Fort Indian Gap. "Let me say this," he remarked in an interview about the educational programs. "The Americans have done a lot for me, but whatever we think we need, they don't provide, and whatever we don't need, they provide."[24]

NOTES

1. Gail P. Kelly, *From Vietnam to America: A Chronicle of the Vietnamese Immigration to the United States* (Boulder, Colo.: Westview Press, 1978).

2. Le-Thi-Que, A. Terry Rambo, and Gary D. Murfin, "Why They Fled: Refugee Movement during the Spring 1975 Communist Offensive in South Vietnam," *Asian Survey* 16 (September 1976): 855–63.

3. U.S., Department of Health, Education and Welfare, Task Force for Indochinese Refugees, "Report to the Congress," unpublished (Washington, D.C.: HEW, 1976).

4. Kelly, *From Vietnam to America*, chap. 4.

5. Pierre Van den Berg, "Education, Class and Ethnicity in Southern Peru: Revolutionary Colonialism," in *Colonialism and Education*, ed. P. G. Altbach and G. P. Kelly (New York: Longmans, 1978), pp. 270–300.

6. Joseph Levenson, *Liang Chi Ch'ao and the Mind of Modern China* (Berkeley: University of California Press, 1970).

7. John Liu, "Toward an Understanding of the Internal Colonial Model," in *Counterpoint: Perspectives on Asian America*, ed. Emma Gee (Los Angeles: University of California, Asian American Studies Center, 1976), pp. 160–68; and Phillip G. Altbach and Gail P. Kelly, *Colonialism and Education* (New York: Longmans, 1978).

8. Liu, *Counterpoint*, pp. 160–68.

9. Jeanette Henry, "Textbook Distortion of the Indian, *Indian Historian*, December 1967, pp. 244–50.

10. Interagency Task Force for Indochinese Refugees, "Report to the Congress" (Washington, D.C.: Interagency Task Force for Indochinese Refugees, December 15, 1975); Kelly, *From Vietnam to America*; and Joseph Dodd, "Aspects of Recent Educational Change in South Vietnam," *Journal of Developing Areas* 6 (July 1972): 55–71.

11. Interagency Task Force for Indochinese Refugees, "Report to the Congress," p. 11.

12. Ibid., p. 13.

13. Ngo Vinh Long, *Vietnamese Women in Society and Revolution: The French Colonial Period* (Cambridge, Mass.: Vietnam Resource Center, 1974); and Arlene Eisen Bergman, *Women of Vietnam* (San Francisco: People's Press, 1974).

14. Vietnamese Immigration Collection, State University of New York at Buffalo Ar-

chives, taped interviews, nos. 32, 33, 42, 73, 75, 78, September 1975–October 1976. These are interviews with school officials, immigrants, resettlement workers, and camp officials.

15. Interagency Task Force for Indochinese Refugees, "Report to the Congress," p. 13.

16. Vietnamese Immigration Collection, tapes nos. 9, 10, 29, 30.

17. Vietnamese Immigration Collection, State University of New York at Buffalo Archives, *Survival English*, Box 3, 1975.

18. Vietnamese Immigration Collection, *Survival English*, Unit 1, Lesson 1.

19. Ibid., Level 2, Intermediate, Lesson 4, p. 4.

20. Ibid., Level 1, Unit 4, Lessons 3, 4.

21. Ibid., Advanced Class, Unit 5, "How to Stretch Your Dollar."

22. English Language Services, *English 900*, 16th ed. (New York: Collier Macmillan, 1975), Books 1–3, p. 8; Unit 2, p. 19; Unit 4, pp. 38–42; Unit 5, p. 49; Unit 8, pp. 77–86; Unit 9, p. 93.

23. Vietnamese Immigration Collection, tape no. 30.

24. Vietnamese Immigration Collection, tape no. 5, side 1.

REFERENCES

Altbach, Philip G., and Gail P. Kelly. *Colonialism and Education*. New York: Longmans, 1978.

Bergman, Arlene Eisen, *Women of Vietnam*. San Francisco: People's Press, 1974.

Carnoy, Martin. *Education as Cultural Imperialism*. New York: McKay, 1974.

Dodd, Joseph. "Aspects of Recent Educational Change in South Vietnam." *Journal of Developing Areas* 6 (July 1972): 55–71.

English Language Services. *English 900*. 16th ed. New York: Collier Macmillan, 1975. Books 1–3.

Henry, Jeanette. "Textbook Distortion of the Indian." *Indian Historian*, December 1967, pp. 244–50.

Interagency Task Force for Indochinese Refugees. "Needs Survey, 1976," (A copy of this survey is contained in the Vietnamese Immigration Collection, State University of New York at Buffalo Archives, Box 2.)

———. "Report to the Congress." Washington, D.C.: Interagency Task Force for Indochinese Refugees, December 15, 1975.

Kelly, Gail P. *From Vietnam to America: A Chronicle of the Vietnamese Immigration to the United States*. Boulder, Colo.: Westview Press, 1978.

Le-Thi-Que, A. Terry Rambo, and Gary D. Murfin. "Why They Fled: Refugee Movement during the Spring 1975 Communist Offensive in South Vietnam." *Asian Survey* 16 (September 1976): 855–63.

Levenson, Joseph. *Liang Chi Ch'ao and the Mind of Modern China*. Berkeley: University of California Press, 1970.

Liu, John. "Toward an Understanding of the Internal Colonial Model," in *Counterpoint: Perspectives on Asian America*, edited by Emma Gee, pp. 160–68. Los Angeles: University of California, Asian American Studies Center, 1976.

Rothenberg, P. Racism + Sexism, 1988.

8

Blaming the Victim

William Ryan

Twenty years ago, Zero Mostel used to do a sketch in which he impersonated a Dixiecrat Senator conducting an investigation of the origins of World War II. At the climax of the sketch, the Senator boomed out, in an excruciating mixture of triumph and suspicion, "What was Pearl Harbor *doing* in the Pacific?" This is an extreme example of Blaming the Victim.

Twenty years ago, we could laugh at Zero Mostel's caricature. In recent years, however, the same process has been going on every day in the arena of social problems, public health, anti-poverty programs, and social welfare. A philosopher might analyze this process and prove that, technically, it is comic. But it is hardly ever funny.

Consider some victims. One is the miseducated child in the slum school. He is blamed for his own miseducation. He is said to contain within himself the causes of his inability to read and write well. The shorthand phrase is "cultural deprivation," which, to those in the know, conveys what they allege to be inside information: that the poor child carries a scanty pack of cultural baggage as he enters school. He doesn't know about books and magazines and newspapers, they say. (No books in the home; the mother fails to subscribe to *Reader's Digest*.) They say that if he talks at all—an unlikely event since slum parents don't talk to their children—he certainly doesn't talk correctly. (Lower-class dialect spoken here, or even—God forbid!—Southern Negro.) (*Ici on parle nigra.*) If you can manage to get him to sit in a chair, they say, he squirms and looks out the window. (Impulse-ridden, these kids, motoric rather than verbal.) In a word he is "disadvantaged" and "socially deprived," they say, and this, of course, accounts for his failure (*his* failure, they say) to learn much in school.

Note the similarity to the logic of Zero Mostel's Dixiecrat Senator. What is the culturally deprived child *doing* in the school? What is wrong with the victim? In pursuing this logic, no one remembers to ask questions about the collapsing buildings and torn textbooks, the frightened, insensitive teachers, the six additional desks in the room, the blustering, frightened principals, the relentless segregation, the callous administrator, the irrelevant curriculum, the bigoted or cowardly members of the school board, the insulting history book, the stingy taxpayers, the fairy-tale readers, or the self-serving faculty of the local teachers' college. We are encouraged to confine our attention to the child and to dwell on all his alleged defects. Cultural

324

deprivation becomes an omnibus explanation for the educational disaster area known as the inner-city school. This is Blaming the Victim.

Pointing to the supposedly deviant Negro family as the "fundamental weakness of the Negro community" is another way to blame the victim. Like "cultural deprivation," "Negro family" has become a shorthand phrase with stereotyped connotations of matriarchy, fatherlessness, and pervasive illegitimacy. Growing up in the "crumbling" Negro family is supposed to account for most of the racial evils in America. Insiders have the word, of course, and know that this phrase is supposed to evoke images of growing up with a long-absent or never-present father (replaced from time to time perhaps by a series of transient lovers) and with bossy women ruling the roost, so that the children are irreparably damaged. This refers particularly to the poor, bewildered male children, whose psyches are fatally wounded and who are never, alas, to learn the trick of becoming upright, downright, forthright all-American boys. Is it any wonder the Negroes cannot achieve equality? From such families! And, again, by focusing our attention on the Negro family as the apparent *cause* of racial inequality, our eye is diverted. Racism, discrimination, segregation, and the powerlessness of the ghetto are subtly, but thoroughly, downgraded in importance.

The generic process of Blaming the Victim is applied to almost every American problem. The miserable health care of the poor is explained away on the grounds that the victim has poor motivation and lacks health information. The problems of slum housing are traced to the characteristics of tenants who are labeled as "Southern rural migrants" not yet "acculturated" to life in the big city. The "multiproblem" poor, it is claimed, suffer the psychological effects of impoverishment, the "culture of poverty," and the deviant value system of the lower classes; consequently, though unwittingly, they cause their own troubles. From such a viewpoint, the obvious fact that poverty is primarily an absence of money is easily overlooked or set aside.

The growing number of families receiving welfare are fallaciously linked together with the increased number of illegitimate children as twin results of promiscuity and sexual abandon among members of the lower orders. Every important social problem—crime, mental illness, civil disorder, unemployment—has been analyzed within the framework of the victim-blaming ideology. . . .

I have been listening to the victim-blamers and pondering their thought processes for a number of years. That process is often very subtle. Victim-blaming is cloaked in kindness and concern, and bears all the trappings and statistical furbelows of scientism; it is obscured by a perfumed haze of humanitarianism. In observing the process of Blaming the Victim, one tends to be confused and disoriented because those who practice this art display a deep concern for the victims that is quite genuine. In this way, the new ideology is very different from the open prejudice and reactionary tactics of the old days. Its adherents include sympathetic social scientists with social consciences in good working order, and liberal politicians with a genuine commitment to reform. They are very careful to dissociate themselves from vulgar Calvinism or crude racism; they indignantly condemn any notions of innate wickedness or genetic defect. "The Negro is *not born* inferior," they shout apoplectically. "Force of circumstance," they explain in reasonable tones, "has *made* him inferior." And they dismiss with self-righteous contempt any claims that the poor man in America is plainly unworthy or shiftless or enamored of idleness. No, they say, he is "caught in the cycle of poverty." He is trained to be poor by his culture and his family life, endowed by his environment (perhaps by his ignorant mother's outdated style of toilet training) with those unfortunately unpleasant characteristics that make him ineligible for a passport into the affluent society.

Blaming the Victim is, of course, quite different from old-fashioned conservative ideologies. The latter simply dismissed victims as inferior, genetically defective, or morally unfit; the emphasis is on the intrinsic, even hereditary, defect. The former shifts its emphasis to the environmental causation. The old-fashioned conservative could hold firmly to the belief that the oppressed and the victimized were born that way—"that way" being defective or inadequate in character or ability. The new ideology attributes defect and inadequacy to the malignant nature of poverty, injustice, slum life, and racial difficulties. The stigma that marks the victim and accounts for his victimization is an acquired stigma, a stigma of social, rather than genetic, origin. But the stigma, the defect, the fatal difference—though derived in the past from environmental forces—is still located *within* the victim, inside his skin. With such an elegant formulation, the humanitarian can have it both ways. He can, all at the same time, concentrate his charitable interest on the defects of the victim, condemn the vague social and environmental stresses that produced the defect (some time ago), and ignore the continuing effect of victimizing social forces (right now). It is a brilliant ideology for justifying a perverse form of social action designed to change, not society, as one might expect, but rather society's victim.

As a result, there is a terrifying sameness in the programs that arise from this kind of analysis. In education, we have programs of "compensatory education" to build up the skills and attitudes of the ghetto child, rather than structural changes in the schools. In race relations, we have social engineers who think up ways of "strengthening" the Negro family, rather than methods of eradicating racism. In health care, we develop new programs to provide health information (to correct the supposed ignorance of the poor) and to reach out and discover cases of untreated illness and disability (to compensate for their supposed unwillingness to seek treatment). Meanwhile, the gross inequities of our medical care delivery systems are left completely unchanged. As we might expect, the logical outcome of analyzing social problems in terms of the deficiencies of the victim is the development of programs aimed at correcting those deficiencies. The formula for action becomes extraordinarily simple: change the victim.

All of this happens so smoothly that it seems downright rational. First, identify a social problem. Second, study those affected by the problem and discover in what ways they are different from the rest of us as a consequence of deprivation and injustice. Third, define the differences as the cause of the social problem itself. Finally, of course, assign a government bureaucrat to invent a humanitarian action program to correct the differences.

Now no one in his right mind would quarrel with the assertion that social problems are present in abundance and are readily identifiable. God knows it is true that when hundreds of thousands of poor children drop out of school—or even graduate from school—they are barely literate. After spending some ten thousand hours in the company of professional educators, these children appear to have learned very little. The fact of failure in their education is undisputed. And the racial situation in America is usually acknowledged to be a number one item on the nation's agenda. Despite years of marches, commissions, judicial decisions, and endless legislative remedies, we are confronted with unchanging or even widening racial differences in achievement. In addition, despite our assertions that Americans get the best health care in the world, the poor stubbornly remain unhealthy. They lose more work because of illness, have more carious teeth, lose more babies as a result of both miscarriage and infant death, and die considerably younger than the well-to-do.

The problems are there, and there in great quantities. They make us uneasy. Added together, these disturbing signs reflect inequality and a puzzlingly high level of unalleviated distress in America totally inconsistent with our proclaimed ideals and our enormous wealth. This thread—this rope—of inconsistency stands out so visibly in the fabric of American life, that it is jarring to the eye. And this must be explained, to the satisfaction of our conscience as well as our patriotism. Blaming the Victim is an ideal, almost painless, evasion. *It is also "Euro-centric" gender-centric*

The second step in applying this explanation is to look sympathetically at those who "have" the problem in question, to separate them out and define them in some way as a special group, a group that is *different* from the population in general. This is a crucial and essential step in the process, for that difference is in itself hampering and maladaptive. The Different Ones are seen as less competent, less skilled, less knowing—in short, less human. The ancient Greeks deduced from a single characteristic, a difference in language, that the barbarians—that is, the "babblers" who spoke a strange tongue;—were wild, uncivilized, dangerous, rapacious, uneducated, lawless, and, indeed, scarcely more than animals. Automatically labeling strangers as savages, weird and inhuman creatures (thus explaining difference by exaggerating difference) not infrequently justifies mistreatment, enslavement, or even extermination of the Different Ones.

Blaming the Victim depends on a very similar process of identification (carried out, to be sure, in the most kindly, philanthropic, and intellectual manner) whereby the victim of social problems is identified as strange, different—in other words, as a barbarian, a savage. Discovering savages, then, is an essential component of, and prerequisite to, Blaming the Victim, and the art of Savage Discovery is a core skill that must be acquired by all aspiring Victim Blamers. They must learn how to demonstrate that the poor, the black, the ill, the jobless, the slum tenants, are different and strange. They must learn to conduct or interpret the research that shows how "these people" think in differnt forms, act in different patterns, cling to different values, seek different goals, and learn different truths. Which is to say that they are strangers, barbarians, savages. This is how the distressed and disinherited are redefined in order to make it possible for us to look at society's problems and to attribute their causation to the individuals affected. . . .

Blaming the Victim can take its place in a long series of American ideologies that have rationalized cruelty and injustice.

Slavery, for example, was justified—even praised—on the basis of a complex ideology that showed quite conclusively how useful slavery was to society and how uplifting it was for the slaves.[1] Eminent physicians could be relied upon to provide the biological justification for slavery since after all, they said, the slaves were a separate species—as, for example, cattle are a separate species. No one in his right mind would dream of freeing the cows and fighting to abolish the ownership of cattle. In the view of the average American of 1825, it was important to preserve slavery, not simply because it was in accord with his own group interests (he was not fully aware of that), but because reason and logic showed clearly to the reasonable and intelligent man that slavery was good. In order to persuade a good and moral man to *do* evil, then, it is not necessary first to persuade him to *become* evil. It is only necessary to teach him that he is doing good. No one, in the words of a legendary newspaperman, thinks of himself as a son of a bitch.

In late-nineteenth-century America there flowered another ideology of injustice that seemed rational and just to the decent, progressive person. But Richard Hofstadter's analysis of the phenomenon of Social Darwinism[2] shows clearly its functional role in the preservation of the *status quo*. One can scarcely imagine a better fit than the one between this ideology and the purposes and actions of the robber barons, who descended like piranha fish on the America of this era and picked its bones clean. Their extraordinarily unethical operations netted them not only hundreds of millions of dollars but also, perversely, the adoration of the nation. Behavior that would be, in any more rational land (including today's America), more than enough to have landed them all in jail, was praised as the very model of a captain of modern industry. And the philosophy that justified their thievery was such that John D. Rockefeller could actually stand up and preach it in church. Listen as he speaks in, of all places, Sunday school: "The growth of a large business is merely a survival of the fittest. . . . The American Beauty rose can be produced in the splendor and fragrance which bring cheer to its beholder only by sacrificing the early buds which grow up around it. This is not an evil tendency in business. It is merely the working-out of a law of nature and a law of God."[3]

This was the core of the gospel, adapted analogically from Darwin's writings on evolution. Herbert Spencer and, later, William Graham Sumner and other beginners in the social sciences considered Darwin's work to be directly applicable to social processes: ultimately as a guarantee that life was progressing toward perfection but, in the short run, as a justification for an absolutely uncontrolled laissez-faire economic system. The central concepts of "survival of the fittest," "natural selection," and "gradualism" were exalted in Rockefeller's preaching to the status of laws of God and Nature. Not only did this ideology justify the criminal rapacity of those who rose to the top of the industrial heap, defining them automatically as naturally superior (this was bad enough), but at the same time it also required that those at the bottom of the heap be labeled as patently *unfit*—a label based solely on their position in society. According to the law of natural selection, they should be, in Spencer's judgment, eliminated. "The whole effort of nature is to get rid of such, to clear the world of them and make room for better."

For a generation, Social Darwinsim was the orthodox doctrine in the social sciences, such as they were at that time. Opponents of this ideology were shut out of respectable intellectual life. The philosophy that enabled John D. Rockefeller to justify himself self-righteously in front of a class of Sunday school children was not the product of an academic quack or a marginal crackpot philosopher. It came directly from the lectures and books of leading intellectual figures of the time, occupants of professorial chairs at Harvard and Yale. Such is the power of an ideology that so neatly fits the needs of the dominant interests of society.

If one is to think about ideologies in America in 1970, one must be prepared to consider the possibility that a body of ideas that might seem almost self-evident is, in fact, highly distorted and highly selective; one must allow that the inclusion of a specific formulation in every freshman sociology text does not guarantee that the particular formulation represents abstract Truth rather than group interest. It is important not to delude ourselves into thinking that ideological monstrosities were constructed by monsters. They were not; they are not. They are developed through a process that shows every sign of being valid scholarship, complete with tables of numbers, copious footnotes, and scientific terminology. Ideologies are quite often academically and socially respectable and in many instances hold positions of exclusive validity, so that disagreement is considered unrespectable or radical and risks being labeled as irresponsible, unenlightened, or trashy.

Blaming the Victim holds such a position. It is central in the mainstream of contemporary American social thought, and its ideas pervade our most crucial assumptions so thoroughly that they are hardly noticed. Moreover, the fruits of this ideology appear to be fraught with altruism and humanitarianism, so it is hard to believe that it has principally functioned to block social change.

A major pharmaceutical manufacturer, as an act of humanitarian concern, has distributed copies of a large poster warning "LEAD PAINT CAN KILL!" The poster, featuring a photograph of the face of a charming little girl, goes on to explain that if children *eat* lead paint, it can poison them, they can develop serious symptoms, suffer permanent brain damage, even die. The health department of a major American city has put out a coloring book that provides the same information. While the poster urges parents to prevent their children from eating paint, the coloring book is more vivid. It labels as neglectful and thoughtless the mother who does not keep her infant under constant surveillance to keep it from eating paint chips.

Now, no one would argue against the idea that it is important to spread knowledge about the danger of eating paint in order that parents might act to forestall their children from doing so. But to campaign against lead paint *only* in these terms is destructive and misleading and, in a sense, an effective way to support and agree with slum landlords—who define the problem of lead poisoning in precisely these terms.

This is an example of applying an exceptionalistic solution to a universalistic problem. It is not accurate to say that lead poisoning results from the actions of individual neglectful mothers. Rather, lead poisoning is a social phenomenon supported by a number of social mechanisms, one of the most tragic by-products of the systematic toleration of slum housing. In New Haven, which has the highest reported rate of lead poisoning in the country, several small children have died and many others have incurred irreparable brain damage as a result of eating peeling paint. In several cases, when the landlord failed to make repairs, poisonings have occurred time and again through a succession of tenancies. And the major reason for the landlord's neglect of this problem was that the city agency responsible for enforcing the housing code did nothing to make him correct this dangerous condition.

The cause of the poisoning is the lead in the paint on the walls of the apartment in which the children live. The presence of the lead is illegal. To use lead paint in a residence is illegal; to permit lead paint to be exposed in a residence is illegal. It is not only illegal, it is potentially criminal since the housing code does provide for criminal penalties. The general problem of lead poisoning, then, is more accurately analyzed as the result of a systematic program of lawbreaking by one interest group in the community, with the toleration and encouragement of the public authority charged with enforcing that law. To ignore these continued and repeated law violations, to ignore the fact that the supposed law enforcer actually cooperates in lawbreaking, and then to load a burden of guilt on the mother of a dead or dangerously ill child is an egregious distortion of reality. And to do so *under the guise* of public-spirited and humanitarian service to the community is intolerable.

But this is how Blaming the Victim works. The righteous humanitarian concern displayed by the drug company, with its poster, and the health department, with its coloring book, is a genuine concern, and this is a typical feature of Blaming the Victim. Also typical is the swerving away from the central target that requires systematic change and, instead, focusing in on the individual affected. The ultimate effect is always to distract attention from the basic causes and to leave the primary social injustice untouched. And, most telling, the proposed remedy for the problem is, of course, to work on the victim himself. Prescriptions for cure, as written by the Savage Discovery set, are invariably conceived to revamp and revise the victim, never to change the surrounding circumstances. They want to change his attitudes, alter his values, fill up his cultural deficits, energize his apathetic soul, cure his character defects, train him and polish him and woo him from his savage ways.

Isn't all of this more subtle and sophisticated than such old-fashioned ideologies as Social Darwinism? Doesn't the change from brutal ideas about survival of the fit (and the expiration of the unfit) to kindly concern about characterological defects (brought about by stigmas of social origin) seem like a substantial step forward? Hardly. It is only a substitution of terms. The old, reactionary exceptionalistic formulations are replaced by new progressive, humanitarian exceptionalistic formulations. In education, the outmoded and unacceptable concept of racial or class differences in basic inherited intellectual ability simply gives way to the new notion of cultural deprivation: there is very little functional difference between these two ideas. In taking a look at the phenomenon of poverty, the old concept of unfitness or idleness or laziness is replaced by the newfangled theory of the culture of poverty. In race relations, plain Negro inferiority—which was good enough for old-fashioned conservatives—is pushed aside by fancy conceits about the crumbling Negro family. With regard to illegitimacy, we are not so crass as to concern ourselves with immorality and vice, as in the old days; we settle beningly on the explanation of the "lower-class pattern of sexual behavior," which no one condemns as evil, but which is, in fact, simply a variation of the old explanatory idea. Mental illness is no longer defined as the result of hereditary taint or congenital character flaw; now we have new causal hypotheses regarding the ego-damaging emotional experiences that are supposed to be the inevitable consequence of the deplorable child-rearing practices of the poor.

In each case, of course, we are persuaded to ignore the obvious; the continued blatant discrimination against the Negro, the gross deprivation of contraceptive and adoption services to the poor, the heavy stresses endemic in the life of the poor. And almost all our make-believe liberal programs aimed at correcting our urban problems are off target; they are designed either to change the poor man or to cool him out.

We come finally to the question, Why? It is much easier to understand the process of Blaming the Victim as a way of thinking than it is to understand the motivation for it. Why do Victim Blamers, who are usually good people, blame the victim? The development and application of this ideology, and of all the mythologies associated with Savage Discovery, are readily exposed by careful analysis as hostile acts—one is almost tempted to say acts of war—directed against the disadvantaged, the distressed, the disinherited. It is class warfare in reverse. Yet those who are most fascinated and enchanted by this ideology tend to be progressive, humanitarian, and, in the best sense of the word, charitable persons. They would usually define themselves as moderates or liberals. Why do they pursue this dreadful war against the poor and the oppressed?

Put briefly, the answer can be formulated best in psychological terms—or, at least, I, as a psychologist, am more comfortable with such a formulation. The highly charged psychological problem confronting this hypothetical progressive, charitable person I am talking about is that of reconciling his own self-interest with the promptings of his humanitarian impulses. This psychological process of reconciliation is not worked out in a logical, rational, conscious way; it is a process that takes place far below the level of sharp consciousness, and the solution—Blaming the Victim—is arrived at subconsciously as a compromise that apparently satisfies both his self-interest and his charitable concerns. Let me elaborate.

First, the question of self-interest or, more accurately, class interest. The typical

Victim Blamer is a middle-class person who is doing reasonably well in a material way; he has a good job, a good income, a good house, a good car. Basically, he likes the social system pretty much the way it is, at least in broad outline. He likes the two-party political system, though he may be highly skilled in finding a thousand minor flaws in its functioning. He heartily approves of the profit motive as the propelling engine of the economic system despite his awareness that there are abuses of that system, negative side effects, and substantial residual inequalities.

On the other hand, he is acutely aware of poverty, racial discrimination, exploitation, and deprivation, and, moreover, he wants to do something concrete to ameliorate the condition of the poor, the black, and the disadvantaged. This is not an extraneous concern; it is central to his value system to insist on the worth of the individual, the equality of men, and the importance of justice.

What is to be done, then? What intellectual position can he take, and what line of action can he follow that will satisfy both of these important motivations? He quickly and self-consciously rejects two obvious alternatives, which he defines as "extremes." He cannot side with an openly reactionary, repressive position that accepts continued oppression and exploitation as the price of a privileged position for his own class. This is incompatible with his own morality and his basic political principles. He finds the extreme conservative position repugnant.

He is, if anything, more allergic to radicals, however, than he is to reactionaries. He rejects the "extreme" solution of radical social change, and this makes sense since such radical social change threatens his own well-being. A more equitable distribution of income might mean that he would have less—a smaller or older house, with fewer yews or no rhododendrons in the yard, a less enjoyable job, or, at the least, a somewhat smaller salary. If black children and poor children were, in fact, reasonably educated and began to get high S.A.T. scores, they would be competing with *his* children for the scarce places in the entering classes of Harvard, Columbia, Bennington, and Antioch.

So our potential Victim Blamers are in a dilemma. In the words of an old Yiddish proverb, they are trying to dance at two weddings. They are old friends of both brides and fond of both kinds of dancing, and they want to accept both invitations. They cannot bring themselves to attack the system that has been so good to them, but they want so badly to be helpful to the victims of racism and economic injustice.

Their solution is a brilliant compromise. They turn their attention to the victim in his post-victimized state. They want to bind up wounds, inject penicillin, administer morphine, and evacuate the wounded for rehabilitation. They explain what's wrong with the victim in terms of social experiences *in the past*, experiences that have left wounds, defects, paralysis, and disability. And they take the cure of these wounds and the reduction of these disabilities as the first order of business. They want to make the victims less vulnerable, send them back into battle with better weapons, thicker armor, a higher level of morale.

In order to do so effectively, of course, they must analyze the victims carefully, dispassionately, objectively, scientifically, empathetically, mathematically, and hardheadedly, to see what made them so vulnerable in the first place.

What weapons, now, might they have lacked when they went into battle? Job skills? Education?

What armor was lacking that might have warded off their wounds? Better values? Habits of thrift and foresight?

And what might have ravaged their morale? Apathy? Ignorance? Deviant lower-class cultural patterns?

This is the solution of the dilemma, the solution of Blaming the Victim. And those who buy this solution with a sigh of relief are inevitably blinding themselves to the basic causes of the problems being addressed. They are, most crucially, rejecting the possibility of blaming, not the victims, but themselves. They are all unconsciously passing judgments on themselves and bringing in a unanimous verdict of Not Guilty.

If one comes to believe that the culture of poverty produces persons *fated* to be poor, who can find any fault with our corporation-dominated economy? And if the Negro family produces young men *incapable* of achieving equality, let's deal with that first before we go on to the task of changing the pervasive racism that informs and shapes and distorts our every social institution. And if unsatisfactory resolution of one's Oedipus complex accounts for all emotional distress and mental disorder, then by all means let us attend to that and postpone worrying about the pounding day-to-day stresses of life on the bottom rungs that drive so many to drink, dope, and madness.

That is the ideology of Blaming the Victim, the cunning Art of Savage Discovery. The tragic, frightening truth is that it is a mythology that is winning over the best people of our time, the very people who must resist this ideological temptation if we are to achieve nonviolent change in America.

NOTES

1. For a good review of this general ideology, see I. A. Newby, *Jim Crow's Defense* (Baton Rouge: Louisiana State University Press, 1965).

2. Richard Hofstadter, *Social Darwinism in American Thought* (revised ed.; Boston: Beacon Press, 1955).

3. William J. Ghent, *Our Benevolent Feudalism* (New York: The Macmillan Co., 1902), p. 29.

9

Sex and Race:
The Analogy of Social Control

William Chafe

. . . Analogies should not be limited to issues of substance alone, nor is their purpose to prove that two categories or objects are exactly identical. According to the dictionary, an analogy is "a relation of likeness . . . consisting in the resemblance not of the things themselves but of two or more attributes, circumstances or effects." Within this context, the purpose of an analogy is to illuminate a process or relationship which might be less discernible if only one or the other side of the comparison were viewed in isolation. What, then, if we look at sex and race as examples of how social control is exercised in America, with the primary emphasis on what the analogy tells us about the modes of control emanating from the dominant culture? Throughout the preceding discussion, the strongest parallels dealt with the use of stereotypes and ascribed attributes to define the respective position of women and blacks in the society. Thus what if the nature of the analogy is not in the *substance* of the material existence which women and blacks have experienced but in the *forms* by which others have kept them in "their place" and prevented them from challenging the status quo?

The virtues of such an approach are many. First, it provides greater flexibility in exploring how the experience of one group can inform the study of another. Second, it has the potential of developing insights into the larger processes by which the status quo is perpetuated from generation to generation. In this sense, it can teach us about the operation of society as a whole and the way in which variables like sex and race have been made central to the division of responsibilities and power within the society. If the forms of social control used with blacks and women resemble each other in "two or more attributes, circumstances, or effects," then it may be possible to learn something both about the two groups and how the status quo has been maintained over time. The best way to pursue this, in turn, is through looking closely at the process of social control as it has operated on one group, and then comparing it with the process and experience of the second group.

In his brilliant autobiographical novel *Black Boy*, Richard Wright describes what it was like to grow up black in the Jim Crow South. Using his family, the church, his classmates, his jobs, and his fantasies as stage-pieces for his story,

Wright plays out the themes of hunger, fear, and determination which permeated his young life. Above all, he provides a searing account of how white Southerners successfully controlled the lives and aspirations of blacks. A series of concentric circles of social control operated in devastating fashion to limit young blacks to two life options—conformity to the white system, or exile. *

The outermost circle of control, of course, consisted of physical intimidation. When Richard asked his mother why black men did not fight white men, she responded, "The white men have guns and the black men don't." Physical force, and ultimately the threat of death, served as a constant reminder that whites held complete power over black lives. Richard saw that power manifested repeatedly. When his Uncle Hoskins dared to start his own saloon and act independently of the white power structure, he was lynched. The brother of one of Richard's schoolmates suffered a similar fate, allegedly for fooling with a white prostitute. When Richard worked for a clothing store, he frequently saw the white manager browbeat or physically attack black customers who had not paid their bills on time. When one woman came out of the store in a torn dress and bleeding, the manager said, "That's what we do to niggers when they don't pay their bills."[1]

The result was pervasive fear, anchored in the knowledge that whites could unleash vicious and irrational attacks without warning. Race consciousness could be traced, at least in part, to the tension which existed between anger at whites for attacking blacks without reason, and fear that wanton violence could strike again at any time, unannounced and unrestrained. "The things that influenced my conduct as a Negro," Richard wrote, "did not have to happen to me directly; I needed but to hear of them to feel their full effects in the deepest layers of my consciousness. Indeed the white brutality that I had not seen was a more effective control of my behavior than that which I knew . . . as long as it remained something terrible and yet remote, something whose horror and blood might descend upon me at any moment, I was compelled to give my entire imagination over to it, an act which blocked the springs of thought and feelings in me."[2]

The second circle of control rested in white domination of the economic status of black people. If a young black did not act the part of "happy nigger" convincingly, the employer would fire him. Repeatedly, Richard was threatened with the loss of work because he did not keep his anger and independence from being communicated to his white superiors. "Why don't you laugh and talk like the other niggers?" one employer asked. "Well, sir, there is nothing much to say or smile about," Richard said. "I don't like your looks nigger. Now git!" the boss ordered. Only a limited number of economic roles were open to blacks, and if they were not played

---

*Despite the problems created by using a novel for purposes of historical analysis, the interior perspective that is offered outweighs the limitations of "subjectiveness." Wright has been criticized for being overly harsh and elitist in his judgment of his black peers. His depiction of the conditions blacks had to cope with, on the other hand, corresponds well with the historical record. In the cases of both women and blacks, novels provide a vividness of detail and personal experience necessary to understand the larger processes at work in the society, but for the most part unavailable in conventional historical sources.

according to the rules, the job would be lost. A scarce supply of work, together with the demand that it be carried out in a deferential manner, provided a powerful guarantee that blacks would not get out of line.[3]

Significantly, the highest status jobs in the black community—teachers, ministers, civil servants—all depended ultimately upon acting in ways that pleased the white power structure.* One did not get the position at the post office or in the school system without being "safe"—the kind of person who would not make trouble. The fundamental precondition for success in the black community, therefore, was acting in ways that would not upset the status quo. When Richard tried to improve his own occupational chances and learn the optical trade, the white men who were supposed to teach him asked: "What are you trying to do, get smart, nigger?"[4]

The third circle of control consisted of the psychological power of whites to define and limit the reach of black aspirations. The sense people have of who they are and what they might become is tied intimately to the expectations communicated to them by others. The verbal cues, the discouragement or encouragement of authority figures, the picture of reality transmitted by friends or teachers—all of these help to shape how people think of themselves and their life chances. Stated in another way, human beings can envision careers as doctors and lawyers or a life of equality with others only to the extent that someone holds forth these ideals as viable possibilities.

Within this realm of social psychology, white Southerners exerted a pervasive and insidious control upon blacks. When Richard took his first job in a white household, he was given a bowl of molasses with mold on it for breakfast, even as his employers ate bacon and eggs. The woman he worked for asked what grade he was in, and when he replied the seventh, she asked, "Then why are you going to school?" When he further answered, "Well, I want to be a writer," she responded: "You'll never be a writer . . . who on earth put such ideas into your nigger head?" By her response, the woman attempted to undercut whatever sense of possibility Richard or other young blacks might have entertained for such a career. In effect, the woman had defined from a white perspective the outer boundaries of a black person's reality. As Richard noted, "She had assumed that she knew my place in life, what I felt, what I ought to be, and I resented it with all my heart. . . . perhaps I would never be a writer; but I did not want her to say so." In his own time Richard Wright was able to defy the limits set upon his life by white people. But for the overwhelming majority of his fellow blacks, the ability of whites to intimidate them psychologically diminished the chance that they would be able to aspire realistically to a life other than that assigned them within a white racist social structure.[5]

---

*There is an important distinction, of course, between jobs which were tied to white support and those with an indigenous base in the black community. Black doctors, morticians, and barbers, for example, looked to the black community itself for their financial survival; hence they could be relatively free of white domination. On the other hand, the number of such independent positions was small. Although many people would include ministers in such a category, the visibility of the ministerial role created pressure from blacks concerned with the stability and safety of their churches for ministers to avoid a radical protest position. That started to change during the civil rights movement.

The most devastating control of all, however, was that exercised by the black community itself out of self-defense. In the face of a world managed at every level by white power, it became an urgent necessity that black people train each other to adapt in order to survive. Thus the most profound and effective socialization toward accepting the racial status quo came from Richard's own family and peer group. It was Richard's mother who slapped him into silence "out of her own fear" when he asked why they had not fought back after Uncle Hoskins's lynching. To even ask the question posed a threat to safety. Similarly, it was Richard's Uncle Tom who insisted that Richard learn, almost by instinct, how to be accommodating. If Richard did not learn, the uncle said, he would never amount to anything and would end up on the gallows. Indeed, Richard would survive only if somebody broke his spirit and set the "proper" example.[6]

The instances of social control from within the black community abound in Wright's *Black Boy*. It was not only the white employer, but almost every black he knew, who opposed Richard's writing aspirations. "From no quarter," he recalled, "with the exception of the Negro newspaper editor, had there come a single encouraging word . . . I felt that I had committed a crime. Had I been aware of the full extent to which I was pushing against the current of my environment, I would have been frightened altogether out of my attempts at writing." The principal of his school urged vehemently that Richard give a graduation speech written by the principal rather than by Richard himself so that the proper tone of accommodation could be struck; the reward for going along was a possible teaching job. Griggs, Richard's best friend, was perhaps the most articulate in demanding that Richard control his instincts. "You're black and you don't act a damn bit like it." When Richard replied, "Oh Christ, I can't be a slave," Griggs responded with the ultimate lesson of reality: "But you've got to eat . . . when you are in front of white people, think before you act, think before you speak . . . you may think I'm an Uncle Tom, but I'm not. I hate these white people, hate them with all my heart. But I can't show it; if I did, they'd kill me." No matter where he went or whom he talked to in his own community, Richard found, not support for his protest, but the warning that he must behave externally in the manner white people expected. Whatever the hope of ultimate freedom, survival was the immediate necessity. One could not fight another day if one was not alive.[7]

Paradoxically, even the outlets for resistance within the system provided a means of reinforcing it. There were many ways of expressing unhappiness with one's lot, and all were essential to let off steam. The gang on the corner constantly verbalized resentment and anger against the white oppressor. Yet the very fact that the anger had to be limited to words and out of the earshot of whites meant that in practical terms it was ineffectual. Humor was another form of resistance. Richard and his friends joked that, if they ate enough black-eyed peas and buttermilk, they would defeat their white enemies in a race riot with "poison gas." But the end of the joke was an acknowledgment that the only way in reality to cope with the "mean" white folks was to leave.[8]

Indeed, the most practical form of resistance—petty theft—almost seemed a ploy by white people to perpetuate the system. Just as modern-day department store owners tolerate a certain degree of employee theft as a means of making the workers think they are getting away with something so they will not demand higher wages, so white employers of black people appear to have intentionally closed their eyes to a great deal of minor stealing. By giving blacks a small sense of triumph, white employers were able to tie them even more closely into the system, and prevent them from contemplating outright defiance. As Wright observed:[9]

> No Negroes in my environment had ever thought of organizing . . . and petitioning their white employers for higher wages . . . They knew that the whites would have retaliated with swift brutality. So, pretending to conform to the laws of the whites, grinning, bowing, they let their fingers stick to what they could touch. And the whites seemed to like it.
>
> But I, who stole nothing, who wanted to look them straight in the face, who wanted to talk and act like a man, inspired fear in them. The southern whites would rather have had Negroes who stole work for them than Negroes who knew, however dimly, the worth of their own humanity. Hence, whites placed a premium upon black deceit; they encouraged irresponsibility, and their rewards were bestowed upon us blacks in the degree that we could make them feel safe and superior.

From a white point of view, a minor exercise of indirect and devious power by blacks was a small price to pay for maintaining control over the entire system. Thus, whites held the power to define black people's options, even to the point of controlling their modes of resistance. *

The result of all this was a system that functioned smoothly, with barely a trace of overt protest or dissension. Everyone seemed outwardly content with their place. At a very early age, Wright observed, "the white boys and the black boys began to play our traditional racial roles as though we had been born to them, as though it was in our blood, as though we were guided by instinct." For most people, the impact of a pervasive system of social control was total: resignation, a lowering of aspirations, a recognition of the bleakness of the future and the hopelessness of trying to achieve major change. In Wright's images life was like a train on a track; once headed in a given direction, there was little possibility of changing one's course.[10]

Wright himself, of course, was the exception. "Somewhere in the dead of the southern night," he observed, "my life had switched onto the wrong track, and without my knowiing it, the locomotive of my heart was rushing down a dangerously steep slope, heading for a collision, heedless of the warning red lights that blinked all about me, the sirens and the bells and the screams that filled the air."

---

*It is important to remember that there existed a life in the black community less susceptible to white interference on a daily basis. Black churches, lodges, and family networks provided room for individual self-expression and supplied emotional reinforcement and sustenance. In this connection it is no accident that black institutions are strongest in the South where, until recently, the vast majority of blacks resided. On the other hand, the freedom which did exist came to a quick end wherever blacks attempted to enter activities, occupations, or areas of aspiration involving whites; or defined as white-controlled. Thus even the realm where freedom existed was partially a reflection of white control.

Wright had chosen the road of exile, of acute self-consciousness and alienation. For most blacks of his era, though, the warning red lights, the sirens, the bells, and the screams produced at least outward conformity to the status quo. In the face of forms of social control which effectively circumscribed one's entire life, there seemed no other choice.[11]

Obviously, women have not experienced overtly and directly the same kind of consistent physical intimidation that served so effectively to deter the black people of Richard Wright's childhood from resisting their condition. On the other hand, it seems clear that the physical strength and alleged dominance of men have been an important instrument of controlling women's freedom of action. The traditional image of the male as "protector" owes a great deal to the notion that women cannot defend themselves and that men must therefore take charge of their lives physically. The same notion of male strength has historically been responsible for restricting jobs involving heavy labor to men. Nor is the fear with which women view the potential of being struck or raped by a male lover, husband, or attacker an insignificant reality in determining the extent to which women historically have accepted the dominance of the men in their lives. Richard Wright observed that "the things that influenced my conduct . . . did not have to happen to me directly; I needed but to hear of them to feel their full effects. . . ." Similarly, women who have grown up with the image of powerful and potentially violent men need not have experienced a direct attack to share a sense of fear and intimidation. "Strength," the psychologist Jerome Kagan has observed, "is a metaphor for power." Thus, despite the substantive difference in the way women and blacks have been treated, the form of social control represented by physical strength has operated similarly for both groups.[12]

An even stronger case can be made for the way in which economic controls have succeeded in keeping blacks and women in their place. In 1898 Charlotte Perkins Gilman argued in *Women and Economics* that the root of women's subjection was their economic dependency on men. As long as women were denied the opportunity to earn their own living, she argued, there could never be equality between the sexes. The fact that women had to please their mates, both sexually and through other services, to ensure their survival made honest communication and mutual respect impossible. The prospect of a "present" from a generous husband, or a new car or clothes, frequently served to smooth over conflict, while the implicit threat of withholding such favors could be used to discourage carrying conflict too far.[13]

In fact, the issue of women not controlling their own money has long been one of the most painful and humiliating indexes of inequality between the sexes, especially in the middle class. Since money symbolizes power, having to ask others for it signifies subservience and an inferior status. Carol Kennicott, the heroine of Sinclair Lewis's *Main Street*, recognized the problem. After begging prettily for her household expenses early in her marriage, she started to demand her own separate funds. "What was a magnificent spectacle of generosity to you," she told her husband, "was a humiliation to me. You *gave* me money—gave it to your mistress if she was complaisant." Beth Phail, a character in Marge Piercy's novel *Small Changes*, experienced the same conflict with her husband, who was immediately threatened by the idea of her economic autonomy. Indeed, few examples of psychological control seem more pointed than those represented in husbands' treating their wives as not mature enough to handle their own money.[14]

Even the women who held jobs reflected the pattern by which economic power was used to control women's freedom of action. Almost all women workers were concentrated in a few occupations delineated as "woman's" work. As secretaries, waitresses, cooks, and domestic workers, women on the job conformed to the "service" image of their sex. Significantly, the highest status jobs available—nurses and teachers—tended to reinforce a traditional image of women and the status quo between the sexes, just as the highest jobs available within the black community—teachers and civil servants—reinforced a pattern of accommodation with the existing white power structure. Any woman who chose a "man's job" automatically risked a loss of approval, if not total hostility. For most, the option simply did not exist.

Even those in the most prestigious positions illustrated how money could be used as an instrument of social control. If they were to succeed in raising funds, college administrators in black and women's schools frequently found that they had to shape their programs in conformity to social values that buttressed the status quo. Booker T. Washington represented the most outstanding example of this phenomenon. Repeatedly he was forced to appease white racist presumptions in order to get another donation for Tuskegee. As the funnel through which all white philanthropic aid to blacks was channeled, Washington had to ensure that no money would be spent in a way which might challenge the political values of his contributors, even though privately he fought those political values. But Washington was not alone. During the 1830's Mary Lyons, head of Mt. Holyoke Seminary, agreed not to attend trustee meetings lest she offend male sensibilities, and Mary Alice Baldwin, the very effective leader of the Women's College of Duke University, felt it necessary to pay homage to the conservative tradition of "the Southern lady" as the price for sustaining support of women's education at Duke.[15]

In all of these instances, economic controls functioned in parallel ways to limit the freedom of women and blacks. If a group is assigned a "place," there are few more effective ways of keeping it there than economic dependency. Not only must the group in question conform to the expectations of the dominant class in order to get money to live; those who would do otherwise are discouraged by the fact that no economic incentives exist to reward those who challenge the status quo. The absence of financial support for those who dare to deviate from prescribed norms has served well to perpetuate the status quo in the condition of both women and blacks. "I don't want to be a slave," Richard Wright observed. "But you have to eat," Griggs replied.

The strongest parallel, however, consists of the way in which blacks and women have been given the psychological message that they should be happy with their "place." In both instances, this form of control has effectively limited aspiration to non-conventional roles. Although Beth Phail of *Small Changes* wanted to go to college and law school, her family insisted that her highest aspiration should be marriage and homemaking. A woman should not expect a career. Similarly, when Carol Kennicott told her college boy friend, "I want to do something with my life," he responded eagerly: "What's better than making a comfy home and bringing up some cute kids . . . ?" The small town atmosphere of Gopher Prairie simply reinforced the pressure to conform. Carol was expected to be a charming hostess, a dutiful wife, and a good homemaker, but not a career woman. Thus, as Sinclair Lewis observed, she was a "woman with a working brain and no work." The messages Carol received from her surroundings were not designed to give her high self-esteem. Her husband called her "an extravagant little rabbit," and his poker partners, she noted simply expected her "to wait on them like a servant."[16]

Although Carol's personality was atypical, her social experience was not. When high school girls entertained the possibility of a career, they were encouraged to be nurses, not doctors. the qualities that received the most praise were those traditionally associated with being a "lady," not an assertive individual ready to face the world. Significantly, both women and blacks were the victims of two devices designed to discourage non-conformity. Those who sought to protest their status, for example, were subjected to ridicule and caricature. the black protestor was almost certain to be identified with subversive activity, just as the women's rights advocate was viewed as unsexed and a saboteur of the family. (Ordinary blacks and females were subject to a gentler form of humor, no less insidious, as in the characters of Amos 'n Andy's "King Fish" or Lucille Ball's "Lucy.") In addition, it was not uncommon for blacks to be set against blacks and women against women in a competition which served primarily the interests of the dominant group. According to Judith Bardwick and Elizabeth Douvan, girls are socialized to use oblique forms of aggression largely directed at other females, while men's aggression is overt. The stereotype of women doing devious battle over an attractive man is an ingrained part of our folk tradition. Nor is the "divide and conquer" strategy a stranger to the history of black people, as when white workers sowed seeds of suspicion between Richard Wright and another black worker in order to make them fight each other for the entertainment of whites.[17]

In both cases the psychological form of social control has operated in a similar fashion. The aspirations, horizons, and self-images of blacks and women have been defined by others in a limiting and constrictive way. More often that not, the result historically has been an acceptance of society's perception of one's role. The prospect of becoming an architect, an engineer, or a carpenter is not easy to sustain in an environment where the very idea is dismissed as foolish or unnatural. Instead of encouragement to aspire to new horizons of achievement, the message transmitted to blacks and women has been the importance of finding satisfaction with the status quo.

But in the case of women, as with blacks, the most effective instrument of continued control has been internal pressure from the group itself. From generation to generation, mothers teach daughters to please men, providing the instruction that prepares the new generation to assume the roles of mothers and housewives. Just as blacks teach each other how to cope with "whitey" and survive within the system, women school each other in how to win a man, how to appear charming, where to "play a role" in order to avoid alienating a potential husband. When Beth in *Small Changes* rebelled against her husband and fought the idea of tying herself down with a child, it was the other women in her family who urged her to submit and at least give the *appearance* of accepting the role expected of her.[18]

In fact, dissembling in order to conform to social preconceptions has been a frequent theme of women's socialization. As Mirra Komarovsky has demonstrated, college women in the 1940's were taught to hide their real ability in order to make their male friends feel superior. "My mother thinks that it is very nice to be smart in college," one of Komarovsky's students noted, "but only if it doesn't take too much effort. She always tells me not to be too intellectual on dates, to be clever in a light sort of way." It is not difficult to imagine one woman saying to another as Griggs said to Richard Wright, "When you are around white people [men] you have to act the part that they expect you to act." Even if deception was the goal, however, the underlying fact was that members of the "oppressed" group acted as accomplices in perpetuating the status quo.[19]

The most effective device for maintaining internal group discipline was to ostracize those who did not conform. Richard Wright found himself singled out for negative treatment because he refused to accept authority and to smile and shuffle before either his teachers or white people. Beth Phail was roundly condemned by her sisters and mother for not pleasing her husband, and above all for not agreeing to have a child. And Carol Kennicott received hostile glances when she violated her "place" by talking politics with men or seeking to assume a position of independent leadership in the community of Gopher Prairie. The disapproval of her female peers was the most effective weapon used to keep her in line, and, when it appeared that she finally was going to have a child, her women friends applauded the fact that in becoming a mother she would finally get over all her strange ideas and settle down. As Sinclair Lewis observed, "She felt that willy-nilly she was being initiated into the assembly of housekeepers; with the baby for hostage, she would never escape."[20]

The pressure of one's own group represented a double burden. In an environment where success was defined as marriage, and fulfillment as being a happy homemaker, it was hard enough to fight the tide in the first place. If one did, however, there was the additional problem of being seen as a threat to all the other members of the group who had conformed. The resistance of blacks toward Richard Wright and of women toward Carol Kennicott becomes more understandable in light of the fact that in both cases the individual protestors, through their refusal to play the game according to the rules, were also passing judgment on those who accepted the status quo. Thus, historically, women and blacks have kept each other in line not only as a means of group self-defense—protecting the new generation from harm and humiliation—but also as a means of maintaining self-respect by defending the course they themselves have chosen.

Indeed, for women as well as for blacks, even the vehicles for expressing resentment became reinforcements of the status quo. For both groups, the church provided a central emotional outlet—a place where solidarity with one's own kind could be found, and where some protest was possible. Women's church groups provided not only a means of seeking reform in the larger society but also for talking in confidence to other women about the frustrations of being a woman in a male-dominated society. What social humorists have called "hen-sessions" were in fact group therapy encounters where women had a chance to voice their gripes. Humor was frequently a vehicle for expressing a bittersweet response to one's situation, bemoaning, even as one laughed, the pain of being powerless. But as in the case with blacks, venting one's emotions about a life situation—although necessary for survival—was most often an instrument for coping with the situation, rather than for changing it.

Perhaps the most subversive and destructive consequence of a pervasive system of social control is how it permeates every action, so that even those who are seeking to take advantage of the "enemy" end up supporting the system. When Shorty, the elevator man in *Black Boy* known for his wit and hostility to whites, needed some money for lunch one day, he told a white man he would not move the elevator until he got a quarter. "I'm hungry, Mr. White Man. I'm dying for a quarter," Shorty said. The white man responded by asking what Shorty would do for a quarter. "You can kick me for a quarter," Shorty said, bending over. At the end of the elevator ride, Shorty had his quarter. "This monkey's got the peanuts," he said. Shorty was right. He had successfully used racial stereotypes and his own role as a buffoon to get himself some lunch money. But in the process, the entire system of racial imbalance had been strengthened.[21]

Similar patterns run through the history of women's relationships to men. The coquette role is only the most extreme example of a type of manipulative behavior by women that seems to confirm invidious stereotypes. In the classic case of a wife trying to persuade her husband to go along with a desired course of action, the woman may play up to a man's vanity and reinforce his stereotyped notions about being a tower of strength and in control. Similarly, a female employee wishing advancement may adopt a flirtatious attitude toward a male superior. By playing a semi-seductive role and implying a form of sexual payoff for services rendered, she may achieve her immediate goal. But in each of these cases, the price is to become more entrapped in a set of distorted and unequal sex role stereotypes. The fact that overt power is not available and that the ability to express oneself honestly and openly has been denied leads to the use of covert and manipulative power. Thus, a woman may play dumb or a black may act deferential—conforming in each case to a stereotype—as a means of getting his or her way. But the result is pathological power that simply perpetuates the disease. The irony is that, even in trying to outwit the system of social control, the system pervails.

Basic to the entire system, of course, has been the extent to which a clearly defined role was "woven into the texture of things." For blacks the crucial moment might come as soon as they developed an awareness of whites. In the case of women, it more likely took place at puberty when the need to begin pleasing potential husbands was emphasized. In either case, what Richard Wright said about the process of socialization could be said of both groups. "I marveled," he wrote[22]:

at how smoothly the black boys [women] acted out the role . . . mapped out for them. Most of them were not conscious of living a special, separate, stunted way of life. Yet I knew that in some period of their growing up—a period that they had no doubt forgotten—there had been developed in them a delicate, sensitive controlling mechanism that shut off their minds and emotions from all that the white race [society] had said was taboo. Although they lived in America where in theory there existed equality of opportunity, they knew unerringly what to aspire to and what not to aspire to.

The corollary for both women and blacks, at least metaphorically, has been that those unable or unwilling to accept the role prescribed for them have been forced into a form of physical or spiritual exile. Richard Wright understood that continued accommodation with the white Southern system of racial oppression would mean the destruction of his integrity and individuality. "Ought one to surrender to authority even if one believed that the authority was wrong?" Wright asked. "If the answer was yes, then I knew that I would always be wrong, because I could never do it. . . . How could one live in a world in which one's mind and perceptions meant nothing and authority and tradition meant everything?" The only alternative to psychological death was exile, and Wright pursued that course, initially in Chicago, later in Paris. In her own way Carol Kennicott attempted the same journey. "I've got to find out what my work is," she told her husband. "I've been ruled too long by fear of being called things. I'm going away to be quiet and think. I'm—I'm going. I have a right to my own life." And Beth Phail finally fled her home and family because it was the only way to grow up, to find out what "she wanted," to learn how to be a person in her own right in the world.[23]

Although in reality only a few blacks and women took the exact course adopted by Richard Wright, Carol Kennicott, and Beth Phail, all those who chose to resist the status quo shared to some extent in the metaphor of exile. Whether the person was a feminist like Charlotte Perkins Gilman, a pioneer career woman such as Elizabeth Blackwell, a runaway slave like Frederick Douglass, or a bold race leader like W. E. B. DuBois, the act of challenging prevailing norms meant living on the edge of alienation and apart from the security of those who accepted the status quo. Until and unless protest generated its own community of support which could provide a substitute form of security and reinforcement, the act of deviance promised to be painful and solitary.

This condition, in turn, reflected an experience of marginality which many blacks and women shared. In sociological terms, the "marginal" personality is someone who moves in and out of different groups and is faced with the difficulty of adjusting behavior to the norms of the different groups. By definition, most blacks and most women have participated in that experience, especially as they have been required to accommodate the expectations of the dominant group of white males. The very fact of having to adopt different modes of behavior for different audiences introduces an element of complexity and potential conflict to the lives of those who are most caught up in a marginal existence. House slaves, for example, faced the inordinately difficult dilemma of being part of an oppressed group of slaves even as they lived in intimacy with and under the constant surveillance of the white master-class, thereby experiencing in its most extreme form the conflict of living in two worlds. [24]

Ordinarily, the tension implicit in such a situation is deflected, or as Richard Wright observed, "contained and controlled by reflex." Most house slaves seemed to learn how to live with the conflict by repressing their anger and uneasiness. Coping with the situation became a matter of instinct. But it is not surprising that many slave revolts were led by those house slaves who could not resolve the conflict by reflex, and instead were driven to alienation and protest. For the minority of people who misinterpreted the cues given them or learned too late how to cope, conscious-ness of the conflict made instinctive conformity impossible. As Richard Wright observed, "I could not make subservience an automatic part of my behavior. . . . while standing before a white man . . . I had to figure out how to say each word . . . I could not grin . . . I could not react as the world in which I lived expected me to." The pain of self-consciousness made the burden almost unbear-able. As Maya Angelou has written, awareness of displacement "is the rust on the razor that threatens the throat." In an endless string of injuries, it was the final insult. [25]

Dissenting blacks and women have shared this experience of being "the outsider." Unable to accept the stereotyped behavior prescribed for their group, they have, in Vivian Gornick's words, "stood beyond the embrace of their fel-lows." With acute vision, Gornick writes, the outsider is able to "see deeply into the circle, penetrating to its very center, his vision a needle piercing the heart of life. Invariably, what he sees is intolerable." On the basis of such a vision, exile is the only alternative available. Yet, ironically, it too serves to reinforce the status quo by removing from the situation those most likely to fight it. Until the members willing to resist become great enough, the system of social control remains unaltered. [26]

It seems fair to conclude, therefore, that a significant resemblance has existed in the forms of social control used to keep women and blacks in their "place." Despite profound substantive differences between women and blacks, and white women and black women, all have been victims of a process, the end product of which has been to take away the power to define one's own aspirations, destiny, and sense of self. In each case a relationship of subservience to the dominant group has been perpetuated by physical, economic, psychological, and internal controls that have functioned in a remarkably similar way to discourage deviancy and place a premium on confor-mity. "It was brutal to be Negro and have no control over my life," Maya Angelou observes in her autobiography. "It was brutal to be young and already trained to sit quietly." From a feminist perspective, the same words describe the process of con-trol experienced by most women. [27]

The core of this process has been the use of a visible, physical characteristic as the basis for assigning to each group a network of duties, responsibilities, and attributes. It is the physical foundation for discriminatory treatment which makes the process of social control on sex and race distinctive from that which has applied to other oppressed groups. Class, for example, comes closest to sex and race as a source of massive social inequity and injustice. Yet in an American context, class has been difficult to isolate as an organizing principle. Because class is not associated with a visible physical characteristic and many working class people persist in identifying with a middle-class life-style, class is not a category easy to identify in terms of physical or psychological control. (The very tendency to abjure class consciousness in favor of a social mobility ethic, of course, is its own form of psychological control.) Ethnicity too has frequently served as a basis for oppression, but the ease with which members of most ethnic minorities have been able to "pass" into the dominant culture has made the structure of social control in those cases both porous and complicated. Thus although in almost every instance invidious treatment has involved the use of some form of physical, economic, psychological, or internal controls, the combinations have been different and the exceptions frequent.

The analogy of sex and race is distinctive, therefore, precisely to the extent that it highlights in pure form the process of social control which has operated to maintain the existing structure of American society. While many have been victimized by the same types of control, only in the case of sex and race—where physical attributes are ineradicable—have these controls functioned systematically and clearly to define from birth the possibilities to which members of a group might aspire. Perhaps for that reason sex and race have been cornerstones of the social system, and the source of values and attitudes which have both reinforced the power of the dominant class and provided a weapon for dividing potential opposition.

Finally, the analogy provides a potential insight into the strategies and possibilities of social change. If women and blacks have been kept in their "place" by similar forms of social control, the prerequisites for liberation may consist of overcoming those forms of social control through a similar process. In the case of both women and blacks, the fundamental problem has been that others have controlled the power to define one's existence. Thus, to whatever extent women and blacks act or think in a given way solely because of the expectation of the dominant group rather than from their own choice, they remain captive to the prevailing system of social control. The prototypical American woman, writes Vivian Gornick, is perceived as "never taking, always being taken, never absorbed by her own desire, preoccupied only with whether or not she is desired." Within such a context, the "other" is always more important than the "self" in determining one's sense of individual identity. It is for this reason that efforts by blacks and women toward group solidarity, control over one's own institutions, and development of an autonomous and positive self-image may be crucial in breaking the bonds of external dominance.[28]

Yet such a change itself depends on development of a collective consciousness of oppression and a collective commitment to protest. As long as social and political conditions, or the reluctance of group members to participate, preclude the emergence of group action, the individual rebel has little chance of effecting change. Thus the issue of social control leads inevitably to the question of how the existing cycle is broken. What are the preconditions for the evolution of group protest? How do external influences stimulate, or forestall, the will to resist? And through what modes of organization and action does the struggle for autonomy proceed? For these questions too, the analogy of sex and race may provide a useful frame of reference.

Whatever the case, it seems more productive to focus on forms of control or processes of change than to dwell on the substantive question of whether blacks and women have suffered comparable physical and material injury. Clearly, they have not. On the other hand when two groups exist in a situation of inequality, it may be self-defeating to become embroiled in a quarrel over which is more unequal or the victim of greater oppression. The more salient question is how a condition of inequality for both is maintained and perpetuated—through what modes is it reinforced? By that criterion, continued exploration of the analogy of sex and race promises to bring added insight to the study of how American society operates.

NOTES

1. Richard Wright, *Black Boy* (New York, 1937), pp. 48, 52, 150, 157. Quotations used by permission of the publishers Harper and Row, New York.
2. Wright, pp. 65, 150–51.
3. Wright, p. 159.
4. Wright, p. 164.
5. Wright, pp. 127–29.
6. Wright, pp. 139–40.
7. Wright, pp. 147, 153–55, 160–61.
8. Wright, pp. 68–71, 200.
9. Wright, p. 175.
10. Wright, p. 72.
11. Wright, p. 148.
12. Wright, pp. 150–51; Brownmiller, *Against Our Will;* Jerome Kagan and H. A. Moss, *Birth to Maturity* (New York, 1962).
13. Degler, "Introduction," *Women and Economics.*
14. Lewis, *Main Street,* pp. 74, 167; Marge Piercy, *Small Changes* (Greenwich, Conn., 1972), p. 33.
15. Louis P. Harlan, *Booker T. Washington 1856–1901* (New York, 1972); Ralph Ellison, *Invisible Man* (New York, 1952); Flexner, *Century of Struggle,* p. 33; and Dara DeHaven, "On Educating Women—The Co-ordinate Ideal at Trinity and Duke University," Masters thesis, Duke University, 1974.
16. Piercy, *Small Changes,* pp. 19–20, 29, 40–41; Lewis, *Main Street,* pp. 14–15, 86, 283.
17. Bardwick and Douvan, "Ambivalence: The Socialization of Women"; Wright, *Black Boy,* pp. 207–13.
18. Piercy, *Small Changes,* pp. 31, 34, 316–17.
19. Piercy, pp. 30–31, 34, 39; Mirra Komarovsky, "Cultural Contradictions and Sex Roles," *American Journal of Sociology* 52 (November 1946).
20. Lewis, *Main Street,* p. 234.
21. Wright, *Black Boy.* p. 199.
22. Wright, p. 172.

348 *The Prison of Race and Gender*

23. Wright, p. 144; Lewis, *Main Street*, pp. 404–5; Piercy, *Small Changes*, p. 41.
25. Wright, *Black Boy*, p. 130; Maya Angelou, *I Know Why the Caged Bird Sings*, p. 3.
26. Vivian Gornick, "Woman as Outsider," in Moran and Gornick, pp. 126–44.
27. Angelou, p. 153.
28. Gornick, p. 140.

Suggestions for Further Reading

M. Banton & J. Harwood: *The Race Concept*, Praeger, New York, 1975.

S. J. Gould: *The Mismeasure of Man*, W. W. Norton & Co., New York, 1981.

S. Harding & M. B. Hintikka: *Discovering Reality: Feminist Perspectives on Epistemology, Metaphysics, Methodology, and Philosophy of Science*, D. Reidel Publishing Co., Boston, 1983.

C. Kramarae, M. Schulz & W. M. O'Barr (eds.): *Language and Power*, Sage Press, Beverly Hills, California, 1984.

M. Lowe & R. Hubbard (eds.): *Women's Nature: Rationalization of Inequality*, Pergamon Press, New York, 1983.

H. Marcuse: *One-Dimensional Man*, Beacon Press, Boston, 1964.

D. Spender: *Man Made Language* (2nd edition), Routeledge & Kegan, Boston, 1985.

M. Vetterling-Braggin: *Sexist Language*, Littlefield, Adams and Co., 1981.

PART VI

Beyond Racism and Sexism

Developing an adequate understanding of the nature and causes of race, class, and gender oppression is a critical first step toward moving beyond them. Solutions to problems are generated, at least in part, by the way we pose them. That is why so much of this book is devoted to defining and analyzing the nature of the problem. Only when we appreciate the complex, subtle factors that operate together to create a society in which wealth, privilege, and opportunity are unequally divided will we be able to formulate viable proposals for changing those conditions.

What, then, have the selections in this book told us about racism, sexism, and class divisions? First, there is no single cause. Eliminating these forms of oppression will involve changes at the personal, social, political, and economic levels. It will require that we learn to think differently about ourselves and others and see the world through new categories. We will have to learn to pay close attention to our language, our attitudes, and our behavior and ask what values and forms of relationships are being created and maintained both consciously and unconsciously by them. It will mandate that (1) we reevaluate virtually every institution in society and critically appraise the ways in which it intentionally or unintentionally perpetuates the forms of discrimination we have been studying and (2) that we act to change them. In short, we will have to scrutinize every aspect of our economic, political, and social life with a view to asking whose interests are served and whose are denied by organizing our world in this way.

As a first step, we may need to redefine the term *"difference,"* which Audre Lorde suggests in the first selection in this part. While acknowledging that real differences of race, age, and sex exist, Lorde argues that it is not these differences that separate us as much as it is our refusal to acknowledge them and the role they play in shaping our relationships and our society. Denying or distorting those differences keeps us apart; embracing those differences can provide a new starting point for us from which to work together to reconstruct our world. The poem by Cherrie Moraga that follows Lorde's essay provides a good example of what it means to do just that. Moraga writes of discovering differences that were previously hidden from her and of thus finding a new basis for human community.

As we have seen, most of the differences that separate us have been constructed by society to maintain the privileges of some. Although we are born with certain physical characteristics, we are *not* born with a particular gender or racial identity. That identity is shaped by many factors. In the selection in Part I, Richard Wright talks about learning to become a Negro, lessons that were taught him primarily by the white community. Many selections in this book offer accounts of how other people were taught to adopt socially defined roles and/or the price they paid for deviating from them. In her essay on androgyny as an ideal for human development, Ann Ferguson argues that we must transcend rigid sex roles that assign human characteristics so that women and men each possess half of them. The androgynous person is one who is capable of being both strong and nurturing at the same time. Ferguson argues that genuine love relationships are possible only between equals and that only androgynous human beings have the potential for real equality. If Ferguson is correct, we should commit ourselves to raising our children, not as "boys" and "girls" who will grow up to be "men" and "women," but as human beings complete and whole in themselves.

Any significant attempt to eradicate race, gender, and class oppression will require fundamental changes in the ways that wealth is produced and distributed in our society. The next two selections in Part VI argue that a genuinely egalitarian distribution of wealth and opportunity is essential if we are to create a society in which every individual has the chance to lead a life of health and dignity. Both the article on developing an egalitarian family policy and the one on economic justice for women talk about social and economic policies that can bring about the requisite changes.

Ray Franklin's article, "Race, Class, and Gender Beyond the Welfare State," continues this discussion by analyzing six realities that shape the context in which social change can occur. Franklin argues that social policy that fails to recognize these realities is doomed to failure. Although the early part of his analysis focuses on the realities that shape relations between Blacks and whites in contemporary society, his essay concludes with an account of how current race, class, and gender issues could be transformed within a society based on new human priorities and forms of relationship. Franklin's account offers a new vision of work, family, and community beyond the welfare state.

Part VI concludes with Marge Piercy's enormously hopeful poem "The woman in the ordinary," in which she offers a dramatic alternative to the scenario described in her poem "Barbie Doll," which appears in Part III.

These selections are not offered as definitive solutions to the problems described and analyzed in this book. They are meant to provide specific and concrete examples of how we might begin to move beyond racism, sexism, class privilege, and other forms of oppression that deny people opportunity, dignity, and lives of joy. If these solutions seem too lofty and remote, you might wish to look at your school, family, or community and ask what first steps you could take to initiate this kind of transformation. Specifically, you might try thinking about what five practical changes in your immediate world could have a positive impact on race, class, and gender issues and how you could involve others in working to bring about those changes.

Age, Race, Class, and Sex: *Women Redefining Difference**

Audre Lorde

Much of Western European history conditions us to see human differences in simplistic opposition to each other: dominant/subordinate, good/bad, up/down, superior/inferior. In a society where the good is defined in terms of profit rather than in terms of human need, there must always be some group of people who, through systematized oppression, can be made to feel surplus, to occupy the place of the dehumanized inferior. Within this society, that group is made up of Black and Third World people, working-class people, older people, and women.

As a forty-nine-year-old Black lesbian feminist socialist mother of two, including one boy, and a member of an interracial couple, I usually find myself a part of some group defined as other, deviant, inferior, or just plain wrong. Traditionally, in american society, it is the members of oppressed, objectified groups who are expected to stretch out and bridge the gap between the actualities of our lives and the consciousness of our oppressor. For in order to survive, those of us for whom oppression is as american as apple pie have always had to be watchers, to become familiar with the language and manners of the oppressor, even sometimes adopting them for some illusion of protection. Whenever the need for some pretense of communication arises, those who profit from our oppression call upon us to share our knowledge with them. In other words, it is the responsibility of the oppressed to teach the oppressors their mistakes. I am responsible for educating teachers who dismiss my children's culture in school. Black and Third World people are expected to educate white people as to our humanity. Women are expected to educate men. Lesbians and gay men are expected to educate the heterosexual world. The oppressors maintain their position and evade responsibility for their own actions. There is a constant drain of energy which might be better used in redefining ourselves and devising realistic scenarios for altering the present and constructing the future.

*Paper delivered at the Copeland Colloquium, Amherst College, April 1980.

Institutionalized rejection of difference is an absolute necessity in a profit economy which needs outsiders as surplus people. As members of such an economy, we have *all* been programmed to respond to the human differences between us with fear and loathing and to handle that difference in one of three ways: ignore it, and if that is not possible, copy it if we think it is dominant, or destroy it if we think it is subordinate. But we have no patterns for relating across our human differences as equals. As a result, those differences have been misnamed and misused in the service of separation and confusion.

Certainly there are very real differences between us of race, age, and sex. But it is not those differences between us that are separating us. It is rather our refusal to recognize those differences, and to examine the distortions which result from our misnaming them and their effects upon human behavior and expectation.

Racism, the belief in the inherent superiority of one race over all others and thereby the right to dominance. Sexism, the belief in the inherent superiority of one sex over the other and thereby the right to dominance. Ageism. Heterosexism. Elitism. Classism.

It is a lifetime pursuit for each one of us to extract these distortions from our living at the same time as we recognize, reclaim, and define those differences upon which they are imposed. For we have all been raised in a society where those distortions were endemic within our living. Too often, we pour the energy needed for recognizing and exploring difference into pretending those differences are insurmountable barriers, or that they do not exist at all. This results in a voluntary isolation, or false and treacherous connections. Either way, we do not develop tools for using human difference as a springboard for creative change within our lives. We speak not of human difference, but of human deviance.

Somewhere, on the edge of consciousness, there is what I call a *mythical norm*, which each one of us within our hearts knows "that is not me." In america, this norm is usually defined as white, thin, male, young, heterosexual, christian, and financially secure. It is with this mythical norm that the trappings of power reside within this society. Those of us who stand outside that power often identify one way in which we are different, and we assume that to be the primary cause of all oppression, forgetting other distortions around difference, some of which we ourselves may be practicing. By and large within the women's movement today, white women focus upon their oppression as women and ignore differences of race, sexual preference, class, and age. There is a pretense to a homogeneity of experience covered by the word *sisterhood* that does not in fact exist.

Unacknowledged class differences rob women of each others' energy and creative insight. Recently a women's magazine collective made the decision for one issue to print only prose, saying poetry was a less "rigorous" or "serious" art form. Yet even the form our creativity takes is often a class issue. Of all the art forms, poetry is the most economical. It is the one which is the most secret, which requires the least physical labor, the least material, and the one which can be done between shifts, in the hospital pantry, on the subway, and on scraps of surplus paper. Over the last few years, writing a novel on tight finances, I came to appreciate the enormous differ-

ences in the material demands between poetry and prose. As we reclaim our literature, poetry has been the major voice of poor, working class, and Colored women.
A room of one's own may be a necessity for writing prose, but so are reams of paper,
a typewriter, and plenty of time. The actual requirements to produce the visual arts
also help determine, along class lines, whose art is whose. In this day of inflated
prices for material, who are our sculptors, our painters, our photographers? When
we speak of a broadly based women's culture, we need to be aware of the effect of
class and economic differences on the supplies available for producing art.

As we move toward creating a society within which we can each flourish, ageism
is another distortion of relationship which interferes without vision. By ignoring the
past, we are encouraged to repeat its mistakes. The "generation gap" is an important
social tool for any repressive society. If the younger members of a community view
the older members as contemptible or suspect or excess, they will never be able to
join hands and examine the living memories of the community, nor ask the all
important question, "Why?" This gives rise to a historical amnesia that keeps us
working to invent the wheel every time we have to go to the store for bread.

We find ourselves having to repeat and relearn the same old lessons over and
over that our mothers did because we do not pass on what we have learned, or
because we are unable to listen. For instance, how many times has this all been said
before? For another, who would have believed that once again our daughters are
allowing their bodies to be hampered and purgatoried by girdles and high heels and
hobble skirts?

Ignoring the differences of race between women and the implications of those
differences presents the most serious threat to the mobilization of women's joint
power.

As white women ignore their built-in privilege of whiteness and define *woman*
in terms of their own experience alone, then women of Color become "other," the
outsider whose experience and tradition is too "alien" to comprehend. An example
of this is the signal absence of the experience of women of Color as a resource for
women's studies courses. The literature of women of Color is seldom included in
women's literature courses and almost never in other literature courses, nor in
women's studies as a whole. All too often, the excuse given is that the literatures of
women of Color can only be taught by Colored women, or that they are too difficult
to understand, or that classes cannot "get into" them because they come out of
experiences that are "too different." I have heard this argument presented by white
women of otherwise quite clear intelligence, women who seem to have no trouble at
all teaching and reviewing work that comes out of the vastly different experiences of
Shakespeare, Molière, Dostoyefsky, and Aristophanes. Surely there must be some
other explanation.

This is a very complex question, but I believe one of the reasons white women
have such difficulty reading Black women's work is because of their reluctance to see
Black women as women and different from themselves. To examine Black women's
literature effectively requires that we be seen as whole people in our actual complexities—as individuals, as women, as human—rather than as one of those problematic

but familiar stereotypes provided in this society in place of genuine images of Black women. And I believe this holds true for the literatures of other women of Color who are not Black.

The literatures of all women of Color recreate the textures of our lives, and many white women are heavily invested in ignoring the real differences. For as long as any difference between us means one of us must be inferior, then the recognition of any difference must be fraught with guilt. To allow women of Color to step out of stereotypes is too guilt provoking, for it threatens the complacency of those women who view oppression only in terms of sex.

Refusing to recognize difference makes it impossible to see the different problems and pitfalls facing us as women.

Thus, in a patriarchal power system where whiteskin privilege is a major prop, the entrapments used to neutralize Black women and white women are not the same. For example, it is easy for Black women to be used by the power structure against Black men, not because they are men, but because they are Black. Therefore, for Black women, it is necessary at all times to separate the needs of the oppressor from our own legitimate conflicts within our communities. This same problem does not exist for white women. Black women and men have shared racist oppression and still share it, although in different ways. Out of that shared oppression we have developed joint defenses and joint vulnerabilities to each other that are not duplicated in the white community, with the exception of the relationship between Jewish women and Jewish men.

On the other hand, white women face the pitfall of being seduced into joining the oppressor under the pretense of sharing power. This possibility does not exist in the same way for women of Color. The tokenism that is sometimes extended to us is not an invitation to join power; our racial "otherness" is a visible reality that makes that quite clear. For white women there is a wider range of pretended choices and rewards for identifying with patriarchal power and its tools.

Today, with the defeat of ERA, the tightening economy, and increased conservatism, it is easier once again for white women to believe the dangerous fantasy that if you are good enough, pretty enough, sweet enough, quiet enough, teach the children to behave, hate the right people, and marry the right men, then you will be allowed to co-exist with patriarchy in relative peace, at least until a man needs your job or the neighborhood rapist happens along. And true, unless one lives and loves in the trenches it is difficult to remember that the war against dehumanization is ceaseless.

But Black women and our children know the fabric of our lives is stitched with violence and with hatred, that there is no rest. We do not deal with it only on the picket lines, or in dark midnight alleys, or in the places where we dare to verbalize our resistance. For us, increasingly, violence weaves through the daily tissues of our living—in the supermarket, in the classroom, in the elevator, in the clinic and the schoolyard, from the plumber, the baker, the saleswoman, the bus driver, the bank teller, the waitress who does not serve us.

Some problems we share as women, some we do not. You fear your children will grow up to join the patriarchy and testify against you, we fear our children will be dragged from a car and shot down in the street, and you will turn your backs upon the reasons they are dying.

The threat of difference has been no less blinding to people of Color. Those of us who are Black must see that the reality of our lives and our struggle does not make us immune to the errors of ignoring and misnaming difference. Within Black communities where racism is a living reality, differences among us often seem dangerous and suspect. The need for unity is often misnamed as a need for homogeneity, and a Black feminist vision mistaken for betrayal of our common interests as a people. Because of the continuous battle against racial erasure that Black women and Black men share, some Black women still refuse to recognize that we are also oppressed as women, and that sexual hostility against Black women is practiced not only by the white racist society, but implemented within our Black communities as well. It is a disease striking the heart of Black nationhood, and silence will not make it disappear. Exacerbated by racism and the pressures of powerlessness, violence against Black women and children often becomes a standard within our communities, one by which manliness can be measured. But these woman-hating acts are rarely discussed as crimes against Black women.

As a group, women of Color are the lowest paid wage earners in america. We are the primary targets of abortion and sterilization abuse, here and abroad. In certain parts of Africa, small girls are still being sewed shut between their legs to keep them docile and for men's pleasure. This is known as female circumcision, and it is not a cultural affair as the late Jomo Kenyatta insisted, it is a crime against Black women.

Black women's literature is full of the pain of frequent assault, not only by a racist patriarchy, but also by Black men. Yet the necessity for and history of shared battle have made us, Black women, particularly vulnerable to the false accusation that anti-sexist is anti-Black. Meanwhile, womanhating as a recourse of the powerless is sapping strength from Black communities, and our very lives. Rape is on the increase, reported and unreported, and rape is not aggressive sexuality, it is sexualized aggression. As Kalamu ya Salaam, a Black male writer points out, "As long as male domination exists, rape will exist. Only women revolting and men made conscious of their responsibility to fight sexism can collectively stop rape."[1]

Differences between ourselves as Black women are also being misnamed and used to separate us from one another. As a Black lesbian feminist comfortable with the many different ingredients of my identity, and a woman committed to racial and sexual freedom from oppression, I find I am constantly being encouraged to pluck out some one aspect of myself and present this as the meaningful whole, eclipsing or denying the other parts of self. But this is a destructive and fragmenting way to live. My fullest concentration of energy is available to me only when I integrate all the parts of who I am, openly, allowing power from particular sources of my living to flow back and forth freely through all my different selves, without the restrictions of externally imposed definition. Only then can I bring myself and my energies as a whole to the service of those struggles which I embrace as part of my living.

A fear of lesbians, or of being accused of being a lesbian, has led many Black women into testifying against themselves. It has led some of us into destructive alliances, and others into despair and isolation. In the white women's communities, heterosexism is sometimes a result of identifying with the white patriarchy, a rejection of that interdependence between women-identified women which allows the self to be, rather than to be used in the service of men. Sometimes it reflects a die-hard belief in the protective coloration of heterosexual relationships, sometimes a self-hate which all women have to fight against, taught us from birth.

Although elements of these attitudes exist for all women, there are particular resonances of heterosexism and homophobia among Black women. Despite the fact that woman-bonding has a long and honorable history in the African and African-american communities, and despite the knowledge and accomplishments of many strong and creative women-identified Black women in the political, social and cultural fields, heterosexual Black women often tend to ignore or discount the existence and work of Black lesbians. Part of this attitude has come from an understandable terror of Black male attack within the close confines of Black society, where the punishment for any female self-assertion is still to be accused of being a lesbian and therefore unworthy of the attention or support of the scarce Black male. But part of this need to misname and ignore Black lesbians comes from a very real fear that openly women-identified Black women who are no longer dependent upon men for their self-definition may well reorder our whole concept of social relationships.

Black women who once insisted that lesbianism was a white woman's problem now insist that Black lesbians are a threat to Black nationhood, are consorting with the enemy, are basically un-Black. These accusations, coming from the very women to whom we look for deep and real understanding, have served to keep many Black lesbians in hiding, caught between the racism of white women and the homophobia of their sisters. Often, their work has been ignored, trivialized, or misnamed, as with the work of Angelina Grimke, Alice Dunbar-Nelson, Lorraine Hansberry. Yet women-bonded women have always been some part of the power of Black communities, from our unmarried aunts to the amazons of Dahomey.

And it is certainly not Black lesbians who are assaulting women and raping children and grandmothers on the streets of our communities.

Across this country, as in Boston during the spring of 1979 following the unsolved murders of twelve Black women, Black lesbians are spearheading movements against violence against Black women.

What are the particular details within each of our lives that can be scrutinized and altered to help bring about change? How do we redefine difference for all women? It is not our differences which separate women, but our reluctance to recognize those differences and to deal effectively with the distortions which have resulted from the ignoring and misnaming of those differences.

As a tool of social control, women have been encouraged to recognize only one area of human difference as legitimate, those differences which exist between women and men. And we have learned to deal across those differences with the urgency of all oppressed subordinates. All of us have had to learn to live or work or coexist with men, from our fathers on. We have recognized and negotiated these differences, even when this recognition only continued the old dominant/subordinate mode of human relationship, where the oppressed must recognize the masters' difference in order to survive.

But our future survival is predicated upon our ability to relate within equality. As women, we must root our internalized patterns of oppression within ourselves if we are to move beyond the most superficial aspects of social change. Now we must recognize differences among women who are our equals, neither inferior nor superior, and devise ways to use each others' difference to enrich our visions and our joint struggles.

The future of our earth may depend upon the ability of all women to identify and develop new definitions of power and new patterns of relating across difference. The old definitions have not served us, nor the earth that supports us. The old patterns, no matter how cleverly rearranged to imitate progress, still condemn us to cosmetically altered repetitions of the same old exchanges, the same old guilt, hatred, recrimination, lamentation, and suspicion.

For we have, built into all of us, old blueprints of expectation and response, old structures of oppression, and these must be altered at the same time as we alter the living conditions which are a result of those structures. For the master's tools will never dismantle the master's house.

As Paulo Freire shows so well in *The Pedagogy of the Oppressed*,[2] the true focus of revolutionary change is never merely the oppressive situations which we seek to escape, but that piece of the oppressor which is planted deep within each of us, and which knows only the oppressors' tactics, the oppressors' relationships.

Change means growth, and growth can be painful. But we sharpen self-definition by exposing the self in work and struggle together with those whom we define as different from ourselves, although sharing the same goals. For Black and white, old and young, lesbian and heterosexual women alike, this can mean new paths to our survival.

> We have chosen each other
> and the edge of each others battles
> the war is the same
> if we lose
> someday women's blood will congeal
> upon a dead planet
> if we win
> there is no telling
> we seek beyond history
> for a new and more possible meaning.[3]

NOTES

1. From "Rape: A Radical Analysis, An African-American Perspective" by Kalamu ya Salaam in *Black Books Bulletin*, vol. 6, no. 4 (1980).
2. Seabury Press, New York, 1970.
3. From "Outlines," unpublished poem.

2

Up Against the Wall

Cherríe Moraga

The cold in my chest comes
from having to decide

while the ice builds up on *this* side
of my new-york-apt.-bldg.-window
whose death
has been marked
upon the collective forehead
of this continent, this
shattering globe
the most indelibly.

Indelible. A catholic word
I learned
when I learned
that there were catholics and there
were not.
　　　　But somehow
we did not count the Jews
among the have-nots, only protestants
with their cold & bloodless god
with no candles/no incense/no bloody
sacrifice or spirits
lurking.

Protestantism. The white people's
religion.

. . .

First time I remember
seeing pictures of the Holocaust
was in the ninth grade and the moving pictures
were already there in my mind
somehow *before* they showed me
what I already understood
that these people were killed
for the spirit-blood
that runs through them.

They were like us in this.
Ethnic people with long last names
with vowels at the end or the wrong
type of consonants
combined   a colored kind of white people.

But let me tell you
first time I saw an actual
picture glossy photo of a lynching
I was already grown & active
& living & loving Jewish.
Black. White. Puerto
Rican.
        And the image blasted
my consciousness   split it
wide   I
had never thought   seen
heard   of such a thing
never imagined the look
of the man   the weight
dead
hanging
swinging
heavy
the fact   of the white people
cold
bloodless
looking on   It
had never occurred to me
I tell you   I
the nuns
failed to mention
this could happen, too

how *could* such a thing happen?

because somehow dark real dark
was not quite real
people killed
but some
thing not
taken to heart
in the same way it feels
to see white shaved/starved
burned/buried
the boned bodies stacked & bulldozed
into huge craters made by men
and machines
and at fifteen
before that movie screen
I kept running through my mind
and I'm only one
count one
it could be me
it could be me
I'm nothing
to this cruelty.

. . .

Somehow tonight,
is it the particular coldness
where I sleep with a cap
to keep it out
that causes me to toss
and turn the events of the last weeks
the last years of my life
around in my sleep?

Is it the same white coldness
that forces my back up
against the wall—*choose.*
Choose.

I cannot
choose nor forget

how simple
to fall back
upon rehearsed racial memory.

I work to remember
what I never dreamed possible
what my consciousness could never
contrive.

Whoever I am

I must believe
I am not
and will never be
the only
one
who suffers.

3

Androgyny As an Ideal for Human Development

*Ann Ferguson**

Androgyny: The Ideal Defined

The term "androgyny" has Greek roots: *andros* means man and *gynē*, woman. An androgynous person would combine some of each of the characteristic traits, skills, and interests that we now associate with the stereotypes of masculinity and femininity. It is not accurate to say that the ideal androgynous person would be both

*I'd like to acknowledge the help and encouragement of the socialist and feminist intellectual communities at the University of Massachusetts in Amherst, particularly the help of Sam Bowles, Jean Elshtain, and Dennis Delap, who read and commented extensively on earlier drafts of this [selection]. John Brentlinger and Susan Cayleff also provided feedback and comments. Many students who read the [selection] were helpful and supportive. A first version of this [selection] was read in the fall of 1974 at Bentley College, Boston, Massachusetts.

masculine and feminine, for there are negative and distorted personality characteristics associated in our minds with these ideas.[1] Furthermore, as we presently understand these stereotypes, they exclude each other. A masculine person is active, independent, aggressive (demanding), more self-interested than altruistic, competent and interested in physical activities, rational, emotionally controlled, and self-disciplined. A feminine person, on the other hand, is passive, dependent, non-assertive, more altruistic than self-interested (supportive of others), neither physically competent nor interested in becoming so, intuitive but not rational, emotionally open, and impulsive rather than self-disciplined. Since our present conceptions of masculinity and femininity thus defined exclude each other, we must think of an ideal androgynous person as one to whom these categories do not apply—one who is neither masculine nor feminine, but human: who transcends those old categories in such a way as to be able to develop positive human potentialities denied or only realized in an alienated fashion in the current stereotypes.

The ideal androgynous being, because of his or her combination of general traits, skills, and interests, would have no internal blocks to attaining self-esteem. He or she would have the desire and ability to do socially meaningful productive activity (work), as well as the desire and ability to be autonomous and to relate lovingly to other human beings. Of course, whether or not such an individual would be able to *achieve* a sense of autonomy, self-worth, and group contribution will depend importantly on the way the society in which he/she lives is structured. For example, in a classist society characterized by commodity production, none of these goals is attainable by anyone, no matter how androgynous, who comes from a class lacking the material resources to acquire (relatively) non-alienating work. In a racist and sexist society there are social roles and expectations placed upon the individual which present him/her with a conflict situation: either express this trait (skill, interest) and be considered a social deviant or outcast, or repress the trait and be socially accepted. The point, however, is that the androgynous person has the requisite skills and interests to be able to achieve these goals if only the society is organized appropriately.

An Ideal Love Relationship

One argument for the development of androgynous personalities (and the accompanying destruction of the sexual division of labor in production and reproduction) is that without such a radical change in male and female roles an ideal love relationship between the sexes is not possible. The argument goes like this. An ideal love between two mature people would be love between equals. I assume that such an ideal is the only concept of love that is historically compatible with our other developed ideals of political and social equality. But, as Shulamith Firestone argues,[2] an equal love relationship requires the vulnerability of each partner to the other. There is today, however, an unequal balance of power in male-female relationships. Contrary to the claims of the Natural Complement theory, it is not possible for men and women to be equal while playing the complementary sex roles taught in our society. The feminine role makes a woman less equal, less powerful, and less free than the masculine role makes men. In fact, it is the emotional understanding of this lack of equality in love relations between men and women which increasingly influences feminists to choose lesbian love relationships.

Let us consider the vulnerabilities of women in a heterosexual love relationship under the four classifications Juliet Mitchell gives for women's roles:[3] production, reproduction, socialization of children, and sexuality.

1. *Women's role in production.* In the United States [as of the late 1970s], 42 percent of women work, and about 33 percent of married women work in the wage-labor force. This is much higher than the 6 percent of women in the wage-labor force around the turn of the century, and higher than in other industrialized countries. Nonetheless, sex-role socialization affects women's power in two important ways. First, because of job segregation by sex into part-time and low-paying jobs, women, whether single or married, are at an economic disadvantage in comparison with men when it comes to supporting themselves. If they leave their husbands or lovers, they drop to a lower economic class, and many have to go on welfare. Second, women who have children and who also work in the wage-labor force have two jobs, not one: the responsibility for the major part of child-raising and housework, as well as the outside job. This keeps many housewives from seeking outside jobs, and makes them economically dependent on their husbands. Those who do work outside the home expend twice as much energy as the man and are less secure. Many women who try to combine career and motherhood find that the demands of both undermine their egos because they don't feel that they can do both jobs adequately.[4]

2. *Women's role in reproduction.* Although women currently monopolize the means of biological reproduction, they are at a disadvantage because of the absence of free contraceptives, adequate health care, and free legal abortions. A man can enjoy sex without having to worry about the consequences the way a woman does if a mistake occurs and she becomes pregnant. Women have some compensation in the fact that in the United States today they are favored legally over the father in their right to control of the children in case of separation or divorce. But this legal advantage (a victory won by women in the early 20th century in the ongoing power struggle between the sexes for control of children, i.e. control over social reproduction) does not adequately compensate for the disadvantages to which motherhood subjects one in this society.

3. *Women's role in socialization: as wife and mother.* The social status of women, and hence their self-esteem, is measured primarily in terms of how successful they are in their relationships as lovers, wives, and mothers. Unlike men, who learn that their major social definition is success in work, women are taught from childhood that their ultimate goal is love and marriage. Women thus have more invested in a love relationship than men, and more to lose if it fails. The "old maid" or the "divorcée" is still an inferior status to be pitied, while the "swinging bachelor" is rather envied.

The fact that men achieve self- and social definition from their work means that they can feel a lesser commitment to working out problems in a relationship. Furthermore, men have more options for new relationships than do women. The double standard in sexuality allows a man to have affairs more readily than his wife. Ageism is a further limitation on women: an older man is considered a possible lover by both younger and older women, but an older woman, because she is no longer the "ideal" sex object, is not usually considered a desirable lover by either male peers or by younger men.

A woman's role as mother places her in a more vulnerable position than the man. Taking care of children and being attentive to their emotional needs is very demanding work. Many times it involves conflicts between the woman's own needs and the needs of the child. Often it involves conflict and jealousy between husband and children for her attention and emotional energy. It is the woman's role to harmonize this conflict, which she often does at the expense of herself, sacrificing her private time and interests in order to provide support for the projects of her husband and children.

No matter how devoted a parent a father is, he tends to see his time with the children as play time, not as work time. His job interests and hobbies take precedence over directing his energy to children. Thus he is more independent than the woman, who sees her job as making husband and children happy. This is the sort of job that is never completed, for there are always more ways to make people happy. Because a woman sees her job to be supporting her husband and mothering her children, the woman sees the family as her main "product." This makes her dependent on their activities, lives, and successes for her own success, and she lives vicariously through their activities. But as her "product" is human beings, when the children leave, as they must, to live independent lives, middle age brings an end to her main social function. The woman who has a career has other problems, for she has had to support her husband's career over hers wherever there was a conflict, because she knows male egos are tied up with success and "making it" in this competitive society. Women's egos, on the other hand, are primed for failure. Successful women, especially successful women with unsuccessful husbands, are considered not "true" women, but rather as deviants, "castrating bitches," "ball-busters," and "masculine women." For all these reasons, a woman in a love relationship with a man is geared by the Natural Complement view of herself as a woman to put her interests last, to define herself in terms of husband and children, and therefore to be more dependent on them than they are on her.

A woman is also vulnerable in her role as mother because there are limited alternatives if, for example, she wishes to break off her relationship with the father of her children. As a mother, her social role in bringing up children is defined as more important, more essential for the well-being of the children than the man's. Therefore, she is expected to take the children to live with her, or else she is considered a failure as a mother. But the life of a divorced or single mother with children in a nuclear-family-oriented society is lonely and hard: she must now either do two jobs without the companionship of another adult, in a society where jobs for women are inadequate, or she must survive on welfare or alimony with a reduced standard of living. When this is the alternative, is it any wonder that mothers are more dependent on maintaining a relationship—even when it is not satisfying—than the man is?

4. *Women's role in sexuality.* A woman's sexual role is one in which she is both elevated by erotic romanticism and deflated to being a mere "cunt"—good for release of male sexual passions but interchangeable with other women. Because women play a subordinate role in society and are not seen as equal agents or as equally productive, men must justify a relationship with a particular woman by making her something special, mystifying her, making her better than other women. In fact, this idealization doesn't deal with her as a real *individual*; it treats her as either a beautiful object or as a mothering, supportive figure.

This idealization of women which occurs in the first stages of infatuation wears off as the couple settles into a relationship of some duration. What is left is the idea of woman as passive sex object whom one possesses and whose job as wife is to give the husband pleasure in bed. Since the woman is not seen as (and doesn't usually see herself as) active in sex, she tends to see sex as a duty rather than as a pleasure. She is not socially expected to take the active kind of initiative (even to the extent of asking for a certain kind of sex play) that would give her a sense of control over her sex life. The idea of herself as a body to be dressed and clothed in the latest media-advertised fashions "to please men" keeps her a slave to fashion and forces her to change her ego-ideal with every change in fashion. She can't see herself as an individual.

Androgyny as a Progressive Ideal

It is the sexual division of labor in the home and at work that perpetuates complementary sex roles for men and women. In underdeveloped societies with scarce material resources such an arrangement may indeed be the most rational way to allow for the most efficient raising of children and production of goods. But this is no longer true for developed societies. In this age of advanced technology, men's relative strength compared to women's is no longer important, either in war or in the production of goods. The gun and the spinning jenny have equalized the potential role of men and women in both repression and production. And the diaphragm, the pill, and other advances in the technology of reproduction have equalized the potential power of women and men to control their bodies and to reproduce themselves.[5] (The development of cloning would mean that men and women could reproduce without the participation of the opposite sex.)

We have seen how complementary sex roles and their extension to job segregation in wage labor make an ideal love relationship between equals impossible for men and women in our society. The questions that remain are: would the development of androgynous human beings through androgynous sex-role training be possible? If possible, would it allow for the development of equal love relationships? What other human potentials would androgyny allow to develop? And how would society have to be restructured in order to allow for androgynous human beings and equal love relationships?

There is good evidence that human babies are bisexual, and only *learn* a specific male or female identity by imitating and identifying with adult models. This evidence comes from the discovery that all human beings possess both male and female hormones (androgen and estrogen respectively), and also from concepts first developed at length by Freud. Freud argued that heterosexual identity is not achieved until the third stage of the child's sexual development. Sex identity is developed through the resolution of the Oedipus complex, in which the child has to give up a primary attachment to the mother and learn either to identify with, or love, the father. But Shulamith Firestone suggests that this process is not an inevitable one, as Freud presents it to be. Rather, it is due to the power dynamics of the patriarchal nuclear family.[6] Note that, on this analysis, if the sexual division of labor were destroyed, the mechanism that trains boys and girls to develop heterosexual sexual identities would also be destroyed. If fathers and mothers played equal nurturant roles in child-rearing and had equal social, economic, and political power outside the home, there would be no reason for the boy to have to reject his emotional side in order to gain the power associated with the male role. Neither would the girl have to assume a female role in rejecting her assertive, independent side in order to attain power indirectly through manipulation of males. As a sexual identity, bisexuality would then be the norm rather than the exception.

If bisexuality were the norm rather than the exception for the sexual identities that children develop,[7] androgynous sex roles would certainly be a consequence. For, as discussed above, the primary mechanism whereby complementary rather than androgynous sex roles are maintained is through heterosexual training, and through the socialization of needs for love and sexual gratification to the search for a love partner of the opposite sex. Such a partner is sought to complement one in the traits that one has repressed or not developed because in one's own sex such traits were not socially accepted.

The Androgynous Model

I believe that only androgynous people can attain the full human potential possible given our present level of material and social resources (and this only if society is radically restructured). Only such people can have ideal love relationships; and without such relationships, I maintain that none can develop to the fullest potential. Since human beings are social animals and develop through interaction and productive activity with others, such relationships are necessary.

Furthermore, recent studies have shown that the human brain has two distinct functions: one associated with analytic, logical, sequential thinking (the left brain), and the other associated with holistic, metaphorical, intuitive thought (the right brain). Only a person capable of tapping both these sides of him/herself will have developed to full potential. We might call this characteristic of the human brain "psychic bisexuality,"[8] since it has been shown that women in fact have developed skills which allow them to tap the abilities of the right side of the brain more than men, who on the contrary excel in the analytic, logical thought characteristic of the left side. The point is that men and women have the potential for using both these functions, and yet our socialization at present tends to cut off from one or the other of these parts of ourselves.[9]

What would an androgynous personality be like? My model for the ideal androgynous person comes from the concept of human potential developed by Marx in *Economic and Philosophical Manuscripts*. Marx's idea is that human beings have a need (or a potential) for free, creative, productive activity which allows them to control their lives in a situation of cooperation with others. Both men and women need to be equally active and independent; with an equal sense of control over their lives; equal opportunity for creative, productive activity; and a sense of meaningful involvement in the community.

Androgynous women would be just as assertive as men about their own needs in a love relationship: productive activity outside the home, the right to private time, and the freedom to form other intimate personal and sexual relationships. I maintain that being active and assertive—traits now associated with being "masculine"— are positive traits that all people need to develop. Many feminists are suspicious of the idea of self-assertion because it is associated with the traits of aggression and competitiveness. However, there is no inevitability to this connection: it results from the structural features of competitive, hierarchical economic systems, of which our own (monopoly capitalism) is one example. In principle, given the appropriate social structure, there is no reason why a self-assertive person cannot also be nurturant and cooperative.

Androgynous men would be more sensitive and aware of emotions than sex-role stereotyped "masculine" men are today. They would be more concerned with the feelings of all people, including women and children, and aware of conflicts of interests. Being sensitive to human emotions is necessary to an effective care and concern for others. Such sensitivity is now thought of as a "motherly," "feminine," or "maternal" instinct, but in fact it is a role and skill learned by women, and it can equally well be learned by men. Men need to get in touch with their own feelings in order to empathize with others, and, indeed, to understand themselves better so as to be more in control of their actions.

We have already discussed the fact that women are more vulnerable in a love relationship than men because many men consider a concern with feelings and emotions to be part of the woman's role. Women, then, are required to be more aware of everyone's feelings (if children and third parties are involved) than men, and they are under more pressure to harmonize the conflicts by sacrificing their own interests.

Another important problem with a non-androgynous love relationship is that it limits the development of mutual understanding. In general, it seems true that the more levels people can relate on, the deeper and more intimate their relationship is. The more experiences and activities they share, the greater their companionship and meaning to each other. And this is true for emotional experiences. Without mutual understanding of the complex of emotions involved in an ongoing love relationship, communication and growth on that level are blocked for both people. This means that, for both people, self-development of the sort that could come from the shared activity of understanding and struggling to deal with conflicts will not be possible.

In our society as presently structured, there are few possibilities for men and women to develop themselves through shared activities. Men and women share more activities with members of their own sex than with each other. Most women can't get jobs in our sexist, job-segregated society which allow them to share productive work with men. Most men just don't have the skills (or the time, given the demands of their wage-labor jobs) to understand the emotional needs of children and to share the activity of child-rearing equally with their wives.

How must our society be restructured to allow for the development of androgynous personalities? How can it be made to provide for self-development through the shared activities of productive and reproductive work? I maintain that this will not be possible (except for a small privileged elite) without the development of a democratic socialist society. In such a society no one would benefit from cheap labor (presently provided to the capitalist class by a part-time reserve army of women). Nor would anyone benefit from hierarchical power relationships (which encourage competition among the working class and reinforce male sex-role stereotypes as necessary to "making it" in society).

As society is presently constituted, the patriarchal nuclear family and women's reproductive work therein serve several crucial roles in maintaining the capitalist system. In the family, women do the unpaid work of social reproduction of the labor force (child-rearing). They also pacify and support the male breadwinner in an alienating society where men who are not in the capitalist class have little control of their product or work conditions. Men even come to envy their wives' relatively non-alienated labor in child-rearing rather than dealing with those with the real privilege, the capitalist class. Since those in power relations never give them up without a struggle, it is utopian to think that the capitalist class will allow for the elimination of the sexual division of labor without a socialist revolution with feminist priorities. Furthermore, men in the professional and working classes must be challenged by women with both a class and feminist consciousness to begin the process of change.

In order to eliminate the subordination of women in the patriarchal nuclear family and the perpetuation of sex-role stereotypes therein, there will need to be a radical reorganization of child-rearing. Father and mother must have an equal commitment to raising children. More of the reproductive work must be socialized—for example, by community child care, perhaps with parent cooperatives. Communal living is one obvious alternative which would de-emphasize biological parenthood and allow homosexuals and bisexuals the opportunity to have an equal part in relating to children. The increased socialization of child care would allow parents who are incompatible the freedom to dissolve their relationships without denying their children the secure, permanent loving relationships they need with both men and women. A community responsibility for child-rearing would provide children with male and female models other than their biological parent—models that they would be able to see and relate to emotionally.

Not only would men and women feel an equal responsibility to do reproductive work, they would also expect to do rewarding, productive work in a situation where they had equal opportunity. Such a situation would of course require reduced work-weeks for parents, maternity and paternity leaves, and the development of a technology of reproduction which would allow women complete control over their bodies.

As for love relationships, with the elimination of sex roles and the disappearance, in an overpopulated world, of any biological need for sex to be associated with procreation, there would be no reason why such a society could not transcend sexual gender. It would no longer matter what biological sex individuals had. Love relationships, and the sexual relationships developing out of them, would be based on the individual meshing-together of androgynous human beings.

NOTES

1. I owe these thoughts to Jean Elshtain and members of the Valley Women's Union in Northampton, Massachusetts, from discussions on androgyny.

2. Shulamith Firestone, *The Dialectic of Sex* (New York: William Morrow, 1970), chap. 6.

3. Juliet Mitchell, *Woman's Estate* (New York: Random House, 1971).

4. Socialization into complementary sex roles is responsible not only for job segregation practices' keeping women in low-paid service jobs which are extensions of the supportive work women do in the home as mothers, but also for making it difficult for women to feel confident in their ability to excel at competitive "male-defined" jobs.

5. Thanks to Sam Bowles for this point.

6. Firestone, op. cit. The boy and girl both realize that the father has power in the relationship between him and the mother, and that his role, and not the mother's, represents the possibility of achieving economic and social power in the world and over one's life. The mother, in contrast, represents nurturing and emotionality. Both boy and girl, then, in order to get power for themselves, have to reject the mother as a love object—the boy, because he is afraid of the father as rival and potential castrator; and the girl, because the only way as a girl she can attain power is through manipulating the father. So she becomes a rival to her mother for her father's love. The girl comes to identify with her mother and to choose her father and, later, other men for love objects; while the boy identifies with his father, sublimates his sexual attraction to his mother into super-ego (will power), and chooses mother substitutes, other women, for his love objects.

7. It should be understood here that no claim is being made that bisexuality is more desirable than homo- or heterosexuality. The point is that with the removal of the social

mechanisms in the family that channel children into heterosexuality, there is no reason to suppose that most of them will develop in that direction. It would be more likely that humans with androgynous personalities would be bisexual, the assumption here being that there are no innate biological preferences in people for sexual objects of the same or opposite sex. Rather, this comes to be developed because of emotional connections of certain sorts of personality characteristics with the male and female body, characteristics which develop because of complementary sex-role training, and which would not be present without it.

The other mechanism which influences people to develop a heterosexual identity is the desire to reproduce. As long as the social institution for raising children is the heterosexual nuclear family, and as long as society continues to place social value on biological parent-hood, most children will develop a heterosexual identity. Not, perhaps, in early childhood, but certainly after puberty, when the question of reproduction becomes viable. Radical socialization and collectivization of child-rearing would thus have to characterize a society before bisexuality would be the norm not only in early childhood, but in adulthood as well. For the purposes of developing androgynous individuals, however, full social bisexuality of this sort is not necessary. All that is needed is the restructuring of the sex roles of father and mother in the nuclear family so as to eliminate the sexual division of labor there.

8. Charlotte Painter, Afterword to C. Painter and M. J. Moffet, eds., *Revelations: Diaries of Women* (New York: Random House, 1975).

9. It is notable that writers, painters, and other intellectuals, who presumably would need skills of both sorts, have often been misfits in the prevalent complementary sex sterotyping. In fact, thinkers as diverse as Plato (in the *Symposium*) and Virginia Woolf (in A *Room of One's Own*) have suggested that writers and thinkers need to be androgynous to tap all the skills necessary for successful insight.

4

Changing the Situation:
Steps Toward an Egalitarian Family Policy

Richard H. de Lone

. . . to criticize inequality and to desire equality is not, as is sometimes suggested, to cherish the romantic illusion that men are equal in character and intelligence. It is to hold that, while their natural endowments differ profoundly, it is the mark of a civilized society to aim at eliminating such inequalities as have their source not in individual differences . . . which are a source of social energy, [and] are more likely to ripen and find expression if social inequalities are, as far as practicable, diminished.

R. H. TAWNEY, *Equality*

. . . The principle of equal opportunity has not only failed to help us produce greater equality of distribution (which is not necessarily even implied in the principle); but has failed in its own terms, as the differential odds that face children born in different social circumstances reveal. Equal opportunity as a principle has encouraged the marriage between children's policy and egalitarian policy. Specifically it has encouraged reformers to rely on strategies of individual assistance to children (and sometimes their families) as the antidotes to social inequality.

Implicit in attempts to solve inequality by helping individuals is the belief that social inequalities are caused by individual differences. This is a more sophisticated version of the notion that we are all masters of our fates and it is a natural companion of market economic theory. What this view, in both its cruder and its more sophisticated versions, fails to consider sufficiently is that causality also runs the other way, that social structure influences development. Accordingly, reformers' efforts to change social structure and its dynamics through changing individuals are often attempts to battle against the tides.

The disregard of Americans for social structure and the distributive mechanisms of society is a logical result of our atomistic social theory of liberal culture. The whole process—from disregarding the influence of structure to blaming individuals for inequality—has been recapitulated in the operations of various helping institutions which, in their own structure, in their interaction with the larger social structure (such as the interaction of schooling with the occupational structure) or in the ways they mirror and re-create characteristics of that larger structure have too often produced help that also hurts. Whether in the "helping" institutions or the society at large, structure in a variety of forms undermines good intentions. . . .

If, as we have speculated, the individual is an active participant in his or her development, and if development proceeds not through "inputs" but through situations, efforts to enhance development by aiming programs at individuals are misconceived. These include almost all service-based strategies. Services are essential, and some important changes in services will help alter the structure of children's situations. But at the risk of repetition it must be emphasized that services cannot substantially affect social inequality through "improving" individuals. Nor does it help to wish that we could improve their families.

To the extent that families help transmit inequality, they are scarcely more than intermediate mechanisms shaped by structural inequalities. To put the matter most simply, families do not breed inequality—they reflect it. In constructing a guiding theory of social reality, the child derives in part from what his or her family *is* a sense of what he or she *will become*. Thus, efforts to change what families "do" to children will have little effect on children's futures, at least with respect to social equality. But efforts to alter what families "are," specifically with reference to their social and economic status, may affect them in two ways. First, an equalization of the distribution of social benefits will by definition affect the social status of adults and of children as they become adults; second, it will alter the settings that influence children directly and through their families—in short, it will change the whole developmental context. Changing the circumstances of families changes the situations of development. . . .

Individually aimed service programs that seek to promote equality by "improving" individuals rely on a deterministic philosophy that takes no account of the individual's autonomous participation (as theory builder) in his or her own development. They miss the essential equilibrium of the developmental situation: the balance between development and social structure. To put it another way, an intervention must be extremely powerful to alter that equilibrium—sufficient in scope to influence both the life chances and the theory of social reality that a child constructs out of the continuity and congruity of messages provided by social structure and history. . . .

If social programs cannot alter the developmental situation from "within" the child—that is, if programs of individual or family assistance cannot alter significantly and systematically the process by which an individual constructs a social theory of reality and participates in his or her own development—social policy can, at least in theory, alter the social structure from which a child derives information for that theory. To provide a crude example, the situation of racial discrimination is not affected by our providing services or counseling to black children or their families, nor is racial discrimination likely to be eliminated by our trying to change the attitudes and capabilities of individual black children. But if the "tangible facts" of the employment barriers and inequalities of social and economic status that now exist for blacks were, by the wave of some magic wand, removed, we would expect the developmental patterns of black and white children to be similar. . . .

. . . [W]e believe that a necessary condition for equalizing the circumstances of development, for providing every child with a potentially full future, and for eliminating the insults and injuries of inequality is the changing of some of the basic patterns of society, including its mechanisms for distributing income, opportunity, power, and experience. The creation of a more equal society is synonymous, in our view, with the creation of a more egalitarian setting for development. . . .

. . . [A] policy that aims to equalize the life chances and developmental situations of children must meet two primary conceptual tests. First, it must both acknowledge and come to grips with the inegalitarian premises of the economic side of liberalism. Second, it must promote changes in the situations of development through alterations in social structure. These two conceptual tasks are closely allied operations, if our basic argument is correct, since inequalities in the economic structure, manifest in the class and caste systems, are the framework of the master settings of development. Together, they imply the need to equalize the actual conditions of adults as the prerequisite for creating parity (not sameness) in the developmental situations of children and to achieve a new equilibrium between development and social structure. No other kind of intervention seems likely to be of sufficient scope to alter the historically rooted probabilities, social dynamics, and developmental mechanisms that lead children from different classes or caste groups to such divergent adult futures.

From the vantage point of the individual child, an egalitarian policy should aim for greater equality in the conditions of experience in the present—both quantitative (e.g., material welfare of the family) and qualitative (e.g., the class- or caste-bound nature of experience as reflected, for instance, in cognitive requirements). Further, it should eradicate class- and caste-linked probabilities governing life chances. To make this last point another way, it should lead to an equalization of options and realized opportunities among classes and castes (and, with specific reference to occupational opportunity, sexes). Essentially this means reducing to insignificance in fact the caste and class lines which Americans have long held insignificant in rhetoric. These two broad aims—equalizing the conditions of experience and equalizing life chances—are, of course, closely related since the dynamics of a society in which there is serious inequality of condition lead inexorably to inequality of life chances through the differential situations of development.

The key to a strategy for policy that meets these conceptual tests and that meets these criteria for individual empowerment can be captured in a single word: *redistribution*. This means redistribution not only of income and other basic resources, based on an acknowledgment of the relative nature of deprivation, but also of power—a concept that is often thought of as "political" but that clearly has economic dimensions as well. To be relatively poor, for instance, is to have severe limits on one's ability to influence the decisions of officials in publicly funded service systems, some of which the poor are far more likely than the more affluent to come in contact with (such as the courts) and others of which they are far more likely to be excluded from (such as the schools). This powerlessness of the poor is evident at the level of policy (for instance, the basis on which eligibility for a welfare program is determined or the mode of pupil classification in school) and at the level of individual decision makers (for instance, the vice-principal who issues a suspension, the family court judge who separates a child from parents). In a world where public services are a substantial adjunct to families, this is no small issue for children. Likewise, to be poor is by definition to have little influence in the economic decisions of a society and to barter in the political marketplace from a position of weakness, trading votes for promises with little recourse when they are broken. (This issue helps explain correlations between voting frequency and income.) . . .

What can public policy do to confront such a basic and deeply entrenched problem? We believe the rights traditionally defined by liberalism as limited to the political sphere must be extended into the economic sphere through the political and legislative processes. . . .

In less abstract terms, public policy must attempt to reduce the economic and experiential distance between classes through policies of full employment, targeted economic development and investment policies, affirmative action, and income redistribution. . . .

Beyond economic redistribution . . . lies the ultimate goal of an egalitarian society: to create a world in which each child and parent have the opportunity not only to make decent lives but, in making their lives, to help make history. This would be a world in which the power to influence and shape the collective destiny, a power now concentrated in the hands of relatively few, was diffused among the many who currently have little more than the power to "muddle through."

5

Toward Economic Justice for Women

The Women's Economic Agenda Working Group of the Institute for Policy Studies

When the private economy fails to provide opportunity or security to the majority of women—when in fact it threatens further impoverishment and heightened insecurity—then there is no alternative but to press for public action. Even in a time when government is hostile to social activism and apparently indifferent to women's economic plight, we need to envision the kinds of programs that *could* work for women. We need something that goes beyond a defense of existing programs or a demand for restoration of old programs: We need a programmatic vision that draws specifically on women's experience, and on the insights we have gained from the feminist struggle for dignity and equality. In particular, we believe that programs addressed to women's economic status should be based on the following principles:

- We need to recognize the varieties of American families. Families maintained by women alone are not "pathological" or "broken" because they do not have a man living in them. All families deserve social supports to strengthen them.
- As a nation, we need to treat children as the precious resource that they are. All children are "legitimate" and none should be denied adequate nutrition, health care or educational opportunity on the basis of their race, sex or parents' marital status.
- We need to value the work women do, paid as well as unpaid, as homemakers and caregivers. There should be recognition and financial reward for the time taken out of the labor force by mothers when their children are young. At the same time, because the care of young children occupies a relatively short time in the lives of most women, all women need an opportunity for education and vocational preparation to achieve their occupational potential. Ultimately, both men and women should have the economic security to make occupational choices freely and to share the responsibility for raising children.
- Public programs to enhance women's economic status should be designed to counter not only sex discrimination but also other powerful systems of oppres-

376

sion that limit women's economic prospects. These include racism, discrimination against older citizens, and discrimination against the disabled.
- Finally, we must, as a nation, move beyond the harsh laissez-faire assumption that each person is an economic island, and that dependency on others is a mark of failure or inferiority. We reject the division of people into categories labeled "dependent" and "independent." Dependence is a universal experience; even the most ruggedly "independent" person usually has others who provide the food and shelter, or the invisible logistic support that makes such "independence" possible. Whether bought with marriage or money, such independence is spurious. Rather than perpetuate and glorify the myth of individual independence, we would build toward a society structured to acknowledge our collective responsibility to each other. It is our interdependence, after all, that makes us human.

Is it possible to design government programs that are consistent with our principles? Conventional wisdom says "no," and it is true that government programs to aid economically vulnerable individuals have been deeply flawed. The price of receiving benefits on means-tested programs such as AFDC and Food Stamps is often personal humiliation and an invasion of privacy. Yet this does not mean that there is something inherently undignified about reliance on public social programs. As the black women who spearheaded the welfare rights movement of the 1960s argued, AFDC was *designed* to be humiliating to its beneficiaries and miserly in its benefits, precisely to discourage enrollment by all but the most desperate. If programs were designed to *encourage* utilization and if they were designed to be accountable to their clients, there need be no indignity, and no stigma.

Government programs have often been punitive, but they could equally well build people's self-esteem and empower individuals and communities. The experience of so many "alternative" services, such as feminist health centers, refugee and storefront community centers, shows that services do not have to be professionally dominated and impersonally administered to work. Instead, they can be designed to promote clients' participation and decision making. Grass-roots alternative services cannot substitute for government spending (in fact, most have been dependent on government spending through OEO, CETA or other programs), but they can provide models for the creation of participatory and democratically administered social programs.

Our focus here is on feminist solutions to women's economic problems, but this does not mean that public social programs should be, or will continue to be, primarily a women's concern. Women's economic vulnerability is heightened by our responsibility for children, but men—especially minority and blue-collar men—share in the adverse effects of high technology, corporate mobility and the shift to a service economy. In a more automated, computerized future, a growing proportion of both men and women will no longer be able to find economic security in the workforce—either because there are not enough jobs or not enough secure, well-paying jobs. That future can be disastrous or it can be promising—depending on whether we are prepared to abandon our increasingly obsolete distinctions between "dependence" and "independence," and "work" and "non-work," and recognize that the welfare of each of us is part of the responsibility of all of us.

Getting There From Here: Key Agenda Items

We propose a three-part economic program, both as a long-term goal consistent with the principles listed above and as a focus for short-term organizing efforts: (1) Income support, through a single, consolidated system at an adequate standard of living. (2) Public sector job creation aimed at building up both the physical and social infrastructure of communities, and based on the principle of pay equity. (3) Public sector leverage to create and improve private sector jobs for women.

Each element of this program is essential, and the three together are mutually reinforcing:

- Income support is essential for the survival of unemployed and underemployed women already in poverty. We see income support as a key agenda item and not as a stop-gap measure until more and better jobs become available, for two reasons: First, income support is the only way to provide concrete recognition of the work—usually women's—of homemaking and childraising. Second, in a more automated and computerized future, public sector income support of one form or another will become increasingly essential to the economic security of all those workers, male and female, who are displaced by the new technology. Technological innovation in the workplace can have a positive and liberating effect, but only if we have income support to protect displaced workers, job training and new forms of employment for them.
- Public sector job creation is essential not only to generate employment but to meet vital needs for human services and a liveable environment. Many areas of need—such as health care and housing for low-income families—are not sufficiently profitable to attract private investment. These needs can only be met outside of the for-profit sector, through public enterprise and development.
- Public sector leverage to expand and improve women's job opportunities in the private sector is necessary if for no other reason than that most women are employed in the private sector, and must ultimately win their economic battles there. But only public measures—both incentives and sanctions—can help working women hold their own against employer initiatives such as unfair union-busting tactics, homework, and detrimental applications of technology.

Both income supports and public sector job creation can improve women's status within the private sector workforce and augment public sector leverage. The stronger the safety net of income support and human services, the less vulnerable working women are to exploitation and intimidation on the job. And economic rights won in the public sector—such as pay equity—exert an upward pressure on conditions and benefits in the private sector. Thus the three elements of this program work together; in what follows, we outline each in greater detail.

Unemployment and Income Support Systems

The present system of income support is (1) fragmented, with different programs for the elderly, the unemployed, families with young children, and the disabled; (2) inadequate in the levels of support provided; and (3) structurally biased against women. This bias is built into the two-tiered structure of the present income support system: a primary system, including unemployment compensation and social security, which was designed to help unemployed and retired male wage earners; and a secondary system, which was designed primarily for families without male breadwinners and includes AFDC and other means-tested programs.

Within the primary system, unemployment compensation excludes disproportionate numbers of women workers, largely because they do not have a history of uninterrupted, full-time employment, and provides inadequate support for those who are eligible, forcing many to turn to the secondary system. Similarly, social security payments, calculated solely on the basis of paid employment, penalize women whose work was primarily or partially unpaid labor. The secondary system provides less than minimal support, and in other ways operates to lock women into, rather than to provide a bridge out of, poverty.

Unemployment insurance was founded on the principle that people who lose their jobs are innocent victims and therefore should be helped rather than punished during the period of income loss. This was to be done through a combination of adequate and non-stigmatizing income support, aid in finding appropriate work, and/or training to develop new skills. Unfortunately, this set of services and support has always been limited to a relatively privileged group of workers—full-time, regular workers. The irony, of course, is that it is marginal workers, disproportionately women and minorities, who most need these services as well as the income provided through unemployment insurance. Those ineligible for benefits must turn to the secondary system with its low benefit levels, harsh eligibility requirements and inadequate health care and other services—all of which perpetuate poverty rather than empower the recipients.[1]

On the premise that all who work, including those whose work is the unpaid labor of creating a home and/or taking care of dependents (old and disabled as well as young) are equally deserving of support and aid, we advocate the development of a single, universal, non-stigmatizing income support system. Because it values all work, such a system would provide an adequate standard of living for *all* workers, as unemployment was intended to do for a limited group of workers. It would also provide for those who, through no fault of their own, e.g., physical or mental disability or injury, are unable to support themselves. As a number of surveys show, however, the majority of those needing income support, including those on welfare, would like to be self-supporting through their own earnings as quickly as possible. Thus income support programs must include provisions that recognize the special needs of women seeking to enter the workforce.

We propose the following approach to unemployment and income support systems:

1. The development of *one income support system* that provides an adequate standard of living for all who are unable to enter the paid workforce, who cannot find paid work or who cannot find work that pays enough to sustain an adequate standard of living—and which does not discriminate against those, such as elderly women, whose work has been unpaid.

2. The development of *policies and programs that recognize the legitimate social contributions of child-care and other familial responsibilities,* such as care of the elderly, done mostly by women. These programs would include at a minimum:
   - tax credits for employer-aided child care (e.g., employer-subsidized child care, employer child-care benefits and family leave benefits, as well as employer-provided child care).
   - eligibility for income support when child-care needs and familial responsibilities cannot be reconciled with employment conditions, and lead to job loss (such as a shift change to a time when day care is unavailable, or job loss for one spouse when the other's job is relocated).
   - an extension of eligibility for income support during unemployment to part-time workers.
   - partial compensation for those unable to support their families on their earnings, whether because of low wages, too few hours, and/or a high dependency burden.

3. *Recognition of and affirmative action to address special disadvantages faced by women in the workforce,* such as sex discrimination and harassment, including:
   - resources and training on how to recognize, combat and redress the problems of sex, race, age and other forms of discrimination.
   - adequate resources for the development of job training and placement, with an emphasis on training needs specific to women (including training for non-traditional jobs and provisions for child care).

4. Support of *experimental projects to use income support benefits as training subsidies or as start-up capital* for individual small businesses, community enterprises or worker-owned businesses.
   This system would evolve through an expansion of the present unemployment compensation system. As with similar systems in Europe, it would include those entering the labor market for the first time, or reentering it after a period of full-time child care. Through services, job training and income

support at a level sufficient to maintain dignity and well-being, it would seek to integrate such people fully and effectively into the workforce.

Public Sector Job Creation

Job creation in the public sector could begin to solve twin problems facing our society: widespread unemployment and the critical need for basic human services, such as dependent care and home health care.

The public sector has traditionally been a source of better paid jobs for women and minority workers. More susceptible to outside pressure to enforce affirmative action, the public sector has not been able to disregard the demands of women and minority workers. Over the past five years, for example, the public sector has been the focus of efforts to implement pay equity for women, a crucial component of the fight against discrimination.

An innovative approach to public sector employment programs could also improve the quality of public services and contribute to revitalizing depressed communities. Among the many national precedents for public service jobs are WPA, Senior Community Service Employment Program, and Public Service Employment under CETA. But misconceptions surround the jobs in these programs. Often seen as limited to dam and road construction, or dismissed as "make-work," public service jobs have in fact included human services like child care, which was provided by the government during World War II for "Rosie the Riveters," and programs like Head Start in the sixties and seventies. Caring for the nation's children can hardly be considered "make-work."

One criticism of the public service employment programs of the 1970s is that they did not improve the long-term employability of unskilled participants. However, these programs made it possible for a variety of community organizations to start or expand community development programs and to address many unmet social needs. Ideally, a public sector employment program should enhance the skills and income of participants as well as fill public needs. It can accomplish both of these goals if it is tied to the longer-range development plans of the nation's communities.

At present, major public needs go unmet in our country, both in the physical and in the social infrastructure which form the foundation of a healthy community economic base. Physical infrastructure needs include refurbishing water systems, repairing roads and bridges, and many other construction projects. These construction jobs should be made available to women on an equal basis with men. But public works jobs such as these are only part of what is needed to rebuild declining communities and maintain healthy ones.

As recent experience with programs to revitalize low-income neighborhoods has shown, a community's economic development proceeds from a social as well as a physical infrastructure—including job training and placement, health services, child care, care for the elderly, housing services, and programs for youth.

The problem is that human-centered jobs, mostly held by women, have been consistently undervalued and most job creation efforts have instead emphasized rebuilding the physical infrastructure. Even in such programs, with predominantly male jobholders, more funds have often gone into equipment than into employment. Rebuilding the infrastructure, while breaking down sex barriers in those jobs, is an important national goal, but equally important is the improvement of the quality of life of children, the elderly, the handicapped and the infirm.

A commitment to rebuilding the social infrastructure of low-income communities and to maintaining it throughout society would benefit women in three major ways. First, by creating jobs that require experience many women possess, such programs would expand their employment options. Second, because women and their children comprise the majority of residents in low-income neighborhoods, a social infrastructure program designed to enhance the community's potential for economic development would improve the lives of these women and their families and thereby further expand their employment opportunities. Third, because the job of maintaining the social fabric of families and communities has traditionally fallen on women, many of whom are employed full-time outside the home, these programs would promote a more equitable sharing of social responsibilities.

To advance the economic position of women, we advocate the following innovative approach to public sector job creation:

1. The development of *programs to build the social infrastructure of our nation's communities* through an expansion of day care, health services, services for youth and for the elderly, and other programs tied to long-term community development.
2. The development of programs for *youth training and employment,* such as a youth conservation corps and programs that would tie youth employment to the development of the social infrastructure outlined above.
3. The expansion of *efforts to maintain and expand the physical infrastructure,* particularly in depressed communities, with an accompanying commitment to hire women in non-traditional jobs.
4. A commitment to the *maintenance of existing community services* in vital areas such as public transit and mental health.
5. The *enforcement of pay equity standards in all public employment* as provided for by Title IX of the U.S. Code of Civil Rights. The implementation of pay equity in the public sector, which will eventually have ripple effects into pay scales for women in the private sector and will establish precedents for litigation in private firms.

Building the Social Infrastructure:
Three Vital Areas: Health Care

Building the social infrastructure will require public effort in a number of areas, but none are more important than health, housing and education. In each of these areas, women have special needs and face special problems of discrimination. Programs to provide services in these areas can also generate jobs at many levels of skill and education; for example, in housing construction and maintenance, and in community health education and counseling. But the first priority must be to provide services and meet the needs which, in these areas, have reached crisis proportions.

HEALTH CARE   Health care costs are a source of anxiety for almost all Americans. For many poor and near-poor women, it makes more sense to remain on AFDC and retain Medicaid eligibility than to take a job that offers limited or no health insurance. Medicaid itself is gravely inadequate. Coverage varies arbitrarily from state to state, and, since the passage of the Hyde Amendment in 1977, abortion—an option that is vital to all women's self-determination—is not covered at all. Furthermore, Medicaid eligibility requirements exclude large numbers of people who have no way of paying for their own medical insurance or health services. Thus, for example, the alarmingly high rate of black infant mortality reflects the inability of many poor black women to obtain such a vital and necessary service as prenatal care.[2]

We believe that it is time to replace the present patchwork of Medicaid, Medicare, and assorted private insurance programs. As a starting point for a renewed national commitment to health care as a human right, we support a single, tax-supported program offering universal, comprehensive health care for all Americans.

We propose the following approach to health care:

1. A *National Health Service*, publicly managed and community-accountable, such as proposed in the Dellums bill.
2. *Health programs that* draw on the wealth of experience of the women's health movement and feminist health centers, which *emphasize prevention and patient participation and empowerment*, as opposed to bureaucratic and professional dominance.

Building the Social Infrastructure:
Three Vital Areas: Housing

HOUSING   An increasing source of poverty and even family disruption is the housing crisis faced by families with children—especially those headed by women. In the rental market discrimination against families with children is growing and poses a problem particularly for people of color, and in regions where many new immigrants have settled, the Sun Belt and the Southwest.[3] In the public sector housing subsidies have been drastically reduced; particularly, the Section 8 subsidy, which enabled poor families to escape the poverty ghettos of housing projects by helping them pay the rent on housing wherever they chose to live.[4] And in both public and private housing sectors, the homes of poor people are being destroyed or taken and not replaced to make way for development and gentrification.

Together, the shelter crisis in the public and private sectors has become a crisis of existence for the poorest families, because a family that does not provide shelter for their children can lose them, and those without addresses cannot receive official help. In the recession of 1982, media attention focused on the most recent poor—such as laid-off steel and auto workers—and it was commonly assumed that those who had already been in poverty were no worse off than they had been. Yet there is a great deal of evidence that those at the bottom dropped from poverty to destitution and family disruption, with children going into foster care and ex-AFDC mothers showing up in shelters as part of the new homeless.[5]

A shelter program for women in poverty should include:

1. Extension of the 1968 Fair Housing Act to include a *prohibition of discrimination against families with children*.
2. *Housing subsidy* programs, building in the maximum amount of choice and flexibility, e.g., housing counseling that facilitates choices outside of racial and economic ghettos.
3. Programs that protect women against the loss of not only shelter but also community and equity upon divorce, particularly in "community property" states where the family home is sold in order for the joint property to be split. A *subsidized buyout* program, whereby the government or private lenders buy out the non-custodial parent's equity, would prevent the disruption of a divorce-occasioned move for the children as well as maintain stability and equity for the custodial parent, usually the mother.
4. *New forms of housing*, with child-care centers, joint laundry centers, and other facilities designed for married as well as single mothers' work and family needs.

Building the Social Infrastructure:
Three Vital Areas: Public Education

PUBLIC EDUCATION   For women and girls, access to high quality, non-racist, non-sexist public education remains a top priority. The notion of "excellence in education" means little to women without access to equal educational opportunities. Moreover, in a labor market characterized by constant change, education must both prepare workers with basic skills to take them through the several occupations they are likely to hold, and provide a life-long experience that has a realistic and productive association with the world of work.

To ensure educational excellence and equity for the country's poorest citizens, women and their children, we advocate:

1. A strong federal role in public education at all levels through the *strengthened enforcement of laws* that guarantee access to quality education regardless

of sex, race, national origin, religion and disabling condition, including Title IX of the Education Amendments of 1972, Title VI of the Civil Rights Act of 1964, Section 504 of the Rehabilitation Act of 1973, and the *Lau* Decision.

2. Programs to *decrease high school dropout rates among female students*, particularly among those young women who are, or are about to become, parents.
3. *Comprehensive career education* programs (K–higher education) that will provide students with a working knowledge of the world of work, make the connection between that world and their educational experience, and encourage female students of all races and minority male students to consider a broad range of occupations.
4. *Financial assistance* for continuing education and training—vocational, undergraduate, graduate and professional. This should include the elimination of education-related financial assistance, such as scholarships, as an income source in the qualifying process for means-tested programs.
5. Free, quality *child care support* services at all education levels.
6. *Restructuring teacher education* programs and establishing human development certification requirements aimed at sensitizing educators and training them to provide a non-stereotyped affirmative education.
7. Continued and increased funding of the *Women's Educational Equity Act Program* (WEEAP) which supports the development of non-sexist, multicultural instructional, counseling and other education supplemental materials.
8. Targeted programs to improve the *access of females and minority males to quality technical vocational education*, particularly in new and emerging technologies.

Improving Women's Options in the Private Sector

While public sector jobs have provided, and can continue to provide, women with increased employment opportunities, any agenda for economic equity must also address the position of women in the private economy. We need policies that go beyond vague prescriptions for stimulating economic growth and beyond traditional affirmative action programs, though these should be strengthened, not abandoned. These policies must aim both to generate new, high-quality jobs and to improve existing jobs.

Public policy can improve women's options in existing jobs in a number of ways: by enforcing women's right to organize, by raising the minimum wage, by encouraging improvements in the quality of work-life, and by establishing and enforcing the principle of pay equity. The right to organize is key to advancing women's economic status. While unionization alone will not equalize men's and women's wages, increased unionization in occupations that employ large numbers of women could provide a basis for a new tier of middle-level jobs. On the average in 1980 unionized women workers earned 30 percent higher wages than non-union women workers.[6] In addition, collective bargaining can be used to make a range of other gains: to increase workers' participation in decision making about the applications of new technology, to create job ladders for upward mobility, and to win benefits such as child care.

A major obstacle to organizing is the increasing assault from management. As mentioned earlier, the use of unfair labor practices by employers has risen dramatically over the last decade. Because the penalties for pursuing unfair tactics are so inconsequential for management, they have little incentive not to do so. The problem is both that existing labor relations laws are not enforced promptly and effectively, and that these laws are themselves in need of reform to truly guarantee the right to organize and bargain collectively.

As industrial decline accelerates job loss in many areas, the need grows for innovative approaches to job creation. Many states are experimenting with new financing mechanisms for young or expanding enterprise, targeting new business creation with minority and/or women's ownership, tax credits for firms that create new well-paying jobs, and state involvement in research and development. To expand opportunities for women workers, these state development efforts must be aimed at creating high-quality jobs, not simply more jobs.

Local communities are assessing their economies in detail and considering what options are available to expand and strengthen their economic base. The more women's, minority and labor organizations participate in these efforts, the more likely their outcome will contribute to the pursuit of economic justice.

Unlike previous recessions, the recent recession left many workers in declining industries permanently displaced. Among these dislocated workers, women have found it more difficult than men to find work with pay at or above the jobs they have lost.[7] A variety of new programs, including severance benefits, relocation assistance, and special counseling and training, have been proposed to help dislocated workers make the transition into new employment. To benefit women, such programs must take into consideration the additional barriers to reemployment women face, such as housing discrimination and the need for child care for parents entering training programs. However, a danger exists that programs designed for dislocated workers will create a two-tier system in which dislocated workers receive most of the benefits to the detriment of long-term disadvantaged workers, who include a large number of women.

The solution to this dilemma lies in improving the employment security system for all workers. Improved training and education opportunities should be available to both dislocated and disadvantaged workers and should also be an integral part of the expanded social welfare programs discussed above.

Another area of concern for women is the introduction of new workplace technology, which has a tremendous impact on the character of new jobs being created. While technology has more often been used to deskill work than to upgrade it, this need not be so. Economist Eileen Appelbaum argues that, by rushing to production methods that use low-cost labor, industry is sacrificing the long-run productivity gains that only investments in worker expertise can bring.[8] How technology might be used to enhance work and to strengthen opportunities for upward mobility should be a top research priority.

Finally, workers' needs vary over their lifetime and employers should respond to changing patterns of work and family responsibilities. Flex-time allows workers to design their work schedules around other responsibilities, and could potentially relieve commuter traffic congestion. Paid parenting sabbaticals, such as those available in several European countries for both men and women upon the birth of a child, allow parents to balance work and family responsibilities without the stress of a sudden drop in family income. Some states are now using unemployment benefits to subsidize worksharing as an alternative to layoffs. Another important reform is flexible pension plans, so that workers who change employers and/or move in and out of the labor force over their lifetime enjoy the security of pension benefits.

In designing programs to improve the economic position of women in the private economy, we should assure that our short-term agenda contributes to our long-term goals: increased participation of workers and communities in the economy and economic equality for all members of society.

We propose the following programs for improving women's options in the private sector:

1. Enacting *comprehensive labor law reform* that supports the rights of workers to organize and bargain collectively.
2. Expanding *federal, state and local initiatives in economic development* that will create well-paid, quality jobs with equal access for women.
3. Expanding *federally supported job training programs* in the private sector such as the Jobs Training Partnership Act (JTPA).
4. Reforming the *employment security system* to improve services for both displaced and disadvantaged workers.
5. Encouraging the development of *new workplace technologies* that upgrade the skill level, flexibility and pay of jobs.
6. Increasing *workplace flexibility* through flex-time, paid parenting sabbaticals, subsidizing shared employment with unemployment benefits to avoid layoffs.
7. Altering *pension systems* to respond to the needs of workers who change employers and workers who move in and out of the labor force.

Conclusion

We have argued that, if current trends continue, the economic condition of the majority of women can only worsen. The alternative is concerted social action to empower women and guarantee their economic security. To this end we have proposed a number of programs that we believe should be rallying points for feminist economic action.

Most of the programs we have proposed—expanded and reformed income support, child care, health, housing, public sector job creation—have been on the agendas of mainstream American feminism and liberalism for two decades or more. What we have added here is an emphasis on the specific needs and experiences of women, in the context of current economic trends. We believe that these programs are practical, affordable and, above all, necessary. In fact, programs comparable in scope have long since been instituted in many of the European democracies.

Yet in this country the direction of public policy is running counter to the needs of women, minorities and the poor. Expanded social programs have come to be seen as too costly for our nation. The existence of widespread poverty and near-poverty—once considered a national disgrace—is increasingly accepted, or ignored. Even within the women's movement, there has been some retreat from the vigorous advocacy of social programs articulated, for example, at the National Women's Conference in Houston in 1977.

Here we have not attempted to estimate the likely cost of the programs we propose. In part this is because our proposals are general and broad-stroked, and would need a great deal of refinement before numbers could be assigned to them. But there are also inherent difficulties in costing out programs which, first, are interactive, and, second, in some cases, qualitative departures from past approaches. For example, public sector job creation will partially offset the need for income supports for the unemployed; and efforts to gain leverage over private sector employment and to expand worker- and community-owned enterprises could reduce the need for direct job creation by the public sector. Similarly, of course, spending for publicly subsidized child care would allow many thousands of women, who are now dependent on public income support, to enter the workforce. And, in ways that are intuitively obvious, but are not quantifiable, better jobs and income supports lead to improved health status and ability to make use of educational opportunity; while improved health care and education enable people to seek better jobs.

In addition, the costs of qualitatively different services cannot easily be derived from the cost of conventional programs. For example, an expanded national health program modeled on existing private insurance programs or even Medicaid and Medicare could be prohibitively expensive. But the cost of a national health program that emphasizes preventive care, health education and the employment of non-medical personnel would be far lower. Similarly, it would be enormously costly to provide housing to all who need it at current market prices. Public housing development, by eliminating the costs that represent private profit, is the only feasible approach. Finally, we have emphasized the need for all programs to encourage individual empowerment and participation. Although it is impossible to assign a dollar value to such intangible aspects of social programs, we believe that the most efficient approach to meeting any need is through programs that involve their beneficiaries as active participants.

But, ultimately, we do not believe that the burden of providing a detailed financial justification for expanded social programs should rest with us. In a relatively affluent nation, the need for such programs should be a sufficient justification for developing them. The greatest obstacle is not so much the cost, but the perception of scarcity which has come to dominate domestic social policy. The major reason for this perception of scarcity, which acts as a brake on all public sector social initiatives, is the escalation of military spending, which drives up the federal deficit and drains resources for domestic spending of any kind.

Tragically, we seem to have reached a point at which military spending—and with it the militarization of many aspects of our lives—seems to accelerate as if it were no longer susceptible to human control. In fact, a vicious cycle has come into play: Military spending creates a constituency for more military spending, especially in those regions of the country, such as the West and Southwest, that most benefit economically from defense contracts. At the same time, the depletion of social welfare programs intensifies people's dependency on military spending as a way of providing jobs. As the safety net frays, people now employed in defense-related industries become increasingly fearful of cuts in military spending. And, of course, escalating military spending guarantees that social welfare programs will be further depleted.

Increasingly, our economy's self-reinforcing reliance on military spending resembles an addiction. As with any other addiction, recovery can only be achieved through a deliberate and conscious effort.

The cure lies in a new set of social priorities: reinvestment in social welfare and jobs programs, plus conversion of defense-dependent industries to production for peaceful purposes. Is an economy in which substantial public spending is devoted to employing and assisting economically vulnerable people sustainable? Certainly no less so than an economy in which massive public spending is devoted to producing instruments of destruction, including weapons that cannot be used without jeopardizing all human life. For the other possibility is that our nation's dangerous military addiction will "cure" itself—in nuclear holocaust.

Our objections to escalating military spending, however, have as much to do with its purposes as its domestic effects. The justification for military spending is defense, yet according to the Center for Defense Information, only a small fraction of military spending is currently used for any purpose that can legitimately be termed "defense."[9] The major purposes of military spending, which include spending for strategic nuclear weapons and preparations for, and activities related to, wars of intervention, cannot be justified morally or in terms of our national security. Nuclear weapons do not guarantee security; they invite disaster. And the record of recent U.S. military interventions—in Southeast Asia, in Central America and the Caribbean—is a record of cruelty and wasted lives, a source of shame and protest rather than national pride.

It is particularly ironic in this context that U.S. military spending has repeatedly been used to support undemocratic regimes—such as those in South Korea, Taiwan and the Philippines—that are repressive to women workers in their own countries. By impeding organizing efforts and blocking political change that could lead to economic reform, political repression drives down wages in the third world and thus contributes to joblessness and depressed wages here. Support for undemocratic regimes does not "defend" American women workers; it damages them and undermines their economic prospects.

We believe that the "defense" program women most urgently need is a program of defense against the domestic dangers of sexism, racism and poverty. In the face of an economy increasingly centered on death and destruction, we have endeavored to envision the steps necessary to create a society that addresses itself to human needs and values and, above all, human life. As women, we have a central role to play in making this vision a reality, both because of our economic vulnerability and because of our increasingly common aspirations for a peaceful and caring society. The challenge is to transform our emergent political power as women into a force for profound change in our national priorities.

NOTES

1. Diana M. Pearce, "Toil and Troubles: Women and Employment Compensation," *Signs*, Forthcoming, 1985.

2. Southern Regional Task Force on Infant Mortality, "A Fiscal Imperative: Prenatal and Infant Care." Washington, D.C.: Southern Governors' Association, February 24, 1985.

3. U.S. Department of Housing and Urban Development, Office of Policy Development and Research, *Housing Our Families*. Washington, D.C.: Government Printing Office, August 1980, pp. 5.1–5.5.

4. Low Income Housing Information Service, "The 1985 Housing Budget and Low Income Housing Needs," Washington, D.C., February 2, 1984, p. 1.

5. Hon. Patricia Schroeder, "The Impact of the Reagan Cuts on Children, Youth and Families," *The Congressional Record*, July 24, 1984, p. E3268.

6. Freeman and Medoff, *What Do Unions Do?* p. 53.

7. Huntley Collins, "How Women Lost More than Jobs with the Recession," *Philadelphia Inquirer*, March 18, 1984.

8. Eileen Applebaum, "The Future of Work: Expectations and Realities." Philadelphia: Temple University Department of Economics, June 9, 1983.

9. Robert S. Norris, "More Bang, More Bucks: $450 Billion for Nuclear War," *Defense Monitor*. Washington, D.C.: Center for Defense Information, Vol. 12, No. 7, 1983.

6

Race, Class, and Gender Beyond the Welfare State

Raymond S. Franklin

Assessing the role of Black politics in the context of a troubled welfare state that is experiencing difficulty retaining its white working-class supporters transcends the politics of the 1984 presidential election. If it is true, as commonly argued, that we as a society are at the crossroads of a fundamental change or shift in emphasis, and that new group and class alignments are in the making (such as that implied by the Republicans' southern strategy), then the race and class issues that constitute the shifting involvements of the Black community's leaders are profoundly important. The latent and manifest racism of the American people and the Black response to it will affect the nature of the new arrangements that the near future will bring. Understanding the road ahead may be facilitated by knowing the road we have already traveled. The future does not come from nowhere; it is shaped by the way we prefigure it, a fact which necessarily takes us into examining the contours of the past.

The historic entrapment of the Black population—from African roots to North American enslavement, from enslavement to the development of a rigid agricultural tenancy system, from rural impoverisment to ghettoization—has led to circumstances producing specific forms of racism. Significant portions of the Black community have been periodically "locked" into social and economic enclaves that nurtured racism in a variety of vulgar and subtle forms, including self-denigration and dependency. Although some manifest racial sentiments and practices have withered or fallen into disuse, others have been retained or have been transmogrified to fit new circumstances.

In the course of these historical changes, we have not only witnessed shifts between race and class, and not infrequently the fusing of the two, but also altered our mode of production and changed our political institutions. As a result, large numbers of white workers are related to our political institutions in ways that make them extremely "sensitive" to Black demands for redistributive policies that affect white political interests, especially their tax burden and their own entitlements from the politicized nature of the welfare state. Thus, Black struggles to get out from under the shadows of race and class subordination through political action often strike fear into the more affluent white blue-collar workers and many members of the white middle class more generally. I note these social facts and tendencies because they contribute to the structural context in which Blacks are seeking to make their own political history. This context consists of realities not chosen by Blacks themselves. Social action based on a failure to consider them will have unintended consequences as grave as not possessing past knowledge relevant to making one's own history. There are six such realities that need simultaneous consideration in the decade ahead if Blacks are to succeed in their long-standing battle for social justice and equal living arrangements.

Permanent ghetto thesis. The Black ghetto is a permanent cluster that is not going to be readily changed or dispersed by piecemeal reforms in the form of marginal housing or job programs. One consequence of social segregation in our twelve to fifteen largest metropolitan areas is the breeding of, for understandable reasons, extremely balkanized and provincial politics. It is a tendency to be resisted because it is self-defeating. Issues vary with cities (New York is not Birmingham), but the Black population of each will need to work at its own method of transcending group particularism by an orientation that embraces social class issues more generally. For example, schools in Black neighborhoods are no doubt the worst in the metropolitan areas, yet schools are profoundly inadequate in form and content in all working-class neighborhoods. If racist feelings are to be overcome, white workers need to be made part of the solution, if they believe costs are to be incurred in the course of change. Blacks, in the course of articulating their own agenda, must speak in a voice that ideologically and programmatically communicates to workers as a whole.

Too large, too small bind. The Black population is caught in a dilemma in that it is too large to be integrated into the American mainstream because that would involve unacceptable costs to influential segments of the white majority—especially the middle layers—and too small to achieve power by its own effort. Success requires that Blacks forge strong coalitions, but making what are perceived to be excessive demands undermines such coalitions. This problem partly explains Blacks' shifting involvements from class or integrationist alignments to separatist ones. The main political implication of this predicament is that both integrationist and separatist tactics and strategies are incapable of achieving their respective goals. In this sense, both orientations are limited, since neither adequately deals with the problem of cultivating workable and sustaining means to realize social goals that are momentarily blocked by those with more power.

From class to race to gender. Because the overrepresentation of Blacks in the lower and lumpen-proletarian classes, a condition that reproduces itself in a variety of institutionally determined ways, is intimately associated with race, the status of Blacks other than those in the lower class are affected, i.e., middle-income blacks specifically and black women more generally. In this way, race/class connections not only determine the myopic perceptions of the white community vis-à-vis the Black one, but they determine divisions and attitudes within the black community itself.

The Black population is defined not only by its social segregation in the metropolitan areas, but also by its overcrowding in low-income and relatively unskilled positions. In the minds of middle America, race and class get juxtaposed. The middle layers of white America cannot readily dissociate in everyday social exchanges these two phenomena, and therefore whites resist entry of middle and/or working-class Blacks into "their" communities, "their" schools, and "their" places of work. The possibility of middle or stable working-class Blacks integrating on equal terms with whites of comparable class positions easily degenerates into race exclusion and put-downs, even in the absence of class differences.

A similar, albeit more complex, process works to affect the status of Black women. Their position is determined by a combination of race and gender factors on the one hand, and the class position of Black men on the other. As a result, Black women suffer the burdens of survival as single persons or single parents to a greater degree than their white cohort.

Crumbling walls of the central city. The convergence of the above three tendencies has endangered the viability of our central cities. The story has been told many times. The migration pattern between regions and within metropolitan areas has led to concentrations of Blacks in many of our major central cities and the concentration of whites in outlying suburban areas. The metaphor describing Detroit—a white-walled tire with a black center—has its relevance for many American urban areas. Accompanying the exodus of middle-income whites is the exodus of wealth, which has meant the deterioration of the central city's social capital, as well as a decline in its spirit of enterprise. What Blacks, therefore, are inheriting is the management of local governments that are perennially on the verge of bankruptcy. The process is not new in the history of the Black population's relative deprivation. Just as Blacks have often attained entry into declining industries (too little, too late), they now appear to be in sight of political control of a level of government that is on its last legs.

White freedom vs. black social justice. In our society, discrimination against Blacks takes place under the banner of freedom to choose. Milton Friedman's ideological success is not without reason. Freedom of choice for a white consumer means the freedom to avoid living next door to Blacks. The employer's freedom to combine labor and capital in production means freedom not to hire or promote Black labor and freedom to avoid the social costs connected with the movement of a plant from the central city.

To the Black population, these white market freedoms have meant the negation of their own freedom—if not to exist, at least to live decently. Thus, salvation to Blacks, employed and unemployed, has too often existed outside the private market. But once the solution to the Black condition is viewed as existing outside the market, it is automatically seen to fall inside the domain of political action, which takes the form of demands for equity entitlements of a redistributive nature as citizens of the state; it takes the form of asking the state to interfere with white market choices. In this sense, the exercise of white market freedoms becomes pitted against Black demands for social justice. The creation of conflict between two kinds of moral imperatives—freedom versus social justice—lends itself to deep ideological differences between the Black and white populations.

Crisis of the welfare state. The federal government, often viewed by the Black population as its ultimate source of hope, is plagued, for reasons unrelated to the Black/white differences, with dilemmas leading to incoherent urban and related policies. The national instruments of political economy are presently saddled with the perceived need to shrink their role in urban affairs. Inflationary fears, even in the absence of inflation, and the excessive federal debt associated with larger than desired annual deficits tend to make the federal government's demand management policies ineffective in stimulating employment opportunities for the bottom third of the Black labor force that is unemployed, casually employed, or employed at dead-end jobs in our central cities. The welfare state is unable to achieve the kind of market conditions that are necessary for sustained Black employment gains and, at the same time, the mitigation of discrimination within the context of Black/white competition for jobs.

New Directions

Any Black movement aimed at changing American society needs to incorporate the above six realities into its strategies to establish social justice and equal life chances. The sine qua non of a viable Black struggle in the future requires the development of a broad social consensus that will give coalition politics more cohesiveness. Coalitions work without social consensus when the separate groups, even when they are unequal in power, have mutual respect for each other. But in Black/white relations, the centrifugal forces within the class structure and the political system are awesome. Overcoming them is no easy matter under the most advantageous circumstances. Waiting for a crisis, as some are prone, that will hopefully bring people together involves a very limited understanding of both American society generally and Black/white relations specifically. Aside from the fact that a crisis may not come to a head in anticipated ways, the worsening of objective conditions may not necessarily affect all strata of the working and middle classes uniformly; people confronting adversity do not automatically "discover" economic commonalities. If such were the case, the poor of all races would have had their heads together long ago. Unshared anxieties and suffering can divide people further rather than bring them together. Thus, seeking consensus on ideological or moral grounds in the course of pursuing coalitions among various Black/white interest groups must proceed simultaneously.

On the most general plane, Americans need to rescue the decay taking place in the public sector. This involves an effort at achieving a greater commitment to civility in public discourse and purposes rather than to isolated, individualistic plans for development. It means thinking about the public sector in terms of an opportunity to contribute service rather than using government to achieve private ends. Since public life, at least for our major metropolitan areas where problems in one portion of the city rapidly spill over into other ones, is city life, we need to reconstruct the sinews that bind people together. This cannot be accomplished without cultivating a social-regarding ethos. While whites must see their interests in a larger framework, in a less protective one that too often reads "my" schools, parks, and neighborhoods, Blacks will have to move from a demand for ghetto-based programs to ones that envision the rebuilding of the whole urban complex. Such an orientation involves more than an employment plan for blacks and other minorities embracing road repairs, cleaning and beautifying parks, building public housing and more transportation facilities, and not least, reforming entitlement programs. These are, of course, important necessities; they should not be underestimated. But more often than not, the benefits and costs of such projects are defined in terms that are too provincial. What is required is a more "holistic" vision that encompasses the social, as well as the physical, context in which diverse groups and individuals can fulfill their hopes for more meaningful lives through public and civic participation. If white affluence has taught us anything, we know that it can and does exist in the midst of an alarming amount of emptiness of heart and loneliness of soul. The more affluent treadmill no doubt is different from the one that runs poor people's lives, but it is nevertheless anxiety-ridden and often meaningless. This suggests that the better-off middle layers (blue-collar, white-collar, and professional workers) must be part of the solution to the restoration of the public sector and public life. Health facilities, for example, advocated just for poor Black neighborhoods where the need is no doubt profound end up being overused and underfinanced and, therefore, "prove" that public health stations are destined to fail. Health is the kind of problem that can very well destroy middle-class families as well as poor ones. By universalizing health facilities without class distinctions, not only is proper funding assured, but also their common and nonsegregated use is assured, in ways that are self-evidently needed by everyone.

Allied to the infrastructural and related social needs of our cities is the necessity of more environmental amenities. We need to learn not only how to respect and enjoy each other, but also how to care more about the physical spaces in which we build and reproduce our social and family life. This involves extending our time horizons and our thoughts about how activities that suit us and fall within our own geopolitical spaces affect those living in other places—for example, our neighbors on the other side of the river or those across town. Sooner or later, "their" industrial wastes are going to affect "our" drinking water. Getting "them" to care about our water requires beginning to support "them" in some of their environmental needs, which momentarily seem distant from "ours."

The third general direction that we need to pursue is more equity in the distribution of income. Equal opportunity to have unequal results is too limited a goal for the simple reason that de facto unequal outcomes affect the distribution of opportunities in the next generation of competition between individuals and groups. The difference between the average income of the top ten percent and the bottom twenty percent can be narrowed considerably without due concern for disincentives.[1] To the equalization direction, we need to add income security through guaranteed employment. More equality will induce a shift in our incentive system from materialistic drives to moral or noneconomic ones; at least, it will bring about a better balance between economic and noneconomic motives in the allocation of people and resources. Income security will undermine the fear of falling off the edge; it will take some of the anxieties out of life and perhaps remove some of the pressures associated with the perceived need to "make it" while the going is good because of the fear that tomorrow will be too late.

None of the above can develop without the reinforcement of an educational system and a concept of learning that stretches over the individual's whole life span. With a change in the amount of "leisure," the notion of periodic sabbaticals, rather than layoffs, should be extended from tenured members of a university faculty to the whole labor force. This means changing the composition, role, and meaning of college. Credentialism has reached its useful limit; it is now time to focus on the substance of learning. Keeping up with the world should not only mean training for a new job, but also learning about the art of living. This, we hope, will enable us to achieve excitement in our lives through an active involvement or engagement in sport, science and technology, and cultural events rather than in dope or boozing, I-hate-communism campaigns, and mindless, flag-waving nationalism.

Beyond these general recommended directions for the reconstitution of a new America, we need to undertake a profound rethinking of the relationship between work and nonwork activities, with much more attention on those in the latter domain. With respect to nonwork, my central concern is family and community, two areas that preoccupy large numbers in both the Black and white population.

The full rationale for focusing on nonwork would take me too far from my immediate objectives. Suffice it to say that a great many studies from the late 1950s to the present indicate that work is not a central life interest to most people.[2] That is to say, work is viewed as a necessary but not an emancipatory interest. The work site is not one where individuals hope to exercise discretion, express affect, organize one's own time, cultivate projects for self-development, or just have fun. In the daily experiences of most people, work is controlled either through a hierarchically arranged administrative apparatus or technological imperatives. Control is more or less accepted as inevitable. Although humanizing the workplace is possible and in fact has occurred, work is still within the limits of a control system. Thus, emancipatory interests are not expected from the workplace, and therefore, expectations about work experiences are not major sources of disappointments. In the work sphere, most people are fairly realistic. What they seek from its routines is neither salvation nor happiness, but an income—one that is sufficiently large and steady to purchase consumer goods and services that are used in the nonwork sphere. Here individuals are allegedly free to exercise choice, build their own castles, express themselves through hobbies, and find affection in families and purpose in communities. Unfortunately, something else happens. There are some inherent difficulties in the nonwork sphere that are bound to produce disappointments that people try to "rectify" by the very means that stimulated the false hopes. I shall concentrate the remaining portion of my argument on this problem and its resolution.

As productivity has increased over the long run in the work sphere, most people have been induced to use this increase in productivity in the form of more goods and services rather than in leisure or time-related consumption. Although many of these newly acquired consumer goods could be defined as necessary, an increasingly larger proportion are related—not to the satisfaction of essential needs—to the acquisition of status goods and services or the purchase of what Fred Hirsch identifies as positional ones.[3] The unique character of such goods and services is that their enjoyment or utility is closely tied to the extent of their use by others—the suburban neighborhood is quiet if it is not overcrowded with low-cost apartments on each corner of the block; a B.A. degree facilitates a better job if not everyone is permitted to acquire one. Not only is working at a routine job a means to expected pleasures derived from consumption, but so is a consequential portion of consumer goods and services a means to define one's relative position in the group. Competition for such goods and services, in the end, involves pursuing a moving target. Much energy (times and resources) is expended in protecting and forwarding status that differentiates people's rank in the consuming hierarchy. But because everyone is induced to do the same, and eventually achieves some degree of entrance into the positional economy, the worker's relative standing changes little. There is often much motion and little movement. Standing up to see better at a football game works only when no one else follows suit. Otherwise, everyone ends up exactly in the same poor viewing position as before, with one difference: A lot of energy has been employed to stay in the same place. The process is destructive to the catharsis expected from the expressive-affective relationships and the intrinsic pleasures expected from using consumer goods and services. This, of course, is what consumerism, writ large, is all about. How status-related material pursuits turn against fulfillment in community and family, havens that people sought to offset the tedium and hierarchical control characteristic of work, can be illustrated with two scenarios.

Community. Just as work is separated from consumption, with the former "valued" primarily as an instrument to the latter, community interests have become separated from family needs, with similar results. Community is supposed to be a locus where close networks are built, where trust and comfort in relationships are established, where traditions based on rootedness link the past with the present, and where neighbors can be relied upon for support in the event of an unforeseen mishap. But these experiences that we hope to get from community rarely occur because they are perennially undermined by a specific kind of disjuncture between family and community.

The organization of space on which community life centers is continually fractured or transformed into quicksand by industry and real-estate developers.[4] Land, like goods and services, is bought and sold for reasons other than communitarian experiences. The commodifiers, so to speak, keep breaking up the foundations on which social life is constructed. The local and national government, it should be noted, participates in this process in order to keep the economy growing in wanton ways. The process destroys the ability of families to integrate with each other in stable social spaces. Thus, families are forever being forced to pick up and find other places in which to establish themselves, either because their present community is being changed by the market, or because ones close by are being destroyed, causing a large number of adjacent dwellers to "invade" surrounding communities. Since space is so rapidly changed, altered, defaced, or devoured by larger industrial and real-estate interests, communities have a most difficult time sustaining themselves. Families are induced to think about their purchased home in instrumental terms— that is, in the same way that work has become a means to enter the positional economy of consumer goods and services. People are forced to view their home not as a place to establish rootedness and bondedness with neighbors—but as a source of status, an instrument to capitalize in event of a move, a means to provide for retirement, and an opportunity to send their children to better schools to enhance their chances of success. Thus, families are quick to "protect" their investment interest, or abandon it for better instrumental opportunities. The latter propensity often leaves abandoned communities in a state of decay or disarray. Older and less well-off families are often caught in the rapid crosswinds of what is perceived as destructive change. In any event, the need for exit or the development of protective and defensive mechanisms divide people, especially white workers from Black ones, when the former believe that their property values are being threatened by "invading" Blacks who are also victims of commercial disruption. The whole process was succinctly summarized by an Irish worker from Brooklyn who reflectively responded to an inquiry about Blacks coming into "his" neighborhood:

> Economics, I think is the biggest strain because, in this area, a man's whole idea of an investment in the economy of the United States is the house he owns. He invests [$20,000 in 1950 it's worth $40,000 in 1970]. He's really knocking them dead in the economy, right? . . . But when he feels threatened, this money, this investment that he's made, he's desperate. He says what the hell are they doing to me. This is where I put my money. I didn't put it in General Motors. I didn't . . . you know. . . . A man realizes this. . . . They say . . . they're going to devaluate on him. I don't say that it's got any validity, this feeling. What I'm saying, is this is the way they feel. This is where their money went, and this is what they're trying to protect.[5]

Thus, the struggle to maintain the positional character of your community turns it into an investment, a means to another end, rather than something to be savored or enjoyed for its own inherent qualities and purposes. It is protected as a means to make a "killing" in order to move on to an even "nicer" neighborhood, or as a means of accumulating wealth. The process pits group against group, or one segment of a class against another. The final outcome is that one's sense of community is destroyed or never achieved, and often the victims, Blacks and whites, or larger commercial interests become enemies of each other.

Family. As workers flee from their traditional communities, often located in our central cities, in order to acquire more middle-class life-styles, they incur rising tax and debt burdens. As they seek more status-related goods and services, they change the meaning of what constitutes an adequate standard of living. In the process, the costs of maintaining and advancing family life dramatically increase. Paradoxically, workers who "make it" find that they cannot make ends meet. This induces an increase in the labor-force participation among working-class wives and mothers who generally find jobs in the low-wage sectors of the economy. White male workers who are already predisposed to view Black welfare recipients and unwed teenage mothers as tax burdens without empathy are now further agitated by the unexpected need to send their wives into the labor force. As one steelworker angrily blurted out in a conversation: "If my wife can work her butt off to help pay our home mortgage, why can't those niggers do the same?"

Those with personal frustrations not infrequently seek scapegoats. The consequences of multiwage white working-class families racing to keep up or making ends meet include not only the intensification of racist sentiments and a decrease in their support for the redistributive policies of the welfare state, but also more general changes in the nature and quality of family life. Working time for women increases markedly, because they are now doing paid and unpaid work.[6] Employed working-class women, without support services or male partners who fully participate in household chores, increasingly find themselves harassed. Just as communities have become impersonal aggregations of individuals as a result of their fluidity and instrumental market character, many everyday services, once supplied in the home or through community networks, now are purchased in the market through impersonal exchanges. The result is less, not more, time for expressive-affective relations in family life. "Short fuses" in family relations burn everywhere and produce what some sociologists found to be an ill-defined malaise that appears to be unrelated to work per se.[7] The family unit, which is supposed to provide the most elementary meaning to life and work, becomes increasingly impersonalized and infested with market-related anxieties. When the family ceases to function as a reprieve from the relatively dull routines of work, then the main institution that facilitates a "transcendence of narrow egoism in love and care, a link with the past and an orientation to the future" is considerably weakened, if not destroyed.[8] The separation and divorce rate, not to exclude child abuse, reflects this weakening process. Demagogic conservative imagery is built on the loss associated with the decline in family life. Unfortunately, conservative solutions that emphasize the extension of the market are part of the problems that have caused the decline in families and communities. Conservatives in this sense, despite their current power, belong to the past.

Conclusion

The solutions to both building communities and reconstituting family life are inherent in the way I have chosen to identify the problems. Less exit from communities will lead to the exercise of more voice—that is, people will stay and meet the sources of their problems rather than flee from them. Staying in place for longer periods of time breeds rootedness among families and trust between neighbors.

Working with people to achieve shared goals becomes something to be savored, because it involves collective efforts with known and familiar faces.

Children need parents, and adults need each other. The answer is not to send the "little lady" back into the kitchen, but to get off the status-competitive treadmill, which will change the goals of work by decreasing the amount required. This change will simultaneously give new meaning to productivity increases. As we become more efficient and capable of meeting the essential needs of the have-not portions of the population, we should seek leisure or time-related consumption for both parents. As this is occurring, we should also increase the supply of child-care facilities and introduce flexible working time for two-parent and single heads of households. All these changes are directed at increasing nonwork time for the maturing of expressive-affective relationships.

There is one profound obstacle to overcome if we are to move in the direction that I have suggested: The market system as it is presently constituted has a strong bias against time-related consumption. In fact, all of its biases are in the opposite direction, toward the possession and accumulation of goods and services in the form that induces the need to work more, whether job opportunities are available or not. Changing this bias means changing secular values in ways that will inevitably confront and conflict with those promulgated by the business system and its commercial ethic. Although the task is not impossible, it does involve a radical introspection of what we as a people are about.

The realization of a future beyond the present welfare state will not automatically solve all the issues raised in the first part of this chapter. However, I believe that this progress will establish the conditions that will enable us to reduce the divisive cleavages along race and class lines. All these suggested guidelines for the future, in my view, are consonant with the Black population's backlog of unmet needs. Whether Black political action will converge with that of other concerned groups to bring about the social mix to transform America's racial structure is not ordained by the rules of progress nor the logic of history. The pervasive present—dismal, uncertain, and confusing—is upon us. The habit of extrapolating from it is likely to produce a horizon overcast with ominous clouds, but our projections need not proceed without a hopeful vision of future possibilities.

NOTES

This essay is a shortened rendition of the final chapter of a forthcoming book, *Shadows of Race and Class*. The parts dealing with family, community, and positional goods are adapted from an unpublished manuscript by B. Silverman and R. Franklin titled "Workers and Affluence: The Limits of Liberalism."

1. See L. Thurow: "A General Tendency Toward Inequality." American Economic Association Meetings, December 1985.

2. See R. Dubin: "Industrial Workers' Worlds: A Study of the Central Life Interests of Industrial Workers," *Social Problems* (January 1956). For updated versions, see R. Dubin, J. E. Champoux, and L. W. Potter: "Central Life Interests and Organizational Commitment of Blue Collar and Clerical Workers," *Administrative Science Quarterly*, 20 (1975), 411–421;

also, D. Halle: *America's Working Man: Work, Home and Politics Among Blue-Collar Property Owners*, University of Chicago Press, Chicago, 1984.

3. F. Hirsch: *Social Limits to Growth*, Harvard University Press, Cambridge, Massachusetts, 1976.

4. See I. Peterson: "Amid Boom, Black Enclave Shrinks," *New York Times*, October 28, 1986, B-1,4.

5. From "An End to Innocence." WCBS-TV special broadcast. Producer-director, Warren Wallace (September 17, 1969).

6. V. Fuchs: "Sex Differences in Economic Well-Being," *Science*, April 25, 1986, 450–464.

7. G. J. Staines and R. P. Quin: "American Workers Evaluate the Quality of Their Jobs," *Monthly Labor Review*, 102, 1 (January 1979), 3–12.

8. E. Andrew: *Closing the Iron Cage: The Scientific Management of Work and Leisure*, Black Rose Books, Montreal, Quebec, 1981, 178.

7

The women in the ordinary*

Marge Piercy

The woman in the ordinary pudgy downcast girl
is crouching with eyes and muscles clenched.
Round and pebble smooth she effaces herself
under ripples of conversation and debate.
The woman in the block of ivory soap
has massive thighs that neigh,
great breasts that blare and strong arms that trumpet.
The woman of the golden fleece
laughs uproariously from the belly
inside the girl who imitates
a Christmas card virgin with glued hands,
who fishes for herself in other's eyes,
who stoops and creeps to make herself smaller.
In her bottled up is a woman peppery as curry,
a yam of a woman of butter and brass,
compounded of acid and sweet like a pineapple,
like a handgrenade set to explode,
like goldenrod ready to bloom.

*From *Circles on the Water* by Marge Piercy.

Suggestions for Further Reading

B. P. Bowser & R. G. Hunt: *Impacts of Racism on White Americans*, Sage Publications, Beverly Hills, California, 1981.

Z. R. Eisenstein: *Feminism and Sexual Equality*, Monthly Review Press, New York, 1984.

M. Marable: *Black American Politics from the Washington Marches to Jesse Jackson*, Schocken, New York, 1985.

L. C. Pogrebin: *Growing Up Free*, Bantam Books, New York, 1981.

S. Shalom: *Socialist Visions*, South End Press, Boston, 1985.

Acknowledgments (*continued from copyright page*)

Institute for Policy Studies: Excerpt from "The Feminization of Poverty," in *Toward Economic Justice for Women*, by Women's Economic Agenda Working Group, 1985. Excerpted by permission. Copyright by The Institute for Policy Studies.

"Blacks in America: A Statistical Profile," August 28, 1983. Copyright © 1983 by The New York Times Company. Reprinted by permission.

"Overview: Race and Ethnicity," reprinted with permission of Macmillan Publishing Company from *Sociology*, 2nd edition, by Beth Hess, Elizabeth W. Markson, Peter J. Stein. Copyright 1985 by Macmillan Publishing Company.

"Sun Chief, Autobiography of a Hopi Indian" from *Sun Chief, Autobiography of a Hopi Indian* edited by Leo W. Simmons (Yale University Press, 1942), pp. 88–89. Reprinted by permission.

"The Native American Experience: The World of the Native American Child" from *Red Children in White America*, University of Pennsylvania Press, 1977, portions of pp. 15–37. Reprinted by permission of the University of Pennsylvania Press.

Pages 224–229 from *Nilda* by Nicholasa Mohr. Copyright © 1973 by Nicholasa Mohr. Reprinted by permission of Harper & Row, Publishers, Inc.

Francisco Jimenez, "The Circuit," *The Arizona Quarterly* (Autumn 1973), by permission of the author.

"The Asian Women in America," by Gloria L. Kumagai from *Explorations in Ethnic Studies* (1978) vol. 1, no. 2. Copyright 1978 by the National Association for Ethnic Studies, Inc. Reprinted by permission.

"Farewell to Manzanar" from *Farewell to Manzanar* by Jeanne Wakatsuki Houston and James D. Houston. Copyright © 1973 by James D. Houston. Reprinted by permission of Houghton Mifflin Company.

"A Cultural Aversion," by Carol Wang from *In These Times*, volume 9, no. 41, October 30–November 7, 1985, pp. 23–24. Reprinted by permission of Pacific News Service. Copyright Pacific News Service.

"Being Black Is Dangerous to Your Health," from "A Special Report on Black Health," by Denise Foley from *Prevention* magazine, March, 1985. Reprinted by permission of *Prevention* magazine. Copyright 1985 Rodale Press, Inc. All rights reserved.

"Barbie Doll," from *Circles on the Water* by Marge Piercy. Copyright © 1969, 1971, 1973 by Marge Piercy. Reprinted by permission of Alfred A. Knopf, Inc.

"is not so gd to be born a girl" by Nzotake Shange from *Black Scholar*, Vol. 10, May–June 1979. Reprinted by permission of the author.

"Poem for the Young White Man Who Asked Me How I, an Intelligent, Well-Read Person Could Believe in the War Between the Races," reprinted from *Emplunada* by Lorna Dee Cervantes by permission of the U. of Pittsburgh Press. © 1981 by Lorna Dee Cervantes.

"Is the Binge-Purge Cycle Catching?" by Susan Squire, *MS.* Magazine, October 1983. Reprinted by permission of The Putnam Publishing Group from *The Slender Balance* by Susan Squire. Copyright © 1983 by Susan Squire.

"When the Boss Wants Sex," by Yla Eason, March 1981. Copyright © 1981 by Essence Communications, Inc. Reprinted by permission.

"He Defies You Still—Memoirs of a Sissy" by Tommi Avicolli, in *Radical Teacher*, #24, pp. 4–5 and in *Men Freeing Men*, edited by Francis Baumli, Atlantis Press. © 1985 by Tommi Avicolli.

"Real Men Don't Cry and Other Uncool Myths" by Phil W. Petrie, November 1982. Copyright 1982 by Essence Communications, Inc. Reprinted by permission.

"Divorce Law and Policy: The Rising Backlash," by Marianne Takas, published as "Divorce: Who Gets the Blame in No Fault," *MS.* Magazine, February 1986. Reprinted by permission of Marianne Takas. Copyright © 1986.

"At a Welfare Hotel, Mothers Find Support in Weekly Talks," by Sara Rimer, February 5, 1986 by The New York Times Company. Reprinted by permission.

"Listening" by Sey Chassler from *MS.* Magazine, August 1984, pp. 51–53, 98–100. Reprinted by permission of Sey Chassler.

"The Indian Removal Act, 1830," reprinted from *Documents of United States Indian Policy*, by Francis Paul Prucha, by permission of the University of Nebraska Press. Copyright © 1975 by the University of Nebraska Press.

"Declarations of Sentiments and Resolutions, Seneca Falls Convention, 1848," excerpts from *Up from the Pedestal*, by Aileen S. Kraditor. Reprinted by permission of Times Books, a division of Random House, Inc.

"The Anti-Suffragists: Selected Papers," excerpts from *Up from the Pedestal* by Aileen S. Kraditor. Reprinted by permission of Times Books, a division of Random House, Inc.

People vs. Hall, 1854, from *American Racism: Exploration of the Nature of Prejudice* by Roger Daniels and Harry H.L. Kitano, Prentice-Hall, 1970. Reprinted by permission of Roger Daniels.

"The Black Codes" from *Black Reconstruction* by W. E. B. Du Bois (Harcourt Brace Jovanovich, Inc., 1935). Reprinted by permission of David G. Du Bois.

Bradwell v. Illinois, 1873, from *Cases and Materials on Sex-Based Discrimination*, 2nd edition by Herma Hill Kay with permission of the West Publishing Company.

"Stereotypes: Conceptual and Normative Considerations," by Judith Andre, Director, Institute of Applied Ethics, Old Dominion University. Reprinted by permission of the author.

"Self-Fulfilling Stereotypes," by Mark Snyder, *Psychology Today*, July 1982. Reprinted with permission from *Psychology Today* magazine. Copyright © 1982 American Psychological Association.

"Racism in the English Language," reprinted, by permission, from *Racism in the English Language* by Robert B. Moore, Council on Interracial Books for Children, 1976. Write the Council at 1841 Broadway, New York, 10023 for a free catalog of antiracist, antisexist materials.

" 'Pricks' and 'Chicks': A Plea for 'Persons' " by Robert Baker. Reprinted by permission of the author.

Pp. 156–168 from "The Sacrificial Lamb" in *Pornography and Silence: Culture's Revenge Against Nature* by Susan Griffin. Copyright © 1981 by Susan Griffin. Reprinted by permission of Harper & Row, Publishers, Inc.

"Social Effects of Some Contemporary Myths About Woman" by Ruth Hubbard, reprinted from *Women's Nature*, ed. by Marian Lowe and Ruth Hubbard, Pergamon Press, 1983, pp. 1–8.

"The Schooling of Vietnamese Immigrants," by Gail P. Kelley. In *Comparative Perspectives of Third World Women: The Implications of Race, Sex, and Class*, Beverly Lindsay, ed. (Praeger Publishers, New York, New York, a division of The Greenwood Press, Inc., 1980). Copyright © 1980 by Beverly Lindsay. Used by permission.

"The Art of Savage Discovery: How to Blame the Victim" from pp. 3–29 of *Blaming the Victim*, by William Ryan. Copyright © 1971 by William Ryan. Reprinted by permission of Pantheon Books, a Division of Random House, Inc.

"Sex and Race: The Analogy of Social Control" by William Chafe. From *Women and Equality: Changing Patterns in American Culture* by William H. Chafe. Copyright © 1977 by Oxford University Press, Inc. Reprinted by permission.

"Age, Race, Class, and Sex," from *Sister Outsider* by Audre Lorde, The Crossing Press, 1984. Copyright © Audre Lorde, 1984.

"Up Against the Wall," by Cherríe Moraga from *Loving the War Years* (Boston: South End Press, 1983). Reprinted by permission.

Ann Ferguson, "Androgyny As an Ideal for Human Development," from Mary Vetterling-Braggin, Frederick Elliston, and Jane English, eds., *Feminism and Philosophy* (Totawa, NJ: Littlefield, Adams & Co., © 1977), pp. 45–69. (Reprinted by Rowman & Allenheld, 1985.)

"Changing the Situation: Steps Toward an Egalitarian Family Policy," adapted from pp. 172–203 of *Small Futures* by Richard H. de Lone (Harcourt Brace Jovanovich, Inc., 1979).

"Toward Economic Justice for Women: A National Agenda for Change" by The Women's Economic Agenda Working Group, Institute for Policy Studies, Washington, D.C., 1985.

Race, Class and Gender Beyond the Welfare State by Raymond S. Franklin, Queens College, The City University of New York. Reprinted by permission of the author.

"The woman in the ordinary," from *Circles on the Water*, by Marge Piercy. Copyright © 1969, 1971, 1973 by Marge Piercy. Reprinted by permission of Alfred A. Knopf, Inc.